● Tregaron

Llangeitho

Cwm Iou

Chancefield ●

Talgarth ●

Tredwstan ● ● Trefeca

landovery

Abergavenny ●

Trefethin ●

New Inn ●

● Neath

Newport ●

Swansea

Bridgend   CARDIFF

Llan-gan

Bread of Heaven

Bread of Heaven

The life and work of William Williams, Pantycelyn

Eifion Evans

BRYNTIRION PRESS

© Eifion Evans, 2010

First published 2010

ISBN 978 1 85049 240 5

All scripture quotations are from Authorised (King James) Version

Cover design and layout: Creative Media Publishing Limited

Published by Bryntirion Press, Bryntirion, Bridgend CF31 4DX, Wales
Printed by MPG Books Limited, Bodmin, Cornwall PL31 1EB

For Tom and Rhiannon

Contents

Contents

Acknowledgments

The preparation of this work stretches back over many years, and my debt to others who have written on Williams, is great; some of them are mentioned in the Preface, but in addition I must acknowledge the inspiration I have drawn from the friendship as well as the example of the late Gomer M. Roberts. While writing this book, his work on Williams has never been further than arm's length away. Much of the ground-work had been done as I was preparing the book on Howel Harris which appeared in 1974, and on Daniel Rowland, published in 1985. The translation into English of Williams's *Theomemphus* for publication in 1996 was a kind of 'trial run' for this. It is also a pleasure to pay tribute to the courtesy of the staff at The National Library of Wales, Aberystwyth, over a period of some forty years.

Many friends urged me in various ways to persevere: Brian Higham, Geraint Jones, Sulwyn Jones, David Ollerton, and Terry Williams in particular. Cecil Williams and the family at Pantycelyn have always been cordial in their welcome on numerous occasions, while another of William's descendants, Lewis Jones, Myddfai, and his wife Bethan have supported the project with great interest and practical help.

I am deeply indebted to Dr E. Wyn James and Dr David Ceri Jones for reading the manuscript, and giving me the benefit of their scholarly expertise and spiritual insight. The work is considerably enriched by their helpful evaluation. The Rev Graham S. Harrison's meticulous editorial skills and theological acumen have been invaluable. Dr David Norbury, Dr D. Eryl Davies and Mr Huw Kinsey at Bryntirion have shown great diligence in bringing about the book's publication. Its shortcomings are entirely my own.

As always, my greatest debt is to my wife and family, for their unfailing affection and encouragement. The book is dedicated to our only daughter, Rhiannon, and her husband Tom, as joint-heirs of The Great Awakening which bridged the water between Wales and America.

Preface

William Williams, the subject of this biography, was an eighteenth-century clergyman from Wales, famed for his hymns. His life spanned the period of religious revival in eighteenth-century Wales that saw the emergence of Methodism, and he was one of its leaders. Although known chiefly outside Wales for his hymn, 'Guide me, O Thou great Jehovah', often revised to 'Guide me, O Thou great Redeemer', his leadership role in the Methodist Revival, and especially his writings have made him a significant figure in Welsh history and culture. His life and labours deserve notice in a wider sphere on account of his major contribution to an understanding of Christian experience and to the public expression of Christian worship. It would be true to say that he moulded the Christian spirituality of an entire nation for generations. His hymns are still sung, and the distinctive Methodist conviction and mind-set which he forged persist to this day.

Apart from a few years being educated away from home, Williams spent his life in his native county of Carmarthen. It is a county of rich pastureland, market towns and the impressive Black mountain range, known in Welsh as 'Bannau Sir Gaer' (the Carmarthenshire Beacons). Its people's amiable, gentle disposition is reflected in the softness of their language. In terms of religious influence, it boasts a galaxy of men born within its boundaries, with influential names that linger, often with the place of their residence added for good measure. They include Rhys Prichard or Vicar Prichard, Llandovery; Griffith Jones, Llanddowror; Dafydd Jones, Caeo; David Jones (later, of Llan-gan); Morgan Rhys, Llanfynydd; and Thomas Charles, whose name has subsequently been linked with Bala, to mention a few, and to confine the choice to the period relevant to this book. They are names that will be met with later, but the subject of the book must not be forgotten: William Williams, Pantycelyn, or simply Williams, Pantycelyn, or even Pantycelyn, such is his universal and lasting fame. Pantycelyn is the name of the farm where he lived for most of his married life, and one of his descendants continues to farm the land today.

Mention of Wales for some will conjure up nothing more than a geographical area within England. This is a mistaken, if understandable, assumption. Since the Act of Union of 1536 Wales has been deemed one with England, but the identification is unwarranted. Wales is a separate country with a distinct language and culture stretching back over many centuries to a Celtic origin, as its strange-sounding place-names may suggest. A Principality within the United Kingdom, roughly the same size as the State of Massachusetts, today it has a population of nearly three million. Within the compact area of its land the scenery has variety and beauty. A land famed for its song, its sheep and its coalmines, its history has been forged by Roman occupation, the spread of Christianity, attempts to Anglicize its population, and latterly a resurgent independent spirit. Within that separate identity the nation enjoys regional variation in terms of language, geographic features, and distinctive characteristics. In the eighteenth century quite a substantial number of Welsh people could not understand or speak English. Today, the picture is different, with Welsh a minority language, and everyone familiar with English.

The book is not only about Williams and the Welsh in general. It also deals in particular with the Welsh Calvinistic Methodism of which he was part, and to which he made an immense contribution. It is important to make clear at the outset that Welsh Methodism was not English Methodism, having emerged independently, and developed separately. The abiding Methodism of England, following the Wesley brothers, was Arminian; Welsh Methodism was Calvinistic. The Methodism of George Whitefield was also Calvinistic, and he worked closely with his Welsh counterparts, but unlike Wesleyan Methodism, that of Whitefield and the Countess of Huntingdon in England, another Calvinist, did not long continue as a significant body. Whitefield, with his labours in America, was also a vital link with the wider Great Awakening, of which Welsh Calvinistic Methodism was a part, and with which it had close affinities. As a result, Williams could easily identify with the simultaneous ministry of Jonathan Edwards in New England, and benefit hugely from his written reports of it. There was abroad at the time a strong conviction that the mighty God of revival in the American colonies was also at work in a powerful a manner in the Welsh counties.

An attempt has been made to set Williams in the appropriate ethos to which he belonged. Methodism may have drawn quite extensively on the veins of Pietistic influences in which individualistic, 'other-worldly', and subjectivist tendencies were conspicuously prominent. But this needs some qualification when dealing with Welsh Methodism, simply for the reason that it was modified by a solid Calvinistic theology and spirituality. Welsh Methodists aimed at reproducing New Testament Christianity, and if this bore evidence of the practices of Pietism, it was a Christianity safeguarded by the constraints of a vigorous Reformed pedigree. This is the reason why frequent references to John Calvin's writings appear in this work. The Welsh Calvinistic Methodists, in the estimate of this writer, are firmly in the Reformed tradition. Their strength lay in what they brought to that tradition with their insistence on holding together God's sovereignty and human personality in the work of grace. In this sense they considerably enhanced that tradition, and Williams was in the forefront of that contribution.

Welsh Calvinistic Methodism continues to this day, although its preferred name is 'The Presbyterian Church of Wales', reflecting a drift away from its roots of experimental Christianity to ecclesiastical organization. It is also important to emphasize that during Williams's lifetime, Welsh Methodism's Calvinism, like all true Calvinism, was concerned with 'the whole counsel of God' rather than with the definition or preservation of a party spirit. The evidence for this is irrefutable as the life and ministry of Williams unfolds. For this reason, the book deals with Calvinistic Methodist beliefs and practices rather than with ecclesiastical structures. Williams could not faithfully be portrayed in any other way.

For the benefit of readers for whom Williams is comparatively unknown, it may be appropriate at this point to include assessments of Williams's contribution by some leading authorities. They all agree in using superlative categories to do so. For Bobi Jones, Williams 'is the greatest Welsh writer between the end of the fifteenth and the beginning of the twentieth century, and at least two-thirds of his renown is founded on the thousand or so hymns he wrote ... They were written to be sung in public and to provide spiritual instruction and articulation for hundreds of congregations; but the energy and sensitivity that are so evident in very many of these songs poured out of an urgent and extraordinary personal inspiration ... if one thing emerges from the study of Pantycelyn, it is this: not only did he have a penetrating creative faculty and a sensitive taste for language, but he probably possessed the most precise analytical brain in the Wales of his time.'[1] Prominence is also given to Williams's hymns by Glyn Tegai Hughes in an article on Williams's influence: 'the constant and powerful undercurrent of Pantycelyn's hymns is the emphasis on the divinity of Christ's love and man's total dependence on God's saving grace ... Williams's hymns were the real Confession of Faith of the Methodists, and they became in the course of the nineteenth century some kind of Confession of Experience for the majority of Welsh believers.'[2]

Saunders Lewis, writing from a Roman Catholic standpoint, saw Williams's genius as mystical, having close affinity with what was known as Romanticism. Poets within this movement drew heavily on a highly introspective and individualistic motivation. Written in 1927, Lewis's conclusion proved influential and controversial. Sixty years later it was shown to be deeply flawed by R. Tudur Jones, with his assertion that 'it was not the experience that was amazing, but what was conveyed through it ... the means (that is, the experience) is subjective, but the substance (that is, Christ) is objective.'[3] In another work, Jones says that Williams 'holds a unique position ... He was a man of rich culture and profound religious experience. What made his contribution to spirituality unique were his gifts as an author. He stands in the front rank of European hymn-writers and at his best he expresses in an incomparable way the richness of the spiritual life fostered by the Evangelical Revival. His significance extends beyond his hymns.'[4]

Jones's sentiments regarding Williams's significance is important. It is not merely the fact that Williams's hymns by their popularity have dominated the heritage he bequeathed, but also, as R. Geraint Gruffydd admits, 'his work, like the work of every genius, is full of surprising things and hard to explain.'[5] To appreciate that significance, then, involves consideration of Williams as preacher, spiritual counsellor, and prose writer as well. It is for this reason that Derec Llwyd Morgan's comments about Williams are so appropriate: 'he is not first among equals at all, but a giant, a giant far above the ordinary ... I referred to him as a giant, a giant of a pioneer. Give him yet another name: revolutionary, a revolutionary artist ... Those who were blazing the trail in the revival realized that the newness of their religious expression needed a fresh style of literature to be its handmaid ... in the forties of the eighteenth century Williams is an example of a talented young man who providentially discovers his proper task; and the fusion of these two things, the talent and the task, generating within him a totally unexpected and indispensable dynamic.'[6]

A Welsh essay on the life and death of Williams by Thomas Charles of Bala in his *Trysorfa Ysbrydol* ('Spiritual Treasury') published in

1813 provided an early, if brief, fund of material. Edward Morgan's fuller account, *Ministerial Record; or Brief Account of the Great Progress of Religion under the ministry of William Williams, of Pantycelyn, Carmarthenshire,* appeared in 1847. It stemmed from his interest in Daniel Rowland of Llangeitho and David Jones of Llan-gan, his account of the former appearing in 1840 and of the latter a year later. J. R. Kilsby Jones introduced his *Holl Weithiau Prydyddawl a Rhyddieithol y Diweddar Barch. William Williams, Pant-y-celyn* ('Complete Poetic and Prose Works of the late Rev. William Williams, Pantycelyn') in 1867 with a short memoir, as did N. Cynhafal Jones in his two-volume edition of the works of Williams Pantycelyn, *Gweithiau Williams Pant-y-celyn,* in 1887 and 1891. The first volume of a work under the joint authorship of John Morgan Jones and William Morgan appeared in 1890 with a valuable chapter on Williams. This was translated into English by John Aaron and published in 2008 under the title *The Calvinistic Methodist Fathers of Wales.* No evaluation of Williams could ignore Gomer Morgan Roberts's two-volumes on Williams, *Y Per Ganiedydd (Pantycelyn)* ('The Sweet Singer [Pantycelyn]'), which appeared with the subtitles *Trem ar ei fywyd* ('A survey of his life') in 1949, and *Arweiniad i'w waith* ('An introduction to his work') in 1958. These are comprehensive and reliable to such an extent that any subsequent writer might be charged with plagiarism. In 1964 the Board of Celtic Studies of the University of Wales issued Williams's two epic poems, edited by Gomer Morgan Roberts, followed by a second volume in 1967 with Williams's prose works, edited by Garfield H. Hughes. Both appeared with the title *Gweithiau William Williams Pantycelyn.* In this English work I have sought to introduce him to an English constituency in keeping with the subtitle of the book. This in some measure accounts for its length, and the necessity for translations at various points has been another reason.

Literature on Williams is vast, mostly in Welsh, and chiefly concerned with an evaluation of his contribution as a poet and hymn-writer. This is not without reason; his writings are written predominantly in Welsh, and his reputation is chiefly that of hymn-writer. In turn, however, it creates some difficulties when writing about him in English while at the same time seeking to convey his overall contribution to what by the end of the century came to be known as 'the Great Awakening'. This has involved much translation of original material, with varying degrees of success, but the prime consideration has been to maintain the integrity of the original. Translations by others have been acknowledged.

Original manuscripts were often written without grammatical and typographic consistency, and in the main these have been modernized or corrected, in the conviction that the original form may be viewed by consulting the appropriate reference. Bible verses are quoted in the King James Version of 1611 since this would have been the equivalent in Williams's day of the standard Welsh Bible of 1620.

It will soon be apparent to the reader that the author's standpoint, historically and theologically, is in full sympathy with that of Williams himself. With regard to history, in an early essay Gomer M. Roberts concluded that 'Williams did not write from the perspective of history, but from that of Methodism' when he portrayed the period prior to the Great Awakening as 'blackest night.'[7] This is only partly true: Williams was not only a competent hymn-writer, he was also a good historian, careful to view events within the framework of God's standards as well as God's providence. Every effort has been made to write this book within the same constraints. As for the aim in writing, a declaration by John Calvin of the motive behind his literary work bears repetition: 'I am sensible that it would have been much more agreeable to the taste of many, had I heaped together a great mass of materials which has great show, and acquires fame for the writer; but I have felt nothing to be of more importance than to have a regard for the edification of the Church.'[8] A modern writer on Williams has expressed a similar conclusion with regard to Williams: 'Williams's craft is an aesthetic handmaid to his message ... his purpose behind all that he wrote is the same, namely "to feed God's flock in the wilderness."'[9] The present writer shares that objective as well, however short achievement may have fallen of desire.

Mention of 'God's flock' confirms that Williams did not write to impress the public with his wide reading, or to entertain congregations with poetic flair. His only purpose was to bring his readers and congregations face to face with God. Iain H. Murray records an incident in the life of Dr D. Martyn Lloyd-Jones which bears this out. In the summer of 1949, after unremitting ministerial labours, and low in spirit, Lloyd-Jones was urged to rest. Recuperating at Bristol, he had an experience of spiritual reassurance in his room which dissolved his fears and strengthened his soul. Some two weeks later, while on holiday near Bala, North Wales, he 'had retired early one Saturday evening. Alone ..., he was reading the Welsh hymns of William Williams in the Calvinistic Methodist hymn book when he was again given such a consciousness of the presence and love of God as seemed to excel all that he had ever known before. It was a foretaste of glory.'[10] This was the reason why, at a conference for Christian ministers, Lloyd-Jones could say that Williams's hymns 'have an incomparable blend of truly great poetry and perfect theology.'[11] On an equally personal note, and extending those sentiments to the whole range of Williams's works, this author can say that they have often revived the soul with a deep, powerful impression of the majesty and mercy of God.

Abbreviations

Cal	Boyd Stanley Schlenther and Eryn Mant White, *Calendar of the Trevecka Letters*, Aberystwyth, 2003
CH	*Cylchgrawn Cymdeithas Hanes y Methodistiaid Calfinaidd/ The Journal of the Historical Society of the Presbyterian Church of Wales* (1916-76; New Series 1977-). See also TMS
CMA	Calvinistic Methodist Archives, National Library of Wales, Aberystwyth
Cyn	N. Cynhafal Jones, *Gweithiau Williams Pant-y-celyn*, Cyfrol I, Treffynnon, 1887; Cyfrol II, Newport, 1891
DWB	J. E. Lloyd and R. T. Jenkins (eds.), *The Dictionary of Welsh Biography down to 1940*, London, 1959
GMR1	Gomer Morgan Roberts, *Y Per Ganiedydd [Pantycelyn]*, Cyfrol I, 'Trem ar ei fywyd', Aberystwyth, 1949
GMR2	Gomer Morgan Roberts, *Y Per Ganiedydd [Pantycelyn]*, Cyfrol II, 'Arweiniad i'w waith', Aberystwyth, 1958.
GWP1	Gomer Morgan Roberts (gol.), Gweithiau Williams Pantycelyn, Caerdydd, 1964
GWP2	Garfield H. Hughes (gol.), *Gweithiau Williams Pantycelyn* Caerdydd, 1967
HHD	Howel Harris's Diaries, Calvinistic Methodist Archive, National Library of Wales, Aberystwyth
Kilsby	J. R. Kilsby Jones, *Holl Weithiau y Diweddar Barch. William Williams*, Pant-y-celyn, Llundain, [1867]
Morgan	E[dward] Morgan, *Ministerial record: or, Brief Account of the Great Progress of Religion under the Ministry of Rev. W. Williams, of Pantycelyn, Carmarthenshire*, London, 1847
NLW	National Library of Wales, Aberystwyth. Followed by MS indicates a Manuscript number or collection
ODNB	Lawrence Goldman, Brian Harrison, Colin Matthew (eds), *Oxford Dictionary of National Biography*,

	60 Volumes, Oxford, 2004
Theo	Eifion Evans, *Pursued by God: A selective translation with notes of the Welsh religious classic, Theomemphus by William Williams of Pantycelyn,* Bridgend, 1996
TL	The Trevecka Letters, Calvinistic Methodist Archives, National Library of Wales, Aberystwyth
TMS	The Trevecka Manuscript Supplement. This appeared in two series issued at intervals as part of CH (see above)
Trysorfa	Thomas Charles, 'Buchwedd a Marwolaeth y Parch William Williams, o Bant y Celyn, Sir Gaerfyrddin', *Trysorfa, &c.*, Ionawr, 1813

1.

'Truth in the head'

'A respectable, honest farmer' is the description given of William Williams's father by Thomas Charles, his first biographer.[1] Another tribute speaks of him as 'one of the ruling elders in Cefnarthen church … a sober, just and quiet Christian, and one that had an easy passage through the wilderness of this world to the desired country.'[2] Such was John Williams, a man considerably older than his wife, Dorothy, who bore him six children. William was born in 1717, being the only one of three boys to survive to adulthood. They farmed Cefn-coed, in the parish of Llanfair-ar-y-bryn, some three miles to the east of Llandovery in Carmarthenshire. It was only a mile or so from Dorothy's home farm of Pantycelyn which she was to inherit after the death of her two brothers.

Farmhouses of the time would have been whitewashed, the land used for grazing sheep and horses, but also some cattle which were usually black and small. Pastureland was fertilized with lime, easily available in a county where there were several limekilns. Cereal production was chiefly barley and oats, and these were consumed as oatcakes or barley bread, together with butter and cheese. Until the second half of the century there were substantial tracts of woodland, but these were denuded with the demands of the developing coal, iron and tin industries. At home, the women were occupied with spinning, carding and cloth weaving, but also in knitting stockings, Llandovery being famous for selling the latter commodity. It was a busy town in the rich pastureland of the Towy river which flowed to the sea at Carmarthen. At the beginning of the century Llandovery had 'about a hundred houses meanly built', and several inns. Markets were held on Wednesday and Saturday, and during the year there were three fairs, on St George's Day (23 April), Whit-Tuesday and 17 December.[3] The parish church was Llandingad, with Llanfair-ar-y-bryn as an attached chapelry whose parish extended eastward.

The town was used by the drovers as an important staging post between the west and Brecon as they drove their cattle to urban centres in England. Llandovery was also a commercial centre, and one of the drovers, David Jones, was to set up a Welsh bank in the town in 1799, 'Banc yr Eidion Du' ('the Bank of the Black Ox'). Other travellers, less familiar with the area, and more concerned with comfort than commerce, had grave misgivings about the roads. Signposts were often misleading, landmarks sometimes indistinguishable, and the road surface varied from mediocre to atrocious. Maps were cluttered and inaccurate, and the spelling of some Welsh place-names, notoriously difficult at best for an English publisher, was unrecognizable. From the 1760s turnpike trusts were established to take over the main arterial routes in South Wales, in the vain hope that they would improve road conditions. The trusts were composed mainly of farmers and the gentry, and for their maintenance they could exact a toll from users, but the anticipated goal was seldom realized.[4] The county town, Carmarthen, some thirty miles to the west, was thought of by some as 'the London of Wales', while Swansea, a similar distance to the south, was a thriving industrial town and a busy coal-exporting port.[5] For his travels on horseback, Williams would have used more familiar and direct tracks through forests, across rivers, and over mountains. The delights and dangers of those journeys sometimes found expression in his hymns.

The Williams family worshipped at Cefnarthen, an Independent church with a rich Nonconformist tradition and a strong membership. A report to the bishop in 1710 states that, 'of 150 families belonging to Llanfair-ar-y-bryn, one half of them are supposed to be Presbyterians.'[6] During Williams's boyhood there were theological tensions within the congregation on the meaning of God's grace. The Arminian party, following the minister, Roger Williams, held that man was free to co-operate or otherwise with God's grace, so that salvation was a partnership between God and man. Consistent with this affirmation of man's free will, was the possibility of defection from grace. In contrast, the Calvinists maintained that God's grace was sovereign, the Holy Spirit working faith and repentance in the soul, and producing an irresistible, irreversible and triumphant salvation. Following the death of Roger Williams in 1730, these tensions were reflected in the choice of three ministers, one of whom was Calvinist. Matters came to a head towards the end of 1739, and by July the following year the Calvinist section had constituted themselves a separate congregation, meeting at Clunypentan farmhouse, a short distance from Cefn-coed. John Williams was one of the founding members of this new cause. A permanent place of worship for them was erected in 1749 at Pentre-tŷ-gwyn on Pantycelyn land given by William Williams and his mother. Many years later Williams was to put in poetic form the havoc wrought by doctrinal controversy and neglecting the demands of brotherly love:

> It set men's thoughts in turmoil, divisions followed fast,
> The church split into parties, for union could not last;
> Zeal for obscure issues, in those already blind,
> One pulpit's favoured doctrine flayed by the other kind. [7]

Such controversy diverted the energies of the churches from the task of saving souls. It may also have been a negative factor in a later decision by Williams to become an Anglican clergyman rather than a Nonconformist pastor. One thing is clear, during these early years Williams remained a stranger to saving faith.

This is not to say that sound teaching and true worship were absent from Nonconformity. Various Exhortations to family worship were in circulation at the time.[8] Six major editions of the standard Welsh Bible had appeared between 1660 and 1730, with 40,000 copies printed. It had been translated into Welsh originally by William Morgan in 1588, and revised jointly by John Davies and Richard Parry in 1620. As for an English Bible, Williams possessed a copy of the Geneva or Breeches Bible of 1582. This was the most influential version, with 126 editions prior to the appearance in 1611 of the King James Bible.[9] As well as providing an accurate text, the Geneva Bible included marginal comments in keeping with the Reformed theology of Calvin and his successor, Theodore Beza.

For a devout Christian public, the Puritan writings of the previous century formed a rich resource of spiritual nourishment. Welsh editions of 'best-selling' titles included Richard Baxter's *Call to the Unconverted* (1659), Joseph Alleine's *Sure Guide to Heaven* (1693), Lewis Bayly's *Practice of Piety* (1629), and John Bunyan's *Pilgrim's Progress* (1688). These combined theological depth with personal application, emphasised the individual's need for spiritual new-birth, taught the initiative of grace in salvation, and provided practical counsel for godly living. Various tracts against the evils of the time were sponsored and distributed by the SPCK, (the Society for the Promotion of Christian Knowledge) in the early 1700s: *Exhortations against Lying; Dissuasive from the Sin of Drinking; Dissuasive from Play Houses; Caution against Profane Swearers; Persuasive towards*

3

the Observation of the Lord's Day; Rebuke to the Sin of Uncleanliness. Tracts against Popery and the Quakers were available from the same source.[10]

Even more accessible and appealing to Williams would have been the Welsh poems of a Llandovery clergyman of the previous century, Rhys Prichard. He was affectionately known as 'Vicar Prichard', a Calvinist Anglican, reforming crusader and open-air preacher all rolled into one. Bearing the title *Cannwyll y Cymry* ('The Welshman's Candle'), fourteen editions had been published between 1658 and 1730.[11] The poems had stirred the imagination of the ordinary people with their lively, simple style and down-to-earth language:

> Sell your lands and sell your chattel,
> Sell your shirt, and sell your cattle,
> Sell, if needs be, all you treasure
> To possess the whole of Scripture.

> Better have no drink, no eating,
> House, nor fire, bed nor clothing,
> Light of day, nor sun's warm shining,
> Than to have no Gospel teaching.

More importantly, the Vicar's poems formed a kind of poor man's manual of theology, expressing biblical truth in easily-remembered, pithy sayings. Doctrinally they were orthodox and Bible-based, and they combined an evangelistic thrust with detailed moral guidance. There was also about them an urgency and directness which had instant appeal. All in all, Prichard's work was a superb model for communicating the Gospel. This was especially true at a time when the spoken word and memory were the chief means of disseminating information. In his use of both language and rhyme, Williams may be regarded as a disciple of Prichard, esteeming him 'the first among the poets'.[12]

Together with the psalm and hymn-singing, Williams in his unconverted days would have been familiar with the religious exercises of listening to sermons and catechizing. The chapel architecture of Nonconformity, with the pulpit in a prominent place, unmistakably conveyed the centrality and importance of preaching. Given the theological tensions at Cefnarthen, the sermons would have been controversial rather than devotional. On Tuesday, 1 January 1740, the evangelical Independent minister, Edmund Jones of Pontypool, had preached there on 'Election'. Within seven months the Calvinists

4

separated, and Jones celebrated the first communion service among them with 36 communicants in August of that year. In the same month, Mary, William Williams's sister, married the previous year, was admitted into membership at the age of 19 years, after deliberation and 'with much concern, affection and tenderness' by Jones. There is no record to show that her brother, four years her senior, was in membership.[13] On a broader canvas, Nonconformist sermons were reckoned to be dull and theoretical, objects of derision, and bringing upon their preachers the label 'Y Sentars Sychion' ('the Dry Dissenters'). Their piety at that time has been portrayed as 'dignified, courageous, serious, intellectual and solid. But it was hardly the type of religion that would bring the Christian gospel to those who were as yet beyond its scope.'[14] With some notable exceptions, Anglican sermons were no better, but for a different reason. Here there was no pretence at evangelical orthodoxy, merely polished essays extolling the virtues of reason and morality. The Established Church's ineffectiveness was acknowledged in print by such titles as, *A treatise concerning the Causes of the Present Corruption of Christians, and the remedies thereof*, which was issued in 1700 by the SPCK.[15] Two decades later, Erasmus Saunders's *View of the State of Religion in the Diocese of St. David's* exposed the parish clergy's ignorance, non-residence, pluralism, and inability to speak Welsh. Many church buildings were in a sad state of repair, 'the solitary habitations of owls and jackdaws', and in others it was rare, 'if at all, to meet with preaching, catechising, or administering the Holy Communion.' [16] The religious revival in which Williams was to labour, evidently met a real and profound spiritual need.

Welsh translations of the Prayer Book Catechism were widely available during Williams's childhood, but in Nonconformist circles preference would have been given to those produced by the Westminster Assembly of Divines in the 1640s. These usually bore the title *Egwyddorion a Sylfeini'r Grefydd Gristnogol* ('Principles and Foundations of the Christian Religion'), and at least seven editions had appeared in Welsh by 1740.[17] Their framework followed the pattern of the Apostles' Creed, the Ten Commandments and the Lord's Prayer, but they aimed to provide a Scriptural summary of the way of salvation. Hence, the opening question and answer of *The Shorter Catechism* is a profound lead-in to the meaning of faith and discipleship: 'Question: What is the chief end of man? Answer: Man's chief end is to glorify God, and to enjoy him for ever.' Towards the end of his life, Williams refers to these catechisms, along with the Assembly's Confession of Faith as 'deserving of the greatest respect and acceptance', and as 'some of the most illustrious beauties of the Reformation.'[18]

A number of schools were available for Williams's early education, the nearest being that associated with the Nonconformist church at Cefnarthen. At Llandovery there were schools associated with its parish church of Llandingad and at the chapelry of Llanfair-ar-y-bryn. From an early age he appears to have been a lover of books. His name appears as one of the subscribers to the second edition of *Drych y Prif Oesoedd* ('Mirror of the First Ages') by Theophilus Evans in 1740, a book that set out a romanticised history of Wales, the overthrow of its early form of Christianity by the Papacy, and how the Faith is propagated in its integrity in the Anglican Church. A popular work by Ellis Wynne, *Gweledigaetheu y Bardd Cwsg* ('The Visions of the Sleeping Bard'), which appeared in 1703, reflected the deep-seated anxieties of the age in the matter of death and hell.[19] Williams's library also included copies of Virgil and Ovid, Latin, Greek and French grammars, various dictionaries, and books on history. Literature with a less solemn purpose was readily available in English. Chief among these were Jonathan Swift's *Gulliver's Travels* (published in 1726, and one of the most reprinted books in English) and the almost as perennially popular work of Daniel Defoe, *Robinson Crusoe* (1719). University education was denied to Nonconformists, but there is ample evidence that Williams had a cultured mind.

To 'complete his education', writes Thomas Charles, Williams went to an academy at Llwynllwyd, near Hay-on-Wye, with the intention of becoming a doctor. Two medical men may have influenced the young Williams to pursue a medical career. John Williams, one of the ministers that followed Roger Williams at Cefnarthen, was esteemed for his patience and gentleness, but he was also 'a noted physician and a very skilful surgeon'.[20] The other medical man was John Jones of Myddfai, the last of a family of doctors, who died in 1739. Myddfai is a village three miles south of Llandovery, but his medical practice was based in the town itself.[21]

Llwyn-llwyd was a farm in Llanigon parish, and 'Academy' was a pretentious name for the institution since its activities were held in a barn.[22] It was a Nonconformist institution that provided teaching in the classics and humanities mainly, but with a definite bias towards theological subjects. English, Mathematics, Latin, Greek, Hebrew and Moral Philosophy (Logic and Ethics) were regarded as essential for any professional career at the time. History, Geography, Physics and Chemistry were attracting more interest, with the appearance in 1728 of the *Cyclopoedia* of Ephraim Chambers. At a contemporary Academy in Northampton, anatomy featured in the syllabus for third year students. Although his first language would have been Welsh, Williams was fluent in English. His knowledge of the classics surfaces in quotations on the title-pages of some of his books, and his writings show an interest in the sciences that was extensive. [23]

The two tutors, Vavasor Griffiths and David Price, were both ministers, and their joint labours were shared between two locations, Llwyn-llwyd and Chancefield, each within easy reach of Talgarth in Breconshire. Price seems to have been responsible for overall management, while Griffiths taught the senior students. Williams may have been lodging in Talgarth with a relative of the same name, the minister of Tredwstan, two miles from the town. The Independent chapel at Tredwstan was numerically strong, with 250 members in 1715. The pastor was 'an excellent scholar, and a painstaking, successful minister', and considered to be 'among the most notable and useful ministers of his generation.' However, it was only after 1742 that he 'preached faith', so that during Williams's time at the Academy his sermons would have advocated dependence on human effort rather than on divine grace.[24]

At the time, a recently published book, Bishop Joseph Butler's *The Analogy of Religion, Natural and Revealed* (1736), was causing a stir in theological circles. It soon came to be accepted as an effective broadside against the authority, adequacy and finality of reason which had been claimed by John Locke in his book, *The Reasonableness of Christianity* (1695), and in Matthew Tindal's *Christianity as Old as Creation* (1730). Butler drew attention to the fact that as there are unexplained mysteries in the realm of nature, so also in religion: miracles, prophecies and the work of Christ cannot be rationally understood. He also argued that even as reason is supported by experience in everyday life, and moral sensitivities are monitored by conscience, so also, in an analogous way, spiritual mysteries are only understood by divine revelation. Rationalism had a devastating effect on Nonconformists as well as Anglicans, and Michael R. Watts draws attention to it in this way: 'Beyond the problems of social adjustment which faced Dissenters in the age of toleration lay more serious problems of religious adjustment raised by the transition from the enthusiasm of the mid-seventeenth century to the rationalism of the early eighteenth. In so far as Dissenters were now looking to Locke rather than to Calvin for intellectual support for their faith, and in proportion to their readiness to seek inspiration from human reason rather than the Spirit of God, their zeal flagged and their congregations dwindled.'[25]

When his mind had been enlightened by Gospel truth, Williams came to recognize the bankruptcy of contemporary religion. He, too, would maintain that however convincing the arguments, however extensive the range of man's studies, the power of God's Spirit alone could bring light and life to the soul:

> 'Tis nought to hear of doctrine, though splendid to the mind,
> 'Tis heaven's power only, no less, that I must find;
> Base error and true teaching, to me are both the same
> While I, beneath sin's burden, still grovel in my shame.
>
> How much I need God's power! For this a world I'd give,
> For Satan's full of knowledge; this only, makes none live;
> Without the Word that quickens, and in it heaven's power,
> I'll pine away and perish, though kneeling by the hour.
>
> But oh! it profits nothing, to know truth in the head,
> Mere knowing may not influence, the heart is still not fed;
> To prove it all is different, a taste of pardoning grace
> Would make my life most blessed, my home the happiest place. [26]

A godly home, a disciplined church background, early medical ambitions, and foundational studies at a Nonconformist Academy, all these had significance for William Williams, the future Methodist soul physician and hymn-writer. But it took the earnest labours of a young, fiery evangelist to bring him to faith in Christ. Only then would he 'prove' and 'taste' God's grace for himself so that his life and home would be blessed and a blessing.

2.

'The Language of Canaan'

Williams, according to Thomas Charles, 'studied the art of healing diligently, and to the day of his death he benefited many by his medical advice.' The reason for the radical departure from his original intention to enter the medical profession is also given by Charles: 'But when the Lord called him by grace, he gave himself fully to the work of the sacred ministry. On his way home from the Academy, a.d. 1738, he was called while listening to Mr. H. Harris preaching his important message after the service in Talgarth churchyard.'[1] This man, Howel Harris, aged 24 at the time, and born in nearby Trefeca, was God's instrument in Williams's conversion.

Harris had been convicted of sin at Talgarth church on Palm Sunday, 1735. The words of the vicar, Pryce Davies, about fitness for communion had affected him powerfully and profoundly: 'if you are not fit to come to the Lord's Table, you are not fit to live, you are not fit to die.' At the time he was teaching at a school held at Llangasty church, three miles from his home at Trefeca. He now spent time at the church for another purpose as well, namely, to reflect on his spiritual state, and one day, to give himself to God. Efforts at self-reformation followed, without relief, until Whit-Sunday, when 'the spiritual world, and eternity began ... to appear ... I felt some insatiable desires after the salvation of poor sinners ... all my heart was drawn from the world and visible things ... and could not help telling in going home from Church ... that I knew my sins were forgiven me.' Three weeks later, while in meditation at Llangasty, he felt that 'the love of God was shed abroad' in his heart (Romans 5: 5). Another verse drawn to his attention, Malachi 3:6, 'I am the Lord, I change not; therefore ye sons of Jacob are not consumed', brought reassurance, and a compulsion to share the Gospel with others. In retrospect he wrote:

> All my study was now to show my gratitude to God ... Now the fire of God did so burn in my soul, that I could not rest day nor night, without doing something for my God and Saviour; nor could I go with satisfaction to sleep, if I had not done something for his glory

9

> that day … Thus I spent that summer, 1735. In the beginning of
> November following, I went to *Oxford* and entered at *St. Mary's
> Hall…* My friends now were in hopes I should be effectually cured
> of my enthusiasm (as they called it); but the Lord Jesus had now got
> possession of my heart … when I saw the irregularities, and
> immoralities which surrounded me there, I became soon weary of
> that place, and cried to God to deliver me from thence; and thus,
> after keeping that term, I was again brought to my dear friends
> in *Wales*.[2]

It was not only his friends who accused Harris of 'enthusiasm', the
powerfully emotive word of the day for religious fanaticism. His
brother, Joseph, and the vicar also expressed their disapproval of his
behaviour.

Personal appropriation of biblical precepts and promises, sustained
communion with God, urgent pleas to others to consider their souls'
welfare, all these were now close to Harris's heart. His Christian
profession and practice was now far removed from the decorum and
formality of the parishioners of his day. There were other aspects, too,
that disturbed his contemporaries: in particular, his insistence on the
new birth and his assurance of salvation. In his defence, Harris claimed
that the clergy were strangers to regeneration, and therefore he never
heard them preach it. For the authorities another stumbling block was
Harris's practice of 'exhorting' his neighbours while still a layman, and
his unrestrained evangelistic journeys. Maintaining a balance between
church order and meeting an urgent spiritual need had always
created tensions within Protestantism. In the cauldron of mid
seventeenth-century Puritanism, Richard Baxter maintained that it was
'better that men should be disorderly saved than orderly damned: and
that the Church should be disorderly preserved than orderly
destroyed.'[3]For Harris in the next century, urgency was enough to
vindicate his mission: 'shall I neglect doing present good to follow
private studies? I know not how short my time is, and zeal, that
heavenly gift, is a fire sooner put out by negligence than by opposition
…Though I can't fall to study the languages of Greece and Italy, yet I
am wholly willing to study the … language of Canaan … I am not for
dallying with earthly toys while heaven is so full in my view.'[4] And
Williams mentions as one sign of religious revival that many young
people 'learned the language of Canaan' at such a time of
unparalleled Gospel success. Neither he nor Harris were referring to
Hebrew or Aramaic; they had in mind how citizens of the kingdom of

heaven speak to one another, much as the pilgrims in John Bunyan's classic allegory 'naturally spoke the language of Canaan', which proved a puzzle to the people of Vanity Fair.[5] Conversion brings with it a different culture as well as a new direction.

The vicar warned Harris that non-compliance with the Anglican Church's rules would compel him to report the matter to the bishop, a measure that would 'prove an unmoveable obstruction' to ordination. Faced with this dilemma, Harris was advised by some local friends to consult a Carmarthenshire clergyman, Griffith Jones, whose fame had spread far and wide, and who had himself experienced censure from the ecclesiastical authorities. Fired by a sense of divine calling, Jones had attracted large crowds and, since his zeal could not be contained within his own parish, the censure of his bishop. In his defence, he claimed that his extra-parochial activities were at the invitation of the clergy, and this was accepted. His message was biblical, his preaching forthright and direct. From 1716 until his death in 1761 he was Rector of Llanddowror, becoming famous as a pioneering strategist for Christian education, setting up circulating charity schools, teaching the illiterate to read through the medium of Welsh, and using his extensive catechism to provide Scripture knowledge. In all over 3,300 such schools were established, and their fame spread as far as Russia.[6] He proclaimed Christ as the only Saviour from sin, and urged upon his hearers to turn to God in repentance and faith. His insistence on God's grace rather than man's efforts as the ground of salvation flew in the face of popular religion. In spite of such difficulties he remained a fervent Anglican throughout his life, accepting the constraints as well as the strengths of both the Thirty-nine Articles and the Book of Common Prayer. His labours were recognized as an important contribution to the coming religious revival in Wales, a kind of 'Morning Star', much as John Wycliffe and John Hus had been for the Protestant Reformation. An elegy to Jones's memory by Williams bears witness to this:

> This the man, e'er dawn had broken
> In revival on the land,
> Pure Gospel seed had scattered
> Seeking harvests like the sand;
> Many reapers now have followed,
> Oh! how plentiful the yield!
> Now the sieve and fan are active
> So that good fruit may be sealed.

In the opinion of some 'he was the greatest Welshman of the eighteenth century.'[7] With his own experience of censure and the advantage of maturity and wisdom, Jones counselled Harris to seek ordination, even though it meant delay for his evangelistic activities.

This Harris did four times, without success, but not altogether with regret. He felt that such a settlement would have seriously curtailed the realization of his evangelistic vision. In his words it would have been 'contrary to the spirit I am acted [urged on] by; my desires are general, without any limits.' It appeared to him that the whole country 'lay in a lukewarm, dead condition', and that sermons were scarce and often legalistic. 'Feeling the love of Christ' in his heart, this was transposed by him into 'an absolute necessity of going about to propagate the Gospel' of his 'dear Master and Redeemer.' He was prepared to submit to the bishop on condition that he was given a license 'to go about to preach the Gospel to poor sinners that perish, and to have private societies to build up such as are awakened and to catechize them.'[8] For the authorities it was a concession too far, and he was never ordained.

Williams's elegy testifies to Harris's evangelistic zeal, solemnity, and authority:

> In the thunder was his dwelling,
> In the cloud his awful place;
> (A spirit broken, bruised, but ardent
> Obtains the King of heaven's grace).
> Thence he hurled tremendous lightnings,
> Flaming with terrific sway,
> On the dark, benighted thousands,
> Who in sin's foul regions lay.
>
> Come and hear him preach, describing
> Man's foul heart – so prone to sin;
> Tracing every inward turning,
> Full of error, found within;
> And disclosing many secrets
> To the righteous on their way,
> While enlivening death's cold region
> With the glorious Gospel ray.
>
> Come and hear him now expounding
> Heaven's free, redeeming grace;
> Loudly praising the Redeemer

> Of our poor apostate race;
> Lo! He causes many a pilgrim,
> Sore oppressed with fear and grief,
> To depart in joyous freedom
> From the bonds of unbelief.[9]

The first occasion that Williams heard Harris was like 'a summons straight from glory' to his soul, and he says of Harris's manner:

> In a solemn, serious spirit,
> With eternity in sight;
> Urging, pleading with the people
> From God's wrath to take their flight.

In another publication, Williams acknowledges that his conversion to Christ was by unlikely means, at an unexpected time, and without any preparation on his part (*'A minnau'n ddibartoad'*). God's sovereign purpose and supervision of personal circumstances, as in the case of so many biblical figures, including Paul, Peter, Zacchaeus and Mary Magdalene, were at work in calling him effectually from sin to righteousness.[10] As for the effect on Williams, it was to be defined in terms commonly used by believers when speaking of their coming to faith in Christ:

> I'll not forget the spot, the ground
> Where wine flowed to my soul's foul wounds,
> From heaven's store in endless spate,
> My wound to heal, my dread, abate.[11]

That was written much later, when his perception of the event had matured. At the time its impact, though memorable, was private and personal rather than public. Thus, although it was customary for Harris to gather converts into a convenient society meeting, where their spiritual understanding and progress could be nurtured, there is no evidence that Williams belonged to one of these groups around Talgarth. However, there is no question as to the pivotal nature of the event for Williams's future. His life and labours can only be appreciated by understanding the meaning of his conversion.

Its most enduring feature for Williams was God's initiative, bringing to his soul a message from heaven that was authoritative, convincing and liberating:

Convictions well nigh triumphed, he hardly could bear more,
The heat of accusation, the pain of guilt was sore;
A word was sent from heaven, a word to heed and heal,
Far greater than creation, and bearing heaven's seal.

He must be found, or perish, in time God's word then came:
'Son! all your sin's forgiven, its debt and guilt and shame,
A ransom was forthcoming, atonement has been done,
And payment has been rendered, no debt is left, not one'.

He leapt with joy unsullied, his spirit deeply moved,
For he now that experienced, till now by him unproved;
He raised his eyes to heaven, before of wrath a store,
But now a sea of mercy and love without a shore.[12]

Repeatedly Williams speaks of God's power in his word, bringing with it life and vigour to the soul.[13] This is clear from his portrait of the fictional character, 'Fidelius', the one he describes as closest to a New Testament Christian. It occurs in his work *Tri Wyr o Sodom a'r Aipht* ('Three Men from Sodom and Egypt'), and he does so in this way: 'he lived a prodigal life, until the time of his espousals and of free grace was fulfilled, and God's eternal purpose brought forth the hour of mercy; then heaven called him with a voice that compelled him, like Saul, to listen; he obeyed the word of life, and returned home to live under the wing of the Gospel of grace.'[14]

Theologically, this is regeneration, the sovereign work of the Holy Spirit, in which the soul is passive, spoken of by Christ to Nicodemus in John 3:3 as the new birth. God breathes new life, spiritual life into the soul, and the sure, inseparable evidence of this is conversion. Conversion is the conscious, active and willing response to God's gracious gift of life. It consists in faith, repentance and new obedience. The entire personality is involved: the understanding, affections, will, memory, conscience and imagination; it implies a setting up of God's kingdom in the heart. In conversion, according to Williams, conflicting emotions are resolved, the understanding that was corrupted by Adam's rebellion in the garden of Eden is restored, the will, previously impregnable like a fortress in its stubborn bias against God, now submits, a hitherto blunted conscience is sharpened to respond to God's word, while memory and passions are now brought into order.[15] He reports the perception of it in the words of a fictional convert:

O blessed hour, when my soul was in the greatest

14

extremity, the day dawned upon me. In a moment I felt my sins forgiven. I received the Word in fullest ecstasy, fuller than any prisoner would feel on being released from the sentence of hanging ... At such time my memory is more alert, and innumerable Scriptures flood my mind ... My senses are sharpened; I understand the things of God in clearer light; my reason and emotions are so disciplined, that I am careful not to say or do anything which would cause my brethren to stumble, or the ungodly to blaspheme ... because a sinner, who has been delivered from misery, is praising the God who brought about this salvation.[16]

Williams also describes the subjective experience of conversion in another work, *Theomemphus*. He does so in terms of forgiveness and acceptance into God's favour, and then he proceeds to tell how it motivates praise:

Bliss came at last to Theo, its nature all sublime,
Not found in earthly creatures, or in the realms of time;
For sin a full forgiveness, for sins of deepest dye,
A pardon freely given, by God who cannot lie.

O! Jesus, how can any, to whom you've given sight,
Forbear from singing praises, and hymns both day and night?
And who can still be silent, that feel Christ's saving blood,
Its value and its virtue, to make us right with God?[17]

Significantly, these experiences came to Theomemphus, in the words of the chapter heading in which they are found, 'after hearing Evangelius', and several other sermons, especially those of 'Boanerges'. Between them, 'Boanerges' and 'Evangelius' had made known to him the Law's dreadful terrors and the Gospel's liberating salvation. It was on these objective statements, conveying the whole counsel of God, that Theomemphus based his personal, subjective response of repentance and faith.

The twin aspects of the object of trust and the content of belief come into focus in the conversion of 'Fidelius' in Williams's work : 'It would be hard to find anyone in his area that exalted Christ more than him; he boasted that Christ was righteousness, sanctification, wisdom, and redemption. And he was so adamant about this that the substance of his counsels, the life of his teachings, together with the entire expression of his prayers, were in conformity with the ways of free grace and atoning righteousness …The whole Bible was Fidelius's body of divinity.'[18] The centrality of Christ for Williams is never in doubt, witness the extended title of one of his Welsh epic poems: 'A View of Christ's Kingdom, or Christ is all, and in all'. The faithful Gospel preacher he describes as one for whom 'Christ is the text and Christ the sermon', and he stressed that the aim of his hymns should be, 'that Jesus alone should be exalted and that horrible little word "I" removed from them.'[19] From such statements, it is clear that, for Williams, Christ and His work have pre-eminence for the believer, and that the Christian life is an ongoing relationship with Him in personal trust and communion. As for the Bible, Williams held it to be

> The full and precious parchment, where safely lies impressed,
> The plan of God's salvation, before the world was blessed.[20]

The Bible, then, made clear the plan of salvation, and through preaching - in Williams's case, that of Harris - the Holy Spirit makes the truth alive, relevant and personal to the sinner. The mind is brought to understand spiritual realities, a new instinct or principle is planted in the heart, and the sinner responds willingly to God's initiative. That new principle is faith:

> The faith that God has planted, a principle divine,
> A witness by its nature which cannot hence decline;
> It firmly grasps what's living, believes the blood once shed
> Shall never lose its power, is living, and not dead.[21]

This faith gave Williams insight into life as a pilgrimage to glory, as a conflict with the flesh, the world and the devil, and as a privileged, accountable citizen in the kingdom of God. Henceforth, for him, too, the language of Canaan now had meaning. It was also the indispensable tool with which he would guide others to that promised land.

16

3.

'Ruffi, Gymmos, and Asafetida'

Before considering the implications of Williams's conversion, Thomas
Charles's account itself deserves more attention because it leaves some
matters undecided. If his conversion took place while he was still at the
Academy it would undoubtedly have given his studies a new direction.
It would also have kept him in touch with Howel Harris. However, a
period of regular contact between them at that time is unsupported by
Harris's diaries, simply by the lack of references to Williams.
In contrast, references to Howel Davies, converted under Harris's
preaching early in 1737, are fervent and frequent. Davies is 'a
companion so faithful and diligent', 'a dear friend ... my
fellow-soldier.'[1] Such allusions continue until November of that year
when Davies moved to be with Griffith Jones at Llanddowror to
prepare for ordination in 1739. Besides this, when Harris prays for
God's help to Williams at his first curacy, he refers to him as 'the young
minister (sent I hope of God)', as if he is speaking of a comparative
stranger.[2] It may also be asked, was Williams speaking of himself when
he sets out the 'reflections' of Theomemphus, the hero of his epic poem
on conversion, 'after hearing Evangelius – meditating in the woods,
and praying'? This would at least suggest an interval between the effect
of Harris's sermon and the later familiarity which existed between
them.[3] Harris seems to have remained unaware for some time of his
instrumentality in Williams's conversion, but he is
acknowledged as such in the elegy that Williams wrote for Harris.[4]
Writing in his diary in 1745, Harris refers to both Davies and Williams
as his 'spiritual children.'[5]

On the other hand, did Charles's words, 'on his way home' mean that
this was the last time for Williams to return home from the Academy,
with his studies for a medical career behind him? If so, a period of two
years elapsed between Williams's conversion and ordination. This
opens up several possibilities. Did he spend those two years as an
apprentice physician somewhere, at nearby Hay-on-Wye, for example,
as has been suggested? Williams's name does not appear in the records
of contemporary registered physicians either at Hay-on-Wye or in the

Llandovery area. This does not exclude the possibility, however, since the name of a friend of Williams, William Read, the apothecary of Pontypool, is also absent.[6] Others have suggested that Williams spent some time as a schoolmaster at Llansawel, but the timing of his stay at this village, the home of his future wife, is in dispute, as being either before or after his curacy within the Established Church. Those who mention this may perhaps be confusing the hymn-writer with another William Williams who, at a later date, 'providentially got a school at Llansawel.'[7]

When Williams left the Llwyn-llwyd Academy for the last time it seems likely that one consideration would have been to help at home on the farm since his father's eyesight had failed in 1736. Responsibility for the farm at Pantycelyn as well, from 1731 the property of Williams's mother, would have added to the workload of the Williams family. A sister of Williams, Mary, was also at Cefn-coed to help, but she was married in December 1739 to Morgan Price of Bronnydd. Both husband and wife became members of the new Calvinist church at Clunypentan, and the church book records of her death in 1751 that she was 'a valuable and useful woman ... much lamented by all', and had left four young children.[8] Farm labourers and maidservants would have been part of the household, but Williams himself would have been, and must have remained throughout his life, involved in all aspects of farm management.

With such hired help, Williams would have had time to practise his medical skills in the area, especially when the death in 1739 of John Jones, the Llandovery physician, raised the issue of a successor. Following a House of Lords ruling in 1701 apothecaries were deemed to be practitioners of medicine, giving advice on treatment as well as supplying medicines. They had to serve an apprenticeship of seven years and pass an examination before they were licensed by the Society of Apothecaries.[9] By 1761 Llandovery could boast of having four apothecaries, but for the period immediately after Jones's death, the emerging skills of an aspiring apprentice would have been welcomed.[10]

During the two crucial years 1738-1740 Williams's commitment to the Christian ministry was growing. At the same time, medical matters and practice may have been receding in their importance and demands on his time, but they never went away altogether. There was no reason for them to do so. It was an age when medical knowledge was less exact, and few ordinary people were able to pay the fees of physicians.

Not a few clergymen found time to indulge and expand their medical interests. It was said of Griffith Jones that he not only fed and clothed the poor 'in considerable numbers, but was likewise a physician to their bodies, as well as their souls. He had by long study, arrived at a great proficiency in medicines; and had large quantities of drugs sent him from London, which he made up, and dispensed to the poor *gratis*; and, through God's blessing, with great success.'[11] Others, such as John Wesley, Daniel Neal and Rowland Hill were also renowned for this. Wesley's *Primitive Physick* of 1747 proved popular, going through several editions. In it, he 'essentially offered instructions in the most direct and simple form, organizing his cures, illness by illness. He kept his *materia medica* simple and within the compass of potential readers.'[12] It is certainly true that Williams's medical references have an air of familiarity and sure-footedness.

In the long poem *Golwg ar Deyrnas Crist* ('A View of Christ's Kingdom'), Williams sets out the marvels of God's handiwork in the anatomy of the human body, from its formation in the embryo to its resting place in the grave. He speaks of veins and arteries, muscles and nerves, bones and flesh, and the circulation of the blood through the heart, and all this on account of the power and wisdom of God.[13] In another book, jealousy is said to drive many to hysteria, depression, jaundice, mental instability and even death.[14] Several of Williams's hymns make free use of medical categories to convey spiritual ailments and remedies: sin is portrayed as poison, Christ as Physician, salvation as healing, and Christ's death on the cross as sin's cure.[15] In the elegy he wrote for William Read in 1769, 'the Physician, Doctor and Apothecary', Williams refers to symptoms, diagnosis, fevers, prescriptions, drugs, medicines, and ointments. And in an imaginary 'letter' to his family from 'the western streets of the Holy City, through the "Star of the Day" gate', Read confesses that he now knows 'about the human frame, its constitution, diseases, their causes and cures, a thousand times better than ever before.' At least one medical book, *A Dissertation of the Nerves*, by W. Smith, had been the property of Read, before it was passed on to Williams.[16] As well as books on General Medicine in Williams's library, there were more specific titles, on the nerves, on fevers, and on midwifery. The mortar used by Williams in preparing the drugs of his choice has been preserved; how he prescribed them, to whom, and with what success cannot now be determined.[17]

When in his sixtieth year, Williams wrote to his son, William, affectionately called Billy, about healthy living. In the letter he placed physical ailments in a spiritual context:

> There is no complaint so distressing as the nervous one, which came upon me by too great attention to reading, writing, over-exertions in travelling and preaching, and by not being sufficiently careful of myself when over-heated or cold. I have been afflicted with it for several years. What gave me great relief, under God's blessing, were opening medicine, exercise in the open air, composure of mind, and digestible food. I avoided taking ardent spirits, and used but little table beer. I endeavour to put off every thing that has a tendency to tire, vex, harass, dishearten, or alarm me; for these are the very food of the nervous complaint. But whenever I am attacked by it, I take the above medicine, and it clears my stomach of all acid, sour, unpleasant matter. Then I relish my food, breathe better, and get warmer in bed. Thus, my dear son, I improve, by God's blessing. I believe your distemper is the same, and that it was in the same way it arrested you. Endeavour to take as much exercise as possible for it; by that means the animal spirits go through the nerves in a lively manner; and when these are any where stopped, the complaint is brought on in another part. But remember, my dear son, that notwithstanding all, it is the Lord that orders, that sends these complaints, and takes them away, by and through means. Therefore lay your case chiefly before him; and pray to him; for the earnest prayer of a righteous man availeth much. I hope my prayers for you are not unanswered. Let not your mind dwell long upon anything.

Williams also mentions pills that he used to treat the condition: 'Ruffi' (with Aloes and Myrrh as the active constituents), 'Gymmos, - and Asafetida mixed with them' (often given for nervous disorders). Aloes was widely used at the time as a purgative. Ten years later, similar advice was given to his other son, John:

> The nervous disorder which continually haunts your mother, myself, and your brother, has taken possession of your nerves also. I wish you had seen Buchan on that malady, which goes under the several names of Hypochondria, Hysterics, and Melancholy. Take great care to go soon to bed, to rise early, and to walk out often. Don't sit long at your books, and don't vex for anything, let it go as it will; eat a little often, but not much at a time. [18]

In the closing chapter of his long poem, *Theomemphus*, Williams lists some of the agents that death, 'the King of Terrors', has at its disposal, in order to convey to his fictional character, the Theomemphus of the title, the transient nature of this life. Among them are consumption (pulmonary tuberculosis), rheumatism, gout, epilepsy, jaundice, smallpox, and pneumonia. For these, when death gives them commission, there is no physician, no doctor, 'no gum from India, no drugs from Peru' that can prevail. By the time Williams wrote the poem in 1764, Williams could say that he had studied death for many years, its ancestry in the Garden of Eden, its power and, until God's 'heavenly grace' intervened, its tyranny. Now he knew that death was only God's servant, already conquered on the cross by Christ, and ultimately to be swallowed up in that victory.[19]

Such knowledge would not have been achieved during Williams's time at the Academy, or in the crucial period following his return home. Medical matters clearly retained their interest for him throughout his lifetime, but thoughts of the Christian ministry became increasingly persistent. Farm work would have been a priority, but during the winter months there would have been more leisure to consider other matters. Life at home in this way would have been conducive to Bible study, meditation, and working through what must have been a growing inward constraint to proclaim the Gospel that had already changed his life. One thing is certain, by 1740 he had become aware of an irresistible call to the ministry of God's Word, and to the more solemn and far-reaching work of healing spiritual ailments.

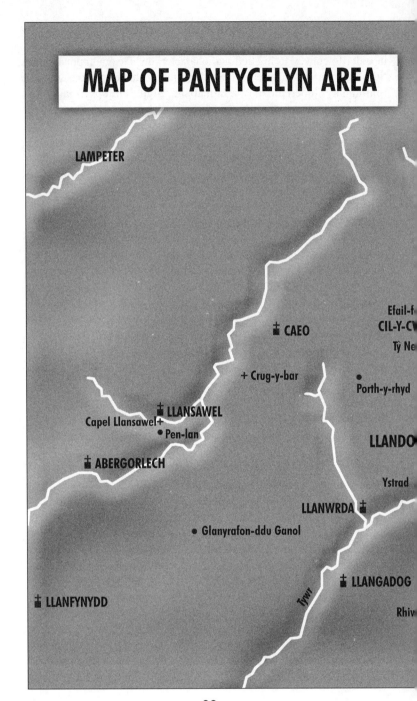

MAP OF PANTYCELYN AREA

LAMPETER

‡ CAEO

Efail-f
CIL-Y-CW
Tŷ Ne

+ Crug-y-bar

● Porth-y-rhyd

‡ LLANSAWEL

Capel Llansawel +
● Pen-lan

LLANDO

‡ ABERGORLECH

Ystrad

LLANWRDA ‡

● Glanyrafon-ddu Ganol

‡ LLANGADOG

‡ LLANFYNYDD

Tywi

Rhiw

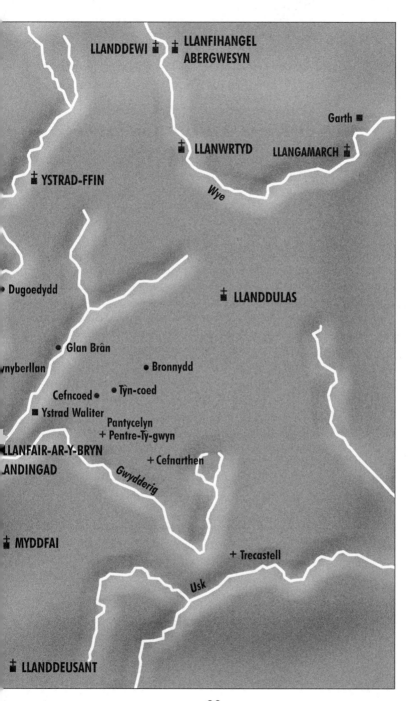

LLANDDEWI

LLANFIHANGEL
ABERGWESYN

Garth

LLANWRTYD   LLANGAMARCH

YSTRAD-FFIN

Wye

Dugoedydd

LLANDDULAS

Glan Brân

nyberllan

Bronnydd

Cefncoed   Tŷn-coed

Ystrad Waliter

Pantycelyn
+ Pentre-Ty-gwyn

LLANFAIR-AR-Y-BRYN

ANDINGAD

+ Cefnarthen

Gwydderig

MYDDFAI

+ Trecastell

Usk

LLANDDEUSANT

23

4.

'An office of vast importance'

Edward Morgan introduces the dilemma which faced Williams on his return home from the Academy in this way: 'Soon after this great change, an office of vast importance came under his most serious consideration, attended, under the divine blessing, with unspeakable usefulness, called the ministry of reconciliation.'[1] Several passages in Williams's writings convey the high esteem in which he held that calling, even though at times he uses fictional characters to make his point. His 'Fidelius', the ideal Christian, looked on ministers as 'sent down from heaven to feed God's flock in the wilderness.'[2] 'Martha Philopur' represents a young believer who seeks advice about genuine revival experiences. She expects that her minister, 'Philo Evangelius', is sufficiently equipped to 'lead her away from every deviation in experience or interpretation of Scripture'.[3] Another reliable guide in spiritual matters, 'Theophilus' in Williams's *Drws y Society Profiad* ('The Door of the Experience Meeting'), acknowledges the temptation for all and sundry to take on an office so highly respected among God's people, but reckons it would be 'a great loss to the Church of God to be deprived of' gifted laymen. He also sets out the criteria by which they are to be distinguished: 'So long as their doctrines are sound, and they continue humble in spirit, living lives becoming to the Gospel of Christ, it is no small sin to despise them, though they have no great learning and are lacking in knowledge both literary and historical. Yet, while they have the substance in them – that is, the Spirit of the Lord – you must esteem them highly in every way that is fitting and right for ministers of the Gospel.'[4] For Williams, no single description is adequate to embrace all the responsibilities involved in being one of God's ambassadors to sinful humanity. In *Theomemphus*, the Christian ministry requires that a man be at once a 'Boanerges', preaching the terrors of the law, an 'Evangelius', offering grace and mercy in Christ, and a 'Dr Alethius', a spiritual physician able to diagnose the soul's illness and prescribe the appropriate medicine.[5] A similar compounding of ministerial abilities appears in *Crocodil Afon yr Aipht* ('The Crocodile of Egypt's River'): 'Lively Ministry, Close Discipline, Stern Rebukes,

24

Spiritual Oversight, who are the most honest men in the wide world'.[6]

During his lifetime Williams would become familiar with many such, not the least of these being Griffith Jones. George Whitefield was another such worthy Gospel minister, 'the man whom heaven did adorn with glorious gifts', who 'Loudly published Gospel peace and grace / Procured in full unto the chosen race'.[7] Links between Whitefield and Wales had existed before his first visit to the Principality in March 1739. Born in Gloucester in 1714, he had been converted while a student at Oxford. At the University he received financial help from Sir John Philipps of Picton Castle, Pembrokeshire. Unable to suppress his passion for bringing sinners to Christ, he considered his ordination to be a roving commission in pursuit of that goal. A man of deep personal piety, large compassion, indefatigable zeal and exceptional preaching gifts, Whitefield soon came into prominence as one of the leaders of the Methodists. As early as 1739 he regarded Harris as 'a burning and shining light ... an indefatigable promoter of the true Gospel of Jesus Christ'. He 'wanted to catch some of his fire', and worked closely with the Welsh Methodists for the rest of his life.[8] They shared a common theology, and Whitefield married Elizabeth James of Abergavenny, on whom Harris had also set his affections for a time.

Williams testifies to two other men who gave lustre to the ministerial office. The first of these was Howel Davies, converted under Harris's ministry in 1737. Regarded by many as 'the Apostle of Pembrokeshire' on account of his labours in that county, Williams referred to him as one who 'preached the Gospel with a lively, liberated spirit'. With true zeal for Christ and for the souls of men he preached throughout the length and breadth of Wales, perspired in the heat of densely-populated London, and persevered in the cold and tumult of Bristol. His rebuttal of heresy was no less fervent, and his pastoral warnings were timely in the face of severe trials and harmful influences. With his departure, says Williams, his flock should trust Christ, the Physician who can apply a plaster as extensive as the wound.[9]

The second to receive such high praise as a Gospel minister from Williams was David Jones, one of the second generation of Welsh Methodist leaders. A Carmarthenshire man by birth, for his forty-three years ministry in the Vale of Glamorgan he was affectionately called 'the Angel of Llan-gan', the location of his parish. Williams says that for him, 'Jesus was the text and Jesus the sermon', and that his preaching could 'melt the rocks with his vigour, and yet with his gentle Gospel make the stoutest oak to bend like the most supple reed.'[10] Such were the ideals of a Gospel preacher. Even though the portrayal of them came much later, Williams's decision to seek ordination would not have been taken lightly.

Given the allegiance of the Williams family to Dissent and William's time at a Dissenting Academy, the obvious sphere for ministry would have been within churches of the same persuasion. It therefore comes as a surprise to find that Williams sought and obtained ordination in the Anglican Communion. For this there were certain requirements, some of them noted by Howel Harris in a letter to his brother, Joseph, in 1736: 'the Canons require (and our own bishop is strict, too) to have a Certificate from the minister's hand that we are full 23 [years of age] … the neighbouring clergy must know me for three years ere they'll sign my testimonial.'[11] Williams attained that age in 1740, the year in which he became a leader in the 'societies'.[12] The society at Llanfair-ar-y-bryn was one of the first to be gathered in Carmarthenshire prior to 1739, and before the end of 1740 there were some five or six in the Llandovery area.[13] Harris visited them regularly during that period, and it is quite likely that this contributed to Williams's growing acquaintance with him. Williams would certainly have sought counsel from sympathetic Anglicans, and Griffith Jones would have been an obvious choice. The extent of such influences on Williams's decision to become an Anglican, however, is still a matter of speculation.

Association with the societies on Williams's part conveys the clear impression that he identified with them in conviction and experience, and a willingness to acknowledge the validity of what would in time become a characteristic of Methodist soul culture. Their attraction for Williams would have been the liveliness of their spiritual life. This would have been in sharp contrast to the deadening effect of the doctrinal controversy at Cefnarthen. A carefully thought-out persuasion of church order and organization would not have been the determining factor in his decision to seek Anglican orders. Even though it meant that he followed his mother's side of the family in their ecclesiastical affiliation, this consideration would have been secondary to his passionate pursuit of spiritual reality.[14]

For ordination Williams needed testimonials to his character and learning from appropriate clergymen. From 1733 Luke Gwynne had been vicar of Llandingad with Llanfair-ar-y-bryn, and during 1739-41 several of Griffith Jones's charity schools were active in his parish. The

Gwynne family of Glanbran were hostile to the Methodists, but Williams's involvement in the movement would not have attracted public attention at the time. There would have been closer affinity with Joshua Thomas, the curate at Tir Abad, not far from Cefn-coed, who was known to Howel Harris. Harris heard him preach at Llanwrtyd in August 1739, and at the end of October felt constrained to pray for 'poor Jos. Thomas and dear Mr. Rowland.'[15] The same could be said of Lawrence Payne, from 1732 Vicar of Defynnog, a village less than ten miles to the east. Such local Anglican clergymen could have provided Williams with the necessary testimonials for his ordination.[16] It was on Payne's invitation that 'the dear Mr. Rowland' to whom Harris refers, preached at Defynnog in 1737, an occasion that proved significant in the development of Welsh Methodism.

Daniel Rowland had been converted under Griffith Jones's ministry shortly after becoming a curate in the country parish of Llangeitho, Cardiganshire, in 1734. His preaching at first was characterized by a vigorous application of threatening texts setting out God's wrath against sin. With a clearer understanding of the meaning and work of grace in his own heart, he soon began to apply the Gospel remedy with equal vigour. Vast crowds flocked to Llangeitho on account of his preaching, and it became for the rest of the century the scene of extraordinary religious fervour. Several distinct periods of revival were witnessed there, and the monthly communion seasons were times of special blessing. At Defynnog in 1737, Howel Harris was in the congregation, and he recorded that Rowland preached with 'amazing power and authority'. To Harris it seemed as if the preacher was 'surrounded with glory in the pulpit'. His account of this first meeting with Rowland ends with the statement: 'here began my acquaintance with him and to all eternity it shall never end.' Rowland's life was not without trial, enduring censure from ecclesiastical authorities who sought to limit his preferment within the Church and his freedom of movement, as well as persecution from the world. The highest praise was given to his preaching gifts by reliable and experienced contemporaries: 'in his pulpit he is a second Paul'; 'the greatest preacher in Europe'; 'the greatest minister in the whole world'.[17] It was with Rowland that Williams was to work closely for the greater part of his ministry, sharing with him the trials and triumphs of Gospel witness.

A clergyman of very different convictions, Theophilus Evans was appointed vicar of Llangamarch in 1738. He had previously served at

Defynnog and Tir Abad, and in 1740 he was also responsible for the perpetual curacy of Llanwrtyd, which, for reasons of size, was linked with two small churches at nearby Abergwesyn. He was the author of *Drych y Prif Oesoedd* ('Mirror of the First Ages'), a book which 'showed that it pays to live a good life; that history shows God punishes sin', and extols the virtues of Anglicanism. The book first appeared in 1716, and Williams subscribes to its second edition in 1740.[18] Evans's translation into Welsh of the Bishop of London's *Pastoral Letter* of August 1739 also appeared in 1740. Its chief purpose was to oppose the 'enthusiasm' of the Methodists, George Whitefield in particular, charging them with claims to special inspiration and prophecy, pride, doctrinal deviation and prejudice against the clergy. Whitefield's immediate Answer to this, in which he 'honestly meets all the charges brought against him', likewise appeared in a Welsh translation in 1740.[19] A few years later Evans took up the attack upon the Methodists in his book *The History of Modern Enthusiasm*, published in London in 1751, with a second edition in 1757. Although it was directed against Whitefield, the inclusion of Welsh Methodists 'by association' was hardly veiled.

While Theophilus Evans opposed all that the Methodists stood for, he seems to have been at that time either unaware or unheeding of the emerging Methodism around him. A letter written to Howel Harris early in December 1741, while Williams was curate at Llanwrtyd, gives evidence of Evans's ambivalence:

> I went up on Saturday morning to Llanwrtyd and Brother Rowland came there and preached ... with great power ... on Sabbath day morning Mr. Evans from Brecon, who is the owner of the church, came to preach there. His text was, 'My grace is sufficient for thee'. I never heard such a sermon in my life, the devil made him as bold as a lion, calling the ministers of Jesus Christ false prophets, hot-headed fools, and such like expressions ... After he had done he was prevailed upon to let Brother Rowland to preach again that night.[20]

It was this clergyman who offered Williams the curacies of Llanwrtyd and Abergwesyn for an annual stipend of £10. It is possible that Williams was recommended to him by the Nonconformist minister of Llanwrtyd at the time, Thomas Morgan. Morgan was a former student of Vavasor Griffiths, and seems to have helped him teach at Llwyn-llwyd during the period when Williams was at the Academy.[21] The ordination took place at the Bishop's Palace in Abergwili, near Carmarthen, on Sunday 3 August 1740. On the following day Williams received the license to serve his curacies, duly authenticated by the Bishop's seal, and declaring that

> we do by these presents give and grant to you in whose fidelity, morals, learning, sound doctrine, and diligence, we do fully confide our License and Authority, to continue only during our pleasure to perform the office of curate in the Chapels of Llanwrtyd and Dewi Abergwesyn in the County of Brecon and Diocese of St. David's and performing other Ecclesiastical duties belonging to the said office according to the form prescribed in the Book of Common Prayer … and not otherwise, or in any other manner. You having first before us subscribed the Articles and taken the Oaths which in this case are registered by Law to be subscribed and taken.[22]

Having spent a number of years as clergyman in the area, Evans was clearly satisfied with Williams's character and attainments, and may not have enquired too closely about his theological convictions. For the time being, the bishop, too, found Williams acceptable.

With regard to Williams's character, Edward Morgan has this to say:

> He was a most consistent Christian, and his mind delighted in the service of his God; no less than three times a day did he keep family prayer, and his conduct was truly serious, charitable, and godly … He was a good looking man in his youth, somewhat lively, and about the middle stature. His temper was warm; but in general he was kind and affectionate towards all, especially children and young people. He would make presents to [give to] little ones, to encourage them to proceed in good ways. He was very accessible, and, therefore, frequently visited, and consulted by the young, in matters of great importance and delicacy. Wisdom, piety and kindness shone forth in his general conduct, and in his private walks, as well as in the church.[23]

Together with his being 'a literate person', and declaring his conformity to the Liturgy of the Church of England, such a person would have been an acceptable candidate for ordination to Nicholas Claggett, Bishop of St. David's at the time. In other respects, however, Claggett, shared the conviction and attitude of Theophilus Evans. A sermon on religious education, preached at a meeting of the Charity Schools, shows that Claggett believed that man 'with a little care and culture' was capable 'of knowing and loving God', apart from a regenerating work of God's Spirit or the necessity for an objective atonement to satisfy for sin.[24] His hostility to the Methodists became clear when he sent a copy of *The New Weekly Miscellany* for Saturday,

31 October 31 1741 to Daniel Rowland. Its leading article, written by an anonymous writer from Aberystwyth, attacked Rowland by name as an extreme fanatic, in league with Whitefield. It accused him of pride and greed, and of driving people to despair or presumption by teaching such doctrines as election, regeneration, and assurance of salvation.[25] Opposition to those who preached the Gospel in its purity was clearly widespread. Given the marked differences between the convictions of Williams and his superiors, it is not surprising that his ministry within Anglicanism, while providing opportunity, would also create tension.

A summary of Williams's ministerial activities is given by Thomas Charles:

> His oratorical gifts were considerable, his preaching was evangelical, experiential and sweet – searching diligently into false doctrines and false experiences, drawing a clear distinction between a true and false spirit. His imagination was vivid, his eye wise and penetrating, with many heavenly influences acting on his spirit in his public ministry, as well as in his dealings with men about their souls and in the private societies.[26]

His ministerial charge was in a remote, sparsely-populated area some twelve miles from his home at Cefn-coed and just over the border in Breconshire. No accommodation was available to him at Llanwrtyd or near the other two churches some three miles distant, and he was therefore obliged to make Cefn-coed his base.

Shortly after his settlement at Llanwrtyd, Harris heard him preach from the text Ezekiel 33:11, 'Say unto them, As I live, saith the Lord God, I have no pleasure in the death of the wicked: but that the wicked turn from his way and live; turn ye from your evil ways; for why will ye die, O house of Israel?' Harris's notes convey the impression of youthful zeal, uncompromising candour and a fiery passion in his delivery. The sermon is rich in biblical allusion and fervent in its personal application, and Harris was profoundly moved:

> He showed, first, that all the ungodly must die, their death an eternal separation from God. Secondly, being imprisoned forever with devils, to all eternity. Thirdly, be pained forever in flames, Revelation 14:10. Why must the ungodly die? (a) Because the wages of sin is death; (b) they are unclean and not capable of heaven. He has none to pay his debts, having rejected Christ. (O Lord, take the scales from my eyes that these great truths may go to my heart); (c) that God has no will or pleasure in the death of a sinner ... Fourthly, that our damnation is of

ourselves. When he said of the misery of the damned it affected me ... a glorious day!

On Christmas Day that year Harris heard 'of the great power lately given to Brother Williams, curate of Llanwrtyd ... was so filled that I could not help jumping and dancing as David before the Ark.'[27] In 1741 Williams was in touch with Griffith Jones, supplying testimonials to Jones's schoolmasters in the area.[28]

Meanwhile, storm clouds were gathering around Williams. His father, a 'sober, just and quiet Christian, and one that had an easy [silent] passage through the wilderness of this world to the desired country', died on 1 April 1742, aged 86. Williams himself had been ill with smallpox, and Harris was deeply concerned about his condition:

> [January 12] O bless dear Brother Williams of Llanwrtyd; seeing him young, cried, 'O my dear Lord! Give him strength and light and power to help him through ... [February 13] Thinking of Brother William Williams, the minister that is sick. O happy he if he shall come home [that is, to glory] ... [February 14] In prayer, earnest for Brother Williams, minister of Llanwrtyd, now sick ... [February 15] Had help to resign Brother Williams to die as seeing the work of God [in] all ... [March 24] Brother Williams, curate here [Llanwrtyd] is sick of a fever, having just recovered of the smallpox.[29]

Before the end of April, two wardens of his church at Llanfihangel Abergwesyn made an official complaint against him 'for absenting himself on several Lord's days and not performing divine service in the said parish church.' No reference was made to his illness or bereavement, and the complaint may have been grounded on a failure on his part to arrange for someone to take his place. He was sufficiently recovered to be expected at Builth early in September, and to be with Rowland at Llangeitho in October. By the end of that eventful year, Harris's reports testified to widespread blessing, not the least being William's full recovery: 'There is a general revival everywhere, but such acts as I never heard of as here with Brother Rowland. This morning I parted with Brother Williams, curate of Llanwrtyd; with him likewise is amazing power. He burns with love and zeal.'[30]

Several allusions in Harris's diary during 1743 confirm the impression given already that in spite of ecclesiastical censure Williams's ministry was being owned of God over a sustained period of time:

> [11 February] I went toward Llanwrtyd … there I heard how Bro. Rowland and Bro. Williams had been beaten and abused much indeed … Brother Williams preached on Luke 7:47: he showed the difference between Christ in the head and Christ in the heart … My soul was inflamed with love in listening … The spirit of Brother Rowland is fallen on Brother Williams. O! what earnestness had he! [12 July] In the chapel Bro. Williams opened 2 Cor. 4. He was amazingly helped, uncommon power. [6 October] Souls are daily taken by Brother Williams in the Gospel Net. [2 December] Brother Williams preached on Exodus 15:25. He spiritualized the Israelite's journey. There came very great power indeed, and there was great crying out. Blessed be God for the love and gifts given Brother Williams. [7 December] Hearing how the Lord was with Brother Williams in an uncommon manner. [20 December] I heard Brother Williams preaching home and gloriously on the New Jerusalem.[31]

Williams was being identified with Rowland, not only in gifts but also in persecution, as Harris reported to Whitefield: 'I have seen Brother William Williams on his return from Brother Rowlands. He informed me of the enemy being let loose on them, while they were discoursing near the seaside in Cardiganshire. A company of ruffians came upon them, armed with guns and staves, and beat them unmercifully; but they escaped without much hurt. The ruffians were set on [that is, sent or encouraged] by a gentleman of the neighbourhood. No wonder the enemy rages, when he sees his kingdom so attacked.'[32]

Persecution from the world was hardly surprising, given the nature of the Gospel with its clear denunciation of ungodliness. Opposition from the Church authorities was more disturbing, and Rowland refers briefly to the matter in a letter dated 20 October 1742:

> I heard since that I am put into the Court for discoursing at an Alehouse. Brother Williams is put in too for not living in the parish where he officiates … Brother Williams was here last Sunday. I love him more and more because of his simple, honest, plain way of dealing with the people. His parishioners are highly incensed against him. I trust we shall have him out before long.[33]

The church wardens' criticism of Williams's non-residence was unfair but not untrue, and merely provided them with a technical excuse to cover an underlying opposition to the biblical thrust of his ministry. On mature reflection, Williams's own view of this period in his life is given by Thomas Charles:

> The Bishop refused to ordain him on account of his irregularity in preaching anywhere, as well as in the churches of his pastoral care. With hindsight in later years he did not commend this irregularity. He deemed it to have been a rash step, and reckoned that he would have been far more useful if he had exercised caution and discretion. God, however, can bring about his purposes even through man's folly, and it may be that his wise counsels were best served in the manner in which they happened.[34]

With calls and opportunities for preaching the Gospel increasing, and bearing in mind the example of clergymen like Griffith Jones and Daniel Rowland, how could Williams not respond, even if such extra-parochial activities were caricatured as fanatical and frowned upon by the ecclesiastical establishment? For Williams, as for these other clergymen, Peter's constraint in similar circumstances was enough, 'we cannot but speak the things which we have seen and heard' (Acts 4:20), and when intimidated by human authorities, conscience dictated that 'we ought to obey God rather than men' (Acts 5:29).

Other charges brought against Williams were neglect of his duties in the lesser parishes under his care, and non-residence. They were 'exhibited' at an ecclesiastical court in June 1743, the alleged 'offences' dating back to April 1742. They hardly took account of the debilitating effect on him of smallpox in the February, or of the 'fever' which had followed in March. Williams's 'Personal Answer', dated 20 July 1743 provides a detailed, point-by-point defence, concluding with the hope that the charges will be dismissed. In his reply he maintained that he faithfully held Sunday services, much as his predecessors had done. The two churches at Abergwesyn, supplying the needs of not more than thirteen households, were a mere hundred yards apart, and it was more practical to serve them alternately with both congregations in attendance. On other occasions, such as special church festivals, it was impossible to gather a congregation. He catechized the children at Llanwrtyd, but in the other two parishes the parents neglected even 'to give their children any manner of school education.' As for non-residence, there was no 'proper or convenient place for his habitation or abode in such parish.' In spite of his competent, courteous, and convincing rebuttal, at a later court he was 'pronounced to have been guilty of neglect in the discharge of his duty'. When he was refused ordination to the priesthood in August 1743, it was not on the technicalities brought by the church wardens, but on account of his Methodism. Church documents suggest that he was to have been

33

ordained priest and presented to another parish, Aber-nant in Carmarthenshire, but on the list of ordinands for the occasion the words 'a Methodist, refused', appear alongside his name.[35] Some person or persons with higher authority than the wardens, Theophilus Evans perhaps, had intervened to prevent his progress within the Church of England.[36]

5.

'The despised Methodists'

With Williams's Methodist affiliation becoming more and more public, and with official censure already hanging over his head, Williams's ordination as priest in August 1743 would have appeared only remotely possible in the spring of that year. His Methodist friends were aware of this, and at an Association meeting early in April 1743, they took a decision which changed Williams's life. It was a meeting at which George Whitefield presided as 'Moderator'. Whitefield was aware by this time of Williams's labours and had felt 'a sweet union' with him.[1] The first decision of the Association read simply, 'our Saviour being sought unto for direction, it was agreed that the Reverend Mr Williams should leave his curacies, and be an assistant to the Reverend Mr Rowlands.'[2] Thomas Charles states that it was 'chiefly George Whitefield who urged him to leave the Church and go out into the byways and fields.' Charles continues:

> From that time until his death he continued to travel throughout Wales to preach God's message to the darkened inhabitants of the Principality wherever anyone would listen, and he did so for about half a century. Ordinarily, he went each month to Llangeitho to help Mr D Rowlands administer the Sacrament of the Lord's Supper to the vast crowds that came to the communion from all parts of Wales. The strongest brotherly affection between them was sustained throughout their lifetime, as may be seen from the elegy that he wrote to that man shortly before he himself died.[3]

For the rest of his life, Williams gave himself to an itinerant ministry. Whitefield's advice had been based on the conviction that 'whenever there shall be a general Revival of Religion in any country, itinerant preaching will be more in vogue.' He had every opportunity to encourage Williams at the end of April to take this step, as he was preaching at Llandovery on Saturday and Sunday 23rd and 24th. It was a conviction that grew stronger with the years, and in a 1753 letter he gave vent to his feelings, 'had I a thousand souls and bodies they should be all itinerants for Jesus Christ.'[4]

35

While the Methodist decision was made in April, its implementation took time. Williams asked a correspondent at the end of August 1743 to acquaint Harris, in London at the time, with the fact 'that he applied to the Bishop last week for full ordination and had letters of approbation of many clergy, and his parishioners, but was refused on account of his being a Methodist, and going about to preach.'[5] While the complaints of his Abergwesyn parishioners against him were still under investigation, Williams prepared his defence. It was in January 1744 that the ecclesiastical court finally imposed censure on him.

Meanwhile, the Methodist leaders were itinerating, preaching was often fruitful, converts were being gathered and nurtured, and Harris, particularly, was consolidating the movement's organization. Rowland, unlike Harris, was an ordained clergyman with parochial responsibilities. Even though there were frequent calls for his ministry from an ever-widening area, there were also 'sermons frequently besides Sundays' at Llangeitho.[6] Since Williams lacked full priest's orders, he could only assist at the Communion Service and would not be allowed to administer the Sacrament himself, but he accepted the limitations this imposed upon him. Given the conviction which all the Methodists held, namely the desperate need for Gospel light in a society darkened by sin and ignorance, together with the priority of spiritual life over ecclesiastical order, the lack of priest's orders may not have appeared to Williams at the time as a serious deficiency.

Methodism in 1743 differed in many respects from the Methodism of Oxford a decade earlier. In 1734 Whitefield had written, 'God enabled me to do much good to many, as well as to receive much from the despised Methodists ... The world, and not themselves, gave them the title of Methodists, I suppose, from their custom of regulating their time, and planning the business of the day every morning.' In his *Journal* he frequently refers to them as 'the despised Methodists', but they were supported and encouraged by some godly people, the Welshman Sir John Philipps among them. They were by most, however, perceived as over-scrupulous and over-zealous. Another charge, made in 1739 by the Bishop of Gloucester, that Whitefield, like other Methodists, was belittling the clergy, was vigorously denied. In Whitefield's reply he claimed that it was the clergy's 'falling from their [Thirty-nine] Articles, and not preaching the truth as it is in Jesus, that has excited the present zeal of those, whom they, in derision, call the *Methodist preachers*.'[7] What had begun in Oxford as an individually-driven desire to be and do good, had become a divinely-motivated passion to save souls. Furthermore, Welsh Methodism was a home-grown version of this later phenomenon, emerging as an independent, vigorous and spontaneous movement of revival.

The Welsh movement's evident progress was reflected in its geographical spread and strength. Harris claimed in November 1740 that there were 50 societies in South Wales.[8] In terms of members, in 1743 for example, they numbered 28 at Llanwrtyd and 64 at Llangeitho.[9] Rowland's monthly communion occasions at Llangeitho over the years became phenomenally popular with some 1500-2000 in attendance.[10] As for sympathetic clergymen, they included Thomas Lewis of Llan-ddew in Breconshire; Thomas Jones of Cwm-iou, and John Powell of Llanmartin and Wilcrick, in Monmouthshire; John Hodges of Wenvoe in Glamorganshire; John Davies of Llanddarog, Carmarthenshire; and Howel Davies in Pembrokeshire.[11] They looked on Griffith Jones as their mentor, even though his Methodism was by association rather than conviction, and his strictures were, on occasion, severe. They shared his evangelical convictions, relied on his vast experience, and often drew on his wise counsel. Critical though he was on occasions of the itinerant preaching of Rowland, Harris and Howel Davies, the Methodists still owed him an enormous debt. He was instrumental in Rowland's conversion, Davies spent some time as his curate, Williams's wife had derived much spiritual benefit from her time in the Llanddowror Rectory, and Harris visited him as often as he could. Frowned upon by the Church authorities as 'the Methodist Pope', a title neither deserved nor appropriate, he persevered with its order and liturgy. The origin of Methodism was even foisted on him, and he was held responsible by one anonymous writer as the one who had 'put a windmill into Whitefield's head, and sent him Don Quixoting up and down the world', as a kind of footloose, charlatan preacher.[12]

When the Methodist leaders agreed that Williams should become an assistant to Rowland, in no way did they mean to imply that they were abandoning Anglicanism. They all agreed in their commitment to it, with the expectation that its blemishes and failings could be reformed. But by this time Methodism involved theological and pastoral convictions that were perceived by the authorities as alien to contemporary Anglican beliefs and practice. Methodists, for their part, maintained that they agreed wholeheartedly with the Thirty-nine Articles, and were content to use the Book of Common Prayer. In their evangelistic zeal they were only addressing the desperate plight of their generation as responsible ministers of the Gospel. What others regarded as wild enthusiasm in them, they attributed to enthusiastic, personal dealings with God; when they were criticized for their irregular methods, they exposed the neglect of the clergy in the face of the alarming danger and eternal destiny of precious souls.

What, then, were the features of Welsh Methodism, and how were they shaped? 'Methodism' was a term that came to be applied to people who had experienced in an individual sense the salvation from sin to be found in Christ. Usually this would be brought about through a Gospel preaching that was attended with much of the divine presence, bringing an awareness of spiritual and eternal realities. This involved personal accountability and guilt for sin, the realization of an eternal dimension to existence and destiny, and amazement at God's provision of forgiveness, reconciliation and acceptance to the believer in Jesus Christ. It was fluid, dynamic, and evangelical in its essence, and by mid-century had affected parts of all the southern counties of Wales. More importantly, it affected the individual's entire mind-set and behaviour, his relationship to God and to others, his aim in life and his comfort in death. In a more theological framework, Methodist conviction emphasised regeneration (the new birth), justification by faith, acceptance of biblical truths, and personal holiness.

The use of the word 'experienced' must not be taken, as some have done, to imply an emotional, subjective and perhaps even irrational, spur-of-the-moment response to an equally emotional encounter with God that was devoid of any cerebral involvement. This may have been true for some, but Methodist safeguards filtered out a superficial profession. Methodist conviction and practice insisted on sound exposition of biblical material that was aimed primarily at the intellect, and only then directed at the feelings, the conscience and the will. Anyone familiar with the writings of Williams, the sermons of Rowland, and the Catechisms of Griffith Jones will readily acknowledge that they are intellectually robust. But these men knew that the ultimate obstacle for the reception of their message was not illiteracy, since spiritual blindness and prejudice against the truth characterized the fallen human condition. A real, lasting and life-changing encounter with Christ could only be wrought by the Spirit driving Gospel truth home to the entire personality. This was the reason why acceptance into membership of the society was only possible after a period of 'trial'.

A few months may appear to be a short enough time to test genuine conversion, but to many in those unusual times the perception of an enlightened mind, a changed heart, and the prospect of new life was immediate. This aspect of Methodism proved to be a stumbling-block to many within the religious establishment, Episcopalian and Dissenting alike. For them it was a false, presumptuous, arrogant kind of religion, for which the word 'enthusiasm' was appropriate and on which religious sanction, if not condemnation, was appropriate and deserved. John Wesley's conversation with a stranger on one of his travels in 1739 may be taken as representative of the Methodist response:

> A young gentleman overtook me on the road, and, after a while, asked me if I had seen Whitefield's Journals. I told him I had. 'And what do you think of them?' said he. 'Don't you think they are … enthusiasm from end to end? I think so.' I asked him, 'Why do you think so?' He replied, 'Why, he talks so much about joy and stuff, and inward feelings. As I hope to be saved, I cannot tell what to make of it.' I asked, 'Did you ever feel the love of God in your heart? If not, how should you tell what to make of it? Whatever is spoken of the religion of the heart, and of the inward workings of the Spirit of God, must appear enthusiasm to those who have not felt them; that is, if they take upon them to judge of the things which they own they know not.'[13]

In speaking of the reality of such immediate experiences, the Methodists were not claiming a special revelation or mystical ecstasy that was not susceptible to objective evaluation. They affirmed that the source of their enlightenment was the teaching of Scripture, and their experiences were portrayed in, and subject to evaluation by, biblical categories for true faith.

They also claimed that the movement of God's Spirit in the land, of which they were a part, was an authentic reviving of God's work. Williams dates the 'breaking out of light like a fresh dawn' to 1738.[14] By this he meant the beginning of several periods of spiritual awakening in Wales, as well as the time of his own enlightenment in the things of God. Whitefield reported a similar work at the end of that year in London, and calls it 'a great pouring out of the Spirit.'[15] Griffith Jones had witnessed such a time of heightened spiritual activity locally at Laugharne in 1714 when his congregations numbered three or four thousand, but in 1735 he bemoaned the low condition of the church and urged in a letter, that 'since we have reason to fear that God is now about leaving our land and departing from us … it is now, if ever, we should stir ourselves up to lay hold on him, as the prophet says, and by earnest resolution, fixed thoughts, and flaming affections, solicit his return and stay with us.'[16] When Williams mentioned 1738 he may have had in mind a remarkable occasion at Llangeitho early in Daniel Rowland's evangelical ministry while he was reading the Litany. At the words, 'by Thine agony and bloody sweat, by Thy cross and passion, by Thy precious death and burial, by Thy glorious resurrection and the coming of the Holy Ghost', a powerful and overwhelming influence came upon minister and congregation alike, so that many fell to the ground with grief for their sin.[17] A similar 'great revival' broke out in the parts of Montgomeryshire visited by Howel Harris in the summer of 1738, and at the beginning of the following year Harris, writing from Glamorganshire, could speak of 'a great revival in Cardiganshire', adding that 'in this County, where I am now the revival prospers.'[18] A letter from Harris written at Llangeitho on 4 December 1742 speaks of revival in other places as well as Llangeitho and Llanwrtyd:

> There is a general revival everywhere ... Brother Howel Davies ... is most gloriously owned in Pembrokeshire; and tomorrow fortnight I trust I shall hear the laborious old soldier, Mr. Griffith Jones, who has been owned to batter Satan's stronghold near thirty years, and still holds on, and is wonderfully owned in his ministry ... Mr. Thomas Lewis of Brecon ... has been much blessed of the Lord indeed, and grows sweetly ... I hope to hear one of the most solid, experienced ministers I ever heard, another old church minister, Mr. Jones of Cwm-iou.[19]

Other letters from the same period speak of 'great crowds that flock to hear everywhere', and of many 'in great liberty, and have vast fire and life among them.' While 'power', 'fire', and 'life' were words frequently used by the Methodists to convey an extraordinary manifestation of God's presence and power, they never claimed for themselves any ability to produce such conditions. Rather, they invariably ascribed them to God's initiative and grace. It was, in Williams's words at the end of 1745, 'a harvest time for faith.'[20]

With 'many rejoicing in Christ', Methodist concern to ascertain the reality of their profession of faith found expression in the 'society' or 'fellowship' meetings that they set up. These were local groups that met on a regular basis under an appointed, mature leadership to monitor, nurture and discipline the converts. Williams traced his involvement with them to the year 1740.[21] While such meetings had a teaching purpose, and were occasions of worship through prayer and singing, their primary aim was to share experiences under the guidance of the leader. An open letter to the societies from Whitefield that year gave prominence to this aspect. It also laid out guidelines for their constitution and discipline. On their object, and in giving counsel about fellowship, he has this to say:

> The only end which I hope you all purpose by your assembling yourselves together, is the renewing of your depraved natures, and promoting the hidden life of Jesus Christ in your souls... Content not yourselves with reading, singing, and praying together; but set some time apart to confess your faults, and to communicate your experience one to another... To this end, you would do well, as others have done, to form yourselves into little companies of four or five each, and meet once a week to tell each other what is in your hearts; that you may then also pray for, and comfort each other, as need shall require. None but those who have experienced it, can tell the unspeakable advantages of such a union and communion of souls. I know not a better means in the world to keep hypocrisy out from amongst you. Pharisees and unbelievers will pray and read, and sing psalms; but none, save an Israelite indeed, will endure to have his heart searched out.[22]

The societies were despised by the formal religionists of the day for this very reason. In the words of John Harris, one of the 'exhorters', 'After public exhorting it was revealed to me that nothing grieved the devil as much as private societies, and that was evident by his instruments, the carnal people of all denominations; they hate it above all things.'[23] The Methodists insisted that they were not embryonic churches but 'societies in the Established Church', and that their leaders or 'exhorters' should not be called 'ministers'.[24] The issue of their identity created a tension within Methodism which sometimes generated misunderstanding and even separation. It was an issue which the Methodists in Wales did not resolve until early in the next century.

Inevitably, the ability of a society to fulfil its ideals varied considerably, depending on how able or willing its members were to articulate their experience, and also on the discernment and knowledge of its leadership. An early attempt with this in mind was made by Harris in February 1741 at a meeting in Llandovery when two ordained clergymen, two Dissenting ministers, and four exhorters were present, with 'many more' of the latter to be accepted later in the proceedings. It is not clear whether Williams was present, but it is reasonable to assume this since his home was nearby, and Harris stayed there

41

overnight shortly after the meeting. Rules were drawn up that emphasised the sharing of Christian experience, mutual oversight, encouragement and love. Admission to their fellowship was not on the basis of opinion, that is, head knowledge alone, but 'anyone who could give satisfaction regarding their saving acquaintance of Christ' would be received. God's Word was to be the rule by which all things would be determined, and a monthly day of prayer and fasting should be observed for the work. The fourth rule set out the theological pillars on which the Methodist edifice was to be built: 'Since we trust we are led by the same Spirit, the Lord made us of one mind with regard to doctrine: for free grace; weak faith and strong faith; election; perseverance in a state of grace; dominion over sin; complete perfection in Christ, and in part in us, progressive in degree.'[25] A year later the Welsh Methodists published *Sail, Dibenion, a Rheolau'r Societies neu'r Cyfarfodydd Neilltuol a ddechreuasant ymgynull yn ddiweddar yng Nghymru* ('The Basis, Purposes, and Rules of the Societies or Private Meetings which have lately started coming together in Wales'). [26] A further thirty years were to elapse before Williams wrote *Drws y Society Profiad* ('The Experience Meeting'), a more detailed and mature manual for the societies, widely regarded as a 'classic of the spiritual life'. [27] Its penetrating analysis of genuine Christian experience and guidelines for managing spiritual growth will be examined in a later chapter. The Welsh Methodists did not publish written testimonies of conversion similar to Jonathan Edwards's *Faithful Narrative* of 1737 and William M'Culloch's *Short Account of the Remarkable Conversions at Cambuslang* of 1742. [28] Their accounts were made verbally in the societies, reported in summary in letters, and depicted fictionally by Williams in his writings. During the 1740s, with the work of revival flourishing and expanding, there were more urgent and pressing matters bearing down upon the Welsh Methodists.

6.

'Association no separation'

The need for careful supervision of society leaders was recognized as crucial at an early stage. For this purpose, Harris was ideally gifted, more so than any of the Methodist clergymen, and he duly organized regular 'Association' meetings for the purpose. Williams had attended and preached at them from their early days, and served from time to time as 'Moderator'. The first exclusively Methodist Association had met early in 1742, and George Whitefield sent its members a letter of counsel, an assurance of his prayers, and a recommendation that they should meet on a monthly basis. 'The affairs you meet about are of the utmost importance ... Some of you are ministers of the Church of England, but if you are faithful, I cannot think you will continue in it long. However, do not go out till you are cast out; and, when cast out, for Jesus Christ's sake, be not afraid to preach in the fields ... As for those who are not ordained, I cannot say much, only pray that each may take his proper place ... All this may be done without separation from the Established Church, which I cannot think God calls for as yet.'[1] The letter was read and its suggestions were adopted as guiding principles for Calvinistic Methodism in both England and Wales.

The bond between the Calvinistic Methodism of the two countries was further strengthened when Whitefield was appointed Moderator of the Welsh Association whenever he was available to preside. The first occasion of his doing so was in January 1743, when both English and Welsh representatives of the work met at Watford, a country house near Caerphilly. The occasion is portrayed in a well-known imaginary painting that dates from 1912, and shows the leaders gathered around a table with an open Bible in front of the central figure, George Whitefield. 'It is a notable fact', says Whitefield's biographer, Luke Tyerman, 'that the first Calvinistic Methodist Association was held eighteen months before Wesley held his first Methodist Conference in London.' Watford was the home of Thomas Price, a leading member of the Glamorgan societies, and a magistrate. His daughter-in-law, Grace, died of pleurisy when 37 years of age, and Williams wrote for her one of his most poignant and powerful elegies. He compares her funeral to a wedding, adding that it was as if she had left her earthly husband for the heavenly Bride who 'made atonement for her life, and cleared all her debts on Calvary.' She died singing one of Williams's hymns.[2]

While this first joint Association had formalized Whitefield's involvement in the Welsh work, it had also opened for Harris a door of opportunity in England. The second joint Association, also held at Watford, further cemented the union between Calvinistic Methodists in England and Wales, but also drew Rowland and Williams together. The decision that Williams should become Rowland's helper proved highly significant. It not only resolved for Williams the present dilemma of ecclesiastical sanction, but also strengthened for the future a rallying point at Llangeitho. Preaching, prayer and business were the common features of these Associations. At their business sessions, journeys were planned, leaders appointed, reports of societies scrutinized, and careful records kept. They were to prove crucial for the progress, and indeed, the survival of the revival in Wales.

Most society members only understood Welsh and with Griffith Jones's schools spreading, the number of literate members was increasing. This opened up a new opportunity which the Methodists grasped eagerly by providing suitable reading material in Welsh. Sermons were one obvious source of instruction for the young converts, and some of Rowland's sermons appeared in 1739. Translations of English religious classics, or of such works as the Welsh Methodists deemed necessary or timely, such as Whitefield's sermons, were prepared at their instigation or with their recommendation.[3] John Bunyan's *Doctrine of Law and Grace and The Holy War*, Elisha Coles's *The Sovereignty of God*, and Ralph Erskine's *Sina and Zion*, had all appeared in Welsh by 1745, to be followed some years later by Ebenezer Erskine's *Assurance of Faith*, translated by Williams. The other major contribution to religious literature in Welsh before 1750 was the appearance of several collections of hymns, and in the provision of original hymns in Welsh no-one would surpass those that issued from Williams's pen.

Letters giving accounts of Methodist activities and experiences were published as a regular paper, for some years appearing weekly, between September 1740 and 1748. From the time of its earliest appearance, Harris encouraged the printer and used the publication as a means to propagate news of the revival's spread. The paper changed its name from time to time: *The Christian's Amusement; The Weekly History; An Account of the Progress of the Gospel*; and *The Christian History*. It was the product of the printing press of John Lewis, a Welshman who lived in London.[4] Writing from the metropolis in October 1742 to Thomas James, one of the Breconshire exhorters, Harris speaks of its distribution: 'I wrote to dear Mr. [Marmaduke] Gwynne last post, and a scrip to Mr. Williams of Llanwrtyd. I sent *The Weekly History* to him bound up as desired, and to brother Williams unbound, and a volume of Erskine's Sermons which I desired him to send you. These are for Brother Richard Jenkins in Montgomeryshire, which he did send to me for.'[5] Its contents were often personal even though intended for a wider readership, the source being protected by anonymity, as in this letter, bearing the title: 'From a person in Wales, to one at Deptford. Cardiganshire, Aug. 11, 1744', even though it was signed with the initials 'W. W.', and was probably from Williams, Pantycelyn:

> I am glad to hear that you are well. I hope that you do glorify God in your health, by denying yourself, and departing from all iniquity. And that you have the Holy Spirit to lead, guide and govern you; and that your eye is fixed on eternal happiness. It is that will make you long more and more to be there, and to walk with God continually while here, freed from the world and all its pleasure, in an holy fear and evangelical love, waiting upon the Lord, saying, 'When shall this mortal put on immortality, and this corruptible put on incorruption?' It is the view of this that increases eternal life in our souls, and makes us become as pilgrims on the earth, and go on cheerfully towards the heavenly Jerusalem. My dear sister, there is an ocean of happiness prepared for us, and what we experience here is but as a drop, or a taste of that which we shall enjoy. A sight of His love is the cause of our love; and our thirst after Him is but the effect of His thirst after us; and our diligence in seeking Him, is the effect of His diligence in seeking of us. A sight of this will break our heart, and make us look upon ourselves as nothing in His sight. It is not our works that is the works of redemption, but the works of Jesus Christ. Oh that we were always as nothing in His sight! Then indeed would He fashion us as the Potter doth the clay. Then let us yield ourselves up to Him more and more day by day. For it is right that we should be *nothing*, and HE ALL in ALL! For it is no more we that live, but Christ that liveth in us. Then are we truly His temples; and He is within, and self without; Christ on the throne, and self crucified. This is my cry, and this is my voice; and I am sure God's ears are open to my prayers. Here I am in measure; I want to be more established. This is sweet to all those that know it, and are going out of sin and self. I hope you know this mystery more and more; for as the soul loveth the Lord, so it hateth *self*; and as the soul tasteth the Lord to be sweet, so it tasteth self to be bitter. For by going into God, we go out of *self* more and more. Thus let us go on comfortably

45

> hand in hand to the kingdom of God. Thank the Lord for forgiving me
> all my sins, and pray that I may walk in the Spirit all my days, and bring
> forth the fruits of holiness to His praise.[6]

Harris similarly recognized the paper's usefulness as a means of
providing counsel, allowing letters to individuals to be published in
order to benefit a wider constituency. The next extract was intended
primarily for 'Mrs. E. P.', but in Harris's mind she was representative
of others who, he trusted, would benefit from its appearance in print:

> O what would my soul give for being made instrumental to comfort any
> of the poor dear precious lambs that are equally dear to the dear
> Shepherd ... If you feel yourselves hard under the Word, and as you
> think, not edified, I believe it is a common case, for we are often taught
> some lessons in those frames [feelings, conditions], which we could not
> learn before; and that was the way God manifested Himself to us at that
> time. All wounds are not healed in the same manner. When Christ
> comes down some of His lambs He feeds with tenderness, others at the
> same time He seems to frown on; some He heals, and some He wounds
> at the same time, and with the same love to all these. You will come to
> see that His hidings, your crosses, etc., flow as much from His love as
> His tenderest smiles. Indeed, He changes not.[7]

There was even talk of translating this weekly paper into Welsh, the
language of the majority of society members. The project was
abandoned, but in spite of this, by the end of 1745 each society in Wales
was encouraged to obtain a copy.[8] Clearly, its usefulness was in
proportion to the competence of the leader in the English language.

This matter, in turn, raised the issue of intellectual ability among the
leaders of the societies. The issue had to be addressed. Even for the
limited sphere of a 'private exhorter', there was careful assessment of
any prospective labourer. In March 1743, therefore, the Association
agreed 'that when one proposes himself for an exhorter he should first
exhort in the private societies; first, to have the approbation of some
grave, experienced Christian or Christians that have often heard him;
second, the judgment of some three or four private and public
exhorters and ministers; third, to be examined as to his grace, call,
qualifications, gifts and doctrine.' An example of how this worked in
practice is found in the minutes of an Association in August, 1744, at
which Williams was Moderator: 'after a close examination of brother
Edward Bufton about his knowledge of the divinity of Jesus Christ, and
of his bearing his people's sins away on the tree, and of the

46

perseverance of the saints etc., by the revelation of the Holy Ghost and of the misery of all mankind by nature; and having been satisfied of his grace and call to speak for the great God, we agreed that he should assist brother Beaumont as a private exhorter.'[9] It was taken for granted that the 'exhorters' should be self-taught, men whose progressive Scripture knowledge would be buttressed by 'the best and most lively theological authors' and by dealings with mature Christians. One such character was the fictitious 'Mirandus' in the Preface to Williams's serialized work, *Pantheologia*, which commenced in 1762. Mirandus had become 'a star in his locality, a lamp in the church, the worthy head of his household, a guide to the blind, a source of strength for the weak, a help to the needy, and a light to the ignorant.'[10] Williams was in 1749 appointed to instruct 'such as are near and about Llansawel [Carmarthenshire]' for 'two days in the week or a week in the month to improve themselves in grammar, divinity, logic, philosophy, and all knowledge necessary to make them more useful.'[11]

Another thorny issue was that of the ecclesiastical irregularity of the public exhorters, who exercised an itinerant ministry as laymen. Some were called 'bold, visionary rustics', others, 'illiterate mechanics, much fitter to make a pulpit than to get into one.'[12] In Wales, Griffith Jones denounced some of the lay-preachers as being 'exceedingly erroneous, harsh, conceited and disorderly; and have ... no appearance of that soberness and humility in their temper, discourse or doctrine, that become true godliness.'[13] In England, Methodist lay-preaching was criticized by the Cornish Evangelical clergyman, Samuel Walker, as tending to schism.[14] Whitefield's position was ambivalent, since closely related to his misgivings about lay-preachers were his convictions in favour of an itinerant ministry. On the one hand, he approved Harris's preaching as one who had 'offered himself thrice for Holy Orders'; on the other he believed that the 'consequences of beginning to teach too soon will be exceeding bad.'[15] By his involvement with the Welsh brethren who, at their Association meetings sanctioned such lay activities, Whitefield allowed the practice, since it was subject to careful evaluation and supervision. The Welsh Methodists found support for them in a book bought by Harris in 1741. Its full title was *The preacher sent: or, A vindication of the liberty of publick preaching, by some men not ordained*, and Harris found its advocacy of the practice convincing. It argued for a covenanting local church, with preaching as an office derived from the congregation rather than from ordination. Williams, the former

Dissenter, would have identified with the book's support for the practice more readily than Rowland and others who thought that only ordained clergy should officiate in this capacity. The book came into Williams's possession, and he replaced an inscription by Harris with his own name. In the same copy he wrote in another place, 'William Williams, Lay Preaching defended.'[16]

Not only was there verbal debate about Methodism within the evangelical constituency: criticism in print of both their convictions and methods appeared from an early date. 'The most authoritative and serious' attack in print on Whitefield was that by the Bishop of London, Edmund Gibson, in 1739. In the form of a *Pastoral Letter to the People of his Diocese*, it warned 'against lukewarmness on one hand and enthusiasm on the other'. Of its fifty-five pages, the first nineteen addressed lukewarmness; the rest attacked 'enthusiasm' and quoted Whitefield's *Journals* as evidence of serious departure from the Church's teaching and practice. The Bishop's allegations were answered by Whitefield's appeal to Scripture and the Church's Thirty-nine Articles. An indication of their importance to each side in the debate is the fact that both were translated into Welsh.[17]

Within Methodism there were also theological differences. The Moravians had profoundly influenced the Wesley brothers, and initially Howel Harris worked alongside them. They were highly esteemed for their disciplined devotion to Christ and missionary endeavour. Influenced by the individualistic, Pietist stream of evangelical Christianity that flowed from Philipp Jakob Spener and Johann Arndt, they held that believers should exercise mutual oversight. This in turn exposed them to a subjective, if not sentimental, strain of spirituality that found expression, on the one hand in a passive piety, and on the other in an obsession with the physical sufferings of Christ. Harris criticized them in 1740 for 'denying any weak faith, any degrees short of full assurance, and full power over sin and full liberty; and that ordinances (the Lord's Supper, for example) are of no avail without a full faith'[18]. In spite of such areas of disagreement, the Welsh Methodists could still enjoy the hymns of John Cennick, a Calvinistic Methodist who joined the Moravians in 1745. Through the biblical preaching of Rowland and others, with its balance of teaching and application, and the writings of Williams, with its insistence on understanding as well as appropriation, the Welsh Methodists avoided, to a commendable degree, the pitfalls of Moravian excess.

Another separation had occurred by 1743, that between George

Whitefield and John Wesley, representing the Calvinist and Arminian Methodists respectively. The identity of Welsh Methodism was further defined by its close affinity to Whitefield's position, whose Methodism by this time was recognizably Calvinist. As early as November 1739 Whitefield had come to this position: 'God has been pleased to enlighten me more in that comfortable doctrine of election ... God chose us from eternity; He called us in time; and I am persuaded, will keep us from falling finally, till time shall be no more.'[19] Harris 'was taught the Doctrine of Election slowly, in stages', during the spring of 1737. He was confirmed in these convictions by three clergymen, Thomas Lewis of Methyr Cynog, Thomas Jones of Cwm-iou, and Daniel Rowland.[20] An important letter from Harris setting out his Calvinist convictions to John Wesley is dated 24 October 1741. Harris met Wesley in Cardiff in March 1742 and maintained cordial relations with him as with Whitefield, because, he said, 'my love is not founded on agreeing in principles but on our belonging to the same Kingdom.' After parting with Wesley he recorded in his diary the issues on which they agreed and those on which they differed.[21] It was always a fragile union, an ideal rather than a reality, as the further efforts to come to an agreement in 1747 and 1749 showed. 'We settled several rules towards an union', Harris wrote after meeting John Wesley at Bristol in 1747. Misgivings surfaced again in 1749, in the words of Harris again: 'I mentioned my fears least he [Mr. Wesley] should ask to be head and form a party. Mr Whitefield mentioned his objection to his [Mr. Wesley] monopolizing the name of Methodist to himself only.' Perhaps the strongest area of agreement was in the matter of general principles, to 'stir up souls to live by faith on Christ', and 'to abide in the communion of the Established Church and to look upon the bishops as fathers till thrown out.'[22] The Williams family had made their position clear in 1740 by their separation from the Arminian section of the Cefnarthen congregation. Throughout his works, whether hymns, long poems or prose, Williams's proclamation of the sovereignty of God's grace is affirmed with confidence and gratitude. A hymn on 'election' sung in the societies in 1742 is complemented by a Williams hymn on the same theme a few years later. They confirm that such Calvinist convictions were a driving force within Welsh Methodism from an early period.[23]

In the early years, the Welsh Methodists made use of often dilapidated, sometimes abandoned, 'chapels of ease' associated with a parish church, following the example of Griffith Jones. Rowland,

Williams, Howel Davies and Peter Williams ministered at several of these in Carmarthenshire for shorter or longer periods of time, as they were allowed: Ystrad-ffin (Cil-y-cwm); Llanlluan (Llanarthne); Abergorlech (Llanybydder); Capel Ifan (Llanelli), and there were others wider afield as well.[24] Such buildings provided not only a preaching centre, but also a 'consecrated' building where the fully ordained clergymen among them could celebrate communion. There were other locations where Williams preached on a regular basis. Thomas Charles relates that 'he preached at Llanlluan chapel over a period of more than 30 years on a monthly basis; similarly at Caeo and Llansawel, apart from when he was visiting churches in North Wales, or on an extensive tour through the South … labouring in the Word and doctrine among the Methodists of Wales.'[25] The Methodists insisted that their societies were not churches, and in making such provision they deliberately avoided giving the impression of separation.

Nevertheless, it was necessary to make some provision for the societies, a need that became more pressing as the work flourished under God's blessing. Methodists in Williams's own county of Carmarthenshire were among the first to resolve the dilemma with a decision to go ahead and build. In June 1746 Williams was staying at Trefeca while on a preaching tour, and he informed Harris, in London at the time, of their intention:

> I promised to write you before now but could not conveniently in that ever since I saw you I have been hardly nothing at home. Last night I came from Cwm-du to Trefeca where I preached, and it was sweet indeed with me and the people. All your family here are well; your mother gives her love to you; your servant and your maid, and also Thomas Jones who comes with me some part of this round. We have had an Association lately at Llechryd where Mr. Rowland, Davies, Price and myself and many of the brethren were together. John Harris and [George] Gambold and [John] Sparks likewise were there. I suppose the latter is very simple [that is, honest, single-minded] and has little or no inclination to the Moravian doctrine. We had a long dispute with brother Gambold as at Glancothi. We found him now as then partly erroneous in some fundamental points of religion, especially holding actual justification from eternity, but in many things nearer to us than we thought. It was said he preached against you when you were last at Pembroke, telling the people they were for having some poison with their meat, some Law with their Gospel, meaning you; but he was not found really guilty of this; certainly he said some such words. We concluded at that Association not to break our union, but to leave him

50

some time more on trial desiring him not to preach such doctrine any more as he did in some places before. I hope this will come to nothing. Dear brother, more union than ever will be in [a] short [time]. I know you say 'Amen'. The work of the Lord goes on here daily; we are for building two houses in Carmarthenshire, one at Cil-y-cwm, the other at Llansawel. May the Lord prosper us. Mr Rowland is to go to Bristol; he will be [away] for a fortnight in going and coming. 'Tis Mr. Davies, myself, and the Reverend Peter Williams that is to be at Abergorlech next time. Dear brother, excuse me in writing; my time is short. 'Tis now about 9 and I am to be at Capel-y-ffin about 10. My soul loves you dearly. I long to see you in Wales. I have some thoughts of going to Ireland, I have some business which I will tell you when you come home, not this first three months if I will at all … This from your faithful brother this side and the other side for ever, W. Williams.[26]

There were many aspects to consolidating God's work: securing doctrinal integrity and preserving unity among them, as well as providing appropriate facilities for the societies. The difficulty and delicacy of the task are reflected in this letter, and also in a comment made by Harris at the time: 'I made a stand about a house going to be erected for preaching, and not to call it as it was for divine service only, but for a school and other divine uses.' Thus Cil-y-cwm was referred to as Tŷ Ysgol, Ysgoldy, Tŷ Seiat, Tŷ Newydd, or Tŷ Cwrdd (School House, Society House, New House, or Meeting House), and the Trust Deeds were directed 'towards the erecting of a house for performing divine worship therein and doing other acts for propagating the Gospel … to perform divine worship in the said house or to do other act or acts for teaching and propagating the Gospel.' In the future they would insist on including the 17th of their Church's Thirty-nine Articles, among others, in the Trust Deeds of their chapel buildings:

> Predestination to life is the everlasting purpose of God, whereby (before the foundations of the world were laid) he hath constantly decreed by his counsel secret to us, to deliver from curse and damnation those whom he hath chosen in Christ out of mankind, and to bring them by Christ to everlasting salvation, as vessels made to honour. Wherefore, they which be endued with so excellent a benefit of God be called according to God's purpose by his Spirit working in due season; they through grace obey the calling; they be justified freely; they be made sons of God by adoption; they be made like the image of his only-begotten Son Jesus Christ; they walk religiously in good works, and at length, by God's mercy, they attain to everlasting felicity.

51

This was not only a statement of theological conviction, it was also an affirmation of intent.

When the Association met at Cil-y-cwm a year later, it was said to have been held at the 'New House'. Harris wrote of it in his diary: 'We were happy and loving together and settled many things toward discipline, which for our want of love could not be settled before, and strengthened each other's hands, reproved and settled some rules about marriage. The Lord having given us a small respite from the great storm.' Following the Association Harris spent the night at Cefn-coed with Williams where he 'had much freedom to speak of many things.' It seemed that Williams's prayers were being answered, and that wisdom and charity in the work of the Lord had prevailed.[27]

7.

'Preaching, persecution and prayer'

The Methodist ideal was not simply to make converts, but to make disciples. All their energies were channelled to this end, their preaching, teaching, fellowship meetings, prayers and structures. Revivals were not merely about the excitement of heightened emotions and profound experiences; this God-sent manifestation of powerbrought about a realchange in people. Such individuals henceforth belonged to another kingdom, the kingdom of God, where Christ's rule was relevant, farreaching, beneficial and ongoing. It would be productive in terms of spiritual worship, a different lifestyle, a believing community, and anticipation of a blessed, eternal destiny. Discipleship involved nurture and discipline by every Bible-sanctioned means possible in an attitude of commitment and humility. It was to this task that the Welsh Methodists dedicated themselves in the productive years that followed Williams's alignment with Rowland at Llangeitho in 1743, and the new-found freedom that he found on leaving his curacies.

What, then, were the means they used to achieve this goal? Gospel preaching within parish boundaries and beyond, encouraging Bible reading and prayer, celebration of the Lord's Supper, society meetings, and the provision of edifying literature were priority considerations. Although Bibles were available they were costly, but people were prepared to make financial sacrifices in order to obtain one, and to make time to learn to read in one of Griffith Jones's schools. Jones's *Cyfarwyddwr Ffyddlon at Orseddfaingc y Gras ('A Faithful Guide to the Throne of Grace')* had appeared in 1738, and the first part of his extensive catechism, *Hyfforddwr i Wybodaeth Iachusol o Egwyddorion a Dyletswyddau Crefydd* ('Instruction for a Saving Knowledge of the Principles and Duties of Religion') in 1741. It was agreed at an Association in April 1744, 'that we should all endeavour to set catechizing everywhere', a decision that was influenced by pressure from Jones. By October the following year, a qualification was added: 'to set up catechizing in the most edifying and enlivening way', a typical Methodist emphasis which showed concern that religion should be in the heart as well as the head. This was further elaborated in January 1747: 'That the brethren should do all they can to stir up the people to a more diligent reading and searching of the Scriptures; and to inform themselves in all the practical principles of the Christian religion, in order to set up catechizing in our families and societies, and in order to help them that they should use all the help they can get, Revd. Mr. Griffith Jones's exposition on the Church catechism, and the [Westminster] Assembly's catechism etc., till such time as the brethren shall draw up a catechism.'[1] In this way the Methodists were providing for their congregations a biblical framework for a better understanding of their sermons.

Nothing was more prominent in the revival than the Methodists' preaching. It assumed feverish proportions in frequency and fervour. Harris's crammed itinerary, Rowland's extensive popularity, Howel Davies's success in Pembrokeshire, could all be attributed to preaching. Its character as well as its prominence is evident in the story of Williams's *Theomemphus*. The Methodist preaching of a 'Boanerges' and an 'Evangelius' was distinguished by its authority, penetration and power. It was in sharp contrast to the theoretically doctrinal, ethical and schismatic sermonising of 'Seducus', 'Orthocephalus', 'Schematicus', 'Arbitrius Liber', 'Orthodoxus', and 'Academicus'. Congregations recognized the difference, and responded to the note of authenticity in Methodist preaching, both in its biblical content and spiritual liveliness. Such vigorous activity was based on the conviction that 'it pleased God by the foolishness of preaching to save them that believe', and that 'faith cometh by hearing, and hearing by the Word of God' (1 Corinthians 1: 21; Romans 10:17). It was this conviction which compelled Harris to resort to 'field-preaching', and Williams to become an itinerant rather than a resident clergyman. It explained extra-parochial excursions by Griffith Jones and Daniel Rowland.

In this way the Methodists revived a Puritan priority. The Puritan constituency, when Sabbath pulpits were refused them, had set up their 'lectureships', so that 'the lectureships made London a city of preachers, and hence a city open to Puritan penetration.' Civic leaders with Puritan convictions and a hunger for God's Word, were prepared to finance 'the settling and establishing of the public preaching of God's Word', so that 'even the most hard-headed businessman among the city fathers must have felt the public monies were well employed.'[2] The same conviction is found among the Welsh Puritans, Walter Cradock, Vavasor Powell, Hugh Owen, Morgan Llwyd, and Stephen Hughes. Their ministries, too, were itinerant, their passion for preaching unrelenting. It is true that for them another factor made it imperative to spread the Word of God, namely, the vacuum created by the ejection of unfit ministers from their livings. In parts of Wales the Methodists were labelled 'Cradociaid' (Cradocians), but this was still a testimony to the resilience of preaching in one century, and its resurrection in another.[3]

The benchmark for all Welsh Methodist preaching was that of Daniel Rowland. Here is Howel Harris, endeavouring to record what must have been an experience of spiritual ecstasy under Rowland's sermon on Isaiah 6:5, in December 1742, 'I am a man of unclean lips, and dwell among people of unclean lips': 'In singing again I was quite melted away to love, and my heart burnt solidly indeed with true heat and love, feeling God there indeed, so as to draw my heart up to God from all; feeling love to all, so that I did not know what to do. Never did my eyes see or my ears hear what power is here! I was at first condemned, but now fed indeed and in an amazing manner, set free indeed by the Lord, and so now set free indeed by faith, and feeling so, I was made sweet to meet the dear lambs who were full of zeal and liberty, burning with coals from the altar of God, and my own soul now burning with fire and zeal, and rejoicing.'[4] Thus, Harris's comments on Williams's preaching two months later must be taken as an accolade of the highest order: 'Yesterday I heard brother Williams preach sweetly and powerfully indeed. The spirit of brother Rowland seems to rest in a great measure on him.'[5]

So much for the spiritual power that attended Methodist preaching, but what was the manner in which they approached this great task? In his elegy to Howel Davies, Williams describes his pulpit ministry to the vast crowds that attended. First there was singing and solemn pleading, like Moses, face to face with God for blessing.

> He reads his text, his words important sound
> Melodious sweet in every ear around;
> Explains the context, shows how they connect,
> And how some parts to others have respect.
> Hark! Hark! How clear his silver trumpet sounds,
> How keen his darts, how every sentence wounds.
> The multitude move! The arrows pierce 'em thro',
> His thunder roars, his fiery lightnings glow;
> The sinner starts, and to himself applies;
> To me alone belongs all this, he cries!
> What shall I do? I am undone, I fell
> From the height of bliss unto the lowest hell!

> Convictions fly like arrows thus around,
> And thousands groan at Sinai's dreadful sound;
> Hard rocks do rend, hark on their doleful cries,
> And see how flows full rivers from their eyes!
> Anon how sweet he lays his threatenings by,
> And points a Saviour to the mournful eye,
> Proclaims salvation with its glorious train,
> To all such souls as Sinai's trump has slain.
> Here comfort swells, a deluge here of grace
> O'erflows their mournings, and their terror chase;
> In silent showers here glorious peace distils,
> And with true joys the trembling mourner fills.[6]

Careful exposition of the text and its application are enveloped in prayer, so that the congregation is overwhelmed with the 'dreadful sound' of the Law and the 'deluge of grace' in the Gospel.

Presenting 'the whole counsel of God' in this way attracted opposition from the world, while it gained a harvest of souls for Christ's kingdom. Williams often faced persecution from hostile mobs: in 1743 in Cardiganshire, he and Rowland faced 'ruffians, armed with guns and staves … and beat them unmercifully; but they escaped, through the care of the great Shepherd, without any great hurt. The ruffians were set on by a gentleman of the neighbourhood. No wonder the enemy rages, when he sees his kingdom so attacked.'[7] Two weeks later, and even closer to home, near Ystrad-ffin, Williams and Harris faced opposition from a magistrate, who 'ordered his steward to read the proclamation against riotous assemblies, and then he ordered us all to disperse immediately.' Harris's graphic account continues:

> I asked him if his Majesty did not allow us an hour; he said he did, but we had best be gone immediately. I said we should pray and then depart; he then said it was his land, and that we should go, and called the man of the house to send me. Then I said he should not find me of an opposing or turbulent spirit, but he asked me who sent me … his steward told him to run his horse over me … then he came on again and looked at his watch and our hour was almost gone; and then I went off, his steward reading the Proclamation again.

Methodist persistence in the face of adversity is undeniable. In October of that year Williams and Rowland were in Anglesey for the cause of Truth, but found that 'the door was shut by the mob so they did not preach'. It was no different for them in 1754, and North Wales was so

56

hostile to the Methodists in those early years that Harris was fearful of going there.[8] Rowland on one occasion was prevented from preaching at Nefyn church when the incumbent gave out the long Psalm 119 for the congregation to sing. On another occasion on Angelsey, Rowland was denied a pulpit because he was not licensed by the bishop of the diocese, and Williams was at the same time hindered because he was not in full orders.[9]

One author suggests that Williams occasionally avoided persecution because of the respect shown to his poetic ability, or perhaps because his opposers feared lest he should expose them to ridicule by the genius of his pen! At one place an innkeeper suggested he disguise himself in different clothes, but having done so Williams was ashamed as Christ's words came to his mind, Mat. 10:33, 'Whosoever shall deny me before men, him will I also deny before my Father which is in heaven'. He discarded the borrowed materials, and on being recognized in his own clothes again, was attacked by the mob. However, the innkeeper protected him and he escaped without serious injury.[10] Sometimes discretion prevailed: Williams was said to have escaped once by being let down from a window in a basket, much like the Apostle Paul from Damascus; another time he took refuge in a barn where he slept the night.[11]

A dread of riots, mobs and disorder found expression in the hostility shown to Methodist itinerant preachers, especially to the laymen. Their strange accents and vocabulary were merely the beginning of woes in rural areas with a parochial outlook. Their preaching in the open air and outside the protection either of the parish church or the licensed chapel for Dissenters raised further suspicion. In the 1740s the situation was further exacerbated by a lurking Jacobitism, with its threat to a kingdom made stable by the Hanoverian succession. Fears of an uprising, led by James II's grandson, 'Bonnie Prince Charlie' or 'The Young Pretender', were real until his defeat at Culloden in 1746, and Methodists were often forced to defend themselves against being involved in the conspiracy. The gravity of this charge of disloyalty to the Crown was not to be underestimated. It was made public by a series of pamphlets published during the closing months of 1743, which Harris saw as 'a new scheme to attempt a final stop to the present Revival under the character of Methodist ... representing them as dangerous of State and Church.' Whitefield replied in print with *An Answer*, and also instigated court proceedings against a hostile crowd which had seriously injured Thomas Adams at Hampton in the

Cotswolds. In his *Answer* Whitefield reaffirmed Methodist loyalty to King George, and defended Methodist open-air preaching.[12] Charles Wesley was accused of treason by a clergyman in March 1744, and was acquitted by a Wakefield magistrate on hearing his assertion, 'I am as true Church-of-England man, and as loyal a subject, as any man in the kingdom', adding that Methodist hymns and prayers were all for King George. In doing so, Charles was echoing his brother John's 'Address to the King' on behalf 'of the Societies in England and Wales, in derision called Methodists'. Such people, said Wesley, were 'part (however mean) of that Protestant Church established in these kingdoms', and 'we are ready to obey your Majesty to the uttermost, in all things which we conceive to be agreeable' to the Word of God.[13] Selina, Countess of Huntingdon, also wrote to the King in 1745, a 'remonstrance' that expressed loyalty in the face of aspersions to the contrary on account of her association with the Methodists. By way of reply the King made clear that he would 'suffer no persecution on account of religion', and that he was 'fully sensible' of Selina's 'attachment to the House of Hanover.'[14]

Williams, for his part, sets the whole affair in a spiritual context in a letter to Harris from his home at Cefn-coed in December 1745:

> Many here nowadays long to know the art of believing; for 'tis little more we have to go against sin, Satan, yea, the French and a Popish Pretender – the wars and tumults abroad and at home, especially the rebellion in Scotland, and the fear of an invasion hath destroyed a great deal of our carnal confidence, self-security, lukewarmness, and worldly-mindedness, and stirred up faith, watchfulness, diligence, with pure zeal for God and His interest, Christ and His Gospel, King George and his peaceable government ... Here are some fears by reason of the rebellion in the north, but it would fill your soul with love to God to see how fervent the poor despised Methodists pray for King George the Second and the present Government. We had a Society last week to fast and pray with our Arms. Certainly God was there. I doubt not but many prayers went to heaven and shall be answered in God's time. I expect daily to hear of the fall of our enemies. We have very many here and Cardiganshire who are willing to wear arms as soon as called for. Certainly this disproves their disloyalty as was accused by some; hence that passage in Mr. Whitefield's Answer to my Lord Bishop of London is confirmed ... In the midst of wars and tumults my dear brother stand still and you shall see the salvation of God. How long before this rebellion ceases, or how far God will permit them to go I know not; I am apt to believe a Popish Pretender will not prevail long.[15]

The gravity with which the Welsh Methodists viewed the uprising is reflected in an Association decision of October 1745: 'Agreed that as many as can should keep next Friday, November 1st a day of prayer on the present occasion against the enemies of our Religion, the Pretender; and those that can't let them keep Friday sevenight; and to set forth before the people the knowledge of the Popish Religion etc.'[16] As far as the Methodists were concerned, it was not only their safety that was at stake, the very foundation of biblical Christianity was threatened.

Distances travelled by the Welsh Methodists on indescribably primitive roads, and in the face of unpredictable weather conditions, suggest phenomenal stamina and impressive dedication to what they considered an urgent task. The fitness of horses and of hostelries was another hazardous factor, and the story is told of Williams's horse dying on one journey. His timid servant tried to mitigate the loss by saying that the horse had gone to eternity. Williams's quick reply was, 'Well, I hope it has left the bridle and the saddle behind!' Williams often travelled with Rowland on preaching tours, and the latter might have been referring to this when he spoke of their limited resources: 'We had but a poor reception and a poor fare while travelling over hills and mountains on our little nags, without anything to eat but the bread and cheese we carried in our pockets, and without anything to drink but water from the springs; and if we had a little buttermilk in some cottages, we thought that a great thing.'[17] In spite of all this, Harris in 1748 had 'visited [in nine weeks] 13 counties and travelled nearly 150 miles every week … and travelled from one morning to the next evening without any rest above 100 miles, discoursing at 12 or 2 in the morning on the mountain, being obliged to meet at that time by reason of persecution.'[18] Less than a year before his death, Williams excused his infrequent correspondence to one of his sons with this reason: 'I am most part of my time from home … I travelled through the 6 counties of South Wales, and some few of them very often [in the last six months] … and now I am just come from a long journey through Carmarthenshire, Glamorganshire, Monmouthshire, and Breconshire, being about 250 miles.'[19] At 73 years of age his zeal for preaching the everlasting Gospel was clearly undiminished.

God's appointed means to gain such blessing was prayer. It featured prominently in the activity, not only of Welsh Methodists, but also of the wider Great Awakening. In February 1740 Harris records in his diary that he was 'filled with zeal to press on my brethren with me to lay aside days for prayer.'[20] In another letter at that time he urged

Elizabeth James of Abergavenny, who was to become Whitefield's wife, to press on others to come together 'to keep a strict discipline and to observe constantly your monthly Day of Prayer.'[21] From June 1744 Association minutes bristle with decisions to keep days of fasting and prayer, a practice frequently found among the godly people of the period. Sometimes there was a particular objective in view, such as imminent persecution or concern about national security. Within a year, however, the 'great lukewarmness' that prevailed in several places became an urgent matter for prayer. It coincided with a call from Scotland for a 'Concert of Prayer', received by Harris in March 1745. The response of the Welsh Methodists to it was immediate and sympathetic. They recorded their agreement at an Association on 29 March 1745: 'As a proposal was sent from Scotland to keep one day in every three months, beginning November 1st a Day of Prayers for two years and to meet every Sunday morning on account of the late work in England, Scotland, Wales and America, both to praise God for it and intercede and pray for its furtherance and to be humbled for the sin that attended it, we agreed to it; to keep the first of May next (the quarter's end) and every Sunday morning with as many as we can have, and also in private to give it a place in our hearts and time as much as we can every Saturday night and to recommend it to others also.'[22]

The 'Concert of Prayer' gained momentum with the publication in 1747 of Jonathan Edwards's *Humble Attempt to Promote Explicit Agreement and Visible Union of God's People in Extraordinary Prayer for the Revival of Religion and the Advancement of Christ's Kingdom on Earth*. In it Edwards rejects any objection of novelty, since a London publication in 1712, based on Zech. 8:21, and with the title 'A Serious Call from the city', had argued for a specific time 'that all who make conscience of praying for the peace of Jerusalem … to entreat the face of the Lord.' It was also in keeping with Edwards's conviction, 'that the prayers of his saints should be one great and principal means of carrying on the designs of Christ's kingdom in the world … when God is about to accomplish great things for his church, he will begin by remarkably pouring out "the spirit of grace and supplication", Zech. 12: 10.'[23]

The title of Edwards's work may have been an echo of a similar work by Isaac Watts, published in 1731, *Humble Attempt towards the Revival of Practical Religion*. In it Watts pleads with his readers, 'O let us stir up our hearts, and all that is within us, and strive mightily in prayer and in preaching to revive the work of God, and beg earnestly that God by a fresh and abundant effusion of his own Spirit, would revive his own work among us.'[24] Scottish evangelicals could have based their plea on a work by John Willison which appeared in 1733, *The Church's Danger and the Minister's Duty:* 'Let us pray for God's *pouring out his Spirit from on high* upon the Ordinances and assemblies of this land, for our affairs will never take a turn for the better *until the Spirit is poured out from on high'.*[25] 'Praying Societies' in Scotland were common, and were often, but not always, linked to preparation for partaking of the Lord's Supper.[26] The Welsh Methodists had their own precedent, an essay by Jeremi Owen published in 1733, which made this plea: 'At this present time it is a sad time for the cause of Christ in the world; it is dark night on the Church; the friends of the Bridegroom … are uneasy, and under holy agitation … They therefore pray without ceasing, every time they make mention of His Name, that He would manifest His authority, and reign … return, return, so that we may gaze upon you, as King of Zion marching triumphantly in the chariot of the everlasting Gospel.'[27] The 'Concert of Prayer' that resulted from the Scottish initiative may be seen as the organized culmination of these several strands of influence. From October 1744 until 1786 prayer for revival was the focus of many evangelical gatherings not only in the Old World but also in the New.[28] It stimulated not only dependence on God's Spirit but expectancy of unprecedented Gospel success.

Isaac Nathan, in his tribute to Williams refers to his prayers as well as his sermons, implying that Williams's strength in the pulpit was drawn from his entreaties at the throne of grace: 'He was the most theological of all the Revivalists, and also the best scholar. But such was the weightiness of his sermons that his preaching would have been dry and sterile, had it not been for four qualities: (1) the sweetness of his voice; (2) his use of imagination to serve the Gospel; (3) applying his message by quoting verses of his hymns, often under sublime unction so that he would weep before he finished the verse, especially if it was about Christ's agony in the Garden or death on the cross; (4) the emphasis on experience was deliberate in his sermon; he spoke as a witness, expressing God's dealings with his own soul … Even though he was highly esteemed as a preacher, people would speak more often about his prayers.'[29] One of Williams's Welsh hymns draws attention to the need for the Holy Spirit's power to attend the preaching, and make the message meaningful, convincing and effective:

Glimpses, Saviour, of Thy count'nance
Brings the lifeless from the dead;
Heaven and hell before you open
When your heavenly smile is read;
Gracious Word, mighty sword,
Breaks apart each binding cord.

Speak, O Lord, Thy glorious message,
With authority and might;
Show Thy voice is strong to conquer,
And put unbelief to flight;
Heavenly flame, blaze in fame,
Triumph here, exalt Thy Name.[30]

Expressed as a petition, the hymn was intended for congregational use,
so that everyone present would listen for God's voice in that of His
messenger, and desire that fire from heaven which alone could set their
hearts ablaze in true worship.

8.

'The fragrance of the Bridegroom's robes'

From both personal acquaintance and experience Thomas Charles was eminently suited to give a description of Williams's preaching. Charles had been converted under Rowland's preaching at Llangeitho and was later in correspondence with Williams. Speaking of Williams, he writes: 'His preaching gifts were profuse, his sermons evangelical, experimental and sweet. He was able to discern false doctrines and spurious experiences, and could distinguish between a true and false spirit. His imagination was powerful; his eye both piercing and keen. Many were the heavenly influences that attended his public ministry as well as his converse with individuals about their souls in the private societies.'[1] Some who heard him in the early years were critical; 'fairly good', was the comment of one of the exhorters, Richard Tibbott in 1744; 'he is very warm, serious, and devout young man, intent upon doing good, but wants to give himself to read and study', was the appraisal of the Dissenter, Thomas Morgan, a few months later. Even Harris at that time had to concede, that 'though this was an excellent discourse [on Zech. 13: 9], yet some things were so delivered that had I been in the flesh [that is, an unbeliever], or not freed by another portion [of Scripture with which Harris was familiar], I could have been brought to bondage for want of more distinctions.'[2] Perhaps the considered assessment of a North Wales exhorter, John Evans of Bala, could be taken as representative of Williams's mature years: 'he was noted for his powerful, fiery flights of imagination, his enlightened, evangelical doctrine, delivered with much spiritual unction.'[3]

As for the message that Williams conveyed, however, there can be no doubt as to its clear biblical content, and its personal application to the hearer or reader. The text is explained, its teaching developed and its message driven home. In an undated but important sermon Williams develops a pivotal theme of Protestant principles, that of imputed righteousness. His text was Psalm 89: 16, 'In Thy name shall they rejoice all the day; and in Thy righteousness shall they be exalted.' Because it is given prominent attention in his writings, it deserves extended analysis. It raises the basic issue of how a sinner can be right with God. This is how Williams begins his sermon:

> *First*, the nature of this righteousness … God's Law was given in the form of a covenant, with promise of life on Adam's perfect obedience, but of death on disobedience. Adam, and all his seed in him and with him, having broken the covenant, came under a curse, so that our salvation was utterly impossible until justice was satisfied, and the broken Law's integrity restored … Under such conditions … God's Son stood Mediator and substitute before the Law for the sinner, to fulfil the command and suffer the curse. God accepted Him as propitiation … Christ, the eternal Son of God, in the fullness of time was born of a woman, and under the Law, and as substitute in our place, fulfilled all the conditions of the covenant; in a word, He obeyed all the demands of the Law; suffered its curse, and so brought in that everlasting righteousness by which alone the guilty sinner is justified before God; and this is the righteousness spoken of in the text …

Words used by Williams here: 'covenant', 'Law', 'mediator', 'substitute', 'propitiation', and 'justified', are frequently found in his writings. They were to be understood in a manner consistent with Scripture usage and assert divine right as well as divine provision. They bring together Christ's Person and work, and the sinner's guilt and salvation. The beneficiaries of this covenant come into possession of 'everlasting righteousness' by the power of the Spirit working faith in them to accept it. This is a transaction, a transfer, an exchange that has the sanction of God's Law, since its demands have been met by Christ in the sinner's place:

> Even though Christ obeyed the Law, satisfied justice, and has brought everlasting righteousness, yet God's elect do not participate of this righteousness until God's power brings them to accept it by faith… The righteousness of the Mediator is transferred to us by imputation … Here is an exchange between Christ and us: He takes our sin and unrighteousness, and instead He gives us His pure, unspotted righteousness … It is an imputed righteousness on the basis of the union between Christ and the believer.

The language here is reminiscent of the 'wonderful exchange' spoken of by John Calvin in his *Institutes of the Christian Religion*:

> that, becoming Son of man with us, he has made us sons of God with him; that, by his descent to earth, he has prepared an ascent to heaven

for us; that, by taking on our mortality, he has conferred his immortality upon us; that, accepting our weakness, he has strengthened us by his power; that, receiving our poverty unto himself, he has transferred his wealth to us; that, taking the weight of our iniquity upon himself (which oppressed us), he has clothed us with his righteousness.

As Williams continues, he is careful to join together the sinner's justification and his sanctification. He speaks of union with Christ as the key; to be joined to Him for acceptance and forgiveness, is also to be joined to Him for growth in grace and personal godliness. It is a union that Williams aptly compares, among others, to that between the body's members and its head, between branches and the vine:

On account of this union believers are a gathered flock within one fold, and under the same Shepherd; a body with many members, yet united in one Head; a family living under one Master; a city owning allegiance to one Prince, and under the precepts of the same law; stones on the same foundation; branches of the same Vine. Having been made one with Christ, God's righteousness covers them.

The sermon is brought to a conclusion with encouragement to embrace Christ's righteousness:

Second, the excellencies of this righteousness. It is perfect and blameless ... a plentiful righteousness ... therefore, sinner, be sure that you possess it, so that you will not be speechless at the last judgment ... It is an incomparable righteousness ... How glorious this righteousness with which the believer is clothed ... It is an everlasting righteousness... Third, how believers are exalted in this righteousness ... above the righteousness of their own works ... above the world ... with its pleasures, flattery and derision ... above the wrath and malice of the devil."[4]

Even in summary these extracts provide sufficient evidence to establish Williams as a preacher in the Puritan mould of careful exegesis, doctrinal development and close application.

Two more sermons are preserved at some length as being Williams's, but they, too, have doctrinal precision rather than fluid presentation. In the one on Galatians 6:14, 'But God forbid that I should glory save in the cross of our Lord Jesus Christ, by whom the world is crucified unto me, and I unto the world', the central significance of the cross is emphasised, together with its implication for the Christian of suffering for Christ in a deceitful and hostile world. The third sermon, preached at the Trefeca College Anniversary in August 1789, also instructive in its tone, has more direct, personal application. The text was Matthew 11:29, 'Take my yoke upon you, and learn of me, for I am meek and lowly in heart, and ye shall find rest unto your souls', and there is encouragement to face the hardest trials armed with Christ's promise and power: 'When we are in trouble, it is natural for us to be agitated and worried, and to thrash out like a trapped wild bull. Believers in such circumstances find that their flesh is weak, while their spirit is willing; but they consider how they should submit, and know where to find grace … Here Christ offers the aid you require, as if He says, "Fear not what awaits you; think what I can do; everything is within my power; I can make the crooked straight, and the rough smooth; I can draw out your affections, bend your will, influence your behaviour, deliver you from sinful fears."' [5]

Contemporary witnesses of Williams's preaching give more lively accounts of his style and in recording their impressions at the time convey something of the preacher's liveliness. On one occasion early in 1744 Williams's preaching to some 200 people was 'attended with great power'. In April he preached on Jer. 50:19 'reasonably well' beside a house in Llanllugan, Montgomeryshire on his way to an Association.[6] Here is Harris, writing after listening to Williams preaching at Llangeitho in August 1744 on Zechariah 13:9, 'I will bring the third part through the fire, and will refine them as silver is refined, and will try them as gold is tried':

> He showed what is the nature of the fire by which he refines his people. Firstly, that he sends a spirit of bondage upon them; not a legal bondage arising from a slavish fear; but the hiding of his face. That he leaves them with faith, but yet removes his face, which is worse than hell to those who love him. Secondly, that he refines them through the fire of providential crosses, giving David and Job as examples. Thirdly, by allowing some liberty to the sin and pollution within us. Which is the most secret fire, and the heaviest burden of all to every Christian. His comments were searching. He showed further the effects of the fire, that it gives light and consumes every sin. A sweet and searching discourse. I see with what tenderness we should deliver truths.[7]

Within a month, Williams had accompanied Rowland on a tour in North Wales, and 'had wonderful liberty and power and no interruption.'[8] Harris's records of the Watford Association in January

1745 show that Williams addressed the dangers and opportunities faced by God's people in a hostile world in a sermon on the Song of Solomon 3:8, 'every man hath his sword upon his thigh because of fear in the night':

> He opened up the whole Book to this point and then described the night that is referred to here as 1. the night of a legal spirit at Sinai; 2. the night of persecution and the night of trial; and 3. the night of tribulation and affliction. He illustrated these things in the history of the Church from ... the Church in Egypt and Canaan and Jerusalem etc. until now, referring particularly to Job, Joseph, etc. He showed that though the enemies of the Church were so numerous, God defended them. He was very powerful when he showed of the persecution that perhaps is at the door ... he showed that this world is a night [compared] to the state of the other world. He penetrated to the quick in exciting all to be diligent, now, while we still have liberty.[9]

That it was a remarkable time, with sixty present, is borne out by the testimony of Herbert Jenkins, who also preached there: 'the Lord was amongst us, and with us of a truth. Many of the hearers were greatly comforted, and went away rejoicing. We were two days together, and had sweet harmony ... good accounts we had of the progress of the work of our Lord ... we parted in peace and in much love.'[10]

A letter from Bristol in April 1746 notes that 'Mr. Williams, a clergyman from Wales has been here printing some hymns and he preached once in Welsh at the Hall. His purpose would have been to visit the printer Felix Farley, who had been entrusted with every part of *Aleluja* except the first, with its fourth part to be published in 1746.[11] Unlike Harris, Williams's forays into England were rare, and most of his time and labour was spent in the counties of South Wales.

In 1747 Williams preached in Welsh at Maesmynys, in Breconshire, followed by Charles Wesley in English. For Charles, on his way to Ireland, the visit had far-reaching consequences. It was here that he met his future wife, Sarah, daughter of Marmaduke Gwynne who lived nearby at Garth. Gwynne had been converted under Howel Harris's preaching some ten years earlier, and at that time Theophilus Evans, who provided Williams with the curacy at Llanwrtyd, served as chaplain to the Gwynne family. Charles was immediately attracted to Sally, as she was affectionately called, and they were married two years later. John Wesley was also on his way to Ireland when he called with the Gwynne family at the end of February 1748. He 'hastened on to

Holyhead; but all the ships were on the other side', and while he was detained in this way, he met 'Mr. Williams, a clergyman from South Wales.' They took the opportunity to preach together, at Rhydyspardyn and at Llanddeiniol on Anglesey.[12]

Williams's published works of prose and poetry also contain passages that might have been initially delivered as sermons. Garfield H. Hughes considers that the section on the parable of the Prodigal Son in Williams's *Crocodil, Afon yr Aifft* ('The Crocodile of Egypt's River'), where the evils of jealousy under the figure of the crocodile are described by examples from Scripture) to be 'one of the most important testimonies we have to the preaching styles of eighteenth century Methodists.' For Williams the parable 'described man's defection from God, and the restoration of the repentant sinner to his father's house, together with the horrible jealousy which all legalistic people hold towards those who receive such grace, and towards God its glorious and wonderful author.' Thus God's love is contrasted with human jealousy:

> Wonder of wonders! The father's love revealing itself before the son's repentance appeared ... Each party showed urgency and fervour, but the father carried the day. God is first and last; here is free grace in the spirit of the new covenant; after the assurance of forgiveness, behold the sweet, evangelical confession, 'I have sinned against heaven, and in your sight' ... but the irrational jealousy of the older brother ... is seen, first, in the old scribes and Pharisees towards publicans and sinners who accepted the spirit and grace of the Gospel ... secondly ... in those who from their youth lived upright lives towards those who came into the church as great sinners ... third ... in old, sleepy Christians who are at ease towards those younger ones who are fervent, zealous and lively ... and lastly, in those elderly congregations which have lost their first love, towards congregations on which the Spirit of the Lord is shining.[13]

In his application Williams directed his remarks to a mixed congregation, believers and unbelievers, young and old, religious and profane. There was no compromise as to the content of the sermon, and in its delivery it offered a full and free salvation to whosoever would repent and believe. In this way Williams was fulfilling Christ's commission to take the Gospel to ever creature without fear or favour.

In *Theomemphus*, Williams portrays several preachers of his day by fictional characters whose names are intended to convey the nature of their message. 'Boanerges' thunders the demands of God's Law in all its sanctions, spirituality and authority. He applies the Law to expose sin, and to stir man's sluggish conscience and natural bias against the truth. This is right and necessary, but a number of false trails are now introduced, each of which has its appeal to the pride of man, but none of which bring peace or relief to a troubled sinner. 'Seducus' leads men astray as he denounces Boanerges and argues that a religion of reason and morality is sufficient.

> 'Religion's but good conscience, live in an honest way,
> Defending poor widows, care for the weak each day;
> Maintaining good relations, no quarrels and no spite,
> No swearing and no tippling, such is the grace that's right.'

'Orthocephalus' insists on doctrinal clarity, and his sermon is orthodox but theoretical, and holds out no comfort to bruised, guilty hearts. 'Schematicus' shows 'zeal for obscure issues', that creates cliques within and alienates those without. The sermon of 'Arbitrius Liber' emphasises man's free will and invites partnership with God in the matter of the soul's salvation. Finally, along comes 'Evangelius', who begins by acknowledging the validity of Boanerges's teaching, and to claim, 'Now I from heaven's counsels am also sent by grace', and to hold forth the Gospel remedy. This declares the sufficiency of Christ's atonement and a call to the vilest sinner to trust Him alone, altogether, always for complete salvation:

> O! grace that's free and changeless, eternally secure,
> The Lamb Who died, was wounded, alone provides sin's cure;
> For guilt and shame true healing, the fear of death subdued,
> And love forever grounded on peace with power endued.[14]

This, then, was the preaching ideal: a combination of Law with grace, and of instruction with application, having Christ at its centre and praise as its fruit.

The high office of preacher of God's Word, in Williams's esteem the highest of all offices, required spiritual as well as intellectual qualities. In a digression from the section that deals with society stewards in his *The Experience Meeting*, Williams deals with the issue of ministerial qualification. Against the backcloth of 'these lifeless Gospel days', Williams admits that unfit and unworthy preachers were numerous. They were boastful, proud, immature, and impatient, and Williams reminds his readers that the Holy Spirit had given 'a sharp warning to beware of teachers who have gone astray in their doctrines, their lives, their aims or their spirit.' He bemoans the fact that 'in all the denominations, many set out to preach, who are much more concerned about honours, personal gain and creature comforts, as you say, than for the glory of God and the good of immortal souls; and their preaching has none of the fragrance of the Bridegroom's robes – none of the holy oil, no note of the voice of the divine Dove.' Hence former meanness of station in life, of peasant stock or humble craft, should not in itself disqualify from this high office, provided there was evidence of grace, godliness and divinely endowed gifts:

> As to these men, it would be a great loss to the Church of God to be deprived of them; and so long as their doctrines are sound, and they continue humble in spirit, living lives becoming to the Gospel of Christ, it is no small sin to despise them, though they have no great learning and are lacking in knowledge both literary and historical. Yet, while they have the substance in them – that is, the Spirit of the Lord – you must esteem them highly in every way that is fitting and right for ministers of the Gospel; and though they were lately only carpenters, shoemakers and cobblers, as you say, they are none the worse for that, any more than the Apostles, who were all unlearned men except Paul himself, if they continue in the true spirit and adhere to the doctrine of the Church. I know that some preachers, who formerly lived by just such poor trades, are today truly dividing the Word of life – able to teach, to convict, to rebuke, encourage, and catechize, and sounding forth the Gospel of Christ in the same spirit as the holy martyrs of old, or the first Reformers from the Popish religion, so that no one need be ashamed of them, and neither priest nor bishop can find fault with them, if they are allowed to speak in their own way – because they do not presume to teach the people anything but Jesus Christ and Him crucified, according to the teaching of the true Faith.[15]

This is not to say that lay preachers were sanctioned without examination. Whitefield in July 1748 'was determined not to join with any to preach (after the delusion and abomination he had seen through young ones going out rashly in a wild fire) till he should be fully satisfied of their teachableness, of their tempers [that is, attitude], and if they are willing to use all means to improve themselves.'[16] Such checks and balances had existed in Wales from the early days; in March 1743 an Association had agreed to silence four laymen 'as being persuaded not sent of God.' Another was allowed only to exhort 'in the nearest private societies, till he shall have a testimony from them, and come to our next Association to be examined.' Williams was deputed on one occasion to notify one particular layman that the Association was 'not so persuaded of his call to exhort … and therefore we give him up to the Lord.'[17] The need to distinguish between a genuine call by God to preach and a merely human desire for public applause required sustained vigilance.

Methodist preaching was a distinctive *kind* of preaching. Careful exposition of the text was involved, yes, and so also were awareness of the congregation's needs, and an appropriate oratory. But the preacher was to *rely* on divine assistance, an attending unction only supplied by the Holy Spirit to make the message effective. What mattered was 'the fragrance of the Bridegroom's robes … the holy oil … the voice of the divine Dove.' What other explanation could there be for the effect on the illiterate, coarse miners of Kingswood, Bristol, of Whitefield's preaching for nearly an hour or so in February 1739? An early biographer comments on the occasion that, 'the first discovery of their being affected was to see the white gutters made by their tears, which plentifully fell down their black cheeks, as they came out of their coal pits. Hundreds and hundreds of them were soon brought under deep convictions, which, as the event proved, happily ended in a sound and thorough conversion.' Whitefield's own perception of the occasion, when he preached to several thousand people in the open air, was that God enabled him to preach with great power. He added: 'The fire is kindled in the country; and, I know, all the devils in hell shall not be able to quench it.' Three months later Whitefield could bear witness to God's transforming power in their lives: 'Instead of cursing and swearing, they are heard to sing hymns about the woods; and the rising generation, I hope, will be a generation of Christians.'[18] Both Welsh and English Methodists shared the same aim for the manner and fruit of their preaching.

Harris, too, spoke of such dependence. Of one preaching occasion he says, 'the power of God came down and souls were awakened'; on other occasions he feared that it was 'only the common work of the Spirit' that had attended his ministry, or that there had been 'much oratory but little power'.[19] In an elegy to one of the lay preachers, Williams graphically compared this divine unction to a heavenly gale, which alone would serve the true purpose of preaching:

> Feeling was his life and essence,
> Heaven's breeze his only aid;

> With no breath of God attending
> Fixed his vessel would have stayed;
> Sturdy oars not his to row with,
> But the gale from heaven above
> All the saints would bring in triumph
> To the paradise of love.[20]

It was considerations such as these that distinguished Williams's preaching. While his hymns have rightly bestowed on his name prominence and lustre, the significance and effectiveness of his preaching should not be forgotten. He preached in a truly Calvinistic Methodist fashion, with power and fruit that could only be attributed to the aid of God's Spirit. Referring to another Methodist preacher (and Bible expositor), Peter Williams, William Williams is reputed to have remarked only a little seriously, 'You, Peter, can preach just as well if the Holy Spirit was in France, but as for me, I can do nothing unless I have Him at my elbow.'[21]

Throughout his sermons, hymns and prose works Williams offers a unified, systematic presentation of the Christian faith. In the development of his preaching gifts there was refinement certainly, but in its content there was consistency. Over the years his theology shows little evidence of change, but much consolidation and growing conviction. Wherever the reader turns there is prominence to the same central themes, unflinching conformity to biblical standards, and a sustained attempt at 'earthing' truth in human experience. But there is also the unspoken and uncompromising awareness that for effectiveness in achieving that encounter between divine provision and human need, Williams depends entirely on the secret operations of God's Holy Spirit.

9.

'Geneva jigs and a Welsh Aleluja'

Among the books in William Williams's library there were two from the previous century by George Wither, which had belonged to Williams's uncle, William Lewis. The title of the second of these began with the word *Halelviah*. It mentioned '*spirituall songs*' and ended with the words '*applied to easie tunes to be sung in families.*' Did the Williams family of Cefn-coed sing these hymns, and did William have the title in mind when his first published collection of hymns was called *Aleluja*? Gomer M. Roberts raised the issue in his discussion of Williams's work, and it seems a reasonable assumption.[1] If the family was inclined to use them, Isaac Watts's *Hymns and Spiritual Songs* would have been available from 1707, his *Psalms of David* from 1719, and both were acceptable in a Welsh Nonconformist household, even though they were in English. Reading, and perhaps singing hymns, privately or in family worship, was not unknown. In his elegy to Grace Price, Williams speaks of her as 'reading and summarizing all my books and noting those hymns which gave her most delight.'[2]

Meanwhile, in the neighbouring county of Brecon, Howel Harris had returned home in November 1735 after an abortive attempt to advance his education at Oxford. In the months that followed he tells us that he was 'occupied in going from house to house ... the people now began to assemble by vast numbers ... the word was attended with such power, that many on the spot cried out to God, for pardon of their sins ... The latter end of this year, a man went about to instruct young people to sing Psalms ... I laid hold of this opportunity, when he had done teaching them to sing, I would give them a word of exhortation, and thereby many were brought under convictions, and many religious societies were by these means formed.'[3] For John Games, Harris's companion, the nightly visits may have been a matter of duty as church precentor, from the conviction that even the limited number of tunes available needed practice when joined to words that did not always fit the metre.[4] By that time, several versions of the metrical Psalms were available to Anglicans. In Welsh, Games had at his disposal a number of editions from 1621 of Edmund Prys's metrical settings. Of these, the most recent edition, *Y Psallwyr, neu Psalmau Dafydd* ('The Psalter, or the Psalms of David') in 1736 was bound with a Catechism and several prayers.

In a selection of Prys's Psalms that Griffith Jones published a few years later, he acknowledged their deficiency as well as their usefulness:

> Until it pleases God (author of all gifts and blessings) to raise up and equip someone, or rather several godly, talented persons, with ability in divine poetry, learned in the true meaning of Scripture, and experienced in the ways and fellowship of God's Spirit and grace, by counsel together to compose a new Metrical Psalms in closer agreement with the means of grace and with the state of God's Church and people in Gospel days, we ought, thankfully and without excuse, to use the Metrical Psalms that we have, choosing with discernment those parts that are more relevant and easier for all to sing with understanding.[5]

Not only was it desirable that the occasionally awkward fitting of words into a rigid metre should be overcome, it would also be an advantage to relate the Psalms to 'people in Gospel days'. This change was already under way, but the emergence of hymns during the Great Awakening, with their variety of metre and expression of Christian truth and experience was to transform congregational singing.

Congregational Psalm singing was a distinctively Protestant expression of religious fervour. John Calvin had spoken of the Psalms as 'an anatomy of all parts of the soul.' Others set tunes to them, sharing his conviction 'that singing has great strength and vigour to move and inflame the hearts of men to invoke and praise God with a more vehement and ardent zeal.'[6] As metrical versions appeared in the language of the people and the repertoire of tunes widened, they became accessible and remembered. They were no longer the sole province of the clergy. Not without reason were they referred to as 'the battle hymns of the Lord' by persecuted French Protestants.[7] They were sung by crowds in the open air at St Paul's Cross in London for hours on end with great relish. Calling them 'Geneva jigs' has been attributed to Queen Elizabeth I and to Roman Catholics.[8] Early versions often included in their titles a statement of bold confidence in their power to influence and transform. The most notable among them, the version of Sternhold and Hopkins in 1562, claimed that they were 'very meet to be used of all sorts of people privately for their solace and comfort: laying apart all ungodly Songs and Ballads, which tend only to the nourishing of vice, and corrupting of youth.[9]

Evidence that Psalm-singing was acceptable among Puritans of the following century is found in 'The Directory for Public Worship' of the Westminster Assembly of Divines, approved by Parliament in 1645. Its concluding section, 'Of Singing of Psalms' emphasises that 'the chief care must be to sing with understanding, and with grace in the heart, making melody unto the Lord.' John Geree's *Character of an Old English Puritane or Non-Conformist* (1646) describes him as one whose 'chief music was singing of psalms, wherein, though he neglected not the melody of the voice, yet he chiefly looked after that of the heart.' Richard Baxter's ministry at Kidderminster was owned of God in such a way that 'on the Lord's Day there was no disorder to be seen in the streets, but you might hear a hundred families singing Psalms and repeating sermons as you passed through the streets.'[10]

A later Nonconformist, Isaac Watts, issued his trail-blazing *Hymns and Spiritual Songs* in 1707. Its publication opened the flood-gate for the expression in song of hymns as well as psalms. This was followed in 1719 by *The Psalms of David*, transposed into New Testament dress, and their popularity with Christian congregations may be gauged by the fact that 'When I survey the wondrous cross' and 'Our God, our help in ages past' still have enormous appeal today. The appearance of such psalms and hymns by Watts created something of a revolution in public worship.[11] Eventually congregations would acquire personal copies of the hymn book so that familiarity would in time produce a measure of musical harmony. The practice of 'lining out', whereby someone sang each line in tune for the rest to repeat, persisted until the 1840s, but fervency and repetition among Methodist societies had secured for hymn-singing prominence as well as legitimacy in public worship.[12]

The transition from Psalm-singing to hymn-singing in Wales was heralded with the publication in 1705 of a collection of hymns by the Presbyterian minister at Oswestry, James Owen, *Hymnau Scrythurol* ('Scriptural hymns'), with a second part in 1717. Another Presbyterian, Thomas Baddy, had published some 'sacramental hymns' in 1703, and in 1725 had added some hymns at the end of his setting of the Song of Solomon in Welsh verse. Williams had in his possession a Grammar which had belonged to Baddy, and a connection between the two families seems possible. Hymns by these two authors, together with a few by Daniel Rowland, Harris, Griffith Jones and others appeared in the 1740s.[13] According to R. Tudur Jones, 'the rapidity with which the Welsh hymn matured until it reached its brilliant climax in Williams's greatest hymns is truly remarkable.'[14] Religious revival and spiritual aspiration, whether of praise or prayer, belong closely together.

The Welsh Methodists quickly adopted hymn-singing as part of their worship; the first rule for the societies in 1742 began with the injunction, 'After singing to God's praise and prayer, 1 Tim. 2:1, that we should open our hearts to one another.' Their early hymns, together with hymns by Isaac Watts would have provided the societies at the time with a limited choice. Williams was later to translate or adapt a number of Watts's hymns. In 1740 a woman by the name of Dorothy Jones, of Llanddarog, Carmarthenshire, was noted for her hymn-singing, and Harris arranged for her to visit the societies to teach them appropriate tunes for the words.[15] In the face of adversity, whether miserable weather conditions or religious persecution, Harris often sang Psalms, and, as they became available, hymns. A favourite was 'Shall I, for fear of feeble man', which he translated into Welsh from the English translation by John Wesley of the original German. His interest in hymns grew after he came across George Wither's *Hymns and Songs of the Church* in 1741. This had appeared in 1623 and represented an attempt to extend versification to biblical material other than the Psalms.

During the early 1740s a spate of hymn books appeared, two collections each being issued by John Wesley and John Cennick. *A Collection of Psalms and Hymns* by the former was published at Charlestown in 1737 and included translations from the German and several hymns by Watts and others. In 1741 a book having the same title was published in the name of John and Charles Wesley and this 'was kept in print during the whole of Wesley's life'. Wesley's *Hymns and Spiritual Songs, intended for the use of real Christians of all denominations* (1753) 'became distinctively the Methodist hymn book' until the appearance in 1780 of *A Collection of Hymns for the use of the People called Methodists.*[16] An advertisement for Cennick's *Sacred Hymns for the Children of God in the Days of their Pilgrimage* in the 1741 Methodist periodical, The Weekly History claimed that they were 'commonly sung by the Rev. Mr. Whitefield'.[17] The title of Cennick's *Sacred Hymns for the Use of Religious Societies* two years later confirms that singing was already becoming a prominent feature in the Societies. After reading a letter from Harris to Whitefield's Society at the Tabernacle in London in March of the same year 'the following verse was sung:

76

> Carry on Thy work with Power,
> Every day and every hour;
> Still let thousands in poor Wales
> Feel that Jesu's grace prevails.
> Hallelujah, Hosannah;
> Hallelujah, Hosannah.'[18]

One who drew on these three, Isaac Watts, John Cennick and Charles Wesley, was George Whitefield. A work that appeared in 1739 bore the title, *Divine melody: or, a help to devotion, selected, approved and recommended by the Rev. Mr. Whitefield*. The work was intended *'for the Pious and Sincere Christian'*, and in a 'Preface' to the work Whitefield acknowledged his indebtedness to hymn-writers, since every Christian is glad 'when he meets with such assistance from others, as may help him to express his grateful sentiments of the divine favour!' The 'Preface' adds that from time to time, the Christian is given some short, interrupted views of those heavenly glories which are reserved for his perfect and eternal fruition in the other world. And when his faith and hope are thus fixed on these immortal objects, his very soul is rejoiced within him; his lips utter the melody that he feels deep in his heart; and he begins a song of thanksgiving to his God, whose love has been displayed to him a poor sinner; to Jesus Christ who has redeemed him from that perdition in which he found himself so miserably involved; and to the Holy Spirit, from whose sweet and gracious influences he experiences so much comfort, joy, and delight.

This hymn-book was intended for personal use, and in what were then small society meetings. Whitefield's 1753 *Collection of Hymns for Social Worship, more particularly design'd for the Use of the Tabernacle Congregation, in London* clearly had public worship as its aim. In the 'Preface' he wrote:

> If you are acquainted with the divine life, I need not inform you that although all the acts and exercises of devotion are sweet and delightful, yet we never resemble the blessed worshippers above more than when we are joining together in public devotions, and with hearts and lips unfeigned, singing praises to Him Who sits upon the Throne forever. Consequently, hymns composed for such a purpose ought to abound much in Thanksgiving, and to be of such a nature, that all who attend may join in them without being obliged to sing lies, or not to sing at all.

In this way, some of the verses in rhyme intended as aids to personal devotion came to be recognized as appropriate for congregational use.

The hymns of Isaac Watts, Charles Wesley and John Cennick would later provide Williams with inspiration, and with fresh metres for composing hymns in Welsh.

In September 1740 Harris heard a hymn on the theme 'God's good will to receive all'. Afterwards he wrote in his diary: 'My soul was so influenced and transported to love that I could not help crying, O Thy loveliness! O the height and breadth and length and depth of Thy love to rebel man!'[19] The occasion was a church service at Llanwrtyd Wells, Breconshire, and the officiating minister was William Williams. Within four years of singing that hymn together, Williams would issue the first nine of some 860 hymns of his own. It is hard to determine exactly when Williams started to compose hymns. A tradition that the Association in 1742 set before its members the task to determine whose skills would prevail is hard to establish. Williams in any case was ill with smallpox at the time.

During this early period the societies were already composing and singing hymns, even though the standard of the writing and the melodies may have been somewhat limited. After an Association at Llanddeusant not far from Williams's home in February 1743, Harris recorded in his diary, 'Surely the Lord was there. In singing hymns we were so set aflame that we could not part and [I] was so overflowed with love to the brethren that I was one spark of fire.' Evidently it was a time of great unity in Gospel worship and work, traceable to the sense of God's presence but expressed in songs of praise.[20] It may well have been in that spiritual ferment that Williams, now recovered from a dangerous illness, felt compelled to try his poetic gifts and join in giving glory to God.

At the National Library of Wales in Aberystwyth, a manuscript of 150 pages of hymns bears the signatures of both Daniel Rowland and William Williams. This manuscript collection of hymns came into the possession of Williams in 1745, some written by himself, some being translations from Cennick, but collected in manuscript form possibly by Daniel Rowland as it bears his name on the inside cover. From page 67, fifty-five of the hymns are in Williams's handwriting, some showing evidence of alterations or corrections. Many of them subsequently appeared in his published collections. Its importance lies in the fact that these are the only hymns of Pantycelyn in his own handwriting that have survived. By 1744 a collection of hymns in Welsh, by various authors, Baddy and Rowland among them, had appeared bearing the title *Hymnau Duwiol, Yw Canu, mewn*

Cymdeithasau Crefyddol ('Godly Hymns, to be sung in Religious Societies'). [21]

Services in the parish churches were to be conducted in Welsh wherever such linguistic predominance existed, and numbers in the emerging religious societies reflected a similar need. It has been estimated that about three thousand Welsh hymns appeared during the period 1740-91.[22] While the older collections of hymns were rhymed statements of doctrine or paraphrases of Scripture, the hymns of Williams and other Methodists harmoniously wedded orthodox theology with personal experience. What better title could there be, then, for the first collection of Williams's hymns, than *Aleluja?* With the full title of *Aleluja, neu Casgljad o Hymnau ar amryw Ystyrjaethau* ('Aleluja, or a Collection of Hymns on Various Topics'), its first part appeared in 1744, and included nine hymns on the themes of praise for salvation and longing for glory. The fact that most of Williams's hymns combined colloquial and literary qualities, rather than in the closely disciplined structures of the classical Welsh bards, reflected his desire to reach the majority of ordinary people in their mother tongue. The metres he used were not confined to those normally associated with the Psalms, opening up new possibilities of poetic expression. This development in turn demanded a wider selection of tunes. As the century advanced their availability increased. They also became more adventurous and provided greater variety.

Proof of the popularity of Williams's hymns is evident. They appeared as over thirty separate publications during his lifetime. Since that time they dominate practically every Welsh-language hymn-book. But it is not only the quantity that impresses. To be of use to God's people, a hymn has to be accessible and easy to understand. Its content must be in keeping with Scripture teaching. Above all, it must be framed in the attitude of intense devotion and be expressed in a manner that would captivate the conscience, affections and will to ensure both response and retrieval. By it, objective reality must become subjective experience, indifference must yield to involvement, and external proposition must become personal possession. The genius of Williams's hymns lies in the fact that they articulate a whole range of Christian experiences and make them soul-stirring and memorable. They were forged chiefly during times of extraordinary religious fervour, and gave expression to elevated spiritual experiences. Describing the effects of one such period of revival, Williams has this to say:

At last he came. 'Our mourning is turned into dancing.' Hearing the word of life is sweeter than market or fair. The six days of labour have turned into a Sabbath, and the Sabbath extends from one end of the year to the other. Salvation in Christ is the only pleasure of multitudes of people. The country's young people have become estranged from fancy clothes. Sleep has fled. Craving for meat and drink has been swallowed up by praise and song. Hymns, psalms and spiritual songs are the sole nourishment of the feasts of the saints. Honour and reputation have been forgotten; prayers, sermons, and especially the singing of God's praises resound through the land. This is more astonishing than earthquakes or all the wars of the world. O blessed summer's day! It is come, it is come.[23]

Revival not only served as a catalyst for spiritual poetic expression, it was also the context in which they were sung with the greatest fervency. The variety of their subject-matter meant that believers could identify with the experienced truth enshrined in them. Some of Williams's collections were issued at times of lesser religious activity and reflect the abiding and amazing power of grace in all circumstances. This imparts to them a universal, timeless quality that embraces all manner of situations through which the believer passes until the realization of an eternal and glorious destiny in the presence of Christ.

It is wrong to think of Williams only as a hymn-writer. His ministry embraced a far wider scope. He was at once a preacher, theologian, soul physician, peacemaker, and leader, but his hymns are his acknowledged and most familiar legacy. According to his first biographer, Thomas Charles, 'his hymns effected a remarkable change in the state of religion among the Welsh people, and in public worship among their congregations. Some verses of his hymns are like blazing coals of fire, warming and firing all the emotions as they are sung, so that they are often repeated until the congregation shouts and jumps with joy.' Charles is careful to emphasise that this happens because the people's minds and hearts are influenced by 'the power and glory of his matter and elevated thoughts.'[24]. In this way he gave objective theological expression to the varied and maturing experiences of the Methodist converts of his day. But he was also mindful that congregations varied, and that the same congregation require different sentiments at different times. As he put it, it would be foolish to 'urge people to sing about the cold of winter while the sun blazes in hottest summer.' Thus the believer's varied experiences are given expression, from aspiration and complaint to assurance and delight. For these reasons his hymns resonate with believers of every age, transcending the ravages of time and the barriers of culture. To appreciate the way in which they become a prominent and effective means of grace, it is right to give them closer attention.

10.

'Nine hymns for a penny'

On the last page of a book published in the summer of 1744 there is an advertisement to which time lends considerable significance. It reads: 'My fellow countrymen, This is to announce that nine godly hymns on various subjects, from the work of the Reverend William Williams, are to be printed with all haste; with the same typeface and paper as these; in duodecimo, price, one penny; and for sale in Carmarthen by John Morgan in Water Street, where this sermon is also available; together with sundry useful books, in Welsh and English.'[1] When the *Aleluja* collection appeared in September of that year, more were promised: 'Dear Countrymen, This is to announce to all that see fit to buy this Collection of Hymns, that another hymn collection (God willing) will follow as soon as this is dispersed, or sooner, of the same dimensions, so that whoever sees fit (by keeping this clean) may bind the two together.' It was Williams's first venture into print, and proved of sufficient popularity to require a second printing before the end of the year. In 1745 the second 'part' appeared, while the sixth and last 'part' appeared in 1747, in all a total of 155 hymns, 43 of which are found in the preserved manuscript of Williams's handwriting. Years later, in 1774, with several other collections already providing soul-stirring material for individuals and congregations, a further nine hymns appeared 'on the new metre called Haleluia'. Apologizing in a letter for the size and quality of the paper, he added, 'yet nine hymns for a penny is not dear to such as love to sing hymns.'[2]

New hymns continued to flow from his pen until 1787, while several reprints, singly or collectively, appeared from time to time. The last of these was in 1790, a year before his death, with the title *Haleluia Drachefn* ('Halelujah again').[3] He issued two collections of hymns in English, *Hosannah to the Son of David; or, Hymns of Praise to God, For our Glorious Redemption by Christ*, published at Bristol in 1759, and *Gloria in Excelsis: or Hymns of Praise to God and the Lamb*, published at Carmarthen in 1772.[4] Some of the English hymns were loose translations from the Welsh, and his two most widely known English hymns, 'Guide me O Thou great Jehovah', and 'O'er the gloomy hills of darkness', are found in *Gloria in Excelsis*. Williams amended the original translation of the former by Peter Williams, and both versions included verses not usually found in later collections. The latter, according to Thomas Charles, was in response to a personal appeal to Williams's hymn-writing skills by the Countess of Huntingdon, for hymns to be used at Whitefield's Orphanage in America. It was sung as 'the first item of the proceedings' at the founding of the London Missionary Society on 22 September 1795. Of the occasion Thomas Charles's biographer says: 'The Welsh Methodists, like Whitefield and his preachers, were essentially missionaries, and the hymn – during the singing of which 'many broke out into sobs and tears' – admirably expressed the large aspirations of the men who had seen the great transformations wrought by the Gospel in Wales.'[5] Both titles had been used for Welsh collections, the former as *Hosanna i Fab Dafydd* ('Hosanna to the Son of David'), having three parts issued in 1751, 1753 and 1754; the latter, also titled *Gloria in Excelsis*, in two parts in 1771 and 1772. Two major collections appeared in the 1760s, the crowning achievements of his hymn-writing efforts: *Caniadau y rhai sydd ar y Môr o Wydr* (1762), ('Songs of those on the Sea of Glass'); followed by *Ffarwel Weledig, Croesaw Anweledig Bethau* (1763), ('Farewell Visible, Welcome Invisible Things').

In one sense the hymns served as a Methodist catechism, less formal and systematic, but effective because they were repeatedly sung from the heart as well as committed to memory. For this reason they needed to distil in a brief compass both truth and experience, so that there was participation as well as information, involvement as well as understanding, and identification between hymn-writer and hymn-singer. For such congregations, society members, adherents and others, the hymn's author was at once a spokesman and representative, with whom there was kinship in the spiritual realm, and correspondence with the realities to which the hymn gave expression. Some were composed on special occasions, such as 'in times of affliction', 'during Advent', and 'on Christmas Day'. One hymn was written for Howel Harris on the healing of the breach between him and the Welsh Methodist leaders, another on hearing of his death. Others were written in response to particular requests; from David Jones, Llan-gan; from the Countess of Huntingdon; from the societies in Cardiganshire and Carmarthenshire.

Williams's purpose in writing hymns was clear:

> The devil shows great diligence and subtlety secretly to entice and direct your thoughts away from God, and from eternal things, to worldly and temporal affairs. Not only is fervent prayer an excellent remedy against this, but also among many other things it is necessary to establish your mind and memory on the Scriptures (which are in God's hand the sword of the Spirit against the devil's schemes). Being aware of these things, and in order to help you in this, I have written for you some hymns, composed as near as possible to the sound and language of the Scriptures, so that in song they might come more easily to mind and be more effective in working on your affections. This was the reason why whole chapters and books in the Old Testament, and some of the New, were written in poetic form. [6]

He is at pains to emphasize the relationship between the hymn-writer's felt presence of God and the hymn's effectiveness. Only in this way would they inflame desire for deeper acquaintance and more intimate communion with the soul's Beloved, Jesus Christ. His presence brings peace, delight, joy, triumph; His absence leaves the soul vulnerable, fearful, and disconsolate.

> I can suffer all affliction,
> And encounter every foe,
> And the depths of flowing Jordan
> Venture also fearless through,
> Only let Thy gracious presence
> Then my feeble soul assist,
> 'Tis Thy strength eternal only
> That can conquer and resist.
>
> In Thy presence we are happy,
> In Thy presence we're secure;
> In Thy presence all afflictions
> We will easily endure;
> In Thy presence we can conquer,
> We can suffer, we can die;
> Far from Thee we faint and languish,
> Lord, our Saviour, keep us nigh.
>
> Thy presence can, without delay,
> Drive all my num'rous cares away,
> As chaff before the wind;

> Compose my thoughts to adore and love
> Thee, as an object far above,
> To Thee alone inclin'd.[7]

In this way Williams reaffirmed the conviction of every believer, expressed in prayer by Moses, Exodus 33:16, 'wherein shall it be known here that I and thy people have found grace in thy sight? Is it not in that thou goest with us? So shall we be separated, I and thy people, from all the people that are upon the face of the earth.'

The frequency of words such as 'Beloved', 'face', 'presence', 'shine', 'delight', 'pleasure', 'wine', 'feast', 'treasure', and 'pearl', conveys Williams's constant involvement, one might almost say, obsession with Christ. His last letter to Thomas Charles makes this quite explicit: 'I used to delight in every book, sermon, and preacher, striving to set forth the glory of Christ's person, and the great privileges of salvation which came through him.'[8] Bearing in mind this testimony, a few examples in his hymns will suffice:

> In Thy gracious face there's beauty
> Far surpassing every thing
> Found in all the earth great wonders
> Mortal eye hath ever seen.
> Rose of Sharon,
> Thou Thyself art heaven's delight.
>
> Jesus alone we will exalt,
> Jesus we will adore,
> And Jesus only be our King
> Both now and evermore.
>
> It is enough, I am content,
> Since Thou, O Lord, art mine;
> More than the glories of the world
> Do in Thy presence shine.
>
> When Thou dost smile in darkest night
> It kindles darkness into light;
> When Thou dost hide Thy gracious face
> A gloomy night o'ershadows grace.[9]

Supremely, therefore, hymns should focus the gaze of the soul on Christ, an aim Williams sets out in a postscript to *Rhai Hymnau a*

Chaniadau ('Some Hymns and Songs') in 1757. His new collection of hymns would be

> more profitable and edifying to all degrees of believers, having modified some lessons which were beyond those believers who have only an ordinary measure of faith and feeling, either to a prayer for such grace, or to admire the Lord who gave it; or else to take away the selfish boasting in the lesser part, so that Jesus alone should be exalted. Furthermore, they have been stripped of that small abominable word 'I' which was in a few of them, putting Jesus and His grace instead, 'not I, but Christ who lives in me', etc. Not quite taking away, either, but rather confirming the 'I' of believing, that is, the personal application of faith, without which faith is no longer faith. In short, as far as possible, to put the sound of Christ and His free Gospel as blood in their veins, and to expose man, his understanding, his power, his light as nothing.[10]

Williams, then, studiously avoids self-centredness in his hymns, but it would be wrong to think that they become impersonal. On the contrary, they are profoundly personal, but in the sense that they aim to bring God's majesty, attributes, activity, promises, into the conscious, spiritual dealings of the soul. Christian maturity and usefulness lie in the believer's focus being drawn to Christ, who He is, what He has said, what He has done. The thrust of his introduction to the third edition of *Aleluja*, which appeared in the following year, is similar:

> I acknowledge that there are some of these first hymns, on the assurance of faith, longing to be dissolved, spiritual joy, together with triumph over enemies, which weak Christians cannot easily sing. This happened not so much because the Lord kept my own soul in good spirits at the time, but chiefly because the Spirit had been so plentifully poured out on those godly people for whom they were written ... When I came to know myself better, and saw what an Egypt of darkness, a sea of uncleanness, a world of pride is man, I determined to exalt the salvation which is in Christ far more, and to abase man and his gifts more. I did my utmost, whatever the nature of the hymn – complaint, plea, holy boasting, or praise, for Christ to be the centre-piece of it all ... I am constrained to give a little advice to those who would give out these hymns ... Some give out verses full of assurance and delight to a congregation that denies the first and has not experienced the second ... Others give out verses of complaint and questioning to a people who have been elevated to the heavenlies, and who feel life in their faith, and Satan under their feet, as if to urge people to sing about the cold of winter while the sun blazes in hottest summer.[11]

Here it is evident that Williams the hymnist is also Williams the counsellor, able both to discern the spiritual condition of individuals and congregations, and to apply appropriate spiritual remedies.

A further example of this appears in his next collection of hymns, *Caniadau y rhai sydd ar y Môr o Wydr* ('Songs of those on the Sea of Glass'). Published in 1762, after a period of spiritual declension within the Methodist societies, he has this to say:

> I am inclined to believe that these will be the last hymns that you will ever have from my hand; if you will only read them through once, that is all I can expect; they will prove edifying or unedifying to the extent that God's Spirit shines on you or departs from you in their use. As for their usefulness, it is much the same as the previous ones, and it will surprise me if those who enjoyed those do not also enjoy these, if not more, at least as much, insofar that the Spirit that permeates them is suited to the spiritual needs of such as have met with sundry outward trials, crosses, and adversities, and numerous inward afflictions and struggles, people who have gone through darkness, leanness, unbelief and such like. Some have been tossed from pillar to post (a condition known in these days to many believers), having nothing of which to boast, except their weakness and the great salvation that is in the blood of the Lamb. Here there is merely a few hymns which even the weakest in the Church can sing, since they are either in the form of a prayer for some of the gifts of the New Covenant, or grief because of sin; whereas many of the first ones cannot be sung by some, on account of the full assurance of faith that is in them with regard to eternal life. As they are, may they be blessed a hundredfold, throughout every locality which has kept the Welsh language under its wings. There are many metres that have not appeared in previous ones, but I hope that you will not neglect to conquer them.[12]

Williams also attached some verses to the title page:

> Both fearing and believing are here held forth in song
> The grip of empty pleasures, yet hatred that is strong;
> And triumph over en'mies, then how they soon arise
> To wound again with vigour, and bring dismay, surprise.
>
> If singing *Aleluja* 'til now the weak found tough,
> To join with those on fire, their faith was not enough;
> Here the most timid Christian, who longs for much more grace,
> May lift his voice with courage, without a loss of face.

Such variety of content proved a blessing and his prayer was answered. An intense and widespread revival followed the appearance of this collection, so that on the last page of his 1763 publication, *Atteb Philo Evangelius i Martha Philopur* ('Philo Evangelius's Reply to Martha Philopur'), Williams reported that

> such was the demand for the hymn-book lately issued, namely, *Caniadau y rhai sydd ar y Môr o Wydr* ['Songs of those on the Sea of Glass'] that twelve hundred of them were sold in a few months, and I am constrained to print a number in great haste, adding to them ten or more new hymns, which were not in the first printing, also on new metres that did not appear then. Since I do not intend to print more than what is enough for the public at this time, it is necessary that those who wish to have them, should subscribe their names together with half the price in advance ... If the Lord has touched any in Gwynedd [North Wales], and for that reason have a desire to sing God's praise, let them send for them; the author will pay for all carriage costs." [13]

This further edition duly appeared before the end of the year.

It was true that a hymn's content should be orthodox theology, and that an appropriate style for effective communication should be studied. However, the over-riding token by which a hymn should be judged as to usefulness and effectiveness was a kind of unction, an indefinable quality that was imparted by the Holy Spirit's influence on the author's mind and heart that determined the words and imagery used. This is confirmed in a substantial preface to the second part of *Ffarwel Weledig, Groesaw Anweledig Bethau: neu Rhai Hymnau o Fawl i Dduw a'r Oen* ('Farewell to visible, welcome to invisible things: or some hymns of praise to God and the Lamb') which deserves to be quoted in full:

> So many hymns have come to us lately that it seems an unnecessary labour to print any more; but let such as think this way realize, that it is not people who have a song in their hearts who consider that there more than enough hymns; much as it is not those who benefit from listening that consider there are more than enough sermons. Those who desire to sing praise to God will not be satisfied with songs of praise, any more than those who are true listeners with listening; and there is no-one that has education, sense and experience that does not know that many gifts are edifying.
>
> Even though most of the hymns that have been written so far have tended to the same substance and teaching, yet insofar as they are endowed with new experiences, fresh light, figurative expressions and new measures, their variety under the eternal Spirit's influence excites

a sense of God's love. The Bible itself would be much smaller if there was no repetition in it. A little addition to any of the four Evangelists would supply the place of the others; half the Psalms would convey the sense of all the others; there would be need neither for many of the chapters in Moses's books, nor for sundry sections of Kings and Chronicles, unless God purposed to bless the repetition of truths and variety in His Word, giving us line upon line, precept upon precept, sermon after sermon, hymn after hymn; and 'to write the same things to you', says the Apostle, 'to me indeed is not grievous, but for you it is safe.'

The greatest tragedy, however, is that many of us presume to touch God's ark without a call; and, possibly from an ambition to be esteemed to have their names in print, and compose hymns without body, joints, soul or marrow, without experience or a spirit that leaves an impression on serious hearts. That uneducated men take to this work is not to be condemned, since God often uses the meanest of men for the greatest tasks; and it was not the attainments of Deborah, Barak, and Miriam that made them, nor David either, such remarkable poets in God's Book, but a lively spirit, and zeal, the enjoyment of God, and experience together with the power of a heavenly breeze stirring within, until the fire blazed forth in sweet songs that will last forever. What is blameworthy is that this spirit is missing in several recent publications.

The glories of the Psalms are their spirit, their faith, their experience, as well as their being given by the Holy Spirit; and not the least of the qualities that made the book of Canticles canonical is the relish that the saints have in it. On the other hand, the strange spirit that permeates the books of the Apocrypha is a clear witness that they were not given by the Holy Spirit. If relish for hymns is lost, they will vanish across the hills of India, where the Welshman will hear them no more.

I humbly advise whoever wishes to send hymns to the printer, 1. to seek true grace for themselves; truly to know God in His Son; apart from which it is dreadful presumption to touch God's ark; 2. To read in English, if they cannot read in other languages, all relevant books of poetry that they can find, in order to expand their understanding, to recognize poetry, wherein its beauty lies, to what purpose it is intended, and the several rules relating to it. 3. Whether they can attain to the last ideal or not, let them read over and over again the prophetical books and the Psalms, the Lamentations, the Canticles, Job, and Revelation, which are not only full of poetic flair, figurative speeches, variety, flowing language, and lively comparisons, but also have a spirit that kindles fire, zeal, and life in the reader beyond all other books in the world (because they are God's books). 4. They should never compose a hymn until they feel their soul near heaven, under the breeze of the Holy Spirit; and the same Spirit will be found to bless the work. Amen.

There are here some new metres, and I shall, in keeping with my promise, give the metres to those few who are able to provide them. Some ten or twelve of them across South Wales are enough, should there be a desire to make them known. Farewell.[14]

Such advice given by Williams demonstrates the close affinity between Williams's hymns and the spiritual experiences encouraged in the societies. As Derec Llwyd Morgan suggests, the 'I', 'me', 'my' of the hymns 'are not always or necessarily the selfish "I", but often the representative "*I*"', with whose experiences the believer could identify.[15] They aimed at fostering the same *kind* of mind-set and soul-culture with clearly-defined characteristics and priorities. It produced a genuine discipleship in terms of personal trust in Christ, commitment to God's Word, growth in grace, a hunger for God, dependence on the Holy Spirit's power, assurance of salvation, and anticipation of glory. The hymns and societies, powerful preaching, and regulated oversight, together made up the Methodist Way. Indeed, E. Wyn James concludes his survey of influences on Williams's hymns by saying that, 'Williams and other hymn-writers of the Methodist movement belong closely together, being on the same wavelength in terms of hymnology and spirituality, and in the same literary and linguistic fold. They are the products of the society, and the language of the society is their language.'[16]

Initially Methodist hymn-singing was confined to Psalm tunes, melodies derived from classical composers like Handel and Purcell, and tunes used by the Moravians.[17] The introduction of new tunes into Wales was a gradual process, but it gathered momentum from the time of Williams's finest hymn collections in the 1760s. R. D. Griffith notes that, 'When Williams began his work as hymn-writer there were only about half-a-dozen metres available in Wales, but by using the few Welsh melodies as well as the English tunes, Williams composed over twenty new metres … Writing hymns to fit the tunes he obtained from England was Williams's usual practice.' [18] *The Divine Musical Miscellany* that appeared in 1754 included 67 tunes and their names suggest Whitefield's influence. John Wesley's Select *Hymns with Tunes annext Designed chiefly for the use of the people called Methodists* first appeared in 1761, with a second edition in 1765. Both of these were a timely resource for Williams at the peak of his hymn-writing productivity. The latter was a handy, pocket-sized volume with over a hundred tunes, and Williams possessed a copy of the second edition.[19]

In 1811 Williams's son, John, brought out *Gwaith Prydyddawl* ('Poetical Work') which was a comprehensive, but not complete collection of his father's hymns. Each hymn was classified as either 'Galarus' (Mournful), or 'Gorfoleddus' (Joyful), and the name of the tune to which it was to be sung was added, the first time for this to happen in Wales.[20] The names included such familiar tunes as 'Darwall', 'Franconia', 'Helmsley', and 'Leoni', together with popular contemporary melodies, 'Lovely Peggy', 'Nutmeg and Ginger', 'Gwel yr Adeilad' ('See the Building'), and 'God Save the King'.

Not only were Williams's hymns biblical in content and experiential in their expression, they were carefully crafted to be sung. A fitting tune, therefore, was desirable to match worthy words. In this respect, too, Williams was following biblical precedent in order to enhance Methodist worship and elevate personal experience. After all, did not the Psalmist often cry out in words like these, 'I will sing of the mercies of the Lord for ever: with my mouth will I make known Thy faithfulness to all generations'? (Ps. 89: 1.) And is it not said of the redeemed in heaven that 'they sung as it were a new song before the throne'? (Rev. 14: 3.) Williams made full use of his God-given talents, conviction, and experiences to ensure that, among the Methodists of his day, there would be ample scope and material to begin such praise this side of glory.

11.

'The eyes of speech'

The frame of mind of those for whom Williams wrote his hymns was distinctly 'other-worldly'. Like their neighbours they perhaps raised families, owned property, paid taxes, suffered pain, cherished hopes and ambitions, and experienced grief and sorrow. All these, and more beside, were their common lot, real enough in themselves and having real consequences, but nevertheless not what gave their life ultimate meaning. The difference was that Methodist believers were heavenly-minded, so that their earthly existence was lived out in the consciousness, delight even, of transcending, eternal values. They lived life before an ever-present, over-ruling, holy God, and saw themselves as an accountable, privileged and eternity-bound people. Therefore it comes as no surprise to read the strange-sounding titles of two of Williams's hymn-collections: 'Farewell Visible, Welcome Invisible Things: or Some Hymns of Praise to God and the Lamb', and 'Songs (of those on the Sea of Glass mingled with fire, who have triumphed over the beast) to the King of Saints'. These are biblically sourced phrases, yes, but for Williams and the Methodists who breathed the spiritual atmosphere of another kingdom, they also gave expression to an abiding reality. In the same way, the titles, *Hosannah to the Son of David; or Hymns of Praise to God for our glorious Redemption by Christ*, and *Gloria in Excelsis: or Hymns of Praise to God and the Lamb*, were meant to convey a relationship with Christ that was progressive and unbreakable. No estimate of the significance of Williams's hymns that fails to recognize these determinative elements will be adequate.

Biblical truth certainly undergirds the expressions of praise and prayer that abound in William Williams's hymns. In an article on 'The Bible's influence on Pantycelyn's hymns', J. Gwyn Jones confirms this:

> Williams's knowledge of his Bible played an important part in moulding and polishing his style. Not only are his hymns replete with Scripture phrases, he also honed his skill by his attempts at setting portions of Scripture to rhyme. He versified portions of the Song of

Solomon and the Psalms, but his efforts were not limited to them. He took considerable liberty in doing so, and also filled out Old Testament statements with Christian meaning.[1]

This characteristic is hardly surprising, given Williams's commitment to the inspiration and authority of Scripture, and the centrality he gave to Christ in his affection as well as in his teaching. The fifth chapter of his *Golwg ar Deyrnas Crist* ('A View of Christ's Kingdom') bears the title, 'The Statute Book of Christ's Kingdom, or Christ all things in the Bible'. For this reason, 'Christ is the Bible's Marrow', and it is a 'precious, golden volume' in which 'no word will go astray', giving 'profoundest pleasure' to the soul.[2]

Furthermore, Williams's own spiritual life, maintained by personal and family devotion, selective reading of the rich heritage of Puritan classics, and the warm fellowship meetings which he attended, would have profoundly influenced his literary output. In particular, his spirituality would have been influenced by his use of the Anglican Book of Common Prayer, however Nonconformist his background, and despite the hostility of that Church's authorities towards him and his fellow Methodists. Harris was not averse to discoursing 'at noon and night on the Lessons' prescribed for that particular day in what came to be known as its 'Calendar'.[3] Williams's initial experience of God's grace, and growing appreciation of its theological meaning was another determinative factor in his spirituality. Elfed ap Nefydd Roberts draws attention to its significance by saying that 'God's grace, not man's effort, is the heart-beat of his spirituality.'[4] Williams drew spiritual succour as well as ideas from the hymns of Watts, Charles Wesley, and John Cennick. Other authors, too, influenced Williams in his spiritual pilgrimage and literary effort, among them George Herbert, John Bunyan, John Milton, Edward Young, and Ralph Erskine.[5] With many of Williams's hymns having the death of Christ as their theme, Kathryn Jenkins did not claim too much when she wrote that 'the Christ-centred spirituality of Williams Pantycelyn is many-sided and has several aspects. The cross is its centrepiece, and triumphant love is its result.'[6]

Closely allied to Williams's use of the Bible was his use of imagery, types, metaphors and figurative expressions. These were useful tools of the poet's trade, authorized and validated by Scriptural examples. They were verbal representations of spiritual truth and reality, and as such avoided the sanctions of the Second Commandment against the visual and physical. John Calvin had spoken of them in this way: 'that the name of the thing signified is given to the sign … is what is called by grammarians a figurative expression … although a figurative expression is not so distinct, it gives a more elegant and significant expression than if the thing were said simply, and without figure. Hence figures are called the eyes of speech, not that they explain the matter more easily than simple ordinary language, but because they attract attention by their elegance, and arouse the mind by their luster, and by their lively similitude make a deeper impression.'[7] It was said of John Bunyan, that, 'far from labouring his effects, Bunyan thought in images. He never really grasped his idea until he saw it personified, and so Biblical metaphors came to populate – literally – the universe he created.'[8]

During Bunyan's century several books had explored Scripture's use of such literary devices, especially since the Protestant interpretation of Scripture had rejected the mediaeval practice of allegorical interpretation as fanciful and misleading. Williams possessed at least four of these: Samuel Mather's *Figures or Types of the Old Testament* (1705), William Guild's *Moses Unveiled or those figures which served unto the pattern and shadow of heavenly things, pointing out the Messiah Christ Jesus* (1619), William McEwen's *Grace and Truth …an attempt to explain … the most remarkable types, figures* (several editions from 1763), and Thomas Taylor's *Christ Revealed: or the Old Testament Explained* (1635).[9] With the aid of these devices, then, Williams transposed biblical persons, places, events, creatures even, into the believer's landscape.[10] Given their familiarity with the narrative and teaching of Scripture, nurtured by sermon and society, Williams's vivid, image-laden verses easily and profoundly resonated with the Methodist converts. At a time when the dominant cultural medium of communication was verbal, and poetry a popular form, his hymns were a potent means of instruction, an effective aid to memory, and a powerful influence to reach all levels of society.

Writers on hymnology have suggested prominent themes and images in Williams's work.[11] Predictably, the themes are biblical ones. That of pilgrimage comes immediately to mind. It reflects the Israelite journey through the desert after the 'exodus' from Egypt, crossing the Red Sea on dry land, and travelling to Canaan. For Kathryn Jenkins, 'it is possible to contend that "journey" is the most important of Pantycelyn's prominent motifs; certainly it has a pivotal place in his works.'[12] A recent author, J. R. Watson, speaks of 'Guide me, O Thou great Jehovah' as 'the greatest of all Exodic hymns', and adds,

94

'Williams has a supreme poetic tact, which allows him to understate the typology, and yet signify it to the attentive reader, so that the singer/reader has to supply the imaginative connections.'[13] The metaphor of a journey through the desert with Williams yields a profusion of related ideas in order to emphasise the darkness, danger, and disorientation he intended it to convey. He makes it explicit in a hymn title, 'The world a desert', and explains that

> The world wherein we dwell,
> Hath lost its ancient fame,
> Its former glory turn'd
> To filthiness and shame ...
>
> Where dreams and shadows do
> Lead simple souls away
> To labyrinths of woe,
> And wilds of black dismay...
>
> And there the lion lurks
> In ambush for his prey...

In another hymn he speaks of

> Our weary pilgrimage below
> Is through a world of sin and woe,
> A gloomy forest wide,
> Where lions roar and tigers sway,
> And dreadful serpents cross our way;
> We'll faint without a guide.
>
> O mighty Saviour! Give Thy hand
> And help us to that blessed land,
> In spite of all our foes;
> Where we shall live, and thrive, and grow
> On milk and honey there that flow,
> Void of terrestrial woes.

There were no lions or tigers in the Welsh countryside, so congregations were expected to draw spiritual parallels: the woeful labyrinth of a sinful heart; the gloomy forest that is this world of deceitful materialism; the wild beasts of satanic foes and temptations that intimidate with fierce strength and subtle ambush. Yet another hymn compounds the sense of helplessness we should feel when it

mentions 'dungeon deep', 'ravening wolves', and 'subtle snares', so
that 'A deadly poison runs / Through all our joys below'. Without a
superior, superhuman – more correctly, divine – Guide, we *will* faint.
They are 'empty joys', polluted by an 'Egyptian stream', with 'Egypt',
the bane of the Jewish nation, representing 'night', 'darkness', 'brazen
gates', 'gloom', and 'bondage':

> The Egyptian stream, curs'd in our fall,
> Now turned to blood I find,
> That raise our passions to a flame
> And fluctuate the mind...

> Stand in the front, Thou glorious King,
> When savage beasts do roam,
> Guide us through every winding maze,
> To Thy eternal home.

> Lighten our path in darkest night,
> With that illustrious ray,
> The fiery pillar in the dark,
> The glorious cloud by day.

Most biblical allusions are general and familiar, like this one of
journey, but occasionally they are specific and even obscure, as when
Williams refers to the dilemma that the people of Israel faced, caught
between 'Pihahiroth and Baalzephon'. Two hymns speak of these, but
the biblical reference, Exodus 14:2, is not given, and this suggests that
Williams could count on substantial Bible knowledge among society
members. Nor are biblical allusions less powerful for being frequent
and sustained. From the time of conversion to Christ, believers are at
odds with the world, living in time and space, but belonging to
eternity and heaven. They are subject to worldly affairs and pressures,
yet they seek to influence and bring society into closer conformity to
God's standards. In the world there are only temporal toys and foolish
vanity; in contrast God's kingdom holds lasting treasures and
pleasures, of which Williams is fond of speaking:

> Good and pleasant are the places,
> Fair unfeigned is the spot,
> In the plan of grace abounding,
> That hath fallen to my lot;

Now my treasures are exhaustless,
Full my cup and running o'er,
And my blessings are in number
As the sands upon the shore.[14]

The Israelite journey from Egypt to Canaan epitomizes that tension.

Tension, yes, and conflict, too. Welsh-speaking congregations will be familiar with verses that begin, 'Mae'r Brenin ar y blaen', and 'Nid myfi sydd yn rhyfela' ('The King is to the fore', and 'It is not I that battle'), both speaking of victory while acknowledging the believer's helplessness in the fight. R. Tudur Jones, in his discussion of 'Conflict and Joy' in Williams's works concludes,

> Thus the Christian is in constant conflict with fears, with contrary circumstances, with his own strong passions, with the enticement of earthly things. But at the root of all else is a conflict with sin. The real enemy is Satan, the Dragon. What hope is there that any Christian will overcome his enemies? The answer is that Christ is the Warrior. Pantycelyn has a great number of images to describe Jesus Christ, but this is one of his most powerful.[15]

Here is a typical expression of Williams's confidence in the face of hostile forces as he travels to glory:

Thou, Lord, my portion art,
My lasting treasure sweet;
'Gainst every woe and fiery dart
A stronghold meet.
'Tis to Thyself I flee,
Thy bosom is my fort,
When foes display their rage to me
Of every sort.

O show Thy power sublime,
Infinite grace and free;
O tell me at this time
I shall a conqueror be;
For unto Thee I flee,
Thy bosom is my nest,
When foes on every hand I see,
In Thee I rest.

97

> Thou, only O my God,
> Eternal, perfect One,
> Dost rule earth, men, all by Thy rod
> And to Thy glory done.
> Guide my weak soul, I cry
> Onward through storm and mire,
> Lead through perplexing ways by Thy
> Pillar of fire.
>
> Thy Spirit, holy Dove,
> Did myriad saints attend;
> Grant me His power divine to prove,
> This favour send.
> As crystal waters, do
> Bring joy to weak and sore,
> Strength and fresh hope to bring me to
> The distant shore.

Victory is secure because the believer is joined to Christ, the Omnipotent God and mighty Conqueror, the One who has already triumphed over sin, death, hell and Satan.

> A most precious victory
> For us He gained,
> By His death and agony
> For the sin-stained;
> Though like sheep from Him we strayed
> Filled with fear,
> He our ransom fully paid,
> Hallelujah![16]

Christ's resurrection not only vindicates His Person, and demonstrated the sufficiency of His atonement; it also guarantees the ultimate security of His people.

Williams's imagery is not merely directed at the world around the believer. There is ample scope to apply it to the human condition and the paramount need of salvation from sin, Williams can trace the 'poison' in earthly joys back to its ultimate source, the venom first introduced into human experience by the catastrophic encounter between the human race's first parents and the serpent, the embodiment of evil, in the Garden of Eden. With striking, memorable imagery, Williams portrays the heart of the Gospel, the meaning of Christ's death on the cross in a verse from his *Theomemphus*:

He came to heal the wounded
Was wounded in their stead;
True heir of heaven was pierced
For those through sin made dead;
He sucked the awful poison
The serpent gave to me,
And from that deadly venom
He died on Calvary.[17]

No statement of what the Bible means by the atonement could be more vivid or more concise. For this reason Kathryn Jenkins concluded that in Williams's spirituality, 'love for the crucified Christ is an important expression of the Gospel experience.'[18]

It comes as no surprise, therefore, that the representation of Christ most frequently found in Williams's hymns is that of 'Lamb'. It corresponds to the biblical portrayal of Christ as the Lamb 'without spot and without blemish', who was 'brought to the slaughter', God's appointed Lamb, 'who takes away the sin of the world'. Purity, perfect obedience, complete sacrifice, effective compensation for sin: all these ideas are conveyed by this figure. The title of both Welsh and English collections of *Gloria in Excelsis* continues with the words, *or Hymns of Praise to God and the Lamb*. He is altogether glorious and praiseworthy:

O heavenly Lamb of God
Surpassing all there is,
With myriad throngs above
Deriving from Thee bliss;
Thy wealth and grace and glorious worth
Fill heaven itself, fill all the earth.[19]

Setting 1 Corinthians 1: 30 in rhyme to a Psalm metre in his early work *Aleluja*, Williams wrote thirty verses, for which the first provided a kind of title:

The spotless Lamb's my godliness,
My righteousness and wisdom;
Redemption, too, from every plague,
My God in heaven's kingdom.

I came to see that He's my King,
My Prophet, Priest, and tower;
My strength, and Advocate above,
My Saviour and my treasure.

Baptize me with Thy Spirit, Lord,
As raging fire burning;
And let such burning, judging might,
Be always on my sinning.

Dispel all ugly sin's remains,
Sealed by Thy gracious dealing;
With grace adorned, a temple meet,
To be henceforth God's dwelling.

He, too, my feeble soul at death
Will be my strong Companion;
In face of death, this, this my plea,
He is my soul's salvation.

Within the veil, beyond the grave,
I'll see His face in beauty;
And in His bosom dwell for aye,
With joy and lasting safety.[20]

The full implications of Christ as the Lamb of God are here worked out, for which the Passover lamb of the Old Testament was a type and shadow. He is the substance and fulfilment, whose sacrifice fully satisfies the demands of God's Law, by which God's eternal purpose of salvation is accomplished. John Calvin's exposition of Hebrews 9: 23 refers to the way in which Christ's sacrifice corresponds to the Old Testament figure: 'The meaning then is this, — as under the Law there were only earthly images of spiritual things, so the rite of expiation was also, so to speak, carnal and figurative; but as the heavenly pattern allows of nothing earthly, so it requires another blood than that of beasts, such as may correspond with its excellency.' [21]

It is not merely Christ's work that has prominence in Williams's work. R. M. Jones, for example, holds that 'two images are predominant in his work, the image of the lover and the image of the traveller.'[22] The believer's enjoyment of Christ may be traced to the initiative, and freeness, and sovereignty of His grace. The Son of Man came to give Himself a ransom for many; the Great Physician is the One who brings healing to the plague of sin; the Gospel is a feast because in Christ there is forgiveness, cleansing, release from sin's tyranny, everlasting life, daily strength, a sure hope of heaven, and much else beside. The following hymn, powerful and poignant, intimately personal and glowing with fervent hope, is deservedly one of the most prized by Welsh congregations, 'Mi dafla' 'maich oddiar fy ngwar':

> My load of sin I now cast down
> Before such pain divine;
> Mountains of guilt Thy cross transforms
> To glorious songs sublime.
>
> Where're I look, to east or south
> To earth's far distant rim,
> Through ages past or yet to come,
> There's none like unto Him.
>
> His hands, so pure, were stretched out wide,
> A crown of thorns He wore,
> That vilest sinners might become
> As linen white and pure.
>
> Ascended now to highest heaven
> To plead there for the weak;
> Soon to His bosom He will clasp
> My soul in succour sweet.
>
> I then shall be on high with Him
> When all the world's ablaze,
> His matchless beauty to admire
> As on His face I gaze. [23]

Williams uses a cluster of words to accompany his expression of affection for Christ. 'Grace', 'ransom', 'forgiveness', 'release', 'strength', 'heaven', frequently occur in Williams's poetic vocabulary. They all encourage fresh, sustained, vigorous confidence in God. The verses that follow are found in 'A View of Christ's Kingdom':

> He's greater than His blessings,
> He's greater than His grace,
> Far greater than His actions,
> Whatever you may trace;
> I'll plead for faith, gifts, cleansing,
> For these I'll yearn quite sore,
> But on Him only, always,
> I'll look and lean far more.

> To see Thy face, Belovèd,
> Makes my poor soul rejoice
> O'er all I've ever tasted,
> Or ever made my choice;
> When they all disappear,
> Why should I grieve or pine,
> While to my gaze there opens
> The sight that Christ is mine? [24]

Not only confidence in God, but also communion with God, and the Song of Songs, for Williams, was a favourite resource for meditation and inspiration.

The element of assurance as a believer's rightful heritage is also woven by Williams into many of the hymns:

> Give me that knowledge pure, divine,
> To know and feel that Thou art mine,
> And Thee my portion call;
> That doubts and fears may flee away,
> And faith unfeignèd win the day,
> And triumph over all.
>
> Tell me Thou art mine, O Saviour,
> Grant me an assurance clear;
> Banish all my dark misgivings,
> Still my doubting, calm my fear.
> O, my soul within me yearneth
> Now to hear the voice divine;
> So shall grief be gone for ever,
> And despair no more be mine.

This earnest passion for closer acquaintance with God, for more of Christ, permeates the Welsh Methodist's worship, personal and congregational. Williams, as their spokesman, articulates it time and time again:

> O Mighty Saviour! Me assist,
> Thy power can destroy
> The strong and subtle foes that would
> My feeble soul annoy.
>
> O speak the word, and all is done,
> My sins shall flee away,
> Just like the curtain of the night
> Before the rising day.

102

> A word drop'd from His gracious mouth
> Revives our hearts with joy;
> He hides His face, and instantly
> Our enemies annoy.[25]

If one authoritative word from God was enough to raise 'the curtain of the night', Williams's choice words for the Methodists sustained their enjoyment of it during 'the rising day'.

The genius of Williams's hymns lies in the familiar idioms and easy style he used to convey the most sublime truth. In this way they captured the imagination, settled in the memory and influenced the will. For this reason they not only characterized their Methodist author, they produced a Methodist mind-set and a Methodist lifestyle that persisted for several generations. It was a soul culture that was both transforming and distinctive. They could be sharp enough to wound the careless, yet soothing enough to heal the smitten conscience. They could raise the soul's gaze from the dungeon of failure and temptation to the palatial delights of God's grace. They drew the erring backslider to restoration, and enabled the humble believer to rejoice. They strengthened the arms of the weak, and brought the struggling soul to the suburbs of heaven. It was given to Williams, more than to any other in Wales during the eighteenth century, to utilize his poetic gifts to glorify God in this way.

12.

'The enjoyment of God'

It was inevitable that the Welsh Methodist Association should entrust Williams, 'the minister of Llanwrtyd', with the supervision of emerging societies and exhorters in that area. Decisions to that effect are found in the Minutes for February and March 1743. The same Association that encouraged Williams to leave his curacies to help Rowland also appointed him 'Moderator' of the monthly Association for Radnorshire and Montgomeryshire where he already exercised oversight of the societies.[1] In a note to Harris, written early in 1743, Williams outlines a proposed preaching itinerary in the area:

> I have contrived with myself about my going to Montgomeryshire and I intend to be at Llanafan Fawr preaching the 24th of January; and from thence on to Montgomery, only do you publish some place for me Monday night about 3 miles or 5 further than Llanafan. Do not publish at Dol y felin lest I shall not come to Llanafan, and if so I must set out from Llanwrtyd Monday morning; and charge to send me a guide to meet me at Llanwrtyd. I intend to be that Friday night at Errwd in my return home.

As a result of the Association decision that Williams should assist Rowland at Llangeitho, the arrangement concerning his supervision of the work in mid-Wales came to an end in June 1744. At that time the Association agreed that he 'should visit the societies in the upper part of Cardiganshire once every six weeks on trial till our next Association.' In February 1745 Harris heard him preach in the north of the county, near Blaenplwyf, 'with much power indeed', and adds, 'O! what a cry was here and full of God, so that his voice could hardly be heard.'[2] In the event it proved a beneficial and lasting arrangement.

With George Whitefield in America, his London Tabernacle had been committed to the charge of John Cennick. When Harris arrived in the capital in November 1745 for one of his many visits, he found that Cennick had joined the Moravians, and the Tabernacle Society now looked to him for leadership, an arrangement which was terminated towards the end of 1749.[3] A letter from Williams kept him informed of matters in Wales. Written from Cefn-coed in December 1745, it includes some personal glimpses as well, and deserves extensive quotation:

> By this time I doubt not but you expect a letter giving a large account of the great Shepherd and little flock in Wales, where the most part of your labours are your crown of rejoicing in that Day where the dear Lamb made you instrumental to the effectual calling of many hundreds to the faith, which I hope will bear trial at last. Indeed had I the ability of giving you an exact and perfect account of the dear lambs here I should have with ease set your heart on fire, for I know such news is a fuel to kindle in you a flame of love, praise, and holy admiration. Dear brother, 'tis less difficult and easier daily to prove that a great work of the Spirit of God is on foot in Wales. Our dear and blessed Immanuel has girt His sword upon His thigh, and, in His glory and majesty, rides prosperously, yea, prosperously indeed, because of truth, meekness and righteousness. Certainly He is in great haste to conquer His enemies, for His arrows are sharp in their hearts; and the people fall under Him; some under His comforting power; some under His convincing power, and some fall under the curse of His hardening power after a long resistance of grace and mercy; but most of the ungodly here fall mute before Him, standing in amazement, being puzzled what this new thing means which continues and increases day by day, for praised be God, the Gospel runs on in some measure in every country of South Wales; but in some parts more successfully, as Carmarthen, Cardigan, and Pembrokeshire, some add themselves daily to the Societies, I hope such as will be saved. But the most part of these that are acquainted with the Lord come up from the wilderness like pillars of smoke perfumed with myrrh and frankincense and all the powder of the merchant. Dear brother, 'tis a glorious sight to look on the saints by faith thus coming up from the world, sin, self; and all leaning on Christ for righteousness, wisdom, sanctification and redemption. We have here the grace of faith daily purged; 'tis a harvest time for faith ... 'Tis obvious to all that observes that the Lord is for exalting free grace, for 'tis the poor, simple, ignorant people in the world's account the Lord owns to confound the wise and the letter-learned doctors of this world. I say 'tis these the Lord owns to do great things. Had this work been begun and carried on only by old learned, prudent people, grace should not be so visible to all as 'tis now. Had the late reformation been among the old professors, and touched but some of the young men, many should be apt to attribute their mortification to their age; their comforts as reward of their former good works; their zeal from reading, hearing, and conversing this many years. But now, as in times past, the Lord [shows] forth His grace more fully: [He] chose the young generation that were

under twenty when [Israel came through] the Red Sea (that is, the) young. The old generation that came from [an] Egypt of immorality, both ministers and people were murdering and unbelieving, and choose rather to die in the wilderness of bondage and darkness, or return to an Egypt of sin to their old companions, than venture on to fight for, conquer, and possess the promised land of Christian liberty. Oh! grace, grace! What is grace, if [it does] not [enable] this young people to fight with a cursed crew of hellish Canaanites, an innumerable army of lusts, to clear their way, as it were by the dint of your sword, to heaven, to swim against an impetuous torrent of corruption. Surely there will be a glorious company other side Jordan in white robes with palms in their hand, singing eternal hosanna to God and the Lamb! ... Never more unity here, ministers, exhorters, and people are all in one; consequently the work goes on bravely everywhere. All the lambs everywhere long to see you. I am to go around Cardiganshire and another to Pembrokeshire, down to Longhouse, before the Association. Brother Rowland is well, a strong pillar in the Church of God, a means to keep the Welsh Methodists from many errors their neighbours have fallen into. Brother [Howel] Davies is well and goes now to Glamorgan; I am to supply him at Llechryd.[4]

Several matters of interest are mentioned in this letter. First in importance is the fact that Williams thinks and speaks in biblical categories. His mind-set is immersed in Scripture parallels and examples, while he consistently traces events to God's initiative and control. Others might explain the revival in terms of secondary causes, but not so Williams. This is important for a proper understanding of revival, whether on a general or personal scale. Consequently, the emergence of Methodism was looked upon by the leaders as 'the late reformation', a work of God so deep and extensive as to constitute a major shift in the religious convictions and life of the day. Furthermore, it had happened mainly among young people, while an older generation remained prejudiced and stubborn in its rebellion against God. And Williams was adamant that God's grace and glory should not be shared with human ability or effort as the means whereby the divine purpose was realized.

This letter had been written from Cefn-coed, the place of Williams's birth, three years after his father's death. By this time his mother had inherited her family home, Pantycelyn, after the death of her brother, William Lewis, in 1731. The Cefnarthen church book recorded of him, 'a single person aged 38, once somewhat loose his life, but of late years more serious and reformed, had strong convictions and vehement

106

impressions under the Word, was after double examination ... at last admitted to church membership ... but did not partake of the Communion, his head being somewhat affected with melancholy.' Some of his books bear Williams's signature, one with the date 1734. It is unclear when Williams's mother moved to Pantycelyn, but it was probably some time after her husband's death in 1742. This would have left Williams with responsibility to farm Cefn-coed, possibly with the help of one of his two remaining sisters; another had married in 1739. There would have been farmhands, too, since the family was financially secure. A certain Rees and Jane Morgan may have lived with them as servants, as their children were baptized at Cefnarthen after 1742, while the parents lived at Cefn-coed. Even in 1756 there is reference to 'Mr William Williams of Cefn-coed', in a letter from a Llandovery physician, James Williams, to Howel Harris. Apparently Harris's wife had been ill and Williams had requested on their behalf a visit to Trefeca, but the doctor's response had been unavoidably delayed. He is now able to make the journey 'provided there is a necessity of it.'[5] The date was seven years after Williams's marriage, and it seems likely that he had moved to Pantycelyn by the time his elder son was born in December 1751.[6] 'When he was about thirty-two years of age', according to Thomas Charles, 'he married Mary Francis, originally from Llanfynydd, but who had been living in Llansawel.'[7]

Mary Francis, the object of Williams's affection, had spent some time as companion to Griffith Jones's wife, and had benefited from the ministry of that man of God at Llanddowror. The length of their courtship is unknown, as are the details of their marriage in 1749. She had a sweet singing voice, understood music, and was often asked by her husband to try out his new hymns to various melodies. She became familiar with his poetic foibles: he might wake in the middle of the night calling on a servant to fetch a candle when the muse stirred his imagination. A candle was not always forthcoming at such critical times. The story is told of him on one of his travels calling for a candle and despite his loud appeals, the maid did not appear. He wrote of her on that occasion:

> I now see this quite clearly,
> Though sound of bells abound,
> And paper mill be grinding,
> However harsh their sound;
> Though brazen pan and cauldron
> Should tumble down the stair,

> Her bed collapse beneath her,
> She'd sleep without a care.[8]

Inspiration brooks no rival, and his elegy to Grace Price, for example, was finished at three in the morning.

Williams and his wife soon settled at Pantycelyn with Williams's mother. He was familiar enough with work on the farm, and possessed at least one book on Husbandry. Even though he no longer received the £12 per annum, the stipend of the Llanwrtyd curacy, it seems likely that he was reimbursed by Rowland for his assistance at Llangeitho. There would have been profit from the sale of some of his hymn-books, and he was known to have carried quantities of tea for sale as well as books, on the back of his horse. Both he and his wife inherited property on the death of their parents. Williams's income therefore was sufficient to finance his ministerial labours.

Eight children were born to William and Mary, the two boys becoming clergymen in the Church of England. One of the girls, Mary Sophia, died in 1758 at just two weeks old, and 'seeing what effect this had on the affections of her mother', Williams wrote an elegy to her memory. Unlike his usual style in writing elegies, it is written in blank verse, and was not published until 1763. Some of his anguish comes across when he confesses: 'All beneath the sun are sighs; a sigh at birth; a sigh to live … man was born to endless woe.' A measure of comfort follows within a few lines: 'And what is death, but an exchange of place … the same Friend, the same God, the same profound, endless peace … To be away from the house is to be at home, To be in the grave is to be in heaven, For all who truly love the Lamb of God. She is one of this vast throng.' Williams ends by professing his love: with a hundred blessings flowing from his marriage to Mary, and now that 'little Mary' is dead, his chief earthly desire is that 'old Mary' may be kept alive.[9] Their eldest daughter, Amelia Maria, was born in 1750, Anne, the second daughter, in 1756; the third daughter, Elizabetha Margaretta in 1761; the fourth daughter, Mariah Sophia in 1762; and Sarah, the fifth daughter to survive to adulthood, in 1764. Of these, Elizabetha, known as Betty, remained a spinster, looking after her brother John at Pantycelyn after their parents' death.

Both sons were educated first by their father, and then at a school kept at Coed Cochion, not far from Pantycelyn, by a Thomas Williams.[10] The elder son, William, later attended Christchurch, Oxford, graduating in 1775. Following his ordination in 1776 he served as a curate in

108

Anglican churches in Cornwall until his death in 1818. There is some evidence that his knowledge of Scripture was comprehensive, and that he was an astute theologian. John was born in 1754 and continued his education at Carmarthen and Ystrad Meurig, the latter an Anglican seminary, before being ordained by the Bishop of St. David's, as deacon in 1779, and as priest in 1780. For a while he served as curate in Llynfynydd, then at Builth. At the instigation of David Jones, the Methodist clergyman of Llan-gan, he taught at a school at Coychurch in the Vale of Glamorgan. He also served for a little over five years as tutor at the Countess of Huntingdon's College at Trefeca. Shortly after his father's death in January 1791 he returned to Pantycelyn and became an itinerant preacher with the Calvinistic Methodists in Wales. His journeys were generally in the southern counties of Carmarthen and Brecon, although he made two extensive tours in the north, in 1800 and 1802. Although he was committed to Methodism, he respected not only the Episcopal Church clergy, but also its lectionary, and read the Psalms set by it for Morning Prayer. John Gill's commentary on the Bible was one of his favourite books, and he was enabled to preach until a month before his death. He produced a collection of his father's hymns in 1811, and died at Pantycelyn in 1828.[11]

Williams and his wife belonged to the Methodist society that met at Cil-y-cwm, the other side of Llandovery from Pantycelyn. It was one of the earliest societies, and the first Welsh Methodist Association was held on 6 January 1742 at Dugoedydd, Cil-y-cwm, in the home of William Lloyd, one of the society members. A report of October 1741 speaks of 'progress in knowledge and experience' among the members. In March 1744 there were 24 members, and within a year they were reported to be 'strong Christians, standing firmly in Christ, and will stand through Christ their King.' Williams was also one of the trustees of the building erected in 1746, to be called 'Soar', but commonly referred to as 'Tŷ Newydd' (New House). On one of his journeys around the country in June 1746, Williams stopped at Trefeca while Harris was in London. In a letter he gives news of the Cil-y-cwm building: 'Last night I came from Cwmdu to Trefeca where I preached, and it was sweet indeed with me and the people ... We are for building two houses in Carmarthenshire, one at Cil-y-cwm, the other at Llansawel. May the Lord prosper us. Mr. Rowland is to go to Bristol, he will be a fortnight in going and coming. 'Tis Mr. [Howell] Davies, myself, and the Reverend Peter Williams that is to be at Abergorlech next time. Dear brother, excuse me in writing; my time is short; 'tis now about 9 and I am to be a Capel y Ffin about 10.' In June 1749 Whitefield preached there on John. 6:36, 'He that believeth shall be saved'. In front of the chapel there still stands a brass sundial which some believed was put there by Harris, bearing the words, now indistinct: 'Y mae'r awr olaf yn nesau' ('The last hour approaches'). Cil-y-cwm was also the birthplace of a contemporary and acquaintance of Williams, Morgan Rhys, schoolmaster and hymn-writer. He typified Methodist convictions when he wrote in a letter, 'As I look back today on the sinful state of my entire life, I was worthy only of eternal hell; the worthiness of Another is the reason why I live, the blood of Another bought me life. For this reason, dear brother, I desire to live henceforth to the One who died for me in love without measure.' Another Cil-y-cwm preacher, John Evans, who died in 1784, is buried in the village cemetery, and for him Williams wrote a short elegy. In it Williams claims that Evans, once so frail, now knows more about the doctrine of free grace than any preacher on earth. Furthermore,

> All his faults are now forgotten,
> For the robe in which he's found
> Has no tear, no seam, or staining,
> From its topmost to the ground.
> From the cross this robe proceeded,
> Woven there by heaven's right,
> Look no longer at his failures,
> Bring his mantle to your sight.

Such were the convictions of the company that Williams and his wife sought for ministry, fellowship and support.[12]

Reports to the Association from James William, 'superintendent under the Rev. Daniel Rowland', give some insight into the state of Cil-y-cwm society in the period 1743-4. The first of these states that it is 'a young society not regularly settled.' The next two reports refer to 24 and 26 members, 'nine free, the rest under the Law', but the comment later is slightly different: 'All of them are under convictions, but so influenced by unbelief, that none of them can say that Christ is their Beloved.' Shortly afterwards it is said of them that 'they are more lively inwardly and outwardly.' Growth in maturity as well as numbers is reported in 1744, so that the membership was now 27. Of these it was said that they were 'taught of Christ, though the devil by various means seeks to separate them. Yet no means prevail and he is disappointed. They meet privately together as they are most free to one

110

another to open their hearts, and bring to light Satan's devices and subtlety; so that through the grace of Jesus Christ and the love of God, they are confident hitherto.' A final report is more general for the group of societies under James Williams's care: 'There is still greater reason to praise the Lord for His goodness to them, by pouring many blessings, and much of His love among them, and in bringing His children onward to a greater knowledge of Himself through Jesus Christ. There are none that I know of [that] draw back, but some are added, notwithstanding the threats of the ungodly. The devil's dogs do run swift, but blessed be God, He chains them hitherto, and the more they persecute, the more zeal etc. the Lord gives His children … so far as I can discern I have not seen so much enjoyment of God among them ever before!'[13] Even though these refer to a slightly earlier period than the Williams's involvement in the society, they give an indication of its spiritual state. The statement about 'much enjoyment of God' would have been both appealing and reassuring.

13.

'The roaring wolves of night'

A letter from Howel Harris early in 1745 gives no indication of the turbulent times that were approaching for Welsh Methodism. In it Williams is described as 'eminently favoured of the Lord. He is a flaming instrument, and is day and night on the stretch for his Master.' Others, too, come in for glowing praise. Howel Davies 'sounds the glad tidings with great success ... He is a lively messenger, and under his ministry the Lord does most wonderfully display His great power in wounding and healing.' The highest accolade is reserved for Daniel Rowland, 'one of the most surprising men that ever I heard ... his gifts and call among the people are superior to any, and so far as he can go, none are so blessed and owned as he is.' All in all, it seems, Gospel work was prospering, the revival was spreading, and unity among God's people was preserved:

> Many indeed live in the suburbs of heaven, and have much of its language and nature, and live indeed near to God ... It is impossible to express what visible signs the Lord continues to give of His gracious presence, what life and power, what holy fire and warmth, what shouts of praise from some, what groanings and mournings from others, what tears of love and joy, and what signs of real happiness appears in the looks of others can only be understood by what experience is in one's own soul ... Hitherto, the uniting Spirit has prevailed over our corruptions here; we have been kept one in heart and mind, though the enemy has often attempted without success. We all speak the same things and when any erroneous spirit did at any time appear, the Lord soon dispelled the vapours with the beams of truth. I think we all agree with the good old orthodox Reformers and Puritans.[1]

This was written some seven years after the time when Williams reckoned that 'light had broken as the dawn', but already there were signs of dissension. Writing in retrospect in 1763 he describes the revival's decline and recovery in this way:

> But alas! The love of many grew cold. In a few years the congregation was divided down the middle; and Satan came in among the sons of

God for several years after this. In every pulpit there were dark, threatening clouds, the sound of groaning, mourning and woe; the silver trumpets were giving an uncertain sound, so that no-one prepared for battle, until the burden became unbearable. Then the hour came. The Father's promise was fulfilled. O blessed morning! This is what you now see... and none but God alone is its author.

In keeping with this portrayal of God's intervention to remedy the situation, one of Williams's hymns says that God's presence stills 'to silence / All the roaring wolves of night.'[2] Harris would go his own way, and it was left to the other leaders, Rowland, Williams, and Davies, to prevent serious disintegration of the work. This period, of some ten years' duration, partly due to what is sometimes referred to as 'The Disruption', proved difficult and painful, but the period while it lasted was not altogether devoid of blessings.[3]

In the mid-1740s tensions between the Welsh leaders were becoming more frequent and serious. Given Harris's intense temperament, the urgency he felt as he faced precious, lost souls, and the solemnity of an eternal destiny of bliss or woe that awaited mankind, he found it hard to accommodate a lesser sobriety in behaviour or in preaching. Two letters highlight this growing tension. The first, written in 1744 by one of the exhorters, Richard Tibbott, raised several matters of concern.

What was particularly blameworthy in our Association was the carnal attitude and superficial spirit, idle, fruitless words, and the trivial talk, which gave rise to argument and dissension. It resulted in our neglect of that work for which we had met, and which was far more necessary and important. We therefore wasted our time, and instead of strengthening each others' arms, we weakened and discouraged each other with controversy, especially when Mr. Rowland and Mr. Harris disagreed, the chief pillars of our fellowship ... And if, when we exhort others we convict them of their levity, and of their idle and unnecessary words, and say to them, as Christ said, that they will have to give an account for them in the Day of Judgment, how dare we ourselves do the same things? ... Mr Rowland and Mr. Harris were also especially guilty in giving and receiving reproof. Even though we have made rules about reproving one another, when it was administered on that occasion it was grievous, inasmuch as it was done in the flesh and not in the spirit. And if we cannot keep our own rules, it is not strange that others cannot do so either ... Levity and quarrelling are clean contrary to the Gospel, and to Christ's commandments to His disciples ... Such behaviour undermines our doctrine and our rules. [4]

113

The other letter was written by James Beaumont a few months later, in April 1745: 'I am sorry that we gave such a bad example to the heathen world by our great extravagances at our last Association. I was told that a carnal minister, that was present the first day we met, should say thus: "It is a time of fasting with us, but a time of feasting with you", meaning the Methodists. This reflection ought to be received by us as a reproof from the Lord for our profuse living at that time when we ought to have been fasting and praying.'[5] It was to be a recurring theme during this period, sometimes accompanied with other complaints.

At the Newcastle Emlyn Association in January 1747, Harris had some misgivings about Williams's preaching: 'He preached exceeding sweet, only mentioning about the Law a little dark, and saying God scourges His children for their sins (not opening it clear), and how we are part in Christ – perfection, and part in ourselves – sinful.' Nevertheless, Harris acknowledges, 'my soul was indeed humbled, and I was made poor. I drank of my dear Lord's poverty of spirit … I felt sin had no power over me. I was drawn out to mourn over the land and the Church.'[6] A week later Harris rebuked Williams for what he considered to be legalistic tendencies in his sermon on the Parable of the Ten Virgins (Mat. 25:1-3). Harris went on to complain that Williams's Gospel purity and zeal had declined. Williams defended himself by maintaining the purity of his motives, and censured Harris for a fluid theology which sowed much confusion.[7] Among other things, Rowland was rebuked because all his knowledge was 'only out of books', for 'carnality and formality … not increasing in the knowledge of Christ and appears to be increasing in selfishness.' At one meeting Harris made the rather pointed remark that 'at this point brothers Rowland and Price departed, and directly the Lord came down … I showed the brethren that God did not come down upon us until Rowland and Price etc. had departed, and that it was their unbelief and selfishness on this point that was keeping God away.'[8] Even Whitefield came under censure at London in 1749: 'I told him how he seemed to me not to grow in the knowledge of Christ, nor to sink deeper to the mystery of the Fall, or of the Recovery, but to preach only to the carnal and the weak, and to touch the affection … I told of his lightness and despising the brethren, the preachers. Nor did he behave as a brother to me since I came up, but as to a servant.'[9]

The work of God is always carried on by flawed instruments, even though endowed with grace and gifts. It is not surprising that these evidences of fallen human nature should emerge in all the leaders: pride, frivolous conversation, and a clash of personalities. In his elegy to Harris, Williams draws attention to jealousy, using a metaphor which he later expanded into a book, 'The Crocodile of Egypt's River':

> When a door in Wales was opened,
> Wider than was seen before,
> Hosts of ministers soon followed
> In your wake – full many a score;
> But alas! the crocodilish
> Serpent's poison in your heart
> Meant that others took your sickle;
> From the work you stood apart. [10]

Ten years into the revival in Wales, it was becoming increasingly evident that Llangeitho, rather than Trefeca, was the centre to which the multitudes were being drawn. Harris was an itinerant exhorter, whose successful labours were diffused, while Rowland had a settled location, with Williams as helper in what was rapidly emerging as the spiritual heart of the work. Geraint Tudur documents Harris's growing antipathy towards anyone who seemed to rival his claim to be first in the field of Gospel labours in the revival, and concludes that, 'unable to claim the overall leadership of the movement owing to his unordained status, he stressed his precedence in time, especially after 1745, to secure for himself a prominent position among the other, mostly clerical, leaders.'[11] Envy is a powerful and destructive force, and in Harris it followed a pattern exemplified in Scripture in the growing alienation of King Saul and David: 'Saul was very wroth, and the saying displeased him; and he said. They have ascribed unto David ten thousands, and to me they have ascribed but thousands: and what can he have more but the kingdom? And Saul eyed David from that day and forward' (1 Samuel 18: 8-9) In turn Harris's attitude affected not merely relationships in the Methodist camp, but also events and, more seriously, convictions.

One area of disagreement was that of discipline in the societies. Harris's criterion for expulsion from the society was a subjective impression gained from a person's convictions and experiences. The other leaders insisted that evidence of grace or lack of it should be drawn from that person's behaviour as well. Thus, while Harris expelled some members, Rowland allowed them to participate at the next communion service. At first this bothered Harris: 'when I turn one out of the society, where I feel I have authority, much of the reproof is lost by his keeping them in the Sacrament afterward.'[12] Later, this brought forth his reprimand: 'I spoke of the holiness of the work, of our disorder, of our lack of discipline, our party spirit; and of our need to agree in private on all things so that we go amongst souls with one voice.'[13] Richard Tibbott accused Harris of a failure 'to distinguish between people and their opinions. There is some bad in good men, but it is wrong to regard good men as bad men on account of their faults ... you took things to extremes against those you withstood, their characters and actions, depicting them as the blackest rebels ... You failed to use all the means for their recovery ... you concentrated too much on words at the expense of sense and substance.'[14] Harris was adamant in holding a different standpoint regarding his discernment: 'When the brethren [Rowland and Williams] offered to cast out the spirit's light, and that we had no rule to go by but outward fruits to cast people out, I insisted on it that there is an eye in the body and spiritual light, and the spiritual man judgeth according to his measure all things.' On this issue Harris was isolated, and Whitefield's words at an Association in August 1748, against depending on 'supernatural revelations and subjective impressions', were accepted as authoritative and final by the Welsh Methodists.[15]

Another sore issue at the time between Harris and the other leaders was his defence of unorthodox views in James Beaumont, a leading exhorter. On the way to an Association with Harris, Beaumont 'argued that the only purpose of the Law is to explain the wretchedness of the sinner; that no one should be exhorted to live virtuously according to the commandments of the Law, but that all should be directed to Christ.' At the time Harris commented that this savoured of Antinomianism, which went further and maintained that the Law has no relevance for Christian behaviour. A society member had been expelled in 1744 by the Association 'after a long debate together and prayer', for holding such views. Beaumont was 'weekly preaching' his errors among the societies in Radnorshire, and creating 'great fermentation', and calling 'sanctification, or the mark or fruits of the Spirit ... knick-knacks by the way; only simple believing, no duties, command[ment]s, etc. will be allowed; no growth in grace.' By 1749, when Beaumont appeared before the Association, Harris argued in his favour: 'I believed him sound at heart, a brother in the Lord, and a preacher sent of God.' Beaumont eventually joined the Moravians, while the Welsh Methodists issued a pamphlet, *Ymddiddan Rhwng*

Methodist ac Antinomian ('Dialogue Between a Methodist and an Antinomian') rejecting this teaching as a departure from Scripture.[16]

Worse was to come. Despite the admonition of his brethren, Harris was deviating further and further from the orthodox position on the doctrine of the Trinity. In 1743, after reading 'a tract', *A Sling and a Stone*, he says, 'I now was brought to see more and more wonders in his infinite Incarnation, Life, Blood, Death, and Resurrection.'[17] It also convinced him that 'every truth, when revealed by the Spirit, is practical, and will have its proper influence on the soul, by humbling the sinner, and exalting the Saviour.' Visiting London the following year, Harris 'found the glory of our Saviour, breaking forth among the people, and many rising out of the Law to see the glory of God in the face of Jesus Christ; the completeness of his atonement, with the mystery and glory of his precious blood!' Williams, too, uses the phrase, sometimes by implication, at others more explicitly:

> Upon the Lord I henceforth would rest while here I plod,
> Of this Thy death is worthy, Thou art infinite God.
> O for my failings answer, and purge me with Thy blood
> In presence of the angels before my Father God.
>
> Lo! Here's the blood that speaketh of better things by far
> Than that of righteous Abel in ages now afar;
> How infinitely wondrous! The blood of the God-man,
> Of which a drop's more precious than worlds combined in one.[18]

In the second verse quoted here, the original Welsh has 'Gwaed Duw yw hwn ei hun' (this is God's own blood), but the context makes it clear that the reference is to the Second Person of the Trinity, not the first. But Williams was a better theologian than Harris, and less susceptible to the 'wind of doctrine' that swirled around the revivalists' world in those days. The societies in London at the time were awash with theological ideas, Methodist, Moravian, Antinomian and Arminian, and in this ferment Harris found it hard to resist what he considered to be most to the glory of God, an emphasis on the mystery of Christ's Deity.[19]

Harris returned to Wales at the end of 1744, and early in the New Year he 'had vast liberty to preach the blood of Christ, seeing it as the blood of God. Never had such a sight of it in my soul, and never had such power to set it forth as now.'[20] Evidently some aspects of the mystery of Christ's Person and work were in the forefront of his mind.

117

He had always insisted that faith was a personal dealing with Christ, based on the abiding and absolute truth of God's Word. But faith was more than holding propositions dealing with a historic Person, it implied acquaintance and closure with a majestic Person, whose greatness was immeasurable; hence the mystery. However, in this very area the boundary between orthodoxy and heresy was a very fine and delicate one, as Church history amply demonstrates. Controversy had raged in the early Church over such matters as the Trinity, and the Person of Christ. Harris now began to use ambiguous and often unbiblical expressions in his preaching, and to show impatience with those who sought to caution him. Rowland did just that early in March, and an Association at Bristol shortly afterwards agreed 'that if we used a phrase that is not in the Scriptures, we should explain it with Scriptural expressions, and as far as possible to confine ourselves to biblical terms.'[21] On his part, Harris did not sufficiently pay heed to things that differ, and his loose phrases about God as One who suffered, and about His blood, brought upon him deserved censure. In his eagerness to portray the majesty of the person nailed to the cross and the infinite worth of the sacrifice, Harris spoke as if God the Father had died. Such expressions fudge the distinction between the three Persons in the Godhead, a travesty of biblical truth labelled by theologians as the twin heresies of Sabellianism and Patripassianism. From May 1750, the Welsh Methodists considered that Harris's failure to recognize this, and his obstinacy in refusing to return to orthodox views, necessitated a parting of the ways, and Harris withdrew to his home at Trefeca.

When Williams used the phrase 'the blood of God', it is in a manner similar to his use of other phrases, such as 'the grace of God', 'the pure love of God', and 'the strength of God'. He is always careful at the same time to convey that Christ is one divine Person, suffering pain and death on the cross in His human nature. The Apostle Paul observed similar constraints in his charge to the Ephesian elders. Having spoken of 'the grace of God', 'the kingdom of God', and 'the counsel of God', he urged them 'to feed the church of God which he hath purchased with His own blood'(Acts 20: 24-28). In a short work which the Welsh Methodist leaders issued at the time, *Ymddiddan Rhwng Methodist Uniongred ac un Camsyniol* ('Dialogue Between an Orthodox and an Erroneous Methodist'), the orthodox position was ably defended: 'God is a Spirit, without body, parts, or sufferings, and so He cannot suffer or die.' Of Christ it stated, 'that the union of two natures (human and divine) in one Person remains, so that our Lord was God-man in the womb, God-man on the cross, God-man in the grave.'[22] It is impossible to gauge what part Williams played in drawing up this document, but it is thoroughly consistent with the teaching found in all his writings.

One more element of this sad episode in Welsh Methodism has to do with Harris's dependence on subjective impulse. He came to regard one of the North Wales converts, Mrs Sidney Griffith, as having what amounted to prophetic insight and guidance. She also shared his convictions about Christ's sufferings, which his wife, Anne, did not. In a letter dated 16 October 1749 Harris comments on this:

> all my cry is abiding and insatiable to have my dear wife up to the light with us to see the glorious Immanuel, and to see all in Him indeed ... I have been just now and am this moment before the throne of our dear eternal Father, and He assures me that He will set all things in a right light before His own children and before the world; and will order all your affairs right in the north and south; and will settle all at Trefeca to His own mind; and will raise my poor Nancy to the light.

For these reasons Mrs Griffith often accompanied him on his journeys in 1749, a practice that betrayed a grave error of judgment on his part, and gave considerable offence to many. On 25 July he wrote in his diary: 'last night I continued singing and preaching all night with Mrs. Griffith and maid. I never felt the like before; for six days the Lord has filled my heart and mouth so as I never had before ... If all the discourses I have had these six days were written down, it would make a volume of pure, clear and strong observations and exhortations.' In August another diary entry elaborates these sentiments: 'I find a total change since I met Mrs. Griffith, raised to a new life, with God in everything. Knowing none after the flesh, my dear wife being given me alone of all the daughters of Eve for my wife ... Mrs. Griffith being my nearest counsellor friend.' [23]

Two years later, Harris faced a showdown with Whitefield in London, and again the diary records the event: 'he said he did not approve of Madam Griffith being with me, that it was contrary to God's Word ... I told him ... that though I am a great sinner, her being with me is not among my sins, that I act in it out of conscience toward God.' On occasions during this period he did confess to a damaging estrangement in his domestic relationships, driving him to prayer: 'Secretly I felt a coldness and indifference toward my wife, child and family; this sent me to the Lord, and I had faith too as to marriage.' Nevertheless he

119

repeatedly insisted that the bond between him and Griffith was spiritual rather than romantic: 'I have nothing to do with Madam Griffith after the flesh', was one such affirmation while she was still alive; another after her death stated that he took her 'from the Lord in the spirit and not outwardly, the whole matter was a matter in the spirit out of and above nature, and did not interfere with any tie of nature.'[24] It is hard to believe that Harris's wife shared these latter sentiments; certainly the other leaders did not. The situation had deeper implications than Harris was prepared to admit.

During the years of separation that followed, responsibility for the continuity of the work rested on the shoulders chiefly of Rowland and Williams. In his elegy to Daniel Rowland, Williams was able to say of this difficult time:

> Some brought Anti-trinitarian
> Heresy, both dark and strange;
> Holding God without the Persons,
> First, Third, Second, yet no change;
> Daniel then stood firm and solid,
> like a pillar, straight and strong;
> Publicly withstanding falsehood,
> Showing clearly what was wrong.[25]

In the opinion of a later clergyman, David Griffiths of Nevern in Pembrokeshire, 'Rowlands and Williams possessed talents sufficient for the government of a kingdom.'[26] Those talents would be severely tested over the next ten years.

Meanwhile, Harris withdrew from public life to set up an extended 'Family' at Trefeca. It consisted of members of societies from all over Wales whose loyalty to him had not been shaken, and who were prepared to join a self-sufficient, self-supporting community of believers under his leadership. They submitted to his spiritual exhortations three times a day and to his discipline. Many crafts were represented among them as well as that of farming the land, and eventually a printing press was also established at Trefeca. 'All members of the Family were expected to forfeit their earthly goods, and place the profits of the various industries in a common fund to be used for the maintenance of all alike.' In 1755, Harris founded the 'Breconshire Agricultural Society', and between the years 1759 and 1762 he served in the Breconshire Militia, 'inasmuch as he felt it his duty to further help in saving Protestant England from Roman Catholic

France.' He was made Captain Lieutenant in October 1760, a rank he enjoyed until he resigned his commission two years later. Typically, Harris joined on condition that he should be allowed to preach, a privilege he used on more than one occasion. At Yarmouth in 1760 he asked the town crier to announce a meeting at the market-place. This is what happened:

> At the time appointed a large mob collected together, furnished with stones, brick-bats, bludgeons, blood, and filthy materials suited to their work, vowing that if the preacher came, he should never get out of the town alive. Mr. Harris, who had been exercising his men at a little distance, when the clock struck, went to the multitude, and enquired what was the matter? They replied that a Methodist preacher was to have come ... Mr. Harris told them that he thought it a pity they should be wholly disappointed, and that if they would favour him with their attention, he would sing a hymn and pray with them, and also give them a little friendly advice. He then mounted a table which had been prepared for him; his men, who surrounded him with their arms, joining him most devoutly in singing and prayer ... Mr. Harris preached with little interruption; the hearts of many of the hearers were softened, and prejudices vanished. Some were awakened to a serious concern for their souls, and led to enquire how they might be saved.[27]

John Wesley recorded in his Journal some months later that Harris at Yarmouth had 'preached every night, none daring to oppose him; and hereby a good seed was sown ... Many were stirred up to seek God, and some of them now earnestly invited me to come over.'[28]

Williams and Rowland did not allow these differences to alienate them entirely from their fellow-worker of such long standing. They were persistent in compassion as well as valiant for truth. Together they visited Harris at Trefeca in September 1754, and although they were welcomed, the visit stopped short of a reinstatement or reunion. Another Welsh Methodist, Peter Williams, who had been converted under Whitefield's ministry in 1748, called before the end of 1754 with a similar response and outcome.[29] After a visit in January the following year, Charles Wesley sent Harris an appeal in verse to return to the work:

> Awake, old soldier! – to the fight half-won,
> And put thy strength and put thine armour on!
> Nor dream thyself a vessel cast aside,
> Broken by stubborn will, and marred by pride.

121

> Most proud, self-willed, and wrathful as thou art,
> Yet God hath surely seen thy simple heart …
> If thou art Harris still, - awake, arise,
> Renew the fight, re-labour up the skies. [30]

When Rowland called in February 1755, it was to encourage Harris to return to the aid of the Welsh Methodists, again with little success. Williams heard Harris preach at Trefeca in January 1756, and apparently confessed to Harris that, 'Stupidity and slumber is come over their people and preachers; and that they have lost the spirit of the reformation, and are going worse; and want me to send somebody among them, and they never thrived since the Breach.' Harris was disposed to be friendly towards him, and had read Williams's *Golwg ar Deyrnas Crist* ('A View of Christ's Kingdom'), adding in his diary, 'My spirit blushed at my own unfruitfulness and blessed God for all the gifts He has given to all.'[31] When John Wesley called at Trefeca briefly in March 1756, Harris told him that 'he preached till he could preach no longer, his constitution being entirely broken.' A few days later Wesley wrote him a letter about selfwill: 'O Howell, let us be more and more aware of this deadly enemy. It contains passions, stubbornness, unpersuadableness … the Lord make us mild, quiet, loving, patient of reproof, advice, contradiction, contempt.'[32] Nor was Whitefield unheeding; Harris records in his diary for 16 July 1756 that he had received a letter from him. A year later Harris and Rowland met at Brecon, and expressed affection and a desire to re-unite, but first they should arrange a conference. A similar qualification was expressed by Harris again when Williams and Peter Williams called at Trefeca in June 1759, and there was talk of restoring some discipline in their midst. These efforts bore fruit, and Harris met Rowland, Williams and others at Trecastle on 4 September 1759. Harris was apprehensive, and the meeting was limited in its achievements. More time was required to remedy what had been a damaging breach.

14.

'Faint, and yet pursuing'

While Williams and others, then, waited God's time for fresh advance in their spiritual campaign against the devil's kingdom, they did not slacken their labours. In this they found considerable encouragement from the occasional visits of George Whitefield. It was not only the presence of someone of his stature among them that was significant; his convictions confirmed the validity of their theology. Furthermore, his preaching not only brought echoes of past triumphs, but produced evidence that the Gospel was still God's instrument of power to change lives.

Despite physical weariness, on account of extensive travelling for some fifteen years to preach the Gospel, Whitefield's passion for preaching was undiminished. Early in 1749 he acknowledged in a letter, 'I am sometimes faint', and added, 'but "faint, and yet pursuing" must be the Christian's motto.' At the time he could report 'that conviction work is going on in England and Wales', and plans were afoot in May for a visit to the Principality, where 'the work is upon the advance.' When he arrived at his wife's house in Abergavenny at the end of May he was glad of a two-day respite 'for the sake of a little retirement.' 'It has been sweet, yea very sweet', he adds, 'so sweet that I should be glad never to be heard of again. But this must not be. A necessity is laid upon me, and woe is me if I do not preach the Gospel of Christ. I therefore purpose tomorrow to begin a three-week circuit and to see what the Lord will be pleased to do by me.' The rest was beneficial, so that a week later he could write from West Wales: 'The Gospel runs and is glorified! I have been enabled to preach fourteen times within these eight days, and the word has everywhere fallen with weight and power ... Congregations grow larger and larger, and all the towns hereabout are quite open for the Word of God ... I wish I had more time in these parts. The fields are indeed white, ready unto harvest ... Last Sunday I believe I preached to near twenty thousand souls ... I think we have not had one dry meeting. The work in Wales is much upon the advance, and likely to increase daily.'[1]

It would be two years before Whitefield returned to Wales. An explanation for the delay is found in his letter to a Welsh correspondent, dated 4 September 1750: 'You must salute dear Mr. R[owland] and the rest of the brethren in my name. As far as I know, we are like-minded as to principles, and I shall be glad to do all I can to strengthen their hands, only let nothing be done through strife or vain-glory ... I would gladly fly to Wales, but perhaps my coming had better be deferred to the cool of the day. Let us not fear. This storm will blow over. Truth is great, and though driven out of doors for a while, will prevail at last.'[2] When Rowland visited Bristol in March 1751, both he and Whitefield preached in the open air 'to vast multitudes, who heard them with apparently deep and serious attention.' The Countess of Huntingdon, who was there at the time, reported that the two ministers were 'owned and honoured of the Lord in the conversion of notorious profligates and self-righteous formalists.'[3] Clearly, the heavenly flame had not been extinguished in the workers, even though the blaze in Wales was subsiding. It evidently confirmed to Whitefield that it was an opportune time to revisit Wales, perhaps in response to Rowland's entreaties, so that on March 30 he had 'thoughts of going to Wales, Ireland and Scotland.'[4] It was to be a prosperous time for Gospel ministry, with little time for his usual letter-writing: 'I fully proposed to have written to you from Wales, but was prevented by travelling and preaching. In about three weeks, I rode perhaps above five hundred miles, and preached generally twice a day. Congregations were as large as usual, and I trust an unusual power accompanied the Word.'[5] His next visit was a year later, where 'abundance of souls, especially in Pembrokeshire, have attended'. The two visits he made to Wales in 1753 differed from one another. At Pembrokeshire in June he saw large congregations, 'and a melting seemed to be among the people.' At Wrexham in October, while thousands came to hear, 'several of the baser sort made a great noise, and threw stones', but he was unharmed, 'and our Lord got himself the victory.' A letter written from London on 2 May 1756 where he had just preached at his newly-rented Long Acre Chapel, 'Whitefield's soul-trap' as it came to be called, says he planned 'to set out for Wales' despite the fact that his body was 'weakened through care and watchfulness, a variety of exercises, and want of sleep.' 'A most delightful circuit' was his assessment of a 1758 summer tour in Wales, seeing a 'great congregation ... of near fifteen thousand' at Haverfordwest, where 'tears flowed like water from the stony rock.' His aim, as he confessed in writing of a 1760

124

1. Cefncoed, Williams's birthplace.

2. Cefnarthen, where the Williams family worshipped.

i

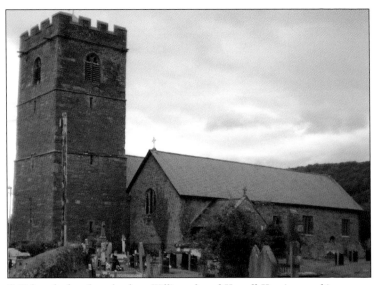

3. *Talgarth churchyard, where Williams heard Howell Harris preaching.*

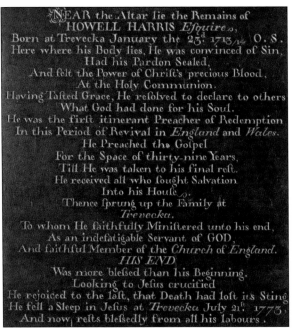

NEAR the Altar lie the Remains of
HOWELL HARRIS *Efquire*,
Born at Trevecka January the 23: 1713/14. O. S.
Here where his Body lies, He was convinced of Sin,
Had his Pardon Sealed,
And felt the Power of Chrift's precious Blood,
At the Holy Communion.
Having Tafted Grace, He refolved to declare to others
What God had done for his Soul.
He was the firft itinerant Preacher of Redemption
In this Period of Revival in *England* and *Wales*.
He Preached the Gofpel
For the Space of thirty-nine Years,
Till He was taken to his final reft.
He received all who fought Salvation
Into his Houfe.
Thence fprung up the Family at
Trevecka.
To whom He faithfully Miniftered unto his end,
As an indefatigable Servant of GOD,
And faithful Member of the *Church* of *England*.
HIS END
Was more blefsed than his Beginning,
Looking to Jefus crucified
He rejoiced to the laft, that Death had loft its Sting
He fell a Sleep in Jefus at *Trevecka* July 21.ᵗ 1773,
And now refts blefsedly from all his labours.

4. *Plaque in memory of Howell Harris in Talgarth Church.*

5. Top: *Griffith Jones, rector of Llanddowror.*

6. Right: *Daniel Rowland statue at Llangeitho.*

7. Left: *Howel Harris of Trefeca.*

8. *Old Llanwrtyd Church, where Williams was curate.*

9. *The first joint Calvinistic Methodist Association at Watford, 1743.*

10. Idealized portrait of Williams by William Mackenzie.

11. Sketch of Williams from memory by John Williams of Llanddarog.

12. Plaque to Rhys Prichard in Llandingad Church.

ALELUJA,

NEU,

CASGLJAD

O

HYMNAU,

AR AMRYW

YSTYRJAETHAU.

O Waith y Parchedig

Mr WILLIAM WILLIAMS.

Eph. v. 19. *Gen lefaru wrth ei gilydd mewn* SALMAU, *a* HYMNAU, *ac Odlau ysprydel, &c.*

Col. III. 16. ———*Gan ddyfgn a rhybuddjo, bawb ei gilydd mewn* SALMAU, HYMNAU, *&c.*

Yr ail ARGRAPHJAD.

CAERFYRDDIN:

Argraphwyd gan SAMUEL LEWIS, yn Heol y Brenin; Lle vell'r cael argraphu pôb Maith o Lyfrau Cymra-aeg, à Saefon-aeg; Llythyren *newydd*, a Phapur *da*; yn gyftal ac yn LLUNDAIN.

M DCC XLIV.

13. Title page of the second issue of William's first hymn collection, 'Aleluja'.

14. Sign at Pantycelyn Farm entrance.

15. Pantycelyn Farm today.

16. The Countess of Huntingdon's College at Trefeca.

17. Selina, The Countess of Huntingdon.

visit was always the same, 'inviting souls to come to Christ.'[6]

While it is true that the geographical scope of Whitefield's visits was limited, it would be difficult to overestimate their effect upon the Welsh leaders. In a decade when they missed Harris's presence and zeal, to have Whitefield's implied approval on their Methodist principles and activities was invaluable. Nor would he have found such numbers ready to listen, or such fervent response, without there being a substantial measure of success on their labours as well. Five visits to Wales are recorded by John Wesley during the 1750s, usually on his journey to Ireland. In 1750 in Anglesey he reported that 'not one scoffer is found in these congregations; but whoever hears, hears for his life.' One morning in South Wales eight years later, he 'scarce ever saw such rain in Europe ... the water ran with a stream capable of turning a mill', but preaching at Newton, outside Swansea that afternoon, 'it pleased God to send a gracious rain upon their hearts.' By the Moravians, 1753 was regarded as the year of John Cennick's 'great work in Wales', chiefly in Pembrokeshire. As with Whitefield and Wesley, preaching was the main purpose of his visits, but was also 'instructing the people of South Wales on the nature of a Religious Society.'[7] The distinctives of Methodism were greater than its divisions. Harris's withdrawal had been a serious setback, but it was not a total eclipse of the work.

Particular testimony to this fact is found in the diary of John Thomas, a Methodist schoolmaster who lived at Tre-main in Cardiganshire. The diary is a very personal record of events that might have been common among the Methodists of the day. They followed their daily routine of home and work, yes, but also attended society meetings and sermons, sang hymns, shared experiences, and even, as in the case of Thomas, read Calvin's Commentaries and Thomas Shephard's *Parable of the Ten Virgins Opened*. Such was the spiritual pilgrimage of those who attended Rowland, Williams and Davies on their preaching occasions. The diary is noteworthy because it provides evidence of sustained, and at times quite elevated, spiritual blessings during the period 1756-59. On the first Sunday of 1757 he heard Williams preach at Llansawel on Matthew 18:20, 'where two or three are gathered together in my name, there am I in the midst of them'. 'He showed', says Thomas, 'that all means are quite in vain without the presence of God', adding, 'Thank God for this sermon.' Two weeks later he was present at a 'remarkable meeting' at Carmarthen, when Williams preached on Zechariah 6:12, 'Behold the man whose name is The Branch ... and he shall build the temple of the Lord', when he adds the comment, 'God was undoubtedly present.' At an Association meeting in October 1759 he heard both Williams and Rowland preaching, and made this observation: 'These two men strike exactly the same chord, namely, God is all; man and everything that pertains to him, is nothing; God eternally exalted and glorious; man and even the best that belongs to him, in the dust, as dung underfoot.'[8] The 'fire' of God could fall, not only on preaching occasions, but also, as Thomas frequently testifies, on society meetings. Of one such occasion he says: 'God had come into the midst ... there was such freedom in my soul ... it persisted in this amazing fashion all night; I could neither eat nor drink ... but praising God full of wonder, and who could do otherwise? For it had become heaven on earth to me.' At another society meeting during a time of prayer, Thomas felt as if a beam of sunshine was flooding his soul, and later he wrote: 'I never thought there so much heaven to be had the other side of the grave as what I now, by sheer mercy, have experienced this side of it.'[9]

Williams's influence was not dormant during this time. It 'is seen in greater or lesser measure' on a clutch of hymn-writers, born within seven miles of Llandovery between 1710 and 1730, among them Dafydd Jones, Morgan Rhys, and John Thomas. Jones (1711-77), born at Caeo, was for a time a drover, but after coming to faith in Christ he settled as a farmer, and became a member of an Independent congregation. A Calvinist by conviction, he was noted as one who had some Methodist fire in his devotion and worship, and was convinced of the assurance of persevering grace. Williams included one of Jones's hymns in the fifth part of his *Aleluja* of 1747. Jones translated into Welsh many of Isaac Watt's Psalms and hymns, and issued three volumes of his own collections in 1763, 1764 and 1770. One of his most popular hymns set Christ's person and work as matters for praise:

> The Messiah has appeared,
> The most precious Friend of all;
> Moses and the prophets hailed Him,
> And on Him His people call;
> He is here, God's Son dear,
> Friend, Redeemer, ever near.
>
> Of our love a Friend so worthy
> Loud our praises hail Him so;
> Bought our life, our debts He settled,
> And our hearts He rids of woe;

Brothers, then, praise again,
Thank Him ever, shout Amen!

He displayed, in his life as well as in his worship, the exuberance which
characterized his Methodist contemporaries, and defended it in rhyme:

Men of the world are asking, and with alarm cry out,
What is this utter folly, this praise to God with shout?
I'm freed from cruel bondage, from this I'll never cease –
To sing in spite of scorners – Christ's blood has brought release!

What if I now start jumping, God's grace to own and mark,
And dance with joy like David, before the heavenly ark?
The lame though long since carried, leaped, danced to celebrate
His healing by the Saviour before the temple gate.

Williams and his fellow labourers were often on the defensive, and for
many reasons, but with gifted apologists of the calibre of David Jones,
they sought to bring their behaviour to biblical evaluation. [10]

Morgan Rhys (1716-1779), schoolmaster and Methodist, was born at
Cil-y-cwm, and issued several hymn collections between 1755 and
1770. Here is a pithy verse of his taken from one of his manuscripts,
translated from the original Welsh:

Build your boat in grace's Day,
'Ere the flood comes, long to stay;
'Tis too late to get the wood
When the world begins to flood. [11]

A hymn of his on Christ's birth still retains its popularity and appeal.
Here are two verses in English translation:

Sweetly sang the stars of morning
On the birth of heaven's King;
Shepherds, wise men, joined together
With their praise and gifts to bring;
Heaven's treasure!
Jesus in the manger born.

To the lost a mighty Saviour,
To the sick, Physician sure;
He delights to pardon sinners,

Brings to such, unfailing cure;
Praise Him!
For remembering dust of earth.

The titles of the hymn collections, the first of which appeared in 1755, reflect Rhys's warm spirituality: 'A View of the Promised Land from the summit of Nebo'; 'A Collection of Hymns on Man's Fall in the First Adam, and of his Restoration in the Second'; 'The features of this world passing, and an Eternity of Happiness approaching'; 'A sight of the City of Refuge; in a collection of hymns to encourage Pilgrims'; 'The Believer's longings for perfection and incorruption'. The beneficiaries named in his will were predominantly members of Methodist societies, Williams, Rowland, and David Jones, Llan-gan among them, a clear indication of the nature of his spirituality.[12]

  John Thomas (1730-1804?), born at Myddfai, was converted under the ministry of Howel Harris. He became a Congregational minister, and his favourite reading included Bunyan's *Pilgrim's Progress* and Rhys Prichard's *Welshman's Candle.* He published *Caniadau Sion* ('Songs of Zion'), in six parts between 1758 and 1786, a total of 187 hymns. One of his hymns may be translated thus:

Behold! A Saviour, great,
Who down from heaven came,
To change the sinner's deadly state,
All glory to his Name!
'Twas in our place He died,
For souls sunk in sin's mire,
All worthiness in Him reside,
Our needy souls require.

To rightly know Him now
Is life that's full of peace;
To prove salvation here below,
This feast will never cease;
To feel sin's wound and pain
By Christ's blood fully healed,
This myriads with their might and main,
Have in an anthem praised.

He translated into Welsh several works, including two of Bunyan's tracts: *The Holy City or The New Jerusalem* (1789), *Christ a Complete Saviour* (1791), and *Reprobation Asserted* (1791). He was also fond of

128

William Romaine's works, translating his *Life of Faith* (1767) and Romaine's sermon at the funeral of James Hervey, *The Knowledge of Salvation Precious in the Hour of Death* (1759). Between 1769 and 1772 he witnessed several revivals under his ministry at Rhaeadr. With pressing calls for his preaching, his settled ministry was laid aside and he moved back to Carmarthenshire to labour as a schoolmaster. [13]

While the emergence of these talented hymn-writers during the difficult 1750s showed the enduring and motivating power of Williams's example, there were other matters demanding his urgent attention. Restoring broken fellowship, removing suspicion and nurturing fresh trust all required patience, perseverance and prayer. Such it proved for the Welsh Methodists, and in a letter to Harris, Williams acknowledged some prejudices among them toward him and the sense of loss that his absence posed. He also expressed, with tact and magnanimity, his defence of Harris and appeal for his return, in a readable fragment in spite of its poor preservation:

> In great need of you at present ... I asked them also whether the ... reformation in the things you ... all answered that they d[esired] ... a little as well as I could ... whe[ther] ... most of us should be under ... bound to go and come, do and ... so that we should be obliged to cancel all our rules, orders ... and directions, whatsoever, from you alone; and to be plain that you should be our master on earth, so far as to deprive us of consulting our brethren, the Word of God, or our own consciences in any spiritual affair. (Pardon, dear Sir, the folly of such suspicions); to which I answered, that you mean no more than carrying such connection and union with us, as would through God's blessing do good both to us and all the Church of Christ; that you intended to be no more a Rabbi or Master than what the Spirit of Christ hath put in you; that you would willingly carry on the grand interest of souls in connection with us as in former times, excepting that you could not go so often abroad; that you designed not in the least to domineer or over-rule the heritage of the Lord ... Dear Sir, come, come soon then, all is ready to receive you. You were never, since you [became] a soldier of Jesus Christ, more accepted in the Church than at this day, by preachers and [people]. The fields are white for the harvest, nothing is wanted but faithful labourers ... you were, and are, owned more than perhaps any in Wales. You shall not go to heaven ... until you settle some affairs in the Church, until you help your ... flock, and discipline the dispersed and scattered sheep.[14]

The sentiments of this letter were echoed in a more official invitation from the leaders, dated 19 May 1762, where Williams's name appears as the first of several signatories, Daniel Rowland and Peter Williams among them: 'We understand by E. Moses [a Trefeca resident and close to Harris] that you intend to resign your present Commission [in the military] and (God willing) once more to fill up your place among us, which we sensibly [that is, feelingly] acknowledge has been long vacant. We have followed you with our prayers through your various tours, and are satisfied you generally appeared double armed, to the furtherance of the Gospel. Glory be to free, sovereign grace! And we unanimously conclude that your inclination to visit our several counties again is the voice of heaven, and we doubt not but all animosities will and must subside, and a spirit of love take place.'[15]

It was a year of great things, with a powerful revival spreading from Llangeitho. Harris must have been deeply moved, writing in his diary at Cil-y-cwm, where Williams's own society met: 'My spirit crying to catch their fire and life, the Lord having awakened many in these parts by a spirit of singing and blessing the Lord, who continue whole nights in that exercise.' Within a year the Methodist leaders, Harris among them, were reunited at an Association meeting at Llansawel on 16 February 1763. Christian charity and unity reigned supreme, and Harris could write: 'Sure this is the year of Jubilee. The time is come, the shadow of prejudices fly away, old love and simplicity return, and what did let and hinder seems to remove, and self seems to come down.' The joy and unity of the event was encapsulated in a hymn written by Williams at Harris's request, which appeared in his 1763 collection *Ffarwel Weledig, Groesaw Anweledig Bethau* ('Farewell Visible, Welcome Invisible Things').[16] Fittingly, it spoke of forgiveness, laying aside all earthly fame, and ascribing all glory to the name of Christ alone.

15.

'A View of the Kingdom'

Welsh Methodists had always been passionate about evidence of the presence and power of God in all their activities. They referred to this as the manifestation of 'authority' and 'power', as the Holy Spirit's 'coming down', or simply as 'fire'. With their ranks depleted by the departure of such a leading figure and influence as Harris, they were deeply concerned about the dangers of disarray and declension. How could they preserve the fruit which God had in such profuse measure bestowed upon their labours? Had their disagreements and, more seriously, their sinful failures grieved the Holy Spirit so that it was futile to expect further revival? Would this great movement, so evidently blessed in the conversion of sinners and in building up believers, now grind to a halt? What was to be done to ensure further inroads into the kingdom of Satan, which was so sorely needed in Wales? Could the 'fire of God' be maintained in the hearts of His people while they waited on Him in prayer for Him to intervene yet again in the land? These were the urgent issues that faced the Welsh Methodists, 'Rowland's People' as they were now called.

It was in the midst of such circumstances that Williams prepared a major work of theology for his fellow Methodists, in the form of a grand epic poem. The cover of the second part of his Welsh hymn collection 'Hosanna to the Son of David', published in 1753, has this announcement: 'I propose to print a small book … with the name, *The Triumph of the Gospel*, as one poem with more than three hundred verses.' When the work of 192 pages appeared in 1756 it bore the title, *Golwg ar Deyrnas Crist* ('A View of Christ's Kingdom'). A second edition, which included corrections and extra material, appeared in 1764. It was this edition that Robert Jones, Rotherhithe, translated and published in London in 1878 with the title *A View of the Kingdom of Christ; or, Christ is all, and in all.* There are in all over 1,360 verses to the poem, each of doubled 7.6.7.6 syllables. For many readers this metre becomes monotonous and tedious, and few would persevere to the end unless they were gripped by the excellence of the subject.

Presumably Williams must have considered poetry as the best and most effective tool for communicating with the readers of his day. His work was written in plain language so as to encourage the reader to persevere, while its rhyme was intended to assist the memory. Williams deliberately embraced both in order, as he says in its second edition, to 'enlighten the reader' and 'enliven his affections', and the poem was 'so arranged that he could run and not be weary'. He would also have agreed with Sir Phillip Sidney's *Apology for Poetrie* in claiming that poetry 'yieldeth to the power of the mind, an image of that whereof the Philosopher bestoweth but a wordish description: which doth neither strike, pierce, nor possess the sight of the soul, so much as that other doth.'[1] So much for the medium; a comment on the work by the literary scholar T. Gwynn Jones, is generous in its praise of the message:

> The poet brings to the task all that he knows, and it must be admitted that there is a certain austere grandeur in the work. Pant y Celyn struggled with the greatest problem which has engaged and ever will engage the human mind. He has subdued chaos, conquered sin, and ascended to Heaven. He has done more. He has overcome self and wretchedness, has known what it is to long with a consuming passion for the clean white flame of absolute invariable goodness and purity; he has realized the utter abandonment of himself to the one sole Saviour, whose being explained to him everything from the merest detail in physical life to the sum and summit of all possible thought. The outbreaks of this sublime passion in the poem are many, and as expressions of utter trust, of absolute unconquerable faith, they cannot be excelled in any literature commonly known. As an element in their complete negation of self, even their frequent and flagrant disregard of form assumes almost a sacred function. There are weaknesses in the poem – repetitions and lapses from verbal austerity; but taken together and read as the record of a passionate soul, it must be allowed to be truly marvellous.[2]

Thomas Charles says of Williams: 'His clear and comprehensive views on the great doctrine of the Atonement are set out gloriously in the poetic essay that he published with the title 'A View of Christ's Kingdom'. He studied so extensively while writing this work, chiefly, that it adversely affected his health for the rest of his life.'[3]

Serious study and wide reading were certainly involved in its composition. Several scholarly disciplines were involved: sound theology, biblical typology, discoveries in astronomy and science, literary skills, and, especially, Christian counselling. 'I did my best', says Williams in his preface to the first edition, 'to read relevant books for the subject as I wrote, and such as were orthodox and sound ... But the book that I clung to chiefly was the Book of God.' The title-words of the work's fifth chapter, 'the Statute Book of Christ's Kingdom', echoed Matthew Henry's convictions in the Preface to his Bible commentary:

> That the holy scriptures were not only designed for our learning, but are the settled standing rule of our faith and practice, by which we must be governed now and judged shortly: it is not only a book of general use (so the writings of good and wise men may be), but it is of sovereign and commanding authority, the statute-book of God's kingdom, which our oath of allegiance to him, as our supreme Lord, binds us to the observance of.

Its authority derived from its author. Old Testament prophecies, types and shadows found counterpart and fulfilment in the New. This confirmed the reliability and authority of Scripture, the unity of God's Kingdom, and the centrality of Christ in God's purpose. Furthermore, Christ was King over the natural creation as well as over the realm of grace. From the furthest star in space to the minutest creature known to science, His rule was absolute and sustained. Williams buttresses his reasons for dwelling on Christ as King of creation with a quotation from James Hervey's *Meditations and Contemplations*: 'I would take every opportunity of inculcating, and celebrating the Divinity of the Redeemer; a truth that imparts an unutterable dignity to Christianity; a truth which lays a most immoveable foundation for all the comfortable hopes of a Christian; a truth which will render the mystery of our Redemption the wonder and delight of eternity; and with this truth everyone will observe, my affection is inseparably connected.'[4]

The work's headline texts, Colossians 3:11 and 1 Corinthians 15:25, speak of Christ's supremacy. The first of these speaks of the real unity between otherwise irreconcilable people when Christ is all to each as the only Saviour, and in all by union with Himself for their life together in the way of holiness. The second text, 'he must reign, till he hath put all enemies under his feet', proclaims ultimate victory and dominion. These were themes, sourced from the same texts, that several Puritan authors had latched on to and expounded; for example, Jeremiah Burroughs in his *Saint's Treasury* (1668), Thomas Watson in his *Plea for the Godly and other Sermons* (1672), Isaac Ambrose in his *Looking unto Jesus* (1658), and, more explicitly, Ralph Robinson in his

Christ ALL and in ALL (1660). Footnotes to the work name some of his sources: divines such as Thomas Goodwin, James Hervey, and William Derham; the philosopher and theologian William Whiston; and the scientists Christiaan Huygens, Isaac Newton, François Pourfour du Petit, and Anthony van Leeuwenhoek. Williams relied heavily on Derham, particularly, for his treatment of astronomy and natural phenomena.[5] For the sections of the work dealing with typology, Williams could draw on at least three books that he possessed: Samuel Mather's *Figures or Types of the Old Testament* (1705); William Guild's *Moses Unveiled; or, those figures which served unto the Patterne and Shadow of Heavenly Things* (1626); and Thomas Taylor's *Christ Revealed; or, the Old Testament explained. A treatise of the Types and Shadowes of our Saviour contained throughout the whole Scripture* (1635).[6] R. Stephens Jones has identified the influence of John Milton's *Paradise Lost* (1668) on some earlier sections of Williams's epic.[7] Similarities between the two works are recognizable, but it is also clear that Williams showed keen discernment in rejecting Milton's shortcomings in his beliefs regarding the Trinity and his Arminianism.

But the work was no theoretical treatise for the intellectually advantaged; it was intended to confirm society members in their faith in the deity of Christ's person, and the completeness of their salvation in Him. There was a danger that, as Harris had taken Christ's deity to the extreme of involving the Father in His passion and death, so on the other hand, the dignity of Christ's person, and the merit of His work could be devalued. This latter departure from orthodoxy 'made Christ far less than God's Scripture makes Him to be'. 'A View of Christ's Kingdom', then, was a considered and deliberate antidote to the doctrinal deviation and subjective excesses within the Methodist ranks of recent years. Williams was addressing a real need. His purpose was to teach and encourage as well as defend. Above all, it was written to convey the essential characteristics of Welsh Methodism. At its heart lay an implicit trust in the salvation that Christ wrought as a matter of sheer grace. This is grounded solely on God's revealed Word in which is found absolute truth and divine purpose for mankind. In that purpose God has appointed His Son to be all in all by virtue of His deity, uniqueness, finality and loveliness.

It may be useful to comment on certain points in the Preface to the first edition, so as to draw out Williams's implied intention and the source of his teaching:

> One purpose I had in mind to write this book about the extent of Christ's Kingdom and the excellence of His Person, the Messiah, was to exhort myself as well as others, to love the great Captain of our Salvation, and to reprove some of their public neglect of Christ, and others of their deliberate indifference about trusting in Him for the soul's justification ... It is a great pity that Holy Scripture, which is so full of Christ, is seldom opened and the Messiah preached ... Every part of the Old Testament is full of Gospel; and yet so little of this is in our head, much less in our hearts ... I did my best when writing the book to consult relevant works as I went along, especially those that were sound and orthodox ... But the Book that I clung to most was God's Book ... What effect this book will have, I do not know; but I do know, that it cost me a great deal of pain and time to produce it ... And that it may be a blessing through a deeper acquaintance with Christ crucified is the earnest desire of your unworthy servant. [8]

To achieve this aim, it was also necessary for Williams to address contemporary deviation from orthodoxy.

> God alone knows how great a number, who possess education and reason, but without grace to rule and guide the one or the other, who maintain that there is no revealed religion except what is found by nature planted in everyone, and able to bring them to heaven ... Again, how much better are those ... who deny the deity of our blessed Lord, the merit of His blood, and the efficacy of His death, and who assert that no more is necessary than to confirm his teaching, much like any other martyr?

The denial of the necessity for revealed religion was a leading feature of the Deism of the day. Deists maintained that human reason was adequate to achieve knowledge of God. Man's understanding of the created order at best could only bring about an acknowledgment of divine existence and power. In his own way Williams was demonstrating the limitations of scientific theory. It proceeds on the assumption that the only reality is material, mechanistic and measurable; and that natural cause and effect works within a closed system, whether chronologically or spatially. Such a discipline is possible only because there is a God-ordained order, which is material, measurable and real, and Williams was far from denying this. Indeed, in this work, he is at pains to demonstrate the marvels of creation: this is God's world, its diversity, profusion, and immensity reflect His infinite wisdom, and power. Even so, there is an element of mystery in the created universe. Thus, while the telescope and microscope reveal worlds otherwise hidden, they also imply

135

that vast areas of knowledge are yet to be discovered.

With this in mind, Williams's exploration of the created order was a demonstration of Christ's supremacy in every sphere. The Preface continues: 'If any ask, why I referred the work of Creation, Providence, and the Day of Judgment to the Second Person of the holy Trinity, I answer, even though they are reckoned to the blessed Father, as to their great purpose and initial decree, and all stemmed from His own scheme and to His glory, yet, in terms of fulfilling His will, He laid it on the God-man, Christ Jesus.' Williams insisted that there was another kind of reality, the dynamic, spiritual reality of the kingdom of heaven, which permeated the former, and at various points produced events that displayed an over-riding of the static order. Material existence is not adequate to explain the condition of one created originally in God's image. Human beings, even though flawed and corrupted by sin, are still different from other created beings because endowed with rational, moral and eternal faculties, and for this reason responsible and accountable. 'A View of Christ's Kingdom' was Williams's way of claiming Christ sovereignty in all God's dealings with a created world, recognizing its natural order and proclaiming God's remedy for its fallenness. It was divine revelation that proclaimed the remedy, and divine intervention in Christ that achieved it. Revelation was progressive but also true: the Old Testament's unfolding of God's dealings for man's salvation was true even though incomplete. God's providential control of human affairs did not exclude the supernatural element of miraculous intervention; and Christ's incarnation, atonement and resurrection, were historic events which involved that supernatural dimension. They had spiritual and eternal significance, beyond the reach of rational evaluation or explanation. 'The purpose of the 1756 epic', says Derec Llwyd Morgan, 'is to portray this magisterial purpose, to show it *in its completeness*. It was not enough to praise the Creator for his Creation, Williams maintained; the question must be asked, what is His purpose?' [9]

That purpose was one of redemption from sin, to which creation and providence were subservient, while Christ was supreme in each realm. In no area of Christian teaching was a clearer and correct presentation more necessary than in this of redemption. Any teaching that detracted from the excellence of Christ's Person and the efficacy of His atoning sacrifice, says the Preface, was to be vigorously resisted:

Besides these, there are others who are grossly mistaken in their estimate of Christ … they say that it is by the purpose or appointment of God the Father only, and not through any infinite value and intrinsic merit of the sufferings of the Son, that there is forgiveness of sin; otherwise, they say, the mercy of the Father is not exhibited … But no scheme of behaviour and purity will prove fruitful unless it stems from faith in Christ. This is what brings life to the soul, and makes for a beautiful and praiseworthy lifestyle, when it issues from a heart that knows Christ. This is what produces understanding and power, making for pure and heavenly objectives.

Here, Williams was affirming the orthodox position with regard to justification that it is by faith alone in Christ alone, rather than by obedience to a new commandment to believe. This was a direct repudiation of the teaching of the Puritan, Richard Baxter. As J. I. Packer noted, 'Where orthodox Calvinism taught that Christ satisfied the law in the sinner's place, Baxter held that Christ satisfied the Lawgiver and so procured a change in the law.' Consequently, in Baxter's view, faith 'is an act of compliance with the precepts of the Divine law now in force, the law of grace which commands all men everywhere to repent and promises an amnesty to those who do it.'[10] For Williams, this was to diminish the excellence, merit and majesty of Christ in another way, since it involved the element of human response in the act of justification. As he insisted in his Preface, forgiveness was by this scheme 'made contingent upon the purpose or appointment of the Father rather than upon the infinite value and intrinsic merit of the sufferings of the Son … Such thoughts of Christ fall far short of the demands of Holy Scripture.' They were also at variance with 'the old orthodox Divines in every age. Such doctrine does not agree with the Articles of the Church of England, with that Church's famous authors; with the [Westminister] Assembly's Catechism, or with the Puritan authors of 140 years ago.'

Similarly, he rejects the merit of human achievement, so dear to Moralists, as the ground of neutralizing the ravages of sin.

> Should all the heavenly seraphs each one take human form,
> Bear pain and dreadful anguish, go through death's awful storm;
> Too small, too short, too narrow, this payment won't atone
> For all the slight, dishonour, to God's pure justice done.
>
> God takes no heed of praying, God heeds no righteousness,
> No sacrifice or incense, no praise or alms impress;
> Nor conscientious effort, nor zeal or holy fast,
> Nor aught to pardon sinners; Christ's death alone will last.

Like lighting one small candle to supplement the sun,
Is adding man's weak merit to what our Lord has done;
For He the books of heaven has cleared by His blood,
Our righteousness is in Him, His Name the Son of God.[11]

All these human substitutes for God's plan of salvation in Christ denied
a miraculous, supernatural element; the one by excluding the need for
divine revelation, the other by making superfluous a divinely initiated
and completed redemption. One more issue is mentioned in the
Preface, the need to expose the false claims of Antinomianism: 'I
intend no part of this book to incline anyone to be feeble, sluggish and
careless about good living and behaviour, or in the matter of using all
the means of grace and ordinances of the Gospel; nor to deny that the
Law is still Mount Sinai's threatening to the ungodly, and for the godly
to discern their duties and failures.'

The sixth chapter, 'Christ's particular kingdom, or, Christ all in the
salvation of His saints', expands the classical Protestant view of
Christ's offices as prophet, priest and king. His word reveals perfectly
the Father's will; His offering up of Himself for His people's sins
makes full satisfaction; His reign reconciles, subdues, governs and
leads His people in triumph. His kingdom is an everlasting kingdom,
which at last He offers up triumphantly to His Father, so that God may
be all in all. Hence Williams's repetitive strain in the titles of the book's
chapters, 'CHRIST IS ALL'. The work was not only an original and
ambitious presentation of a noble theme, it was also definitive for the
new type of Christian emerging in Wales under the name of Calvinistic
Methodist. For this reason it deserves further consideration.

16.

'The King must reign'

For Williams both the nature and length of 'A View of Christ's Kingdom' was significant. In a sense he was nailing the Calvinistic Methodist colours to the mast, a task that deserved careful exposition and extensive treatment. Rowland was doing the same thing by preaching, but Williams was committing himself to the more permanent medium of print. The fruit of his labour would be consulted, studied, memorized even, by a future, as well as his own, generation. For this reason the work needed to crystallize the core beliefs of a Calvinistic Methodism that was soon to become a clearly defined feature of the Welsh religious landscape. Leading principles and firm convictions demanded identification, clarity and precision. Such considerations give enough reason to explore the work more thoroughly.

In the first chapter Williams sets out the ambitious aim of his work. It is to present the ineffable glory of Christ by way of a panoramic survey of His involvement in God's purpose, from before time to its end and beyond. It begins with this extended title:

> *The Kingdom given to Christ, or Christ as all in the Decree; where it is shown*, That the Father in eternity, before the creation of heaven or earth, set forth His own Son to be His pleasure and delight, decreed to clothe Him with human nature, so that in His bosom there might always be One bearing the express image of His Person; also to display His glory, give His name, The Word, ordaining Him head over heaven and earth, visible and invisible, when they would be created; and purposing to grant His Son (in whom He delighted) to create worlds, together with all creatures in and on them, and lastly man. In order to advance His own and His Son's glory, He created man subject to change, and suffered him to fall. Foreseeing man's fall, He appointed Christ the Saviour of mankind; making with Him a covenant to that end; He decreed to clothe Him with a body in order to make in His excellent Person (by His suffering, death, and burial) satisfaction to His righteousness, and a full recompense to the demands of His law; and by these means to receive the promises of grace, forgiveness, and life to believers; and decreeing that He should rule over every creature, and on

all the disposition of Providence; and by the same Decree (by the counsel of His will), either permitting or purposing all that happens, to display His glory, and to set out the attributes of the Godhead. He placed all this Decree to be fulfilled by Christ, and appointed Him to be the Judge of the living and the dead at the end of the world. [1]

Bearing in mind that the author was not yet forty years old, the work displays a substantial measure of pastoral wisdom to recognize real needs within the Methodist constituency, and of theological competence to meet them.

Williams's first concern is to emphasise the deity of Christ, a clear affirmation that the Methodist position in the controversy with Harris was the right one. In a closely-argued footnote Williams spells out the significance of the eternal generation of the Son. The doctrine was necessary for the Covenant of Redemption to be meaningful, to deny the Deists 'license to attempt an overthrow of the entire thrust of the New Testament' and to allow for Christ's appearances prior to the Incarnation. [2]

> Two natures in one Person, betrothed, mysterious now,
> Who afterwards death suffered upon Golgotha's brow;
> Insep'rably united, free ever from alloy,
> Such as no finite creature was destined to enjoy.

The first man, Adam, originally created in the image of God, brought upon himself God's displeasure by sinning, an event with universal, cosmic repercussions, but designed by God to exhibit the greatness of His grace, love, compassion and wisdom:

> He then did man's first parents determine to create,
> With power to hold their station, or choose from hence retreat;
> And these to fall permitting, that through their fall His grace
> Might be revealed in splendour among the human race.
>
> To this end it was purposed the Son one day should be
> A Saviour and Physician, th'apostate world to free;
> To Him assign a people from base and dark mankind,
> Who in His Name believing, life from the dead should find. [3]

Williams returned to man's predicament in sin in the third chapter when he dealt with the Gospel promise in the Garden of Eden after the fall of 'the seed of the woman' that should 'bruise the serpent's head' (Genesis 3:15).

The Second Part of Chapter One sets out 'The Covenant of Redemption between the Father and the Son in eternity; Ps. 40: 6-8; 89: 3-4, 28, 36. Isa. 49: 1, 6; 53: 10-12.' He is careful to designate it the Covenant of *Redemption* rather than the Covenant of *Grace*, since he is still referring to the contract made between Persons in the Trinity, rather than to the application of its benefits on the principle of grace to those for whom they were intended. Here Williams may have been preserving the classic Reformed view at a time when some popular writers were departing from it, Thomas Boston in Scotland and James Hervey in England among them. Jonathan Edwards had expressed his bewilderment at Boston's view on the matter, and John Macleod's comments on Edwards's misgivings are helpful: 'In saying this he might have in view the fact that Boston did not adopt the old and widely accepted way of distinguishing the Covenant of Redemption between the Father and the Son from the Covenant of Grace which is built upon it. It is by the Covenant of Grace in which Christ is Mediator that the believer comes into possession of the good things promised in and secured by the Covenant of Redemption.'[4] The place of covenantal concepts in Williams's theology is discussed in Chapter 31; for the purposes of this chapter their exposition in his 'View of Christ's Kingdom' only are noted.

The terms of the covenant between Father and Son decreed the perfect obedience of the Son to the demands of God's Law for His people, and also that He should suffer the demands of God's justice for their violation of that Law. In making such distinctions between the divine Persons, some may have concluded that Williams was dividing the Trinity. Two footnotes in this section correct this. The first appeals to the Puritan, Thomas Goodwin, in support of a belief in the two natures in Christ, while asserting His one divine Person. The other argues for distinctions within the Trinity while preserving the unity of the Godhead: 'It is good for us to believe that there is one God, all in all, who is involved in every aspect of His work, to whomsoever of the Persons in particular, that its realization is predicated. And in our approach to God, it is good for us to think of the Godhead; to whomsoever of the blessed Persons our worship is directed.'[5] Furthermore, the covenant was agreed before time, not on the basis of any foreseen virtue in the beneficiaries, but solely on account of God's gracious initiative:

No good that He saw in us, for such was found in none,
To give Him an incentive to have the covenant done;
But love, pure and exhaustless, a blaze in ardent flame,
To Adam's fallen offspring, who lost their pristine fame.

But one must death encounter, and one the debt repay,
The debtor thus exchanging, yet the whole debt defray;
Justice to this transaction is willing to agree,
The attribute celestial shall still in honour be.

This is the oath eternal, whereby the Father stood,
Bound willingly to grant Him the purchase of His blood;
And by this oath the Father on His own Son relied
To die for man's transgressions, while they His right denied. [6]

The covenant did not deal with uncertainties or contingencies: made between Father and Son its beneficiaries were specified in its terms. Those for whom the benefits were intended will surely partake of them. From such there will be humble expressions of amazement and endless praise.

The Third Part of Chapter one develops the theme of confidence in God's grace and power to realize in time all that the Covenant purposed in eternity: 'How all the circumstances of the Covenant had been completely arranged in the counsel of the Trinity, etc.'

The contract now concluded, confirmed and rendered strong,
All incidents and happenings that to it did belong;
From earliest creation until the Judgment Day,
Within that secret counsel the Trinity did lay.

God's control of human affairs, his Providence, works for His People's good, namely, the fulfilment in them and for them all that the Covenant decreed. God's people, therefore, will be brought safely through the vicissitudes of a sinful world, and in spite of their own failures, to the eternal paradise prepared for them.

Here there was sealed together in one gigantic roll,
All to the Church should happen, through time, from pole to pole;
Her sufferings without measure, her strong relentless foes,
And the consoling triumph the promise doth disclose.

Grace flowing like a torrent, forth from the Father's breast,
To plan man's rise from ruin, salvation free and blest;
His own Heir to abandon and nail upon the tree,
A place on high preparing for us beyond degree.

> And while they are admiring the depths which none can trace,
> And singing all the wonders of His redeeming grace;
> They yield exclusive honour, in one unbroken theme,
> To Him enthroned forever, and to the Lamb supreme. [7]

For Williams, even in a time of great trials, God's covenant cannot be broken, Christ's kingdom shall endure, and 'the gates of hell' shall not prevail against God's people.

The Second Chapter is one of the longest, with six parts. It sets out Christ's Lordship over Creation, that is, the physical universe at large as well as human beings upon planet earth. Williams summarizes the contents in this way:

> *Christ setting up His Kingdom, or all in Creation*: where it is shown, that the Messiah, having been ordained Head in this way, and the Saviour of the world, was now sent by God's power and His own to create heaven and earth and all that is in them. Firstly, *Chaos*, that is, matter; thereby drawing every element to its own sphere, bringing heat to the sun and shooting stars, making these and the planets dominant and powerful worlds; gathering the waters to the sea and the clouds; setting space around the earth and other planets, binding together the earth as one large globe, having gravity at its centre, and naming it Earth; filling this world, the sea, and air with all manner of creatures; and lastly, creating man as head over all in righteousness, holiness, and authority over the creatures; in his soul and body according to His own image. Heb. 1: 2, 10-13; Eph. 3: 8-10; Jn. 1:3; Col. 1:16, etc. [8]

Ranging from the marvels of astronomy to those of biology, from the use of telescopes to microscopes, the first five parts of the chapter are perhaps more remarkable for their footnotes than their verses. While scientific inquiry was in vogue at the time, it is easy to believe that to gather the information provided by Williams must have taken up a great deal of time. Immense distances between planets are noted, as are their size and orbits; the lengths of the world's mighty rivers are noted; sea creatures are described, from the largest to the smallest. As for the fish in the sea, the eggs of some have been counted: the carp is claimed to have 342,144, and an average-sized cod to have 9,314,000.

It is easy to be side-tracked from Williams's intention by such details, although a little puzzling to know how it would benefit the members in the Methodist societies. But there was a serious purpose: For Williams, Christ is the One by whom all were created and are sustained; nature's profusion and order reflect His omnipotence and sovereignty; all things are His servants; creation and providence are subservient to the purpose of grace. The dichotomy which many introduce between 'secular' and 'sacred' is an artificial one; Christ's Kingdom embraces all, its subjects relate to both, and His grace transforms people who live in space and time.

> My God, beyond my knowledge is all work of Thy hands,
> Unbounded admiration Thine universe demands;
> While I survey Thy wisdom, Thy mighty power and fame,
> I trust all my salvation to Thee and to Thy Name.
>
> My soul, see what a refuge unshaken He became,
> Amidst all things perplexing, my God's grace is the same;
> Here is my nest unruffled, and here my hiding-place,
> In trouble and in danger, there's shelter in His grace.
>
> He can from dust exalt thee, and from the miry clay,
> And cause ills that beset thee, advance thy heavenly way;
> Pour forth the oil of gladness continually on thine head,
> And bring thee through deep waters to pleasure's fountain-head.

This introduces the greatest mystery of all: how can the One who created and controls all things suffer death on a cross of shame to make atonement for rebellious man?

> O love without its equal, what condescending grace,
> That He who stars created, yet should earth's dust embrace;
> To die for Adam's children, who still defied the rod,
> And lived in bold rebellion against Almighty God.[9]

God is the Eternal 'I am', a Spirit without body or parts. Both Incarnation and Redemption are made possible only by the Second Person of the Trinity taking into Himself human as well as divine nature, without mixture, as proposed in the eternal counsel and decree. It remains an unfathomable mystery, compounded indeed by the elements of love, mercy and grace, when man's recovery from sin is proposed and realized. Christ's kingdom is not only mysterious, it is also amazing.

Part Five of the Second Chapter makes the claim that the variety and profusion of created things 'all show the wisdom of the Creator'. Having already spoken, almost in passing, of man's fallenness, another question might be raised: how then, was man created, and how is it that he finds himself now in this wretched condition? Williams's answer spans the Sixth Part of this chapter, and continues in Chapter Three. Man was created in innocence, the centrepiece of God's creation and living in harmony with it. Furthermore, his entire personality, reason, conscience, will, desire and affections were in harmony with God:

> A principle within him of God's most holy mind,
> The seed of the Law moral, all in his heart defined;
> And with good will performing, with bias to obey,
> To study and accomplish, and bend to his King's sway.

All this changed with man's fall into sin, a catastrophe so profound and far-reaching, that nothing could remedy except the death of Christ:

> True bliss for man was forfeit, all that in any wise
> Could serve for life and comfort to us below the skies;
> The day that brought forth treason, the day man did blaspheme,
> From his heart's freewill stemming, against high heaven's Supreme.
>
> He then became my surety, my judgment turned aside,
> The curse that I was under did in Himself subside;
> Restored to me each blessing, which I had lost below,
> And also hundred thousand in heaven I yet shall know. [10]

All this was part of God's unfolding purpose, and Williams leaves the reader in no doubt as to the costliness of that remedy or the certainty of its intended outcome. The Kingdom is in safe hands, for its foundation, its prosperity and its destiny.

This element of certainty comes to the fore in Chapters Four and Five; the one dealing with divine Providence in God's world, the other with divine promises in God's Word. The former guarantees an overseeing, over-ruling of all events to bring about the Kingdom's advance and triumph, the latter confirms the Kingdom's continuity and integrity. Of providence, Williams has this to say:

> Awake all my affections, and occupy your place,
> To love and view with wonder the heavenly Prince of grace;
> The Author of salvation for peace full ransom gave,
> And cares for all my welfare from womb to solemn grave.

Thy providence so boundless! So secret is Thy power!
That I am lost in wonder! I'm speechless in its store!
Foreseeing and arranging the hidden ways of man,
Though he can claim no talent, no gift or skill or plan.

Each morning some fresh reasons and evidence I find
Thy faithfulness to publish, Thy mercies free and kind;
For daily Thou art sealing Thy promises of good,
Those former truths fulfilling that were bestowed by blood.[11]

Throughout these sections Williams relies heavily on Scripture teaching, events and personalities. Providence is shown at work nationally and personally, as a hymn from his *Ffarwel Weledig* ('Farewell Visible Things'), testifies, translating the Welsh word 'rhagluniaeth' (providence) as 'power' in the first verse that follows:

There must be a mighty power,
Silently with thought and love,
Binding me, who knew it never,
To God's pillars, high above;
O great Wisdom,
Thou dost care for all the earth.

Lord, how strange Thy ways and wisdom!
Lord, how marvellous Thy might!
Nothing 'neath the starry heavens
Can withstand Thee or Thy light;
All creation,
Thus revolves at Thine own word.[12]

The section's heading gives two texts, the one from Hebrews 1:3 refers to the dignity of the Son who 'upholds all things by the Word of His power', and the other, Colossians 1: 17, says that 'He is before all things, and by Him all things consist'. God's active supervision of the animal kingdom, and His sovereign control of human affairs are affirmed, however contrary circumstances may sometimes appear. Here Williams echoes the conviction of the Puritan Stephen Charnock in his 'Discourse of Divine Providence': 'Fix not your eye only upon the sensible operations of providence [that is what the senses convey], but the ultimate end. As in a watch the various wheels have different motions, yet all subservient to one end, to tell the true hour of the day and the motion of the sun, so are all the providences of God.'[13] With

146

such convictions, the tyranny of accident, chance, fortune and fate are ruled out. Christ, to whom the affairs and kingdoms of this world are subject, reigns supreme.

The transition between Chapters Four and Five in the book is made in this way:

> In harmony with Scripture, on reading it with care,
> Clear prophecies appear, that are delivered there;
> All threats and every promise, each one shall surely stand,
> In providential order, as God's Son gives command. [14]

The facets of biblical Law are described, and Old Testament prophecies, types and figures are explained. This last aspect of bible teaching was clearly a favourite with Williams, being developed in over forty verses in this work alone. In the Second Part of his hymn collection *Hosanna i Fab Dafydd* ('Hosannah to the Son of David') of 1753 he had already shown 'Christ corresponding to [Old Testament] Shadows' in some forty verses of one of its hymns. Harris heard him preach at Llangeitho on 21 August 1764 and noted in his diary: 'Mr. William Williams preached on Zech [14:16], showing our Saviour anti-type of all the types. He opened of the Feast of Tabernacles, the greatest of their Feasts as this was kept eight days, the other but seven; this showing their having lived in tents, and their being strangers on earth; and that their God would come to dwell in a tabernacle of clay, etc.' Types, figures, shadows were to be related to their New Testament counterpart for the sole purpose of depicting Christ in the fullness of His attributes, offices and saving work, as Williams records in his 1789 elegy to Catherine Jones. Here, in 'A View of Christ's Kingdom', he summarizes it all:

> Thus through the types and shadows Christ Jesus might be seen,
> A Saviour and Physician for sinners all unclean;
> By faith on manna feeding in barren desert sore,
> On Jesus gazing always, the Tree of Life in store.[15]

Williams drew attention to them from the conviction that the believer draws supreme comfort from such exercises.

The fourth part of Chapter Five deals with Christ's Incarnation, the ultimate embodiment of God's revelation, of God's Last Word, of God's saving plan. In this way, by setting out 'The Statute-Book of Christ's Kingdom; or, Christ all in all in the Bible', as the chapter is called, Williams brings to a climax the sense of expectation that has been created in the reader:

> Whatever's been predicted since the world first began,
> Has been fulfilled, or will be, in Christ the Son of Man;
> His Person and His merit, His sufferings on the mount,
> Foretold in the First Test'ment, the Second has brought out.[16]

It is not only Providence that is subservient to Redemption; Revelation, too, announces the glories of the King.

The sixth and final chapter, with eight parts, is another long chapter, and bears the title, 'Christ's Special Kingdom, or, Christ All in the Saints' Salvation'. Against the backdrop of the woeful effects of sin, not the least of which is man's utter inability to save himself from his predicament, Christ alone is shown to be adequate and fitting for the task.

> Sin made a sad destruction, and made the world a prey,
> Confusion and contention in heaven and earth held sway;
> Since that first dreadful moment, when man from God withdrew,
> The earth full of transgression, no wholesome respite knew.
>
> Relentless is His justice, His fierce wrath is hurled,
> 'Tis hard to find a ransom for an apostate world;
> Full payment, if accepted, from imperfection free,
> Weight against weight and measure, full balance there must be.

He is a complete Saviour, and the work of salvation, from beginning to end, is entirely His. For the sinner while here below, He makes full compensation for sin, and, on condition of faith and repentance, confers upon him a divine righteousness.

> Upon thee, Lord, I henceforth would rest while here below
> Thy death alone is worthy, eternal God, I know;
> Stand surety for transgressions, and cleanse me with Thy blood,
> In presence of the angels, before my Father God.

Furthermore, the saint's faith is a divinely-planted principle of motivation and action which affects his whole being, and creates a new orientation to God. This is nothing less than the setting up of Christ's kingdom in the heart, so that Part Three has the title 'Christ reigning within his people; or all things in holiness'.

> Lord, of Thy golden sceptre at length I fain would sing,
> To which all true believers their willing tribute bring;
> Within the heart that kingdom, its tumult to subdue,
> And transform the affections, creating them anew.[17]

The verses that follow make it clear that those faculties of the soul disrupted at the Fall have now been renewed. Consequently, the understanding is enlightened, the stubborn will is made pliable to God's pleasure, the conscience's sensitivity to what is true and right is restored, the memory alerted to heavenly values, and the emotions given stability and a new direction. While the believer remains in a world of sin, and the remnants of his sinful nature continue to hinder his progress, the soul is brought into a state of greater blessing than Adam even in his innocence:

> To bring us into favour, far higher in degree
> Than what was lost in Adam, when ruined at the Tree;
> On safer ground and bottom, conditions gracious, new,
> Excelling all in glory, duration and review. [18]

For the saint on his way to the glory prepared in heaven, Christ pleads at God's throne, He sanctifies and instructs the soul, and is Himself the believer's chief joy and delight:

> To see Thy face, Beloved, makes my poor soul rejoice,
> O'er all I've ever tasted, or ever made my choice;
> When they all disappear, why should I grieve or pine
> While to my gaze there opens the sight that Christ is mine? [19]

Finally, Christ, as Judge of the living and the dead, will declare the eternal destiny of each one, will present His Church to His Father, and in His Kingdom there will be everlasting bliss.

> And then will Christ the Shepherd unto His Father God
> Present a host unnumbered, He purchased with His blood;
> A bride fair and attractive, bright shining as the dawn,
> That followed the true footsteps of her great King alone.
> Lord, grant a faith unshaken that such pure bliss in store
> Will be my soul's possession, when time shall be no more;
> This would my meditation in heavenly things delight
> And kindle my affections, to blazing, pure light.[20]

With this, Williams's panoramic survey of the Kingdom was finished. There is ample matter for meditation, amazement, faith and enjoyment. Objective truth and subjective experience are involved; nature and grace are displayed to full view; and sin's devastation and God's provision are examined. But over all, and through all, and above all, God's eternal purpose in Christ is magnificently portrayed: the majesty of His person, the appropriateness of His offices, the sufficiency of His sacrifice, the victory of His kingdom.

It was, for the beleaguered Welsh Methodists a spiritual tonic, a salutary reminder of their evangelical legacy, and a fillip for renewed endeavour. Howel Harris maintained that it was this work by Williams that confirmed the Welsh Methodists in the deity of Christ.[21] It may well have served to settle Harris's own views, and consequently it may have contributed to the healing of the breach in their midst at the turn of the 1760s. Certainly the depth of its presentation of Christ's person and work was impressive. It was no less breathtaking in its breadth, ranging as it did from eternity to eternity. By its occasional, sublime transport of the reader's mind to dwell on the treasures of God's wisdom and grace it could not fail to impress even the youngest among the Methodist converts. In terms of preserving 'a celestial flame' in their midst, it would be hard to think of a more timely and useful contribution.

17.

'Sound and sweet
and heart-searching'

Listening to sermons, attending society meetings, and singing hymns seems to have been the staple diet of the Welsh Methodists in the 1750s. In spite of difficulties within and dangers without, these means of grace were evidently not in short supply. Nor was Williams idle, and the flow of hymns from his pen was unabated. Two new collections, particularly, appeared during the period with the same title, one of Welsh and the other of English hymns. The Welsh *Hosanna i Fab Dafydd* ('Hosannah to the Son of David') appeared in three parts, the first in 1751, the second in 1753, and the third in 1754, with a total of 109 hymns. Another small collection, with 16 hymns appeared in 1757, with the title *Rhai Hymnau a Chaniadau* ('Some Hymns and Songs'), with an announcement that he would issue in one book most of his hymns, which 'would sound out Christ and His free Gospel as blood running through all their veins; and man, his intellect, his strength and enlightenment as nothing.'

The English *Hosannah to the Son of David; or, Hymns of Praise to God. For our Glorious Redemption by Christ* was published in 1759, with 48 hymns. Williams acknowledged regarding the latter, that some few were 'translations from the Welsh Hymn-Book, but mostly composed on new Subjects.' They included, 'The Cross'; 'Love Unspeakable'; 'God Alone'; 'The World a Desert'; 'Breathing after God'; 'Jesus All in All'; 'Contentment'; and 'Death'. Some show objectivity in their teaching, while others relate experience in a subjective way. They were written at a difficult time, but personal ardour was not lacking:

> O! would He raise my feeble soul
> To a celestial flame.
> I would for Jesus either do,
> Or suffer all the same.

> 'Tis Thou I seek, Thou canst fulfil
> My infinite desire;
> Inflame my gloomy heart anew
> With Thy celestial fire.

Throughout there is breadth to their doctrinal expression and depth in their personal intensity. One that combines these two elements has the title, 'A Prayer for Grace':

> Come, Holy Spirit, now descend,
> And shower from above,
> Upon my dry and wither'd soul,
> Thy everlasting love.
>
> Reveal Thy glories and Thy grace,
> The beauties of Thy name;
> Remove my sin, that heavy load
> Of painful guilt and shame.
>
> Allure my soul above the world,
> Where vanities abound;
> And, lull'd secure upon Thy breast,
> May I be ever found.
>
> Taught to be wise above the wiles
> Of the malicious foe,
> And trample on his secret snares,
> Wherever I may go.
>
> Thou, God, alone canst make me strong,
> Thy Word can faith convey;
> When with Thy strength I am endued
> I'll never more dismay.[1]

These were personal sentiments, certainly, but the longing for widespread effects was no less intense on that account. In his grief at the possibility that God's favour would be withdrawn, Williams was fulfilling a representative as well as an exemplary role. The preservation in their midst of 'a celestial flame' was a priority.

As well as preserving the revival's fruit from decay the Welsh leaders applied themselves to combating error. Early society reports define a person's spiritual state in terms of relationship to the Law of God. Some remained for a time 'under the Law', others were said to 'enjoy full liberty', and of the latter it could be added that 'these are justified and walk in love and zeal'.[2] Those 'under the Law' still considered that they could obey God's Law sufficiently to be right and acceptable in God's sight. Others, realizing their failure to keep the Law, but accepting by faith Christ's perfect obedience and satisfaction in their place, now enjoyed the peace of acquittal from the guilt and penalty of sin. Such faith was perceived not as an isolated act, but as the first acting of a new principle in the soul. This unites with Christ and sustains communion with Him in personal devotion to His Person and practical, loving obedience to His law. Evidence of its influence in the sinner's life, therefore, was to be expected. In order to distinguish things that differ in this area, Harris reported in May 1743 to Whitefield a decision of the Welsh Association: 'We have given Mr. Erskine's *Law-Death and Gospel Life* to be translated into Welsh against our next Association. We thought it would be of universal use to all the lambs with us, as it is very sound and sweet and heart-searching, and would be received by all.' This referred to the sermons on Galatians 2:19 originally preached by Ralph Erskine in 1724 and later published with the full title *Law-death, Gospel-life: or the Death of Legal Righteousness, the Life of Gospel Holiness.*[3] Such a decision would not have been made without careful reading and unqualified commendation by the leaders. The work, translated by John Morgan, a Welsh exhorter and printer, duly appeared under the title *Traethawd am Farw i'r Ddeddf, a Byw i Dduw*, with six hymns by Daniel Rowland at its close.[4]

The Erskine brothers, Ebenezer and Ralph, were Scottish Presbyterian ministers concerned about theological and ecclesiastical trends within the Church during the early 1730s. Together with a few others they seceded from the Church of Scotland to form an 'Associate Presbytery' which, within a decade, had consolidated its position as a separate ecclesiastical body by numerical growth and formal constitution. In 1739 they rejoiced in Whitefield's labours, and by 1744 their sermons were being read by and shared among the Welsh Methodists. Sadly, their initial acceptance of Whitefield's ministry ended in a breach over the issue of church government, and they became critical of the revival, especially at Cambuslang near Glasgow. Their appeal for men like Williams lay in the 'experimental' and 'practical' nature of their sermons, and in the case of Ralph, of his 'sonnets' as well. An indication of their popularity is the fact that between 1743 and 1792 at least ten of their titles were translated into Welsh. Writing to their relative, James Erskine, early in 1745, Harris could say that he set 'a great value on Mr. Erskine's second volume of Sermons and their Gospel Sonnets.' He had requested three copies each of the two volumes and had sent one set to Griffith Jones. One of the exhorters, Thomas Bowen, preferred the second volume, and ordered five copies, while ordering one copy of the first. Williams possessed several editions of their works, from Ralph's Sonnets of 1734 and their joint *Collection of Sermons on Several Subjects* of 1738, to the two volumes of Ralph's Sermons issued in 1764 and 1765.[5]

The title of *Law-Death* is amplified in the Welsh translation to 'A Treatise of Dying to the Law, and Living to God; wherein is set out at length the way in which the Holy Spirit brings the soul from the Covenant of Works to the Covenant of Grace, from the self to Christ.' The reason for its appearance is given in a 'Preface to the Reader': 'the darkness and total ignorance which has blinded the eyes of the vast majority of the earth's inhabitants to the weighty truths contained in the following Treatise, together with the success and blessing that the Lord saw fit to convey to many precious souls in England and Wales, are what constrained me to send it to you, the monoglot Welsh, in your own language.' The doctrine drawn from the sermon's text was simply this, 'That to be dead to the Law, in the point of our justification, is necessary in order to our living unto God, in point of sanctification.'[6] Observations from another sermon by Ralph Erskine, on Haggai 2: 19, highlight the issues which were of concern to the Welsh Methodists at the time: 'You, believers, are delivered from the law as a covenant; and therefore there is none in the world so much obliged as you are to make use of the law as a rule ... But, besides the *precepts* of the law in the hand of a Mediator, there are the *examples* of the saints in Scripture that belong to this square and line for the building, especially the example of the King of saints, Christ Jesus.'[7] Erskine was merely distinguishing things that differ, providing a clear explanation of the relationship between the Law and the Gospel. The Welsh Methodists used it for this reason. It made clear that unbelievers vainly rely on their obedience to the Law to compensate for their transgressions, but the Law does the opposite with the dire consequences of condemnation and penalty. Its demands are too exact, and the sinner's ability too vitiated by sin. Believers, on the other hand, rely solely on Christ's obedience and death in their place, and find acceptance and peace with God. Submission to God's Law follows true believing, as an expression of love and gratitude for acquittal, and of the desire for godliness.

Clarity on the issue was important for the Welsh Methodists, faced with the bare morality urged on unregenerate congregations by some of the contemporary clergy. Such exhortations also played down the purity and spirituality of God's commandments. Preaching the rigours of the Law was not legalism or morality, but necessary to drive home to sinners the gravity and helplessness of their condition. 'As the needle goes before, and draws the thread which sews the cloth; so the needle of the Law goes before, and makes way for the grace of the Gospel, that it may follow after, and take place in the heart.'[8] Unbelievers are all too prone to place their confidence in their own ability, and for such the Law was both taskmaster and tutor to lead to Christ, a point which Ralph Erskine brings out in his Sonnets:

> When by the Law to grace I'm schooled,
> Grace by the Law will have me ruled;
> Hence, if I don't the Law obey,
> I cannot keep the Gospel way.
>
> When I the Gospel news believe,
> Obedience to the Law I give;
> And that both in its fed'ral dress,
> And as a rule of holiness.
>
> The Law is holy, just, and good,
> All this the Gospel seals with Blood;
> And clears the Royal Law's just dues
> With dearly purchased revenues.
>
> Here join the Law and Gospel hands,
> What this me teaches, that commands;
> What virtuous forms the Gospel please,
> The same the Law doth authorize.
>
> A rigid master was the Law,
> Demanding bricks, denying straw;
> But when the Gospel-tongue it sings,
> It bids me fly, and gives me wings.[9]

Once brought to Christ, the sinner's relationship to the Law is changed. No longer under its demands or sanctions with a view to gain God's approval and censure, it is now the revealer and guide for the believer's spontaneous response of delight and pleasure.

> The commands of the Law, in the hand of Christ, have lost their old
> Covenant form, and are full of love. The command of the Law of works
> is, 'Do and live'; but in the hands of Christ, it is 'Live, and do' ... O
> when the believer wins to see by faith, that he hath nothing to do with
> the Law as a Covenant, this makes him delight in the Law of God as a
> rule of holiness; when he sees that he hath not a farthing of debt to pay,
> either to the precept, or threatening of the Law as a Covenant, because
> that debt was paid by Christ's obedience to the death, this makes him
> find himself under the most grateful obligations to serve the Lord, in
> obedience to his Law as a rule.[10]

In this way the leaders were able to fortify the societies against such
subtle deviation from orthodoxy, a kind of 'Antinomianism', which
denied to the Law any function whatsoever in the Christian life.

Within a year of the appearance of the Welsh publication the
Association was compelled to expel someone for Antinomianism:

> After talking a long time with William Rees about some Antinomian
> errors that he is fallen into, and offered to let him stay among us
> notwithstanding if he would promise not to disturb us and the lambs by
> propagating his errors, and when he would not promise this, but said
> (though he owns he has wanderings in prayer etc.) and has not sinned
> several days, etc, and that he has no sin in his understanding, will or
> conscience etc., we agreed that it is our duty to turn him out of the
> bands and society, and to warn all the society against his errors, and to
> have no close fellowship with him; so we solemnly (after a long debate
> and prayer together) turned him out, and had our hearts broken with
> love to him, and concern for the glory of God, with holy fear and
> concern for the lambs. [11]

Early in 1745 Harris in London was concerned about 'universal love'
between the Methodist factions and others, but also about 'how
imperceptibly our dear brethren fell into the many errors of
Antinomianism.'[12] Nor was its poison confined to Britain. Whitefield in
America echoed the concern of the Welsh Methodists: 'Antinomianism,
I find, begins to show its head and stalk abroad; may the glorious
Redeemer cause it to hide its head again, and prevent his children's
spirits being embittered against each other. I am glad to hear the Welsh
brethren continue steady; and that amongst our English friends,
Antinomianism seems only to be speculative; this is a great evil, but not
so great as when it affects the practice, and leads the people of God
unwarily into licentiousness.'[13] In a long letter to Whitefield, Harris

complained that 'the devil attempted to bring in his Antinomian poison to Wales.' His opposition to it, however, was misunderstood: 'being in England called a Legalist because I endeavoured to stop Antinomianism and in Wales called Antinomian and Moravian because I endeavoured to preach that blood which is so precious to my soul.'[14]

The issue was a difficult one, and would not easily go away. Williams was criticized by Harris in 1747 as being 'legalistic and deficient in doctrine, with a veil over his eyes. But on seeing the Lord with him, and himself so simple, I was made thankful for all the gifts given to each of us.' A few weeks later Williams was preaching on 'the foolish virgins' at an Association, and again Harris charged Williams with legalism, adding that 'Williams's Gospel zeal and purity had declined'. In turn, the leaders complained that Harris was tainted with Antinomianism, towards which the Moravians such as John Cennick were leaning. The term may have been a convenient pejorative with which to blacken the theologically ambivalent Harris. However, when he later defended one of the exhorters, James Beaumont, against censure by the other leaders for the same error, the Methodist leaders had no choice but to separate from them.[15]

As a result, towards the end of 1749 the Methodists were preparing a pamphlet to publicize their orthodoxy with the title, *Ymddiddan rhwng Methodist ac Antinomiad* ('Conversation between a Methodist and an Antinomian'). This duly appeared in print, with its rejection of the Antinomian charge of legalism against those who maintained that the precepts of the Law were determinative for Christian behaviour. Methodists deplored the tendency of Antinomianism to turn liberty into license, and charged them with pride for their rejection of clear biblical teaching. With the appearance of Williams's *Theomemphus* in 1764, its danger was exposed in the person of 'Jezebel', and its character defined as 'a life contrary to the Gospel of God, and a buttressing of beliefs which support such corrupt and immoral behaviour.'[16] Another publication that provided personal testimony to the dangers of Antinomianism and gave expression to the orthodox position, appeared years later, in 1767. This was a translation into Welsh of the spiritual autobiography of the hymn-writer, Joseph Hart, under the title *Pererindod: sef hanes y Parchedig Mr. J. Hart* ('Pilgrimage: namely, the story of the Reverend Mr. J. Hart'). It was re-issued by William Williams in 1774 with a revised title, *Antinomiaeth, Bwbach y Rhan Ffurfiol o'r Eglwys Grist'nogol* ('Antinomianism, the Bogey of the Formal Branch of the Christian Church'). Hart recognized the difficulties which Antinomianism presented: 'Pharisaic zeal and Antinomian security, are the two engines of Satan, with which he grinds the Church in all ages, as betwixt the upper and the nether millstone. The space between them is much narrower and harder to find, than most men imagine. 'Tis a path which the vulture's eye hath not seen, and none can show it us but the Holy Ghost.' Among the 'observations' that Hart drew from God's dealings with his own soul were the following:

> ... That the blood of the Redeemer applied to the soul by His Spirit, is the one thing needful ... that self-righteousness and legal holiness rather keep the soul *from*, that draw it to Christ ... that the will of God is the only standard of right and good ... that faith and holiness, with every other blessing, are the purchase of the Redeemer's blood ... that mere doctrine, though ever so sound, will not alter the heart; consequently that to turn from one set of tenets to another, is not Christian conversion; that as much as Lazarus coming out of his grave, and feeling himself restored to life, differed from those who only saw the miracle, or believed the fact when told them; so great is the difference between a soul's real coming out of himself and having a righteousness of Christ imputed to him by the precious faith of God's elect, and a man's bare believing the doctrine of imputed righteousness because he sees it contained in Scripture, or assenting to the truth of it when proposed to his understanding by others. [17]

At the end of the book Williams gives the following reason for the title of his re-issue:

> That many think that Antinomianism is a system that places too much on Christ and too little on man; whereas doctrinal Antinomianism holds that what the Son of God did on the cross is sufficient; those are saved who believe in that, apart from any need for his blessed Spirit to enlighten, comfort, guide, and fully apply salvation to the souls of believers. But in practical Antinomianism, a man believes with his mind all the doctrines of the faith, but has not received Christ's Spirit to renew the spirit of his mind. He lives, like others in the world, to his own lusts and pleasures. Although he confesses Christ to be all with his tongue, he lives after the fashion of this world, and the spirit that works in the children of darkness.

Another book in Williams's library, Anthony Burgess's *Vindiciae Legis*, deals with the issue in some depth, and then urges: 'Let the use then of this be, by way of admonition, that instead of disputing about or against the Law, that we would pray to have the savoury benefit and fruit of it in our souls. Urge God with that promise of writing His Law in our heart. Be thou so far from being an Antinomian, that thou hast thy heart and life full of this holy Law of God; not that the matter of the Law can be the ground of thy justification, but yet it is thy sanctification. What is regeneration, but the writing of the moral law in thy heart? This is that image of God, which Adam was created in. Oh, therefore that we could see more of this holy Law in the hearts and lives of men, that the Law of God might be in men's minds enlightening them, their wills and affections inflaming, and kindling of them.'[18] The words might well have been written by a Welsh Calvinistic Methodist, even by Williams himself.

Closely related to the place of Law in the Christian life was the matter of personal assurance of salvation. Did believing involve more than mental assent to Gospel declarations, and was assurance dependent on erratic feelings and experiences? On the one hand, at a time of great spiritual excitement, emotions were stirred and experiences were as powerful as they were varied. On the other hand there were dangers from relying on a knowledge of the truth while either denying or avoiding its power. Williams discerned this danger in what came to be known as Sandemanianism, after the followers of the Scotsmen, Robert Sandeman and his father-in-law, John Glas. They asserted that faith consisted in a mental assent and acceptance of the Apostolic reports of New Testament events and their significance. In 1760 one of the exhorters, John Popkin, was spreading Sandemanian ideas among the societies. [19] It will be readily perceived that such teaching ran clean counter to the position advocated by Williams and his fellow Methodists, for whom the whole personality was involved in any saving appropriation of Christ's person and work. With this in mind he translated into Welsh a work by Ralph Erskine's brother, Ebenezer, *The Assurance of Faith*. It appeared in 1759 under the title *Siccrwydd Ffydd*, and a second edition was called for in the following year. Its appearance was timely, since it set out the nature of true faith and exposed the dangers of responding in a superficial way to the Gospel. In the great spiritual upheaval that radiated from Llangeitho in 1762, it was also necessary.

That these issues pained the Welsh Methodists is clear from contemporary records. David Jones of Derlwyn had been associated in some way with Rowland, but he too, was expelled from the Methodist ranks for holding Sandemanian tenets. References to this danger appear in several of Williams's works. In a short poetical fragment, 'Gwerthfawrogrwydd Y Bibl' ('An Appreciation of the Bible'), Williams holds that Scripture is the only arbiter of truth, and here the teaching of Sandeman fails miserably:

> He would have you disown feeling,
> Every heavenly breeze of grace;
> And instead hold cold assenting,
> Like the devil, in its place.

> Scripture is the book I treasure,
> Not another can compare;
> This the testimony of Jesus,
> God's Book, making His way bare;
> Sure guide to heaven's glory,
> Lamp to pilgrim's feet, and more –
> Fiery pillar for God's people
> From this world to heaven's shore.

Furthermore, its tenets are said to be as far from 'Pentecost, the baptism of the Spirit and of fire, as Lapland is from Guinea', with 'no room for repentance, or trust, or love.' Sandeman is called 'an idle man from Scotland', driven by 'jealousy from head to foot' to 'drag his lame doctrines across the Tweed'.[20] The evil of jealousy is taken up in one of Williams's prose works as the 'crocodile' in *Crocodil, Afon yr Aipht* ('The Crocodile of Egypt's River'), but in his address 'to the reader' Williams acknowledges that this evil is not confined to Sandeman, even though his poisonous ideas are among the greatest enemies of the Gospel. In one of his elegies, heaven is a 'quiet and safe refuge from the world's clamour, and from the tumult of Satan and Sandeman'.[21]

As an 'advertisement' in the hymn collection *Môr o Wydr* ('Sea of Glass') 1764, Williams regrets that 300 copies of the second edition of *Siccrwydd Ffydd* ('Assurance of Faith') remained unsold, since they were,

> The best books printed in Welsh for these times, when some regard believing as feeling pleasant and happy breezes in God's service, so that when they have lost these, nothing remains but to seek them again, or else suffer under the power of unbelief; and others, who would assert that faith is a bare belief of the words of the Bible, and make of it a dry, dead, sterile, insipid, impotent thing, differing only slightly, if at all, from the devil's believing. Hymenaeus, Philetus, and Alexander the

coppersmith [who troubled the early Church and Paul, 2 Tim. 2: 17; 4:14], brought forth in Scotland, now try and settle in Wales, seeking to draw people away from that experimental faith, which is the mother of all good fruit and virtuous living, to the vain talk and disputable questions of those who undermine faith rather than edify it.

By way of introduction to the book, Williams addresses 'the Reader':

For anyone who has read the many pieces of the author's other works in English, his name alone is a sufficient letter of commendation for this Sermon ... But as The Song of Solomon is also called The Song of Songs since it excels the 1005 songs of his work; even so it could be said of this Author that this Sermon is the most excellent of his work. Here faith is displayed with mid-day brilliance; the difference between it and feeling; its foundations outside of man himself in God, in His Word, His promise, and His covenant; and the confidence that the worst, the blackest, the weakest in grace, yes, those previously without grace, to approach the throne of grace believing; the difference between the confidence of faith and the confidence of presumption; between weak faith and strong faith; man's obligation to use every means to believe, together with many other most important truths for practical religion, are also clearly explained here. From what I know of all the churches in Wales they stand in need of the light that is here set out.

As a means of teaching the true nature of personal faith, assurance and godliness, Williams evidently considered this work to be unsurpassed.

One of the chief Methodist characteristics was that of pressing on for a deeper acquaintance with God, a more intense enjoyment of His love, and closer conformity to His image. In a remarkable manner, this work of Ebenezer Erskine did just that, and it was Williams who provided the Welsh Methodist constituency with it in its Welsh dress, making it accessible to a far wider readership. Herein lay truths that would correct, encourage, build up and challenge the young converts in the societies to prove God's grace in profusion. 'By the assurance of faith', says Erskine, 'Abraham believed that he should have a son in his old age, because God who cannot lie had promised; but by the assurance of sense, he believed it when he got him in his arms ... Faith asserts its interests in a future good, because promised; sense asserts its interest in a present good, because possessed ... By faith I believe my salvation because it is purchased, promised and possessed by my glorious head Christ Jesus; but by sense I believe my salvation, because I find this salvation already begun in a work of regeneration, and advancing in a work of sanctification.' Erskine admitted that the exercise of faith shows fluctuation: 'the faith of every believer is not of the same size and strength. Some have a strong, and others have a weak faith; yea, the faith of the strongest believer, like the moon, has its waxings and wanings; or, like the sea, its ebbings and flowings.' Finally, for Erskine the faithfulness and power of God to keep His promise are the strongest possible grounds for the believer's assurance.[22] Erskine's Welsh translator had no hesitation in subscribing to such sentiments.

At a time of much religious turbulence, Williams not only safeguarded the Methodists from doctrinal deviation and moral disaster, he also held before them the rich inheritance available in Christ to all believers. His was a ministry of edification as well as of consolidation. It, too, was 'sound, and sweet, and heart-searching.'

18.

'Rude and rustic idols'

During the 1750s five children were born to William and Mary Williams, one of the girls dying within a fortnight of her birth. It would have been a period of trauma, adjustment and hard work. In addition to family commitments, there were the two farms, Pantycelyn and Cefn-coed, to be managed, buildings to be repaired, crops to be sown and harvested, and the farm animals to be tended. With Welsh as their first language, the boys were tutored at home during their early years to provide them with a basic knowledge of English, Latin and Greek. Their father's substantial library was freely available to them, and a measure of oversight and discipline as to their reading secured for them a solid foundation for further education. Williams's own literary output continued to grow. During that decade he saw through the press a three-part collection of Welsh hymns, 'Hosanna to the Son of David', the long poem, 'View of Christ's Kingdom', a third printing of the *Aleluia*, his English *Hosannah to the Son of David*, and his translation into Welsh of Ebenezer Erskine's *Assurance of Faith*. In addition to all this activity must be reckoned his sustained labours along with Rowland among the Methodists.

It was also a period when the Welsh Methodists must have been painfully aware that God's work has its times of ebb as well as flow. The Gospel seed was still being sown, but for that decade the harvest seemed poor in comparison to what they had known hitherto. It was towards the end of this period, when God's hand seemed withdrawn in some measure, that Williams's least enduring work was written. He was constrained to address what seemed to him to be gross ignorance among the Welsh Methodists in the matter of recognizing Gospel uniqueness and superiority. He did so by way of a publication that appeared in seven parts over a period of eighteen years, 1762-79. It had a long title: *Pantheologia: Sef Hanes Holl Grefyddau'r Byd; sef y Grefydd Baganaidd, y Fahometanaidd, yr Iuddewig, a'r Grist'nogol; yr hon sydd yn cynnwys y tair canghen, Eglwys Rufain, Eglwys Groeg, yr Eglwys Brotestanaidd, ynghyd ag amryw sectau ymhob un o'r rhain ...wedi eu tynnu allan o'r awdwyr diweddaraf, goreu, a chywiraf,*

('Pantheologia: or A History of all the Religions of the World; namely the Pagan Religion, Islam, Judaism, and Christian, which comprises the three branches, the Church of Rome, the Greek [Orthodox] Church, the Protestant Church, together with several sects in each of these ... drawn from the most recent, the best and most accurate authors').[1]

A work of such detail could hardly have been written on the spur of the moment. It would have involved a major investment in terms of obtaining books, study and writing before its appearance in printed form. Both the idea and the early chapters at least would have occupied Williams's time and energy during the relatively dormant period before the 1762 Revival. Having committed himself to its publication, he had to persevere even though the revival's surge of spiritual activity claimed priority. It must have been difficult both for him and his readers to sustain interest in matters of remote historical and theological fact while they were in the cauldron of a mighty work of God's Holy Spirit.

The title indicates that Williams intended writing a history of religion in its various forms throughout the world. The scope of his 'history' however, strangely omits a section dealing with his own country, coming to an abrupt end with the date 1594 and the establishment of the Church of Scotland. Reference to two Welsh Protestant martyrs, Robert Ferrar and Rawlins White, occurs in the general narrative dealing with the Reformation in England. This suggests that Williams did not consider it necessary to draw attention to a separate Welsh identity. In their Protestantism Welsh conformity and nonconformity had too much in common with their English counterparts to require distinctive treatment. It is more than likely that the diminishing level of interest in his project is the reason for what appears to be a premature ending. In the last year of his life he wrote *A Serious Address* to appeal for funds 'to carry on Welsh Charity Schools' on the same pattern as those of Griffith Jones. It contained a summary history of the Welsh Bible, and a passionate plea to secure greater literacy among the people of Wales. 'Shall a country, privileged with more preaching than England, considering its extent, suffer such indolence?' Wales was a separate country, and the Welsh deserved *distinct* recognition.[2] It may also be true that his perception of his Welsh readers' capacity for information was too high, and that his presentation of the superiority of Christianity was too demanding.

Williams begins by noting that reading the Old and New Testaments raises questions of interest about the culture and customs of biblical lands. While such information may be desirable and helpful, he is quick to qualify this by adding that 'the Spirit of Almighty God alone, and nothing else, can open His Word, and apply it to the heart ... Christianity in man's head is the same as paganism.' In spite of this, Williams proceeded with his detailed investigations, and produced a compendium of comparative religion of substantial proportions. Jonathan Edwards had a similar fascination with the subject, and George H. Marsden says that he 'gathered all the information he could about them.' He adds that much of Edwards's concern 'was to answer the Deist challenge to the particularity of Christianity', and in spite of there being 'remnants of earlier revelations' in them, 'he viewed other religions, such as Islam, as false and pernicious.'[3] Williams, always conscious of the Deists' reliance on the adequacy of reason, aimed at the same rebuttal of the Deist position, and shared the same conclusions with regard to religions other than Christianity.

Paganism, Islam, Judaism and Christianity were considered at the time the four chief rivals for men's religious affiliation. Consequently, the book is divided into four parts, dealing with each in turn. The section on paganism takes in the religious practices of Africa, America and Asia. The final section on Christianity exposes the errors of Roman Catholicism and the Eastern Orthodox Church before closing with an account of the emergence and principles of Protestantism. Over the previous century interest in travel books, dictionaries and religion had produced several volumes in English, and Williams used some of these in translation for his particular purpose among the Welsh Methodists.

As for his sources, Williams writes in the Preface: 'in tracing the origins of Paganism, I have drawn from several of the best authors I could lay my hands on ... Again, to describe Islam, I did my utmost to be fair ... For Judaism I relied on the best books I could get: Dr Prideaux's History, and Dr Watts's abridgement of it were a great help; for the inter-testamental period I had to depend on Josephus ... for the Protestant Reformation I had several honest and godly men to guide me, Clark, Fox, Millar, Bonnet, Knox, and others.' There is some evidence of his use of a book by Thomas Salmon, *Modern history: or, the present state of all nations. Describing their respective situations, persons, habits, ... animals and minerals*, published in three massive volumes in London in 1739. Among the other authors mentioned by Williams are: Bartolomé de las Casas's *The Spanish colonie, or Briefe chronicle of the acts and gestes of the Spaniardes in the West Indies, called the newe world, for the space of xl. yeeres: written in the Castilian tongue by the reuerend Bishop Bartholomew de las Cases or*

Casaus, a friar of the order of S. Dominicke. And nowe first translated into English, by M.M.S.; Thomas Hariot's *A briefe and true report of the new found land of Virginia*; John Harris's *Navigantium atque itinerantium bibliotheca. Or, a complete collection of voyages and travels*; and William Bosman, *A New and Accurate Description of the Coast of Guinea.* [4] It was not his intention that the book should be regarded as an original work, and Harris, writing at the end of 1762 confirms this: 'Seeing Mr. W. Williams's translation of all the religions of the world to Welsh. I blessed God for sending so much knowledge of the poor blind world to Wales.'[5]

The part of the work with which the Methodists would have identified most readily, the story of Protestantism, was the last to appear, and Williams had to concede that by that time he had tried the reader's patience and perseverance. 'It is lamentable that the white, monoglot Welshman in Britain differs so little from the white monkey in India' in his pursuit of knowledge, says Williams, so that 'the illiterate Hottentot far outstrips him in all universal knowledge.'[6] Clearly, Williams intended this as a rebuke to his fellow-countrymen whose reluctance to explore God's world, however superstitious and wayward its inhabitants might be, he considered blameworthy. In the work's Preface he expands on his reason for writing: 'Ignorance is not the mother of religion. But whoever considers that there is no locality in Europe (if the monoglot Welsh know what "Europe" means) which possesses so few books of national and ecclesiastical history in their own language as obtains in Wales … When a monoglot Welshman hears the words "philosophy", "mathematics", "geography" and such like, he scarcely thinks other than that they are words of enchantment.' Furthermore, he bemoans the fact that many who bought the book did so merely on account of their respect for the author of their favourite hymns, but alas, 'hardly look at it, but store it away in some dark corner or other.'[7] Even though it was despised by people from all the denominations, there were some throughout Wales who cherished its encyclopedic contents.

Its purpose is:

> 1. to see that God's free grace alone is able to bring men from the error of their ways. If the light of nature, education, good behaviour could achieve this, so many parts of Europe would not have been so long under the darkness of the Papacy and Islam, nor would the world's universities have been so long without coming to a knowledge of the only true God. Such histories as are found here are presumably sufficient to convince the reader that only God's power, and God's time can bring

man or nation to believe in Christ. 2. To show that only an inward experience of Gospel truth is sufficient to oppose, in the midst of flood and flame, the many conflicts with the flesh, the world and the devil; that all the reasons that scholars around the world have produced to prove that Christ is the true Messiah are not adequate to support the soul in the day of adversity or to lean upon amidst the flames. 3 Perhaps such histories as are here will be useful to some to long for the spirit of religion, and to trust less on the outward trappings of it, which in comparison is an advantage only to some; and if it does one of these things, it will more than repay its cost, to get some in the habit of reading Welsh, as they read some new things, possibly to entice them to read books that will afterwards be more profitable for the state of their souls.[8]

Once more, the work is in the conversational style of a dialogue between two characters, 'Apodemus' and 'Eusebius'. Other characters depict sectarian prejudices: 'Justinus', 'Ignorandus' and 'Coecus' all show strong denominational bias, while 'Moderatus' thinks well of everyone. Its geographical horizon ranges over most of the known world of the time, and its chronological sweep comes to an end with sixteenth century Protestantism. In a footnote, when dealing with Islam, Williams inserts an apology for the work:

It is tragic to think that a vast number of Welsh people have never realized that the world is not covered by the Gospel, nor is it preached everywhere, either by priests in vestments, by Presbyterians in gowns and bands, by Quakers with hats on their heads, or by exhorters standing on stools, from Adam's day to this … my intention here is not to draw attention to the religion of Islam and the Koran, but to produce the greater astonishment at the blindness and pride of man's heart, and to humble each true Christian in the face of distinguishing grace whereby we are not in the same condition as these disadvantaged, darkened souls, who have over-run the greater part of the Old World.[9]

In addition to highlighting Gospel privileges and divine grace, the work was a corrective to the tendency among the Methodists to underestimate the advantages of learning. This tension between spiritual experience and head knowledge surfaces in several of Williams's works, especially in *Theomemphus*. If *Pantheologia* could not compare in popularity with William's other works, he at least satisfied his own objective to resolve that tension.

It is not without significance that Williams's Preface to the work contains a lengthy description of 'Mirandus', the all-round, mature Christian, whose experiences of adversity and trials had driven him 'to trace the roots of teaching, errors, and men's opinions, which means had been used by the Lord to kindle fresh gifts in him, and to make him shine in all spiritual graces.'

> *Mirandus* is a typical example of the benefit to the believer of being taken through many conditions, of extensive travels, to see different opinions and ecclesiastical emphases ... He wandered far and wide to converse with saints of every denomination, to hear ministers with the most excellent reputation, to see the success of the Word, and to acquaint himself more thoroughly with the principles and beauties of the churches. As he pursued these things, he happened to meet with different principles, forms, worship ceremonies, and people with a variety of experiences and conditions in life. By such means, the Lord shone once more on Mirandus's soul, and this last enjoyment far exceeded anything he had proved before ... Mirandus now shines as a *star* in his community, a lamp in the church, a worthy and able head of his family, a guide to the blind, strength to the weak, a help to the feeble, and a light to the ignorant. He is never argumentative about doctrines of the faith; his desire is to experience every truth in his own soul. His chief companions are always those who make much of the principles of religion in their hearts. His attitude towards those of differing principles from his own is always charitable, whenever there is ground to believe that they love, and desire to exalt, the Saviour of the world by the sum of their religious tenets. He has no party zeal in favour of any particular church government or ministry that belittles another. He sucks honey from every flower, and seeks his nourishment from many markets; he is free to enjoy communion with godly folk in many places, even though they do not share the same church order as himself. In short, he is gentle, tender, kind, forgiving, pleasant, generous, moderate, humble, and always at hand to promote the advance of the eternal Gospel.

The Preface concludes by stating that the book's aim is to bring people to see, '1. that only the free grace of God will bring them from the error of their ways ... 2. that only an experience of the reality of religion in the inner man will do to sustain the soul through flood and fire and in the face of innumerable opposition from the flesh, the world, and the devil ... 3. and to create a thirst for the spirit of religion and rest less on its outward ritual.'[10] Here, as in 'A View of Christ's Kingdom', knowledge is the handmaid of religion, regulating a mind-set which produces a life-style that pleases God. Christian maturity avoids both ignorance and prejudice. It is advanced by affliction and investigation. It renounces sectarian pride and thrives in heavenly-minded companionship. In times of spiritual declension, it finds restoration in the pursuit of true knowledge.

But for Williams and his fellow Methodists there were two *kinds* of knowledge. There was that which was accessible to the intellect of the 'natural man', but there was also another kind of knowledge, accessible only to the believer whose spiritual perception was a result of the activity of the Holy Spirit, 1 Corinthians 2: 11-14. It was knowledge received through the study of Scripture in an attitude of waiting on God, through reading 'the most lively authors' in theology, and from 'those who make much of the principles of religion in their hearts ... godly folk.' For this reason it would be wrong to think of *Pantheologia* as having achieved its aim when ignorance and prejudice had been resolved, as a kind of handbook to complete one's knowledge of comparative religion, or perhaps to keep abreast of discoveries in the realm of general knowledge. Its purpose went way beyond that of the dissemination of information, however desirable the exercise or interesting the subject.[11] Williams wanted his readers to recognize the uniqueness of Christianity and the superiority of its Protestant form. Right principles must be firmly planted in the heart, and each person must become one of 'the godly folk', if true religion is to be known, practised and enjoyed. This is why Williams gives particular attention to the errors of Rome, the sufferings of Protestants, and the principles of the Reformation. If he kept his readers waiting until the last issue appeared for that conclusion, the waiting was not in vain. It provides a kind of blueprint for the pursuit of the Mirandus-like ideal.

As Williams moves through the various strands of Christianity, there is ample scope for him to explain biblical questions and to discuss deviations from orthodoxy. Such matters range from sects within Judaism, and the destruction of Jerusalem, to the plight of Salzburg Protestants at the hand of Papists, and the absence of preaching in the Eastern Orthodox Church. Inevitably, the issue that receives the greatest attention is the emergence, character and biblical integrity of Protestantism. 'This great Reformation was one of the wonders of the world, no less than the deliverance of the children of Israel from the land of Egypt with a mighty arm, or the demolishing of the Old Jewish Dispensation by a few poor, uneducated people, save only that they were full of the Holy Spirit; so here also, all Europe great and small lay not only in extreme darkness, but also under severe wrath, prejudice, jealousy and every deadly spirit against Christ and his Gospel; yet in every age of that thick darkness God owned some to make a stand for the truth of his Word, and gave them a spirit willing to forsake all, even their lives, for the sake of the prosperity of the Gospel of Christ.' For further details of the sufferings and martyrdom of these believers, the reader is directed to John Foxe's *Book of Martyrs*.[12] Furthermore, Williams sees Roman Catholic persecution as the inevitable consequence of Roman Catholic teachings. He gives as one example, traceable to a plot devised by the Papist hierarchy, 'the treacherous and infamous massacre of Protestants at Paris in France in the year 1572', that took place on St Bartholomew's Day, 24 August.[13] In case the reader should think that Rome has changed, William quotes in a footnote a letter written from Lisbon by George Whitefield in 1754. He was detained there for a month over the Easter season on his way to America and had ample opportunity to observe the processions that were frequently accompanied by self-inflicted physical punishment.

For Williams this was a confirmation 'that those teachings are today as dark and idolatrous as ever, even though the pomp of their chief apostle is diminished, and that while the Bible is with-held from the ordinary people, they cannot but lie in deep darkness.'[14] For Williams the recovery of Gospel truth and witness in the land goes back to the days of John Wycliffe and had received fresh impetus with the invention of printing. In the providence of God the Bible thus became accessible for the poorest peasant to read, to be enlightened in the truth, and to withstand the errors of Rome.[15] The Reformation's progress on the Continent is charted, followed by that in England and Scotland. Readers would have found its outline of Reformation principles a confirmation of their own:

> They testify that they believe the scriptures to be the true Word of God, and the arbitrator of all religious arguments; that the church is to follow these so far as they are in accord with this Word. That they adhere to the Apostles' Creed, and all Confessions set out by Nicea, Constantinople, Ephesus and Chalcedon ... They believed that justification is by faith alone, which faith is not empty speculation, but genuine belief that is generated by the Holy Spirit, and which enlightens the understanding, and softens the heart to subdue meekly and sincerely to God. They confess to the need for inner righteousness; but that justification and the forgiveness of sin come only on account of Christ's righteousness being imputed to them. [16]

170

It comes as no surprise that Williams, the professed Calvinist, makes his enquirer in the book's dialogue to say, 'especially I would like to hear about Calvin, since those who are orthodox in the Church are called Calvinists.'[17] The request is granted, and John Calvin's preaching, commentaries and other writings are traced to the unequalled diligence and zeal bestowed on him by God.

Puritanism's rise and distinctives also receive attention, but Williams did not consider it necessary to provide similar details specifically for Wales. Contemporary Protestantism in his native country displayed in comprehensive measure those features that were characteristic of neighbouring England. This may explain why the last issue of *Pantheologia* comes to an abrupt end with an account of Presbyterianism in Scotland and persecution on the Continent. By the time of appearance of this in print, 1779, with a total of 654 pages, readers may have felt a measure of fatigue, and some expressed their dissatisfaction, if not outright criticism:

> Methodist minds may regard *Pantheologia* as a *Nonconformist*, on account of its long-winded speech, dragging his words, changing the tone of his voice without any lively spirit; No, friends: that tribe does not give him much acceptance … Nonconformist minds may regard him as a hot-headed *Methodist,* and that he kills time by listening to his father singing hymns; no, that party only accepts it with great effort … Nor does Pan delight in saying that he is of the Established Church, since she is at present corrupt, coveting popularity, but generally throughout the whole of *Wales* only a few attend her temples apart from the priest and the bell-ringer, who are bound to be present. [18]

Whatever the reasons for its unpopularity, Williams persevered with the work in the conviction that 'knowledge … sanctified by the Word of God and prayer, is a means to show more light on the Word, and makes the humble man more useful in the church.'[19] And Methodist readers, given their respect for Williams, might still have derived benefit from the work's sound Christian teaching, despite what many would have considered to be the excess of information that it contained. Compared with the Christ of the Bible, of the Reformation, of the Methodists of his day, all other religions worshipped 'rude and rustic idols'. [20]

19.

'A deluge of grace'

Although the chapter title is drawn from Williams's elegy to Howel Davies, it is an appropriate phrase for the religious revival that began at Llangeitho towards the end of 1761.[1] The Welsh Methodists were no strangers to the effusions of grace that are referred to as 'revivals'. They believed that there was Scripture warrant and precedent for such a 'deluge', or season of refreshing from God's presence. They had experience of it, they prayed for it, and they expected it. They were times of extraordinary spiritual activity, initiated in a sovereign way by the Holy Spirit. They were looked on as additional to, not a substitute for, the regular work of seeking the same end, the extension of Christ's kingdom. The message that proved so effective in realizing this end was the same. The sense of God's presence would be more real, the manifestation of His power would have a higher magnitude, the extent of the Spirit's influence would be far wider, and more might be achieved in days than formerly in years, but it was still God's saving activity. Men were still saved by grace, even though they might receive it in 'a deluge', the word used by Williams for the extraordinary power experienced under the preaching of Howel Davies.

According to Edward Morgan, 'it is very remarkable that W. Williams's Hymns, those most experimental and beautiful compositions, were introduced for the first time at Llangeitho church the *very day* the revival commenced. And some think that, under God's blessing, they contributed very much to the furtherance of the wonderful change that took place after the long and dreary winter that the churches had experienced.' The hymn collection in question, *Caniadau, y Rhai sydd ar y Môr o Wydr* ('Songs of those on the Sea of Glass') was available early in December 1761, and the beginning of the revival should be dated in that year. [2] In these hymns there is greater fluency, stemming from William's growing confidence as a hymn-writer. There is also a greater intensity of desire and longing for God, and more fervent expressions of love for Christ. Seventeen of the hymns are based on verses from the Song of Solomon; some are sacramental hymns, and several have a well-deserved abiding quality.

Their powerful impact during the revival, however, was due to the outpouring of the Holy Spirit at that time.

Morgan adds that the revival 'was renewed soon after Rowlands was turned out of the church.' He continues:

> It [the second outburst of revival] took place under his preaching at Llangeitho chapel. The pouring of the Spirit from above was most surprising in its effects: it seemed as if the whole chapel was filled at the time with some supernatural element, and the whole congregation was struck with some uncommon astonishment, and seized with peculiar emotions. Hundreds of them were bathed in tears; some overwhelmed with grief, and some with joy; some broken in heart and godly sorrow, and some rejoicing with unspeakable joy and full of glory. Some think that the introduction of those remarkable words in Mat. 11: 25-26, ['At that time Jesus answered and said, "I thank Thee, O Father, Lord of heaven and earth, because Thou hast hid these things from the wise and prudent, and hast revealed them unto babes. Even so, Father; for so it seemed good in Thy sight".'] in a very penetrating manner by Rowlands as he was preaching, produced this most extraordinary powerful simultaneous effect on the people. It spread in an amazing manner through all the counties of South Wales. [3]

Clearly this religious revival was both powerful and widespread.

Both Harris and Williams suggest that prayer was another contributory factor to the revival's commencement. Harris records in his diary in August 1763: '… till the Lord did come with these late showers of revival, all was gone to nothing; that this was not by any man but by the Lord Himself, or by some of the meanest of all the exhorters.' In November he elaborates a little on this: 'meeting William Richard, and heard of the beginning of this last revival in Cardiganshire, and how that word went through him when he first cried out at Llangeitho, "I will once more shake the heavens" [Haggai 2: 6; Hebrews 12:26].'[4] Even though Williams fifteen years later in his *Experience Meeting* described a powerful revival in an imaginary setting, parallels with the revival of 1762 are close and convincing:

> This is the way the Lord worked in that part of the world. One time, there were just a few of us, professing believers, gathered together, cold and unbelievably dead, in a meeting which we called a special service, so discouraged as to doubt whether we should ever meet again … forced by cowardice, unbelief and the onslaughts of Satan, we resolved to give up our special meeting; and now we were about to offer a final

173

prayer, fully intending never again to meet thus in fellowship. But it is when man reaches the lowest depths of unbelief that God imparts faith, and when man has failed, then God reveals Himself. So here, with us in such dire straits, on the brink of despair, with the door shut on every hope of success, God Himself entered into our midst, and the light of day from on high dawned upon us; for one of the brethren – yes, the most timid of us all, the one who was strongest in his belief that God would never visit us – while in prayer, was stirred in his spirit, and laid hold powerfully on heaven, as one who would never let go. His tongue spoke unusual words, his voice was raised, his spirit was aflame, he pleaded, he cried to God, he struggled, he wrestled in earnest, like Jacob, in the agony of his soul. The fire took hold of others – all were awakened, the coldest to the most heedless took hold and were warmed; the spirit of struggling and wrestling fell on all, we all went with him into the battle; with him we laid hold on God, His attributes, His Word and His promises, resolving that we would never let go our hold until all our desire should be satisfied. And this came to pass.

Earnest prayers and biblical sermons are no more effective than inspiring hymns, apart from the awakening power of the Holy Spirit. Methodist expectation, as Williams often insisted, was directed to the intervention of God, and not derived from a human source. When Harris mentions 'some of the meanest of all the exhorters', and Williams refers to 'the most timid of us all', they were not speaking in a disparaging way; they were merely expressing the conviction that God, in Pauline terms, uses 'the foolish ... weak ... despised ... that no flesh should glory in his presence' (1 Corinthians 1: 27-29). [5]

Coming as this did after the difficult decade of the 1750s, it must have seemed to the Welsh Methodists as a fulfilment, in their day, of Isaiah 35: 1, 'the desert shall rejoice and blossom as the rose'. Williams waxed lyrical about the circumstances that accompany any genuine work of God, in the real work of 1762 as well as in that imaginary occasion he described later:

There fell upon us the sweet breath of the love of the Lord. We were filled as if with the fulness of the bowls and horns of the altar - the fire was kindled and we gave voice with our tongues. The cloud melted away, the sun shone, we drank of the fruit of the vines of the promised land, and we were made to rejoice. Gone was unbelief - gone guilt - gone fear - gone a timid, cowardly spirit, lack of love, envy, suspicion, together with all the poisonous worms that tormented us before; and in their place came love, faith, hope, a joyful spirit, with a glorious multitude of the graces of the Holy Spirit. Up till now the service was only beginning; for prayer, singing, praise and blessing were redoubled, and no-one felt like bringing things to an end ... now some were weeping, some praising, some singing, some filled with heavenly laughter, and all full of wonder and love and amazement at the Lord's work – to my mind like the time of the Apostles, when the Spirit descended from on high on a handful of fearful people, and strengthened them mightily ... As it was then, so it was here now.

With the reference to the time of the Apostles, Williams clearly had the Day of Pentecost in mind, as recorded in Acts 2, but later in the passage he adds:

During those days I thought many times of the prophecies of the Old Testament, and I never saw them opened out and explained better than by the heavenly authority on our little church at that time, and on the neighbouring districts; like that Scripture in Joel 2:29, 30, etc. – 'And it shall come to pass afterward, that I will pour my Spirit upon all flesh ... And I will show wonders in the heavens and in the earth, blood, and fire, and pillars of smoke'. For to the flesh and the natural man this wonderful work of heaven was as awful and as fearful as blood and vapour, smoke and fire, to timid men. [6]

For Williams and the other leaders the revival's origin and fruit were divine. They willingly conceded that the powerful and unusual manifestations that accompanied it did not in themselves guarantee the integrity of spiritual experience. Nor should the presence of such phenomena discount the revival's authenticity.

There are several testimonies to the extraordinary nature of this revival's character. Despite the widespread criticism, for Williams the experiences were powerful and in the main genuine, and their effect genuinely transforming:

Now the day has dawned, the Lord has breathed on the dry bones, and they move. Multitudes flock to the Word of Life: who can count them? North and south seek one King, and His Name is One, Jesus, King of saints! When the Sun of righteousness arose with healing in His wings, and He flew towards us from on high with wonderful suddenness, the country was kindled by His brightness. Many ministers desired to see that hour; a thousand cried for that Sun to rise. At last He came. Our mourning turned to dancing; hearing the Word of Life is sweeter than market or fair. The six work-days have turned to Sabbaths, and the Sabbath extends from one end of the year to the other. Salvation in Christ is the only pleasure of hosts of people. The country's young

175

people have become estranged from fancy clothes. Sleep has fled. Craving for meat and drink is swallowed by praise and song. Hymns and Psalms and spiritual songs are the only nourishment at the saints' love feasts. Pride of honour and name are forgotten. Prayer, sermons, and especially singing praise to God cover the land. This is more wonderful than earthquakes and all the wars of the world. Blessed summer's day! It is come! It is come!

Williams's reference to an earthquake would have been topical. One took place at Lisbon in November 1755 killing over 100,000 people and virtually destroying the city. Such disasters as well as demonstrating God's mysterious providence, also buttressed Gospel appeals to repentance. Natural disasters were, as Williams was to say in the conclusion of his *Aurora Borealis* of 1774, 'merely the signs of the coming of the Son of Man to set up His kingdom.'[7]

Harris, as always, provides sustained, contemporary comment. At the Llansawel Association on 16 February 1763 he met Williams and Rowland and others, and wrote in his diary:

I heard much of the spirit of singing that is fallen on various parts, and of several awakened in Cardiganshire, Carmarthenshire, etc., and the great flock coming to hear; and I showed that we are not to receive or reject these outward appearances, but see to the real fruit on their spirits and lives, and watch especially if poverty etc. appears … I went among the exhorters … I was home on this spirit of singing and their duty to watch the fruit of it. I showed it may astonish or end in self, and appear to be of the devil … importuned, I went to their chapel and prayed and spoke on Zech. 12: 10, and showed how the prophet foresaw the Gospel Day … then I spoke on this work of singing, that we don't look at this but at the lasting fruit of the spirit of deep poverty and self-acquaintance and coming out of self. If God comes in this way for a time for some wise purpose, who is to hinder Him: His saving and usual way is to come without any outward appearances, calmly, and quietly and still; such as find Him working on their hearts so that they can't refrain. Let them not judge such as receive Him still, and again, let such not judge the other. I spoke home to the carnal, that they should not judge at all, but leave it to such as are spiritual and capable of judging, and take it as a conviction to themselves … This spirit of singing that is come down is as yet not attended with levity and self, as the last; and seeing so many awakened by them and none by me … I see it an honour to go among them. [8]

For the next few months Harris makes frequent reference to the revival:

(29 March 1763): At Cilycwm I discoursed to I believe, 6,000 people at least, with the old and uncommon freedom ... Dined at Cilycwm with the curate and Mr William Williams ... My spirit crying to catch their fire and life; the Lord having awakened many in these parts by a spirit of singing and blessing the Lord, who continue whole nights in that exercise ... (1 April 1763): to Twrgwyn chapel ... Discoursed to a vast crowd; such rejoicing and singing I never saw. (6 April 1763): Builth ... I hear of much awakening in the country. (5 May 1763): To Llangeitho. Discoursed after 1 to about 10,000 people, I think. I find here are added above 200 lately. Above 40 children meet ... There came such a spirit of singing, rejoicing, and leaping for joy as made me desist. (7 May 1763): To Twrgwyn chapel ... In all these parts they sing, rejoice, leap for joy, triumph, and praise the Lord whole nights. I find 'tis of the Lord and I countenance it. (12 May 1763): Haverfordwest ... Now a great awakening in several parts of the country, vast singing and rejoicing. (18 May 1763): Trefeca Association ... Many were here singing and rejoicing from Cardiganshire. All went away happy and in much love. [9]

Harris could not 'understand these outward frames of jumping', and his 'family' at Trefeca was labelled 'cold, barren, dry' by Williams for their emotionally detached spirituality. Yet even in 1770 he found 'amazing flame' in Rowland's ministry, adding that 'above 2,000 and from 40 Welsh miles around' came to Llangeitho on a Saturday to the Sacrament of the Lord's Supper.[10] These extracts provide evidence of the geographical spread, and sustained effects of the revival, especially in South Wales, but it reached other parts as well.

Although the work of Robert Jones of Rhos-lan appeared much later, in 1820, he had been in a favourable position to gather reliable information about Methodist activities in North Wales. Teaching at a school during the day, and exhorting as opportunity afforded, in his *Drych yr Amseroedd* ('Mirror of the Times') Jones traced Gospel success in Wales from Puritan times. On the 1762 Revival he mentions that at Llanbryn-mair, Montgomeryshire, 'multitudes of young people were called and added to the church, as an army with banners.' He later mentions its effects in other parts:

About the year 1762, in the face of great unworthiness and baseness, God remembered His covenant, by visiting graciously a great number of sinners in several parts of Wales; the Sun of Righteousness arose on a great throng of those who sat in the land and shadow of death ... There was a great difference between this revival and that which began

177

at first through Mr Howel Harris; the mode of proceeding in that was sharp and very thunderous; but in this, as in the house of Cornelius long ago, great crowds magnified God without being able to cease, but sometimes leaping in jubilation as did David before the Ark. Sometimes whole nights were spent with a voice of joy and praise, as a multitude that kept holiday. I heard from a godly old woman that it lasted three days and three nights without a break in a place called Lôn-fudr in Llŷn, Caernarfonshire ... these powerful outpourings descended on several hundred, if not thousands, throughout South Wales and Gwynedd [in the North]. [11]

Many in those days made their way from North to South, arriving at Llangeitho utterly fatigued, but their weariness melted away under the ministry of God's Word. Here is the testimony of one such traveller, John Williams, from Dolwyddelan, Caernarfonshire: 'I was fitter for bed than for chapel. But Rowland began to preach. The text was, "And in this mountain shall the Lord of hosts make unto all the people a feast of fat things, a feast of wine on the lees, of fat things full of marrow, of wines on the lees well refined" (Isaiah 25:6). He began to tap the barrels of the Covenant of Grace, and to let out the wine well refined, and to give to the people to drink. It flowed over the chapel. I also drank, until I was as drunk as a fool. And there I was, and scores of others with me, thinking nothing of fatigue, shouting, and some of us jumping, for hours.'[12] Williams expressed similar sentiments in his elegy to Rowland:

> All the crowds are homeward journeying,
> In a glorious frame of mind,
> Having parted with their burdens,
> Left their guilty loads behind;
> Miles of highway full of singing,
> Praises to the Lamb abound,
> Till the barren rocks and valleys
> Echo with the joyful sound.[13]

It was not only visitors to Llangeitho that were powerfully affected: Nathaniel, one of Daniel Rowland's sons came to faith in Christ about this time.[14] The area continued to enjoy these blessings for several years. Harris was told by a certain Benjamin Thomas at the end of 1768 that God's work was thriving 'wonderfully' in Cardiganshire. He reported that at Llangeitho 140 converts met weekly to pray, sing, and open their hearts to one another in the society meeting. Similar scenes were witnessed at Llanddewibrefi, and at Llanddewi Aber-arth after Thomas had preached, they continued singing and praying until midnight.[15]

Inevitably, such fervency produced criticism. A letter sent to a London periodical in June 1763 reported from Carmarthenshire that, 'There is here what some call a great Reformation in Religion among the Methodists, but the case is really this. They have a sort of rustic dance in their public worship, which they call religious dancing, in imitation of David's dancing before the Ark. Some of them strip off their clothes, crying out "Hosannah!", etc., in imitation of those that attended our Saviour when He rode into Jerusalem. They call this the glory of the latter day; and when any person speaks to them of their extravagances, the answer they give is, "You have the mark of the enemy in your forehead!" Such is the delusion and uncharitableness of this people!'[16] An Arian minister labelled these activities as 'wild pranks', while Thomas Morgan, a Dissenting minister, said that 'it appears to all true and serious Christians that they are stark mad, and given up to a spirit of delusion, to the great disgrace and scandal of Christianity.'[17]

Such remarks by sceptical observers were, perhaps, predictable, but how did their sympathizers react? When at Swansea in August 1763 John Wesley was given an account 'of what has made a great noise in Wales.' He was told that 'it is common in the congregations attended by Mr. W[illiams], and one or two other clergymen, after the preaching is over, for any one that has a mind to give out a verse of a hymn. This they sing over and over with all their might, perhaps above thirty, yea, forty times. Meanwhile the bodies of two or three, sometimes ten or twelve, are violently agitated; and they leap up and down, in all manner of postures, frequently for hours together.' Wesley adds, 'I think there needs no great penetration to understand this. They are honest, upright men who really feel the love of God in their hearts. But they have little experience, either of the ways of God or the devices of Satan. So he serves himself of their simplicity, in order to wear them out and to bring a discredit on the work of God.' The account he was given may have been hearsay, and Wesley's comments sound condescending, but evidently he had forgotten his own words on the revival in 1745: 'That, in many places, abundance of notorious sinners are totally reformed, is declared by a thousand eye and ear witnesses both of their present and past behaviour. What would you have more? What pretence can you have for doubting any longer? Do you delay fixing your judgment till you see a work of God, without any stumbling-blocks attending it? That never was yet, nor ever will. "It must needs be that offences will come." And scarce ever was there such a work of God before, with so few as have attended this.'[18]

When a sympathetic English evangelical layman expressed to Rowland his concern at what seemed to be excessive fervour in the congregation, Rowland replied, 'You, English blame us, the Welsh, and speak against us and say, "Jumpers! Jumpers!" But we, the Welsh, have something to allege against you, and we most justly say of you, "Sleepers! Sleepers!"' Alongside this tongue-in-cheek riposte must be placed Williams's measured statement shortly after the 1762 Revival: 'Apart from the heavenly inclination on their spirits inciting their tongues to a lively praising of God, this fire burns in the life and behaviour of so many of them … They are zealous, not for secondary matters of faith, but for the essential issues of salvation. Faith and love are the chief graces they cry for.'[19] God's power and purpose is displayed in a sovereign and saving manner, but ideally its effect should be most evident in godly living. Williams's apology was aimed at demonstrating that the physical phenomena were a passing feature of the revival, and that its lasting effect lay more in changed lives. As an expression of a religion felt, not merely understood, the phenomena were allowed and, given the powerful influences attending the preaching, inevitable. But the whole purpose of the Methodist societies was to evaluate these experiences and encourage stability, submission and growth in the area of practical obedience to God's precepts.

Twenty years later, two short poetic works in Welsh are ascribed to Williams in which he defends the ecstatic fervour of another revival. The title of the first *Atteb i ŵr Bonheddig* (1784), in full translation reads thus: 'Reply to a Gentleman who wrote a poetic rebuke to the spirit that lately descended on some lively congregations, and made them double their singing praise to God and the Lamb; yes, to bless, praise, exult, dance, jump with delight at the joy of their salvation. The author wrote this reply … to encourage Christ's followers, so that they should not lose heart in praising God on account of the opposition of those who lack understanding and experience.' The second, *Atteb i ŵr arall*, published posthumously, had a similar title: 'Reply to another who wrote a rebuke to the outward aspects manifested by people who were overcome by a spirit of singing and praising God.' Biblical precedents are multiplied by Williams to justify such exuberance: the ecstatic songs of Moses and Miriam; David dancing before the ark;

Joel's prophecy of the Day of Pentecost; the shepherds' joy at Christ's birth; and the shouts of the heavenly host described in the Book of Revelation. Gratitude for God's mighty deliverances cannot but evoke this kind of response:

> We came from Babel's prison, by heaven's almighty grace,
> And so a heavenly laughter adorns our glowing face;
> And those who were so tongue-tied, now sing aloud with joy,
> The praise of God our Saviour our tongues shall aye employ.

From the shorter of the two poems comes an exposure of the scorner's hypocrisy:

> Why dost object to dancing, the stringèd harp before?
> The selfsame Spirit moves us, as with the seers of yore;
> It is the Church of England, her wayward sons like thee,
> Who strain their ribs with jigging, a fourstep round and three.
>
> So, foolish man, stop railing, and take the sacred Book,
> And read with care its pages, go pray within thy nook;
> Thou'lt see that true religion, when once it warms thy soul,
> Soon has thy frame responding, as with the saints of old. [20]

Even by Methodist standards the physical manifestations were unusual, some would say that they bordered on the absurd and demeaning, and Williams's strong language implies a defensive stance.

For Welsh Methodism the years following 1762 were a time of great advance combined with the challenge of consolidation. To this latter, Williams applied his literary skills with vigour, as will be seen later. First, however, attention must be given to Williams's own conclusions as to the revival: 'Having considered its every aspect, I am convinced that this work is of God, namely that people sing boldly and fearlessly, praise and worship and bless God, speak well of Him to everyone, reprove sin, stand for His Name before the courts, jump at the joy of their salvation, reveal His goodness to the world. It has been impressed upon me that God's Spirit is the author of this present work, however many hypocrites mix their voices with those of genuine believers ... But you must expect great trials in the days to come, a bitter winter after such a glorious summer.' [21] These words are found in *Atteb Philo-Evangelius i Martha Philopur* ('Philo-Evangelius's Answer to Martha Philopur'), the second of twin pamphlets that Williams wrote at the time in defence of the revival. *Llythyr Martha Philopur at y Parchedig Philo Evangelius ei Hathro* ('Martha Philopur's Letter to her Teacher, Philo Evangelius'), had appeared in 1762, and its 'Answer' was published in the following year. Both, therefore, were written in the midst of that period of extraordinary religious excitement. They addressed an issue that Williams considered of profound importance, namely, the characteristics of a genuine work of the Holy Spirit. While the phenomena attracted attention at the time, as they do in every revival, Williams's concern goes deeper to the manner in which ideas and convictions affect human personality and change human behaviour. For this reason it is fitting to give the matter more extensive consideration in the next chapter.

20.

'A kind of heavenly elysium'

In his task of defending the revival Williams had at his disposal similar works by the New England theologian Jonathan Edwards. These had appeared between 1737 and 1746, the first of which was recommended in a Preface by two highly-esteemed London Nonconformist ministers, Isaac Watts and John Guyse. By February 1738 Harris had read this work, *A Narrative of Surprising Conversions*, 'with great joy', and by November he considered 'the time here [in Wales] now is like New England'.[1] At the end of Williams's letter to Howel Harris in London, dated 7 December 1745, he reports, 'Lately, I have read Dr. [Jonathan] Edwards thoughts of the Work of God in New England, the best book I have seen to that purpose. It gave me [much] light in some things.' The full title of this second work was *Some Thoughts concerning the present Revival of Religion in New-England, and the Way in which it ought to be acknowledged and promoted.*[2] In it Edwards insisted that remarkable revival experiences were not in themselves evidence of fanaticism or spiritual aberration. They were often found in people whose piety was entirely genuine and progressive. He gave as an instance the experience of his own wife, Sarah, even though her name was withheld.

(The person) more than once continuing for five or six hours together, without any interruption, in that clear and lively view or sense of the infinite beauty and amiableness of Christ's person, and the heavenly sweetness of his excellent and transcendent love; so that (to use the person's own expressions) the soul remained in a kind of heavenly Elysium, and did as it were swim in the rays of Christ's love, like a little mote swimming in the beams of the sun, or streams of his light that come in at a window; and the heart was swallowed up in a kind of glow of Christ's love, coming down from Christ's heart in heaven, as a constant stream of sweet light, at the same time the soul all flowing out in love to him; so that there seemed to be a constant flowing and reflowing from heart to heart. The soul dwelt on high, and was lost in God, and seemed almost to leave the body; dwelling in a pure delight that fed and satisfied the soul ... extraordinary views of divine things, and religious affections, being frequently attended with very great effects on the body, nature often sinking under the weight of divine discoveries, the strength of the body taken away, so as to deprive of all ability to stand or speak ... animal nature often in a great emotion and agitation, and the soul very often, of late, so overcome with great admiration, and a kind of omnipotent joy, as to cause the person (wholly unavoidably) to leap with all the might, with joy and mighty exultation of soul ... [3]

Edwards concluded: 'Now if such things are enthusiasm, and the fruits of a distempered brain, let my brain be evermore possessed of that happy distemper! If this be distraction, I pray God that the world of mankind may be all seized with this benign, meek, beneficent, beatifical, glorious distraction!'[4] Williams could rely on these works for sound evaluation and mature counsel regarding the similar religious upheaval that was taking place in Wales. His 'Reply' to Martha's 'Letter' closes with a quotation from *The Distinguishing Marks of the Work of the Spirit of God* of 1741.[5]

It is not without significance that Williams uses female characters to discuss the important issues of the day for the Welsh Methodists. It has been estimated that 'in the early years of Methodism, between 1737 and 1750, women outnumbered men in most societies.'[6] In his 1777 work dealing with the societies, *The Experience Meeting*, Williams speaks of the 'companies of merry, manly youths, crowds of girls in the full strength of their feminine attractiveness and vivacity, men who for the most part are an easy prey for Satan to work upon their fleshly lusts, and to entice them to the pleasures of flesh and blood.' In the revival of 1762 their numbers were considerably increased, and 'Martha' is a fitting and typical representative. Martha's letter begins with a word of testimony. From a sense of guilt for sin she had been brought to the joy of release. She had received the Gospel with greater eagerness than would be felt by a criminal offered released from the gallows. Words describing her convictions are similar to those used by Jonathan Edwards in the 'Application' of his famous sermon on Deuteronomy 32:25, 'Their foot shall slide in due time':

> Martha: I hung above a seething furnace, fire and brimstone, its smoke ascending forever. There was but a hair's breadth between me and being consigned to an eternity with devils. It seemed as though the very stench of hell rose to my nostrils...

> Edwards: O sinner! Consider the fearful danger you are in: 'tis a very
> great furnace of wrath, a wide and bottomless pit, full of the fire of
> wrath, that you are held over in the hand of that God, whose wrath is
> provoked and incensed as much against you as against many of the
> damned in hell; you hang by a slender thread, with the flames of divine
> wrath flashing about it … [7]

Deliverance from this dreadful condition inevitably produced
spontaneous, irrepressible praise and love to the One who brought it
about. Martha compares this compulsion to the woman of Samaria who
called on her neighbours to see Christ for themselves, 'a man, which
told me all things that ever I did' (John 5:29). Such compulsion
overcame Martha's natural reticence and timidity to show her affection,
just as Mary poured ointment on Christ without restraint for the same
reason (John 12:3).

Next in the letter comes a profound and significant statement of the
effect of Gospel preaching on Martha's personality. It is profound
because it deals with human nature in its fallen as well as in its restored
condition, and significant because it deals with spiritual rather than
psychological categories. It could only be initiated and understood in
terms of divine revelation and grace, bringing about the recovery of
God's image in fallen man. To understand this, it is necessary first to
consider Williams's portrayal of the effects of the fall as set out in his
later work, 'The Crocodile of Egypt's River':

> When the mother of mankind first ate the fruit of the forbidden tree, she
> came under bondage to every sin, under all the inherent passions that
> the worst of men experienced; when she was tempted by envy … her
> understanding was darkened, her memory was crippled, her conscience
> fell asleep, all her affections changed their place; new objects filled her
> thoughts, all the faculties of her soul became utterly unruly, so that not
> one kept its proper place; the last became first, and the first last; the
> weakest, tenderest faculties came to dominate, as if the bramble became
> king of all the trees of the forest, and the understanding, reason, and
> conscience were imprisoned in a deep dungeon, not seeing the light of
> day. Now terrors replaced confidence, flesh replaced spirit, love for the
> creature instead of love to the Creator, and the crowning edifice under
> heaven was ruined, as a king's palace reduced to a pile of earth and
> stones without beauty or glory.[8]

This disaster is portrayed by Williams in his 1774 work *Aurora
Borealis*, as having far-reaching effects: 'Man's fall wrought chaos

['afreolaeth'] in the entire creation.'[9] So much for the soul's ruin; what of its recovery? Here is Martha's statement:

> While you preach the Word of Life, I do my utmost to restrain myself, lest I cause others to stumble ... The first opportunity I get, with the love of the Lord burning within me, and I give free rein to my spiritual passions, it is natural for me to shout the Lord's praise, to bless and extol my God, to leap and jump with joy, at such a great salvation as this, which I never knew before. At such time my memory is more alert, and innumerable Scriptures flood endlessly into it, all of this one strain, to praise God for His free grace. My senses are sharpened; I understand the things of God in clearer light; my reason and emotions are so disciplined, that I am careful not to say or do anything which would cause my brethren to stumble, or the ungodly to blaspheme ... While I was under the flood of conviction, it is true that fear worked so much on the weaker powers of my soul, and stimulated my imagination to such liveliness that it was as if I saw a thousand terrifying things against it, and surrounded all my senses with mist and fog until at times I could hardly recognize myself. But when I comprehended forgiveness of sin, all my perceptions, my memory, my conscience and my affections settled into their proper place, and so know that they have a good cause in hand, and there is no need to be ashamed of Christ's cause.[10]

When Williams speaks of 'senses' being sharpened he is not referring to the physical senses of the body, but the inward 'senses' or 'faculties' of human personality: intellect, memory, imagination, conscience, emotion, and will. When God visits the soul, the encounter has a spiritual dimension, one that is prominent in the traditional interpretation of Old Testament texts, such as Psalm 34:8, 'O taste and see that the Lord is good', and Song of Solomon 2: 14, 'Let me see your face, let me hear your voice; for your voice is sweet, and your face is lovely.'

In his Treatise *Concerning Religious Affections* (1746), which Williams possessed in a later edition, but may have accessed sooner, Edwards uses similar ideas:

> The Spirit of God is given to the true saints to dwell in them, as his proper lasting abode; and to influence their hearts, as a principle of new nature, or as a divine supernatural spring of life and action ... And the Scripture speaks of the actual being of a gracious principle in the soul, though in its first beginning, as a seed there planted, as inconsistent with a man's being a sinner (1 John 3: 9) ... From hence it follows, that in those gracious exercises and affections which are wrought in the

186

> minds of the saints, through the saving influences of the Spirit of God,
> there is a new inward perception or sensation of their minds, entirely
> different in its nature and kind, from anything that ever their minds were
> the subjects of before they were sanctified … Hence the work of the
> Spirit of God in regeneration is often in Scripture compared to the
> giving a new sense, giving eyes to see, and ears to hear, unstopping the
> ears of the deaf, and opening the eyes of them that were born blind, and
> turning from darkness unto light … This new spiritual sense, and the
> new dispositions that attend it, are no new faculties, but are new
> principles of nature.[11]

Some have concluded that Edwards was influenced by the ideas of the
philosopher John Locke in this area of practical theology.[12] Edwards
certainly found Locke's books exciting, but there is no evidence that
Williams shared that excitement. There simply was no need for either
Edwards or Williams to rely on John Locke. They had ample teaching
in the Bible to explain and analyse the effect of God's grace on human
personality. Rich exposition of this Scripture material was offered by
their Puritan predecessors. Edwards could draw as well on the New
England theologians Thomas Shephard and Solomon Stoddard.[13]
Williams possessed the relevant works of John Owen, Thomas
Goodwin, and Stephen Charnock on the subject. In a sermon, Owen
says that, 'which way ever we go in this world, our affections are our
sails; and according as they are spread and filled, so we pass on, swifter
and slower, whither we are steering.' In his work, *The Grace and Duty
of Being Spiritually Minded*, Owen develops this theme in several
chapters. The soul's affections are redirected by regeneration to
heavenly things, and their sincerity and vigour promote godly living:
'*Spiritual affections, whereby the soul adheres unto spiritual things,
taking in such a savour and relish of them as wherein it finds rest and
satisfaction, is the peculiar spring and substance of our being
spiritually minded.*'[14] Goodwin's *Work of the Holy Spirit in our
Salvation* refers to 'the heart elevated and suited to all things spiritual':
'whenever God regenerateth any man, and constitutes him a new
creature, lo, the man hath a new eye to see, an ear to hear, and all sorts
of new senses to take in all sorts of spiritual things, as the Spirit shall
be pleased to reveal them to him.' Later in the work, 'Book V'
proposes, 'That besides the Holy Spirit's indwelling in us, and his
motions and actings of our spirits, there are permanent or abiding
principles wrought in our souls, which dispose them for holy actions,
and give spiritual abilities for the performance of them'. Stephen

Charnock's *Discourse of the Nature of Regeneration* describes regeneration as 'a universal change of the whole man ... understanding, will, conscience, affections, all were corrupted by sin, all are renewed by grace. Grace sets up its ensigns in all parts of the soul, surveys every corner, and triumphs over every lurking enemy; it is as large in renewing as sin was in defacing.' John Owen similarly concludes that regeneration 'consists in a new, spiritual, supernatural, vital principle or habit of grace, infused into the soul, the mind, will, and affections, by the power of the Holy Spirit, disposing and enabling them in whom it is unto spiritual, supernatural, vital acts of faith and obedience.'[15] Two books found in Williams's library gave extensive treatment: William Fenner's, *Treatise of the Affections; or The Soul's Pulse* (1642), and Edward Reynolds', *Treatise of the Passions & Faculties of the Soule of Man* (1640).[16] Both Williams and Edwards had these resources at their disposal, simply summarized in the latter's conviction, that 'True religion, in great part, consists in holy affections.'[17] Such teaching enriched Williams's understanding of the full implications of the Holy Spirit's work in the soul, and accounts in some measure for the incisive penetration of his spiritual counsel. It also enabled him to distinguish the genuine from the counterfeit in the powerful manifestations witnessed during revival.

Williams's analysis of the soul's faculties has close similarities with the work of another Puritan, also on his library shelves. This was Anthony Burgess's *Spiritual refining: or A treatise of grace and assurance, Wherein are handled, the doctrine of assurance. The use of signs in self-examination. How true graces may be distinguished from counterfeit.* Certainly, the title would have been both appealing and relevant to Williams and the Welsh situation. Speaking of God's image in man, Burgess says that it 'consisted in an universal rectitude of the whole man, in an holy frame of all the parts, faculties, and affections in a man: now when Adam fell, this curious workmanship was broken to pieces; not part, no affections could do their duty: grace therefore regenerating is to restore and repair these breaches again; the blinded understanding is enlightened, the contumacious will obedient, the stony heart softened, the unruly affections crucified, so that this grace of regeneration makes the most excellent alteration and wonderful change that can be.'[18] The spiritual categories of Puritan theology would have resonated with Williams in a manner which Lockean philosophy could never have achieved. He usually acknowledges an author whose work he found useful and quotes, but Locke is not one of them. Conversely, the books of Goodwin, Owen, John Gill, Walter Marshall, James Hervey and James Ussher get special mention by him at the end of his life as the ones which helped forge his theology.

'Martha', for her part, is made to own that she is but one of many who have experienced these 'new' manifestations. They appeared new because God had been a stranger in the land for so long. It was like a summer's day after a hard winter, so that the 'the Spirit that now shines on the Church is like a blazing fire'. Its seeming newness is a stumbling-block both to religious and worldly people, but in the Millennial reign of Christ, these things shall have even more powerful expression. Meanwhile, observers are as divided as to the authenticity of the revival as they were on the Day of Pentecost. The sustained godly living of the revival's true converts would in time vindicate its divine origin. At this point Martha introduces an impressive array of Scriptures that she considers determinative, for Philo to review. There are sixteen texts or clusters of texts, from the Old and New Testaments, where people respond to the saving ministry of God's Spirit with physical abandon or give fervent expression to praise. They include examples such as Miriam, Ex. 15:20; David, 2 Sam. 6:20, 23; some of the prophets, 1 Sam. 10: 5-7; 19:20; Elizabeth, Luke 1: 41-45; passages from the Psalms and the Song of Songs; Joel 2: 28-9 and its fulfilment on the Day of Pentecost; and Revelation 19 which speaks of the final fall of the Babylon of unbelief and sin. For Martha, so many Old Testament passages 'about shouting, singing, dancing, laughing, clapping hands together, jumping, and such like, are promises to be fulfilled under the New Testament dispensation. However much the prophets set out spiritual realities by outward, physical manifestations, yet such promises as these show that comfort, peace, love, enjoyment, and fellowship with God were to be had to such an extent that it could not but affect the bodies of some believers.' In conclusion, Martha hopes that 'the experiences of the saints will provide better interpretation of both Old and New Testament than any written hitherto.'

Williams begins Philo's 'Reply' with an immediate confirmation that Martha's 'Letter' contained nothing contrary to the truth; its only fault was its brevity. Because revival is a mixed work, controversy is to be expected, and vigorous defence of a truly divine season of refreshing is necessary. 'When has there been a work of God in the world without Satan having his finger in it? ... It is well-known that tares enter when God works powerfully among his churches, and he suffers a thousand small errors in those whose hearts love Him, not hiding His face from them, far more readily than He does the lukewarmness and deadness in congregations that are outwardly most regulated and disciplined.' Here Williams has in mind Paul's first letter to the church at Corinth, and the Spirit's reproof to the church at Ephesus at a later date, in Revelation 2:1-7. With great subtlety, Satan exploits his insight into human nature in order to drive the Lord's people to error. Hypocrites, when God's breeze stirs their natural passions, 'like a ship before the wind, under full sail but without any ballast', are in danger of being driven on to the rocks. On being told that many who showed ecstatic responses later returned to sinful ways, Williams is said to have responded with this anecdote:

> There were three people, two men and a woman, living on the side of the same hill, who began their life at nearly at the same time. Their names were Evan, Betty, and Thomas, and each borrowed a hundred pounds when they went there to live. They thought that in time, with thrift and industry they could repay this money. They did not succeed, but the three failed miserably, and they were threatened with litigation. At last the bailiffs came and took Evan to prison. On the way past Sir John Goodman's house on the other side of the mountain they met Sir John himself. 'Where are you going, Evan?' he asked. 'I fear I have to go to prison for my debts, and I acknowledge that this is just, for I am in debt and have nothing to pay, nor any hope for release ever.' 'Really', Sir John said, 'I am sorry to hear this. How much is your debt?' 'My debt is a hundred pounds plus costs.' 'Well, Evan', said Sir John, 'I will pay your debt.' Then he said to the bailiffs, 'I undertake to pay the entire debt including the costs, let him go free.' It is not hard to imagine Evan's joy and gratitude at this. Having shown most fervently his appreciation to Sir John, he returned home. When he reached the top of the hill above his house, he shouted with all his strength, 'thanks, thanks to Sir John Goodman; thanks to Sir John Goodman.' Betty heard and saw him, and wondered greatly, thinking he was mad. But she went up to him, and enquired the reason. When he told her what Sir John had done, she joined him, shouting, 'Thanks, thanks to Sir John Goodman!' Then Thomas saw them, having heard their shouts. He, too, went up, wanting to know what it was all about. And when Evan told him about Sir John's remarkable reaction, he joined them both in shouting, 'thanks, thanks to Sir John Goodman.' But shortly after, demand was made to Betty and Thomas for the debt; and having nothing to pay, they were thrown into prison, where they both died.[19]

190

For Williams, in genuine Christian experience, heightened emotions must be accompanied by resolute choices. It is never safe to mimic the experiences of others while the reason for it has no personal meaning. Nor are godly people exempt from a similar danger; when the passions of the soul are stirred, all too often their natural passions 'take too much part in the work'.

The undercurrents of criticism are dealt with from time to time in the work. 'Philologus' was one who previously expressed a longing that God would 'make Jerusalem a praise in the earth' (Is. 62: 7), but when it came to pass, he preached against it, an evidence of either ignorance or hypocrisy. Geraint Gruffydd paraphrases another example in Philo's 'Reply' in this way:

> And here we have one of the little cameos in which Williams delights. Pneumaticus (a man full of the Spirit) preaches, and the effects associated with the revival follow: singing, leaping and even prostration. 'The place all that time was full of the presence of God'. But there is in the congregation a gentleman named Fformalistus and his wife Florida (occasional auditors at the Methodist meetings), and they are highly offended. Away they go to take tea with the vicar, to the 'hypocrites' in the meeting house. Then, after tea, they accompany the vicar to church, to Evening Prayer, where they respond with unction to the vicar's exhortation (from the *Book of Common Prayer*) that the people should praise God, and rejoice in Him and even clap their hands and sing His praises with shouts of joy – exactly those things which the 'hypocrites' in the meeting house had been practising. [20]

The reason for this inconsistency, says Williams, is not hard to find. 'It is because their religion is only in their understanding, and never reached their hearts ... With the heart man believes for salvation; that men have believed some form of doctrine, however true, unless those principles which he believed with his mind have also taken root in his heart, so that he loves the Son of God, rejoices in His salvation, denies himself, takes up his cross, follows the Lamb in spite of all disgrace, his knowledge only makes him boastful ... It is because there is no experience of grace that the whole world does not rejoice, leap and sing praise to the Lord.'[21] The alternative to bad emotion, which Williams repudiated, was not no emotion at all, but sanctified emotion. Thomas Manton, another Puritan with whom Williams was familiar, puts it this way: 'Religion doth not nullify, but sanctify, our affections. Some have vainly thought affections to be an after-growth of noisome weeds in our

191

nature corrupted; whereas they are wholesome herbs, implanted in us by God at our first creation, of great use to grace when rightly stirred and ordered.'[22]

Confirmation of the revival's authenticity, says Philo, may be found in reason, church history, and in Scripture. Is it not reasonable to speak much of one we love? And to speak much in praise of the plan of salvation through the blood of the Lamb? Should God's servants be less bold than Satan's servants, for the legions of hell are fierce in their opposition to the glory of God. The natural man is motivated by his sinful propensities; is it not reasonable for the spiritual man to give vent to his divinely-planted desires? Furthermore, church history is replete with similar powerful awakenings: people like Wycliffe and Hus were full of zeal and suffered much persecution, but they opened the door for the Reformation. Philo refers to his own day, to revivals in England, Scotland and New England, so what is happening in Wales is not unique. The Nonconformists are at peace with Anglicans; Quakers are no longer the object of derision; it is the Methodists who now bear the brunt of men's persecuting fury:

> Some professors ranted and raved, heatedly gnashed their teeth and bit their tongues, and the whole cause was because this people loved the Christ whom they did not love ... They spend the whole afternoon with other ladies, and the parish clergyman to entertain them over a cup of tea ... And the main topic of conversation all afternoon was the people who rejoiced and sang praises to God. 'A bunch of hypocrites' was the best name for them ... (in church the same people appeal to all and sundry to praise God) ... and yet they pour out their wrath upon those people who did so from their hearts ... The only reason ... was the spirit which possessed them, that zealous spirit of loving and praising God ... Because they follow the Lord with all their heart.

But the similar work in New England was acclaimed even by the Nonconformists Watts and Guise. Scripture, too, with its prophecies, types, ceremonies, and musical activities all pointed forward to the day of Christ and the coming of the Holy Spirit. 'Then the hour came. The Father's promise was fulfilled. O blessed hour! This is what you now see, Martha, and God alone is its author; and it is that which has been from the days of the apostles until now.'[23]

For his final section, Williams drew on Edwards's works. From *The Distinguishing Marks of a Work of the Spirit of God* he took four passages. The first is from the body of the book: 'A work is not to be judged of by any effects on the bodies of men; such as tears, trembling, groans, loud outcries, agonies of body, or the failing of bodily strength.' The second is from William Cooper's 'Preface', and refers to the doctrinal matters insisted upon: 'The points on which their preaching mainly turns are those important ones of man's guilt, corruption and impotence; supernatural regeneration by the Spirit of God, and free justification by faith in the righteousness of Christ; and the marks of the new birth.' The third makes common reference to 1 John 4:15, the passage on which Edward's work is based, and Williams says: 'I have inquired into the principles of many, and I have listened to their preachers, and they all believe that Jesus of Nazareth was truly God.' The final passage is the one Williams quotes at the end of Philo's 'Answer':

> Some object against it as great confusion, when there is a number together in such circumstances, making a noise; and say, God can't be the author of it; because he is the God of order, not of confusion [I Cor. 14:33]. But let it be considered, what is the proper notion of confusion, but the breaking of that order of things whereby they are properly disposed, and duly directed to their end, so that the order and due connection of means being broken, they fail of their end; but conviction and conversion of sinners is the obtaining the end of religious means. Not but that I think that persons that are thus extraordinarily moved should endeavour to refrain from such outward manifestations, what they well can, and should refrain to their utmost, in the time of their solemn worship. But if God is pleased to convince the consciences of persons, so that they can't avoid great outward manifestations, even to the interrupting and breaking off those public means they were attending, I don't think this is confusion, or an unhappy interruption, any more than if a company should meet on the field to pray for rain, and should be broken off from their exercise by a plentiful shower. Would to God that all the public assemblies in the land were broken off from their public exercises with such confusion as this the next Sabbath day! We need not be sorry for breaking the order of the means, by obtaining the end to which that order is directed: he that is going to fetch a treasure, need not be sorry that he is stopped by meeting the treasure in the midst of his journey. [24]

In Edwards, Williams had a powerful ally for the purpose of defending the Welsh Methodists. Even though New England was geographically removed from Wales, the phenomenon they both defended was similar, and in the conviction that this was of God both were adamant. Grace is free, but it is also universal, and in the mighty awakenings that both these men of God witnessed, they saw the earnest of greater things yet to come. For the present it was a privilege they personally enjoyed and ably defended.

21.

'Pursued by God'

Ever the Christian counsellor and theologian, Williams seldom allows the truth to be theoretical. When faced with God's Word there is need for doctrinal statement, for Scripture exegesis, and for intellectual stimulus, but Williams must drive the truth deeper. As he emphasised in his works on revival, truth must radiate from the mind in order to influence desire, motivation and behaviour. In this he was only taking the classical Reformed position, as epitomized by Calvin's teaching:

> The Gospel ... is a doctrine not of the tongue but of life. It is not apprehended by the understanding and memory alone, as other disciplines are, but it is received only when it possesses the whole soul, and finds a seat and resting place in the inmost affection of the heart ... We have given the first place to the doctrine in which our religion is contained, since our salvation begins with it. But it must enter our heart and pass into our daily living, and so transform us into itself that it may not be unfruitful for us ... its efficacy ought to penetrate the inmost affections of the heart, take its seat in the soul, and affect the whole man.[1]

Émile Doumergue, Calvin's fullest biographer, likens the thought of Calvin to 'an ellipse with two foci. And these are the two foci, as distinct as they are inseparable: the focus of intelligence and the focus of inner experience, these are the two foci of which the combined fires constitute the very flame of Calvinism, the flame which gives light and warmth, and does not consume itself. To eliminate one of the two foci would be extinguish the flame.'[2] For Williams, too, light and warmth should be inseparable. Williams was nothing if not a theologian of the heart. Salvation is a matter of enjoyment and duty as well as of deliverance:

> In Thy righteousness I'll triumph,
> In Thy wisdom I'll be wise;
> In Thy robes I'm perfect beauty,
> In Thy power I'll arise;

> In Thy glorious free salvation
> Only shall my soul rejoice,
> And beyond all other pleasures
> Is Thy sweet melodious voice.[3]

This is a verse from the English collection, *Gloria in Excelsis, or, Hymns of Praise to God and the Lamb* of 1772. It reflects the hymn-writer's confidence in God but also his concern to bring each hymn-singer to a riper experience of God. That individual members of the societies should have a secure ground for assurance of their salvation is reflected not only in his hymns, but also in his literary labours from time to time.

In this way Williams contributed significantly to the Methodist understanding of true Christian experience. In poetic form, a work of 180 pages appeared in 1764 with the title *Bywyd a Marwolaeth Theomemphus o'i Enedigaeth i'w Fedd* ('The Life and Death of Theomemphus, from his birth to his grave'). A selective translation with notes and retaining 507 of the 1,451 verses in rhyme appeared in 1996 under the title *Pursued by God*.[3] In it Williams uses fictional characters, with Latin names, to relate the experience of a typical Methodist convert. It is easy to discern parallels between those characters and the real people in Williams's world: 'Boanerges', preacher of the Law's demands and sanctions, could have been Harris or Rowland; this could be true as well of 'Evangelius', preacher of the good news of salvation in Christ; 'Dr. Alethius', the society leader and soul physician, portrays the skill, discernment and compassion that was so evident in Williams himself; and for other characters a similar identification is not hard to make. It would be true to say that in his ministry Williams embodied all three, provided that the 'Dr. Alethius' element embraced a hymn-writing facility as part of the soul physician's resources. Nor would it be hard for his readers to identify with Theomemphus's story, since it would have been very much their own, only in heightened form. In particular, the way in which he triumphed over the dangers that assailed him, without and within, would have brought fresh confidence for young Methodists to persevere in the way that Theomemphus had done. Here was Christian autobiography presented in readable form, portraying linear progression from an initial conversion to final victory over the last enemy, death.

The use of fictional characters was a commonplace literary device at the time, and Williams would have found precedents in Arthur Dent's popular work, *The Plain Man's Pathway to Heaven*, and in John Bunyan's allegories, *The Pilgrim's Progress* and *The Holy War*. [5] His favourite character, 'Evangelius', takes on several roles: in *Theomemphus* he is the Gospel preacher; in the 'Guide to Marriage' and 'The Answer of Philo Evangelius', he is the careful pastor of God's people; in his elegy to Ann Pugh, a compassionate poet. However, in his Preface to Theomemphus, Williams insists that the work 'cannot be called an allegory, because he is portraying real people', and the only fictional element was the use of the name *Theomemphus* to represent a Christian. As a 'dramatic poem', then, Williams takes his characters through the New Testament landscape of varied experiences, where the believer is 'portrayed ... and pursued by God'. He admits that his work falls short of this ideal, and adds, 'but take Theomemphus on his crutches as it were, and embrace him, for he presses on to eternal life.' He acknowledges his debt to Bunyan's works, 'the best books of this kind which I have seen', pervaded by an 'excellent spirit'.[6] His chief resource has been the Bible, even though he had experience of analyzing, monitoring, and nurturing the Christian experience of society members for twenty-four years.

Following William's description of a 'dramatic poem' for this twenty-chapter work, it could be divided into three 'acts' depicting Theomemphus's spiritual experience. The first relates his condition in unbelief and as a stranger to God; the second, his conversion and experience in God's Church; and the third, his trials in a world that is at odds with God. Some of the *dramatis personae* are listed at the beginning of the work by their Latin names and Welsh meaning. A synopsis of each chapter is provided as a title, and throughout the work, biblical precept and example undergird Theomemphus's transition from a state of sin to grace, and provide his comfort in the face of death. Of supreme importance is the fact that it is by divine intervention and initiative, not by human ingenuity and activity, that 'Theomison', 'hater of God' becomes 'Theomemphus', 'seeker after God'. The faith by which Theomemphus lives is not a human product, generated by an emotional 'high' at a time of religious excitement. It is, rather, a divinely-planted principle that produces, in smaller or greater measure at different times, confidence in God's Word and love for God's way. The dominance of these two elements in the poem reflect the teaching that Williams sought to convey to his readers.

Above all, it is the preaching of that Word that is instrumental in bringing unbelievers to faith, as well as in supporting believers in God's

Way. Hence descriptions of preachers figure prominently in the work. For Theomison the spirituality and the sanctions of God's Law so faithfully preached by Boanerges smite the conscience, and open up the dreadful vista of an unavoidable and deserved hell. A second sermon by Boanerges dwells on the Ten Commandments, their implications as explained in Christ's Sermon on the Mount, and the impossibility of keeping them perfectly. Williams could have been thinking of Rowland or Harris, both of whom, in the words of the Puritan George Swinnock, used 'the needle of the Law to make way for the thread of the Gospel'. John Bradford, the English Reformer, maintained that 'the right way to go unto heaven is to sail by hell', and Jonathan Edwards in New England defended the practice on more than one occasion. [7] 'We use not to stand upon compliment or precedency', says the Puritan preacher Richard Baxter, 'when we run to quench a common fire, nor to call men out to it by an eloquent speech. If we see a man fall into fire or water, we stand not upon mannerliness in plucking him out, but lay hands on him as we can without delay.'[8] For such preachers, this was no subjective enthusiasm or psychological technique, no 'excessive zeal and stress on the emotions', which has been imputed to them, but rather a biblical and realistic portrayal of the danger of the human condition in sin.[9] With such a solemn view of sin, they vigorously eschewed all appearance of trickery and falsehood. They shared the conviction that few will flee for safety unless they are aware of danger, none will take bitter medicine that do not feel the pain of injury or the danger of plague. An honest review of their sermons and writings confirms that they merely passed on the clear teaching of Scripture.

There follows a portrayal by Williams of several false preachers who laid false trails. Leaders of the Awakening on both sides of the Atlantic spoke of the damage done by unregenerate ministers who were strangers to God's grace. One example is found in a Rowland sermon: 'as a heavy judgment upon you, it is that the Lord hath permitted you to have such ministers among you as will countenance you in your sloth, and neglect of Jesus – as depreciate His merits, and speak lightly of His grace, as a sanctifying principle – as run with you into every excess of riot, are the foremost to lead the dance, to circulate the glass, to promote your time-killing pastimes, and to encourage every species of dissipation ... All ministers do not fall under this censure. I only speak of the unawakened among them.'[10] Seducus pours scorn on Boanerges, 'that voice of doom and gloom', maintaining that religion consists of avoiding open sins, and doing good. Orthocephalus combines doctrinal orthodoxy with human ability as the remedy for sin. Schematicus displayed an uncharitable spirit with his zeal for secondary issues, and his preaching undermined any good that may have been done by Boanerges. One more false trail is presented to Theomison, that of the Arminian preacher, Arbitrius Liber, who presents man as still having reliable reason and free will, so that he can recognize what is right and do what is good. This drives Theomison to the verge of despair:

> 'I'm blind, and heaven's footpath I cannot rightly trace
> Unless illumination come from His Spirit's grace;
> I'm weak and cannot labour, and merit ne'er was found
> In man full of corruption, from head down to the ground.'[11]

Sin is no superficial blemish in need of a little human cosmetic adjustment; it is deep-seated, disqualifying and paralyzing, and God's remedy alone will suffice. Salvation is the work of God's 'own hands' not man's.

Theomison's deliverance is near, for 'Evangelius' holds forth that remedy: salvation in Christ, sufficient for the worst sinner, effective in the weakest believer, and praiseworthy to all the saints:

> O! grace that's free and changeless, eternally secure,
> The Lamb who died, was wounded, alone provides sin's cure;
> For guilt and shame true healing, the fear of death subdued,
> And love forever grounded on peace with power endued.

This preaching was different in that it traced all recovery to Christ, was accompanied by the Holy Spirit's power, and produced in Theomison a longing for divine intervention. It is later, 'meditating in the woods and praying', when the Holy Spirit brings illumination, sorrow for sin, and faith in Christ to his soul, that his conversion takes place. The occasion is life-changing, a cause for joy, amazement, and praise:

> O! Jesus, how can any, to whom you've given sight,
> Forbear from singing praises and hymns both day and night?
> And who can still be silent, that feels Christ's saving blood,
> Its value and its virtue, to make us right with God.[12]

This is the end for Theomison, the sinner in a state of alienation from God; he is now Theomemphus, the sinner 'in Christ', and so it is a new beginning. Williams is still only in Chapter 6 of the work.

The rest of the poem takes Theomemphus through experiences that Williams must have regarded as typical for the Methodist converts of his day. First comes 'The story of Abasis', an apparent believer, but as time shows, his initial display of fervour soon passes. Abasis did not really know the deceit of the human heart, and so when another object for his passion comes along in the form of 'the lovely maiden, Phania', his allegiance is soon diverted. This episode makes way for what the Methodists considered a profound necessity: the evaluation of Christian experience in the context of the society meeting. In the case of Theomemphus, the society leader is Dr Alethius, a counsellor of formidable qualities: unequalled in his knowledge of Scripture and human nature; a man of profound discernment, wisdom and compassion. The catechizing is comprehensive: understanding of Christ's saving work, awareness of personal guilt and inability, self-denial and new obedience to God's commandments, a measure of assurance, and an affinity for God's people. Then follows Dr Alethius's counsel, a mix of encouragement and exhortation:

> To you is given a witness, that you to Christ belong,
> His blood from sin has cleansed you, and carries you along;
> Salvation is for sinners, for those without a plea,
> In Christ alone, forever, by faith, through grace that's free.
>
> Be careful not to venture in your own strength ahead,
> To scale the sheer rock-face without a sense of dread;
> There are oft slippery places, and hidden snares abound,
> That only godly fear foresees with vision sound. [13]

This was sound counsel indeed, backed by Scripture warrant in promise and precept, but Theomemphus, like every believer, is inwardly flawed and often floored by the remains of sin, especially presumption and self-trust.

While it is true that these hidden dangers lurk in what is at best a deceitful heart, the next part of the poem emphasises God's investment in the salvation of His people. He never abandons the believer, and Williams affirms their eternal election, the persistence of grace, the goodness as well as the mystery of God's providence, and the restoring power of God's Spirit.

> Divine election sleeps not, though Christians fall asleep,
> Its purposes of goodness, once sown, will always reap;
> It will safeguard God's people, though enemies surround,
> Restore the wandering spirit, though wanderings abound.
>
> The saving of God's people from sin and hell's abode,
> From death and grave's dark terror, to bring them back to God,
> To lead them over mountains, through deserts parched and grim,
> Will make the heaven of heavens an everlasting hymn. [14]

There is honesty as well as realism in this portrayal of Christian experience. Even the preaching of Orthodoxus, although sound and fervent, will not restore the saint from his backsliding and sense of desertion. When God comes afresh with renewing grace, however, the soul is not only comforted, but also made humble and teachable.

Three subtle temptations now lay siege to Theomemphus in his life of faith. The first has to do with marriage, and teaches him to beware of carnal affection, where spiritual objectives are side-lined for the sake of natural desire. A hidden agenda of this kind can lead to blunted witness and bitter choices, as Theomemphus finds when he falls for Philomela in that kind of way. He parts with her after much inner conflict, but later, even a Philomeda, whom he marries with a chastened and balanced affection, disappoints, so that he learns 'to live for God supremely, while I on earth remain'. The second temptation comes in the form of Jezebel, who insists that grace frees the believer from obligation to keep God's Law. This Antinomian heresy was a constant thorn in the Methodist side, and two chapters are given to its ramifications and the way in which Theomemphus overcomes. In an extensive footnote, Williams describes its slippery features, and explains why he personifies it under the name of Jezebel:

> All kinds of people are making an outcry about Antinomianism. Most do not know what it is, any more than what a tangent is in Trigonometry, a satellite in Astronomy, or Latitude and Longitude in Navigation. And even the most astute historians can hardly describe it properly. For this doctrine, if doctrine it can properly be called, changes its principles, convictions, and morality many times in any one age ... In the epistle to the Church at Thyatira, this false spirit is called 'the doctrine of Jezebel' ... Now we are not to think that this was some woman in the church at Thyatira, such as 'Elizabeth' or 'Margaret', who taught the lawfulness of carnal pleasures, but rather it was the unruly

spirit by which some in that church lived daily in all their pleasures, while at the same time claiming that they were the best people, nearest to God, understanding the depths of Satan, while the rest were considered mere babes. For this reason I have called that heresy, namely those principles which allow carnal living, the doctrine of Jezebel. Others may call it Antinomianism, or any name they wish. [15]

He recognizes that the Law is no longer the means of achieving acquittal before God. It is now written on the believer's heart, with love planted by God, its fulfilment, a motivating and enabling power for holy living:

> The law is good and holy, God's stamp on every part,
> A heavenly perfection, the kind found in God's heart;
> Love to the law's commandments, each saint makes this his aim,
> With fervent longing always to honour every claim. [16]

The issue was serious enough to motivate Williams's translation of Joseph Hart's biography published three years later, in 1767. A third temptation is personified in Iratus, whose malice towards Christianity in general, and defamation of Theomemphus's character in particular, evokes a response of anger and a desire for revenge. Once more grace intervenes to restore Theomemphus's spiritual equilibrium, so that he asks forgiveness of his opponent and finds peace restored to his own soul.

Before Theomemphus's story draws to its end, he meets 'Academicus', the learned seminary professor, for whom education is the most important, or even the only, qualification necessary for ministering God's Word. Williams implies that learning without grace has many pitfalls: divorced from godliness it generates pride, covetousness, jealousy, a party spirit, doctrinal aberration, and a powerless morality among them. Not that Williams was against education, but he advocated a certain *kind* of education. Information about God could be accumulated by those who had no personal acquaintance and dealings with Him. Gospel ministry required spiritual understanding imparted by God's Spirit, together with sustained fellowship in the attitude of trust and love. Truth and power, must first be experienced before they can be communicated.

> God's kingdom found no ally in man's philosophy,
> This ridiculed his wisdom, and blurred its clarity;
> Inflicted far more damage than any good it made,
> Its propositions clouding the truth which does not fade.

> The truth from heaven draws power, from God receives its crown;
> Destroys the dragon's castles and tears their towers down.
> The Gospel's sole foundation, authority and might,
> Owes nothing to man's reason, and all to heavenly light.
>
> Though learning has great value, I see this every day,
> Than only the experienced will preach the Gospel way;
> The Spirit makes a preacher, and heaven's choicest sound
> Is heard and felt with power, when heaven's gales abound.[17]

Clearly, this was another area where the Welsh Methodists insisted on the priority of the divine initiative and the inadequacy of human achievement.

In the face of death, 'the king of terrors' as Williams calls it, every believer faces 'the last enemy', and Theomemphus is no exception. What foundation is there for comfort and hope when it assails with one of its deadly instruments? A catalogue of conditions that in Williams's day might prove fatal was to be expected of one with a sustained interest in medicine. But such conditions are of secondary importance to the matter of spiritual reassurance. Here again Williams pursues his subject to a deeper level than the classical Protestant, or even Puritan, response. Where they encouraged the believer to identify evidence of sanctification, marks of grace, and progress in holiness, Williams is convinced that the only infallible source lies elsewhere:

> In death and doubt is power, far greater than is shown
> By marks and signs and virtues, although to others known;
> Another ground, foundation, my naked soul must find,
> Providing safety, comfort, 'gainst foes of every kind.
>
> I cling no more to virtues, to marks of grace within,
> Are they not freely given, by grace, to heaven's kin?
> In me no good lies dormant, vile I, and all unclean,
> No greater, worse transgressor throughout the world is seen.[18]

Williams should not be misunderstood: he is not saying that evidence of a changed life is irrelevant or superfluous, only that it does not constitute an unfailing confirmation of a state of grace and hope of glory. This lies rather in God's Word:

> My strength lies in the promise which God so freely sent,
> Directly from the glory, to sinners, though hell-bent;
> So gracious and longsuffering, and willing to forgive,
> This most unworthy rebel, by grace henceforth to live.

203

> That God is true and faithful, this then my only base,
> The words that He has spoken, these nothing will erase;
> In Christ is resurrection, His death and purity,
> In God my preservation, for all eternity.[19]

With this sure hope, this 'anchor of the soul', then, based on 'the immutability of God's counsel, confirmed by an oath' to the heirs of promise, the believer can die in peace and safety (Hebrews 6: 17-19).

Throughout Theomemphus's journey there is a recurrent theme. It is that 'the word came to him', in his darkest hours, with penetrating, transforming power and lasting effect. In this way Williams conveys the believer's frequent, significant, ongoing dealings with God. It is God's Word that repeatedly, unfailingly quickens Theomemphus, just as it did for John Bunyan, and for every believer.[20] Revelation is not sourced in Christian experience, quite the opposite: the divine word is as necessary as it is productive in its genuine emergence and sustenance. Methodism was not based on emotion, although it acknowledged it; its constituency was real people for whom heavenly revelation was earthed in human hearts.

The symbolism of a journey, too, has important implications. Theomemphus deliberately conveys the impression of progress in the Christian life. While the believer's union with Christ is a settled state, lived in relationship with God, it is also progressive. Within that relationship of belonging there is growing acquaintance and conformity, since the now justified, adopted Theomemphus shows evidence of sanctification. This is an emerging godliness forged by inward kinship and outward discipline that advances steadily, if gradually and imperfectly, towards maturity in Christ. Halfway through the book, Theomemphus is tempted to spiritual pride and self-reliance, with dire consequences:

> Presumption said to Theo, 'Believe that you have grace
> And strength to drive corruption from your heart's every space;
> Believe that fleshly passions no more can wound and maul,
> For sin, once slain, is helpless, it cannot hurt the soul.

Such confidence was a delusion, and the chapters which follow, ten and eleven, deal with the havoc that followed and the difficult path of recovery. In an indirect way, without mentioning any names, Williams was providing his readers with a carefully reasoned case for rejecting John Wesley's claim that sinless perfection was possible in this life. As

204

early as the 1740s the Calvinists had parted company with him on this point, since a perfection that could be lost as well as enjoyed, was contrary to the character and grace of God. Wesley's views floundered on a lack of distinction between assurance and perfection, between justification and sanctification, between maturity and sinlessness. In his 1767 *Plain Account of Christian Perfection*, Wesley asserted that perfection as well as forgiveness were both received by faith. It was a time when many of his followers claimed personal experience of perfect love and obedience. Williams's Theomemphus clearly was not one of that number.[21]

While death is certain for everyone, it does not have the last word. While Theomemphus's earthly pilgrimage has ended, his everlasting bliss in glory has now begun. To this he bears resounding testimony in the epitaph he writes for his tombstone:

> This man was highly favoured, and washed in precious blood;
> His sins were fully pardoned, ten million in its flood;
> Was plucked as from the burning, and when death threatened sore,
> Was lifted from Gehenna; in heaven for evermore.
>
> My body will be raisèd, like my Belovèd's own,
> Free from those ill desires which often made me groan;
> No man beneath the heavens can fully know my bliss,
> And no man can imagine, such heavenly pleasure this.
>
> No darts, no frights, no fears, no sorrow and no pain,
> To sing in heaven His glory, the Lamb that once was slain;
> One of a throng of myriads, who sing with endless praise,
> A love-song as the anthem, a song they'll ever raise. [22]

It was fitting that this last verse should also appear on Williams's own tombstone in the graveyard of Llanfair-ar-y-bryn, his parish church near Llandovery.

22.

'A school of the prophets'

Theomemphus had appeared at a time of immense spiritual upheaval in the Methodist ranks. At the time of writing, Williams was nearer fifty than forty years old, and by this time Rowland and others recognized his leadership skills as well as his poetic gifts. During Harris's absence of more than ten years there had been considerable changes. While at Trefeca, Harris had drawn closer to the parish church, while Rowland had been deprived of his curacy at Llangeitho, affecting the allegiance of the Welsh Methodists to Anglicanism in markedly different ways. These matters surfaced at an Association in August 1765 and Harris's diary conveys his deep misgivings: 'I was convinced I should tell the Association that I cannot come among them in my old place as I do not see among them the same spirit as they set out in; they have left the Church to form a new sect, Mr Rowland at the head of it, and call it Methodist; and to have fallen from the life of faith, and to have no need of discipline and general union, and to judge me for abiding in the Church, a bigot … I went among the preachers to the New House, where the six clergymen sat in a high seat, and the exhorters and a very great number sat on benches below, and I sat among them and refused to go to the seat.' In spite of this Harris noted the next day that, 'after being much pressed indeed by several and asked by Rowland I discoursed, after Peter Williams, on Luke 4:18.' [1]

On the other hand, by many of those whom Harris had been instrumental in calling to faith, his withdrawal and settlement of a 'family' at Trefeca was seen as an abdication of responsibility. Williams may have been articulating their sentiments, as well as his own, when in his elegy to Harris he compared the Trefeca settlement to the monasteries which were pulled down during the Reformation. While Harris was in the military, he was in a position of unquestioned authority, and his dominant, if not domineering, ways may have been aggravated. On his return to the Methodist fold the exhorters found this especially irksome, having by this time been used to a more flexible oversight under Rowland and Williams.

Following the disruption the Welsh Methodists had closed ranks as a matter of necessity, and this, together with continued censure from the ecclesiastical authorities, made a separate Methodist identity inevitable. On his part Harris disowned the name Methodist and all that it implied. He believed that the way ahead lay with a wider constituency, embracing Wesley's people and the Moravians, a proposition not even remotely possible in Wales where doctrinal convictions were solidly Calvinist. All these issues had been dwarfed by the effects of the revival that broke out in 1762, partly healing former divisions, but also setting priorities that demanded urgent attention. Preaching remained a top priority, and one testimony to its continued usefulness during that decade was Whitefield's visit in 1767 to Haverfordwest in West Wales. 'I am just come from my field throne', he writes at the end of May that year: 'Thousands and thousands attended at eight in the morning. Life and light seemed to fly all around.' The letter proceeds to give his itinerary in the area for the next few days: 'On Tuesday, God willing, I am to preach at Woodstock; on Friday, at Pembroke; here again next Sunday by eight, and then for England ... I have been pushing on dear sick Mr [Howel] Davies to go out and preach six miles off. He is gone finely mounted, and I am persuaded will return in high spirits. Who knows, who knows but preaching may be our grand catholicon [remedy for everything] again? This is the good methodistical, thirty year old medicine.'[2] Nothing was allowed to hinder the divine means of bringing sinners to Christ.

With the death in 1761 of Griffith Jones, whose immense influence was celebrated as 'a remarkable bright star' in a fitting elegy by Williams, another constraint on Methodist secessionist tendencies had been removed. One by one the first Welsh Methodist clergymen were passing away, witness the elegies written by Williams in the decade from that date: for Lewis Lewis, whose death in 1764 was 'like a meteor leaving a trail behind it', Howel Davies and George Whitefield in 1770, both of them 'refulgent' stars.[3] Eternity was not only real, as held forth in their sermons, it was also near, as advancing years and death amply demonstrated. Preaching at Llansawel in May 1763 Williams dwelt 'on unbelief as the parent of all sin', making it clear that faith exposes the vanity of the world and its toys, and believers find their true joy in God alone.[4] This theme finds an echo in the title of the collection of 84 hymns published before the end of the year: *Ffarwel Weledig, Groesaw Anweledig Bethau*, ('Farewell to seen, welcome to unseen things'). They expressed not only a note of triumph and assurance, but three were written at Harris's request, and expressed the desire for the spiritual union that should characterize 'all who follow Christ.' With the certainty of a future accountability, it was fitting that a present harmony should obtain among the godly. Besides these things, the intensity of the 1762 revival had hardly abated in its urgency, fervency or solemnity. Revival, too, intensifies the awareness of eternal destinies, and the reality of spiritual things demand and delight the soul's involvement.

If some were taken from the Methodist ranks, others were being added. One of these was David Jones, another Carmarthenshire man, born at Llanllwni, and ordained deacon by the Bishop of St David's in 1758. He served as curate at Tudweiliog in north Wales and Llanafan Fawr, near Brecon in the south. He was ordained priest in August 1760, and his move to Trefethin near Pontypool in 1761 proved crucial to his spiritual pilgrimage. It was here that he came into contact with William Read, the apothecary friend of Williams, who appears to have played some part in Jones's conversion. At this period in his life Jones's 'heart was savingly impressed with the realities of divine truth by the perusal of [John] Flavel's works.' From Trefethin he moved first to Bristol and then to the parish of Crudwell in Wiltshire, until his final settlement as Rector of Llan-gan in the Vale of Glamorgan in 1767. Here he established himself as a gifted preacher, and emerged as a prominent and useful second-generation Methodist leader.[5] For this reason Llan-gan became the counterpart in south Wales of Llangeitho in mid-Wales, a vigorous centre of Methodist witness. Williams spoke of him as 'honest Jones of Llan-gan', whose orthodoxy was sound and reliable. John Williams, son of the hymn-writer, taught school for a time near Llan-gan, a post probably engineered by Jones. The Countess of Huntingdon later often used David Jones to supply the chapels of her Connexion in England. In a letter to her in 1773, Jones mentions an Association in his parish at which Rowland and Williams preached. At the end of the letter he added a Welsh hymn of Williams's, suggesting that some of the students at her College in Trefeca should attempt a translation for her. Addressing the 'dear reader' of a Welsh elegy to Williams by his relative,David Saunders, Jones said it was worthy to be printed in order to 'preserve in the memory of those who heard him speak so sweetly many times about the great Redemption in the blood of the Lamb.'[6]

Trefeca College aimed at providing ministerial training at Trefeca. It was the joint effort of Howel Harris and the Countess of Huntingdon that came to fruition in 1768.[7] The project, however, had been mooted as early as 1740, if an entry in Howel Harris's diary for 1771 is to be believed: 'Of the College, how the laying of it down here was made plain to Lady Huntingdon when she first came over to my house about 7 years ago, and then I mentioned to her how a School of the Prophets had been opened to Mr. Seward and me in 1740 in my house to be near here, and had ever since abode in my heart in prayer. When again it lay dormant for three years, it lay still on my heart, and I put Lady Huntingdon in mind of it and called it College not School.'[8]

William Seward, philanthropist and companion to George Whitefield, had been converted in 1738 and had come to assurance of faith after meeting Charles Wesley. His testimony to Christ explains his Christian generosity: 'I declared that I had found the Pearl of Great Price, even Jesus Christ, and that I had sold what I had to buy it.' His financial acumen and support were a great blessing to George Whitefield from that time to his death in October 1740. In the autumn of that year Seward accompanied Harris on his preaching tour, even though by his own admission, 'I found my call was more to suffer than to preach.' Their joint vision of a 'School of the Prophets' confirms his commitment to Gospel preaching as the great need of the day, and it was his allegiance to the ordinance that cost him his life. While he and Harris stood in the open air for that purpose at Hay-on-Wye, a stone was thrown at his head which rendered him unconscious. Within a few days he died, and his gravestone at Cusop a short distance outside that town, bears the inscription, 'To die is gain'. Before his death he had made financial provision for his daughter, but for Whitefield there was none such. For the Methodists as well as Whitefield his 'martyrdom' was a heavy blow.[9]

Seward's death and the consequential lack of financial resources as well as Harris's preaching schedule meant that the project, however attractive, could not be realised. In the intervening years before its completion, Harris kept it alive in his mind and prayers: 'I had especial freedom to cry for a school at Trefeca to train young men to the Lord. If He would bring one there, that He would make it a blessing to all God's Church, and bring His Catholic Spirit on them all [1749]'; 'Crying for Trefeca ... a great building ... for preaching, and an Academy for preachers. Lord, Thou art able and I leave it to Thee. I had cried that I might serve Him and the people by printing. He seems to have hindered me that way [1761]'; '... need of building New Grand House for an Academy or School of young preachers...[1763].'[10]

Meanwhile, the Countess had embarked on ambitious projects of her own: building chapels attached to her private residences, regarding them as convenient extensions to the rooms where her preachers regularly addressed invited guests. In addition to George Whitefield, William Romaine and Martin Madan had already been appointed her chaplains, and she drew on other clergymen, settled in regular parishes. As her chapels proliferated, so the need for ministry increased, and training men for these vacancies was an inevitable consequence. The chapel at Brighton was built in 1761, that at Bath in 1765 and Whitefield preached at its opening. 'Though a very wet day', he wrote, 'the place was very full, and assuredly the great Shepherd and Bishop of souls consecrated and made it holy ground by his presence.' One feature, a small, curtained-off area, came to be known as 'the Nicodemus corner' since its purpose was to provide anonymity for bishops and other clergymen whose attendance was to be kept secret.[11] In July 1764 the Countess used a visit to south Wales to share her concern to train preachers with Harris, who 'went to Brecon to bring the Countess of Huntingdon to Trefeca ... The Countess stayed many days at Trefeca, greatly approving of the place and of the discipline kept, and informing Harris that she had a desire to establish a college for her preachers there, so that they might go out to preach Christ in the spirit of Trefeca; that they could preach amongst the Methodists and Nonconformists, living in Harris's house and being under his discipline. As he bade farewell to the Countess at Bristol she again questioned him on lower Trefeca and its suitableness as a college, which she called 'a School of the Prophets', with Mr. Jordan, who at the time kept a grammar school at Abergavenny, being principal.'[12]

In March 1768 six students were expelled from St Edmund Hall, Oxford, for their Methodism. They were portrayed as 'enthusiasts who talked of regeneration, inspiration and drawing nigh unto God', but the publications written in their defence soon raised the wider issue of the Calvinism of the Established Church's Thirty-nine Articles. Among those who wrote in this way were Whitefield, Sir Richard Hill and Augustus Toplady. John Wesley saw it as the removal of Calvinist students, and a confirmation of his own views that the Articles were not Calvinistic. For the Countess of Huntingdon, it was a vindication of her Trefeca College project, and added urgency to its realization. Its opening took place on 24 August 1768, the day after work on the building was completed, and the Countess's sixty-first birthday.[13]

The phrase 'School of the Prophets' was a deliberate choice. To the Methodist mind the education necessary to make preachers of the Gospel was of another kind than that provided by the traditional institutions. 'You say well that there are Schools and Academies enough, both in the Establishment and in the Dissenting Way', writes one of Harris's correspondents in his reply to a letter, 'but a School of the Prophets, that's the thing.'[14] While the word 'school' conveyed the idea of disciplined, cerebral study, the qualifying word, 'prophets', implied enlightened, spiritual proclamation. Appropriate preparation for the Christian ministry required theology, yes, but spirituality as well; biblical knowledge, yes, but accompanied by personal fellowship with God and the exercise of gifts imparted only by the Holy Spirit. Geoffrey F. Nuttall saw a two-fold significance to the College: 'in the first place, that it was a new kind of institution: a pioneer in the theological education arising out of the Evangelical Revival ... It was as preachers of the gospel, not as men of learning that the Trevecca students were sent out to itinerate far and wide and to bring light into the dark corners of the land and of lands across the sea ... secondly, that for a generation it became a model for theological education.'[15] Williams's son, John was for some four or five years master at Trefeca until his father died, and regularly wrote to the Countess about the students. Their ministries were mainly exercised in England, even though the first language of many would have been Welsh.

The College opening on 24 August 1768 was a festival of great preaching by Rowland and Whitefield, among others. This was Whitefield's last preaching occasion in Wales, and it must have been difficult for him, coming soon after his wife's death on 9 August. In his funeral sermon to her five days later, Whitefield reminded his London congregation of a particular incident in his early ministry among them, to illustrate the support she had given him: 'Do you remember my preaching in those fields by the old stump of a tree? The multitude was great, and many were disposed to be riotous. At first, I addressed them firmly, but when a desperate gang drew near with the most ferocious and horrid curses and menaces, my courage began to fail. My wife was then standing behind me as I stood on the table. I think I hear her now. She pulled my gown, and, looking up, said, 'George, play the man for your God'. My confidence returned. I spoke to the multitude with boldness and affection. They became still, and many were deeply affected.'[16] With her passing, another of Whitefield's links with Wales was severed.

Williams was present at the College opening, and participated in the proceedings, closing some of the solemnities 'with a suitable address to the awakened and unawakened.' Thomas Charles refers to the occasion in his article on Williams, noting that, 'when the Countess of Huntingdon established her College at Trefeca, he became acquainted with *that elect lady*. She had great respect for him, and in her opinion, as she often remarked, "all things considered, Wales has no greater man in which to boast." When she was there, he visited her on each occasion she spent time in the area.'[17] Williams certainly preached at subsequent Trefeca Anniversary occasions. At the first anniversary, on 24 August 1769, after a sermon by John Fletcher at ten that morning, Williams 'preached in Welsh till between one and two o'clock', while John Wesley preached that afternoon. A report of the proceedings elicited from Whitefield, who was absent, the comment in a letter to Wesley: 'I am glad to hear that you had such a Pentecost season at the College. One would hope that these are earnests of good things to come, and that our Lord will not remove His candlestick from among us.'[18] At the August 1770 anniversary the preachers included, as well as Williams, Rowland and Peter Williams, John Berridge, Walter Shirley and Henry Venn. Immediately prior to the anniversary, Wesley's Conference had adopted a position on the nature of justification that fell short of the Reformed position, and Wesley never again preached at the College.

The following year's anniversary was attended by 'fourteen clergymen', Williams and Rowland among them, as well as 'several Dissenting ministers, exhorters, and lay preachers.' Williams and Rowland accompanied the Countess on a tour of South Wales, preaching 'to large congregations both in the churches and in the open air', in the principal towns of Brecon, Carmarthen, and Haverfordwest. 'At Swansea Mr. Rowlands and Mr. Williams preached to very numerous congregations in the open air. At Newport in Pembrokeshire on Sunday evening, 15 September, Mr. Williams preached in the open air to an immense multitude, many of whom appeared much affected.' Lady Huntingdon arrived at Trefeca five days later, 'filled with wonder and astonishment at the goodness of God her Saviour in preserving her going out and coming in, and enabling her to carry the blessings of the Gospel to those who were sitting in darkness, and in the shadow of death.' On their return to Trefeca, Williams preached twice in Welsh, once at the College and once at Harris's house, and the latter found both discourses 'somewhat searching.'[19] Over the following years, Williams often preached at the anniversary, along with Rowland, Peter Williams, Walter Shirley, Augustus Toplady, and others.

As early as 1769 William Williams had expressed concern as to the availability of suitable students for the College. He was unwilling to give one prospective applicant a testimonial, and in a letter to the Countess suggests that the College should have an auxiliary grammar school. He writes:

> I have promised to write to your Ladyship before this but neglected it, by reason of my roving and ranging over the rude mountains, and wild precipices of Wales, in search of poor illiterate souls chained in the dens of darkness and infidelity … Madam I can't certify anything about this youth … what inward change, or what work of the Spirit of God he has on his heart, I fear none sufficient to recommend him to be a student in a college, whose fundamental design was to train up youth already converted, and professing to know the Saviour, to be more fit ministers of the pure Gospel of Jesus Christ … All which put together, Madam, persuaded me once or twice to desire your Ladyship to consider whether it would be a step further towards promoting the cause in hand, to set up a Grammar school somewhere near the College, to such youth as could not be found of age, proper learning, nor grace clear enough to enter themselves in the College as students.

This was Williams's first letter to a titled lady, and he found refuge for his diffidence in writing by quoting Scripture: 'I know not how to conclude, except it shall be in the words of an old decrepit presbyter of a mean parentage, but canonised after his decease to the title of St John the divine, who concludes his letter to an elect lady thus: "having many things to write to you I would not write with paper and ink, but I trust to come unto you and speak face to face that our joy may be full" – which may be felt and proved at the next association [College anniversary] in Trefeca, is the hearty wish and prayer, my Lady, your Ladyship's most humble servant and poor brother in our Lord and Saviour, Billy Williams.' The signature, Billy Williams, reflects uncertainty rather than familiarity, since in subsequent letters to her, as to his closest friends and other correspondents, his signature was always 'William Williams'. A second letter to the Countess, written in February 1778, speaks of his busy schedule preventing a visit to the College so that he might 'reach home, that I might set out there from immediately to a round in Carmarthenshire for three or four days.' A third letter, written before 1778, also speaks of Williams's busy schedule:

> I have been of late through all the north [of Wales] and travelled about 600 miles in 22 days, and preached constantly twice a day, and often kept a private society. The work of the Lord goes on there bravely; multitudes come to hear the Word, and receive it with joy. I hope there are there thousands of gracious souls; all persecution there is over ...I intend to be at Brecon preaching in your Ladyship's chapel next monthly meeting, where I would be very glad to see your Ladyship. I have heard some talk of your Ladyship going to Llangeitho. I would be glad to know the time, and if it will be any time but the next week, I would be your Ladyship's guide and servant, and my wife also would come along. She has been with me all through the north.[20]

Next to Harris, Williams was the most committed itinerant of the Welsh leaders, and in this respect he could be compared to Whitefield. In his elegy to 'that dear man of God', offered to the Countess, he pays him this tribute: Whitefield was 'one of the most orthodox, active, and faithful ministers of Christ in the British dominions.'[21] Apart from the reference to the British dominions, the same could be said of Williams himself.

In Williams the Countess found a friend but not a servant. Daniel Rowland and Williams limited their involvement with her to College Anniversary occasions and accompanying her on her Welsh tours. Harris was foremost in the links she had with Welsh leaders of the revival, while Howel Davies, David Jones and Thomas Charles were chief among those who on occasions served her chapels in England. For Williams and Rowland particularly the Countess's sallies into Wales were peripheral to the Welsh work. The College at Trefeca was virtually an outpost of the Countess's Connexion, and it was through Harris and Whitefield that the Welsh Methodists came to see the Countess's titled position as a convenient asset to Gospel work.

The cordial relationship between English and Welsh Calvinistic Methodism was strained but not severed when the Countess decided to secede from the Church of England in 1780. Her attempt to secure support from the Welsh Association that met at Llangeitho in August that year fell short of its aim. Peter Williams conveyed his own and the Association's response soon afterwards: 'I was of the opinion, and am still, that your Ladyship had no right, by any privilege of Peerage, to extend your influence, I mean your patronage beyond your personal presence, or the limits of your legal residence ... With regard to the disposition of the ministers at Association especially Mr R[owlan]ds I would as soon hope to persuade the Pope to become Lutheran, as prevail with him to coincide with the late proposal.' [22] Such misgivings did not prevent Nathaniel Rowland and David Jones from attending an ordination within the Countess's Connexion in 1784.[23] Clearly, developments within the Calvinistic Methodist constituency from the late 1760s brought into focus issues that required fresh thinking and controversial resolution. Williams saw them as a challenge to lay foundations that would provide sound landmarks to safeguard the revival's essential convictions and experiences.

23.

'So dangerous an enemy'

The 1762 revival imparted to Williams a fresh passion for communicating biblical truth that was nothing short of incandescent. With theological acumen, mature experience and literary skill, he made provision for real needs among his fellow Methodists, and did so from the vantage point of a deep understanding of God's Word. Some of the reasons for his labours were recent, but not a few were of longer standing. Evidence for this is found in the writings he produced over the following years, as he dealt with the revival's encouragements and problems.

In 1766 Williams translated a pamphlet written in New England that described a revival which the author considered 'to be Heaven begun, even while we are more truly ... than St. Paul, the chief of Sinners.' Written by Samuel Buell (1716-98), it appeared in 1764, and bore the title A *Copy of a Letter from the Rev. M. Buell of East Hampton, on Long Island, to the Rev. Mr. Barber, of Groton in Connecticut (* 'Hanes Llwyddiant Diweddar yr Efengyl, a Rhyfedd Waith Duw, ar Eneidiau Pobl yn North America'). Of course Williams was interested in New England revival movements, but what was it about this work that motivated Williams to translate it? Quite simply, it echoed with remarkable resonance the Llangeitho revival of 1762. People in Wales knew neither Buell nor Barber, East Hampton nor Groton. The work extended to a mere eight pages, but its message was clear and convincing. Revival is a work of God that Buell calls 'this extraordinary Day'. Young and old were powerfully and spiritually affected; religious exercises were sustained day after day with intense desire. The transformation wrought in the most unlikely persons demonstrated irrefutably that it was no ephemeral or emotional excess that was at work.

Williams could identify with Buell in many respects; by conviction both were Calvinists; both had written hymns, both had been influenced by Jonathan Edwards, and both anticipated a future time of prosperity for Christ's kingdom. Furthermore, it is quite likely that it was a common acquaintance, none other than George Whitefield, who introduced Williams to this American author. As early as 1744 Whitefield referred to Buell as 'a young minister whom God hath been pleased to make much use of in the late great and glorious work in New England.'[1] A graduate of Yale, Buell was licensed initially to an itinerant ministry. His preaching at Northampton in Jonathan Edwards's absence and after his return early in 1742 was attended with 'very extraordinary effects', in the words of Edwards.[2] Shortly afterwards his preaching 'five times in Boston publicly to vast assemblies' was 'attended with great success through the blessing of God.'[3] It was Edwards who preached at Buell's installation at East Hampton in 1746, where he remained for the rest of his life.[4] In 1766 Buell wrote a fuller account of the revival, in which he emphasised the divine source, variety of experiences, and the raised expectation of future success that followed.[5] If any confirmation were needed of the affinity between Buell and Williams, it is provided by a statement in Buell's *Spiritual Knowledge of God in Christ:* 'Orthodox speculations and notions in theory concerning God, Christ, and things divine, though ever so exact, give not those amiable apprehensions of divine objects, which the divinely enlightened soul is the subject of.'[6] For Welsh Calvinistic Methodists like Williams no statement could have crystallized their message and mission more clearly.

Buell's pamphlet, translated by Williams, provided ample evidence of the integrity and validity of a work of God, whether in East Hampton or in Llangeitho. In their essential features they were the same, and in other respects there were close parallels:

> For many weeks past God has been preparing His way; his own children have been remarkably replenished with love, holy joys, and unutterable groanings in prayer, for the outpouring of His Holy Spirit upon us. Our assemblies, numerous and solemn, and the arrows of conviction, sermons after sermon, have been fastened in the hearts of sinners. Thus has it been for some time past; but for a week past, heaven and hell have seemed to meet here, and to reign here. God's people have almost all been favoured with such manifestations of divine glory, such communications of light, love, joy and comfort, and been under such labouring pangs, and in such agonies of distress for sinners, that in some instance it seemed as if soul and body would be separated in many, beyond all I have now seen. But oh! The agonies and cries, and importunities of sinners for mercy! Mercy, mercy, Lord! Pardoned mercy, for Jesus' sake, for the chief of sinners! ... Every day, for a week past, the house of God has been repaired to by all our people in general; by nine o'clock, no preaching was appointed, excepting one of

217

the days, when it was supposed there was a thousand people on a weekday in the house of God, and all somehow impressed with a weighty sense of eternal things. Never did I see such an assembly before! God's glory filled the house .... All the town seems bowed before this amazing power and glory, and scarce a single instance of a person out of Christ, above eight years of age, (and several under), but is with solicitude inquiring, 'What must I do to be saved?' Most all of our young people, as well as others, many of them eight, ten, and twelve years of age, are now hopefully converted ... Hundreds are now in distress of soul for a Saviour, complaining of hard hearts and blind minds ... Blessed be God, for about thirty years, I can't but declare, to the glory of God, so far as I can judge from all these things, that the work of God now in East-Hampton, is far the most God-like, Christ-like, excellent and glorious, that ever I knew.[7]

All in all, the correspondence between the two revivals sent out a clear message, that the manifestations of religious activity in both places were the result of an outpouring of God's Holy Spirit. Indeed, the resemblance between the two works, despite geographic remoteness and cultural differences, was remarkable. Williams translated Buell's account from a conviction that it provided the Welsh Methodists with timely support. It vindicated the revival in Wales in the face of criticism from detractors, and confirmed for Welsh believers that the wonderful works of God in their midst were not altogether or always spurious.

Williams's former vicar, Theophilus Evans, had published his *History of Modern Enthusiasm*, with its scathing denunciation of the Methodists, particularly Whitefield, in 1752. A Welsh translation of the anonymous pamphlet *An Earnest and Affectionate Address to the People Called Methodists* ('Annerch difrifol a charedig at y bobl a elwir Methodistiaid'), written to defend the Established Church, appeared more recently, in 1765. In this work distinctive Methodist convictions such as the need to be born again, justification by faith alone, and the direct ministry of the Holy Spirit in believers, together with some of their practices, extempore prayer and some omissions in the words used at Holy Communion among them, were challenged.[8] From the translation of Buell's work it was clear that Welsh Methodists were not alone in their experience of genuine revival, even if they were thought of as fanatics or heretics.

The Methodist constituency in Wales, however, needed instruction in righteousness as well as an awareness of kinship with other believers as to their religious experiences. Following on from Buell's pamphlet,

Williams issued a work of prose that dealt with a very real and practical issue. It appeared in the following year, 1767, with a lengthy title: *CROCODIL, Afon yr Aipht, wedi ei weled ar Fynydd Seion: sef, CENFIGEN, wedi ei holrhain trwy'r Byd a'r Eglwys, tan Geffylybiaeth Bwystfil gormesol yr Anialwch, mor afluniaidd a gwenwynig ei Natur ag un o Fwystfilod y Pwll, &c.* ('THE CROCODILE of Egypt's River, seen on Mount Zion: or, ENVY, traced through the World and the Church, under the Figure of the oppressing Beast of the Wilderness, as ugly and poisonous its nature as any of the Beasts of the Pit, &c.') A verse from Ecclesiastes 4: 4 appears on the title page: 'I considered all travail, and every right work, that for this a man is envied of his neighbour.' Opposition to revival arose partly on account of the envy of formal, lifeless religious leaders, but this deadly enemy threatened God's people from within as well as from without.

Egypt as a location represented the epitome of evil. 'Theomemphus' had traced his origins to Egyptian darkness, with the Egyptian Memphis as representative of the whole land. The meaning of the word 'crocodile' ranges from treachery, falsehood and subtlety to the insincere grief conveyed by speaking of 'crocodile tears'. 'Egypt' figures in the title because its natural habitat was the river Nile. Another of Williams's book titles, 'Three Men from Sodom and Egypt', confirms that life for everyone, sinner and saint alike, is lived in a hostile and dangerous environment, with grace alone providing, not an exit from it but a neutralizing, even conquering, influence against it. So here, the crocodile's subtle, insidious, devastating envy is rampant in a world which has the closest kinship with, and similarity to, Egypt.

The use of 'crocodile' as an emblem for envy is unusual. In the work itself, Williams has this to say for its use:

> Allow me to set it out in allegorical representation so that I can develop it more fully, and show its activity in poor and princely, wise and foolish, young and old, religious and irreligious, in greater detail. Since it is a beast unlikely to be found on Mount Zion, I must have freedom to vary my comparisons, and call it sometimes an ugly beast, sometimes a sly fox, sometimes a deceitful snake, sometimes a handsome idol, but usually a hideous, rapacious, deformed crocodile, which sets it out as well as any ... chiefly because it lurks in hidden places for its prey, and when it snatches it, it first drowns, then tears it to pieces, and then quickly swallows it; and it would be very difficult to find a more appropriate emblem for envy than this.[9]

Given Williams's excursions into encyclopaedic literature for his *Pantheologia*, familiarity with an extensive two-volume work by Edward Topsell on animals might have suggested it. The second of these, *Historie of Serpents, or the Second Booke of Living Creatures*, includes these comments on crocodile tears: 'there are not many bruite beasts that can weepe, but such is the nature of the Crocodile, that to get a man within his danger, he will sob, sigh & weepe, as though he were in extremitie, but suddenly he destroyeth him.' He adds: 'The males of this kind do love their females above all measure, yea even to jealousie, as may appear by this one history of *P. Martyr.*' A book in Williams's library, William Greenhill's, *Exposition of Ezekiel*, likens the Egyptian Pharaoh to a crocodile, and he, too, may have drawn on Topsell's work for the crocodile's description. [10]

Crocodil was written to resolve real, not imaginary or supposed, difficulties, as described in an opening address 'to the reader':

> Perhaps some will be so foolish or precipitate as to think that this little book is an essay that has been shot like a bullet from the breech of a gun at Sandeman and his few followers in Wales. Such people must think that there is no-one else so filled with envy as him … but let it be known to all who read this work, that the author is addressing vast multitudes much closer to home than that distant Scotsman … Let the reader know that this book is written chiefly for the many several denominations of men in Wales who profess godliness, who through their pride, self-esteem, and their envy have made as much devastation in religion as Nebuchadnezar made in Jerusalem when he exiled Zion to Babylon. Anyone with open eyes will see this envy filling the world … You will see that no walk of life, no office, no endowment or gift, is exempt from this envy; otherwise, why are there so many splits, controversies, and upheavals among congregations, other than because this serpent has not been slain. You will see ministers who are of the same doctrine and discipline, cold and distant toward each other. Why cannot one watchman here suffer another watchman there to be praised, unless this root has not been mortified. Why cannot a man of God here rejoice at the success of another man of God there, unless it is for the same reason? And why cannot the whole church rejoice at the elevation and prominence of one another, except for the same thing?

The setting for this allegory is 'God's mountain' or 'Jerusalem', 'Immanuel's land', whose ruler, 'the great Prince' is opposed by 'Lucifer', 'the red dragon'. Against Immanuel, Lucifer's rage was implacably ranged with ferocious intensity, because of His dignity, majesty and sovereignty:

220

Jehovah had set Immanuel as Head, not merely on a great part or half, of heaven, but on the whole; to Him He had given all; hosts, armies, authorities, angels, cherubim, seraphim, of all degrees, under His feet, extending His kingdom to all things visible and invisible: moon, stars, earth, land, sky; and chiefly, above all else He gave Him to be the Prince of mankind, Creator, Sustainer, Saviour, as well as Judge at their end. This Immanuel was the firstborn of all creatures and first-fruits of all creation; He Himself dwelt therein, and it was a worthy shelter for Him. In Him dwelt the fullness of the Godhead, and to Him was given a Name which is above every Name, that is, Wonderful, Counsellor, the Mighty God, the Everlasting Father; so that to Him every knee might bow, whether things in heaven, or on earth, or under the earth. This was the God-man, the delight of the Godhead for all eternity; His human nature was endowed with all gifts and graces that worthily answered His dignity and office and glory. There was no need, as there was no possibility, to endow Him with any greater. This was God's Son; this was the King of Peace! He it was that came in the fullness of time to be born of a pure virgin.[11]

Lucifer's favourite agent is that repugnant creature, the crocodile, representing an insidious enemy to godliness, envy. This is described as 'a spirit's tendency to be grieved, pained, and maliciously inclined when another is successful, or likely to be, and this causes such agitation that he does his utmost against the happiness of that other person; he is incensed against him and against the Giver of his mercies; he wreaks vengeance on him; he seeks by might and main to hinder his success.' While 'the work of the Great Prince of the city is wonderful, His sword triumphs in the world, none can snatch His spoil from His hand, and His love is everlasting', His people are still the target of a hostile foe. 'There is such a thing as leading astray even God's people for a time; the lambs are enticed away from the shepherds' true tents to the wilderness, and remain there until the true Shepherd restores them on His own shoulders. What a multitude have been deceived into false teaching, licentiousness, presumption, prejudice, hardness of heart, carelessness, carnal pleasures, worldly cares, and to that poisonous sin, jealousy?'

The Church at Corinth proves the point, to which Paul sent two letters, on which were written the words 'grief', 'mourning' and 'woe'. This was to rid the church of 'that black gang of fiends that follow envy as smoke follows fire': hatred, strife, adultery, drunkenness, wrath, a party spirit, going to law against each other before unbelievers, and so on. Paul's proposed remedy is to appeal strongly to forsake such things with 'the first-born of all heaven's graces in their stead.' And what is that? Love, with its powerful attending endowments, as described in 1 Corinthians 13.

The havoc wrought by envy is traced throughout the Bible, the most notable examples being Adam and Eve, Cain and Abel, Joseph's brothers, Saul and David, Ahab and Naboth, Haman and Mordecai, the Jews against Jesus, the elder son against the prodigal. Throughout history Prince Immanuel had sent 'life-guards' to seek out this murderer, 'single-eye, godly fear, love of God, brotherly love, faithfulness, a circumcised ear, one-desire, godly jealousy, zeal for truth, humility, faith, patience, and prayer.' Not only 'life-guards', but 'watchmen' also had been commissioned by Immanuel: 'lively ministry', 'strict discipline', 'sharp reproof' and 'spiritual oversight'.[12] This brings to mind the Shepherds of John Bunyan's *Pilgrim's Progress*. The city of 'Man-soul' and 'Prince Immanuel' found in Bunyan's *Holy War* also have obvious parallels in *Crocodil* with similar imagery of the city and the prince.[13]

All the while Williams was writing for a contemporary readership. They were struggling, yes, with criticism of the revival which they treasured so highly; yes, with envy in its various forms, and yes, with doubts. Williams, in his elegy to Howel Harris, expressed regret that the 'crocodilish serpent' had dealt that man of God a crippling blow, so that others had to take up the Gospel conflict in his place.[14] What was God's purpose in all this? Williams was not one to gloss over any dilemma that troubled his society members. So he drew his *Crocodil* to a conclusion by reciting 'the sweetest words of the King':

> Do not lose heart to see enemies every day full of rage and wrath and ranging every weapon against my kingdom; thus it has been from the beginning of the world, and it is my Father's will to suffer these things since all the fury of hell will serve to advance greater glory to Him at the end. It is not because of my inability that they are not subdued under my feet in a moment, but this was fore-ordained to manifest great mysteries hidden from the foundation of the world. They were suffered to appear to prove my people … to show the world whose side they are on … Without these trials their armour would not shine so brightly; apart from hindrances their faith would slumber … It is not good for them to reign in heaven unless they have first struggled on earth … These enemies are suffered also so that my people should not boast; for it is these … which make them realize that my grace is sufficient for them, and that my strength is made perfect in their weakness … But

> chiefly these enemies are suffered by my Father to reveal the bounty of His limitless grace and power, and the infinite worthiness of my death. They would not apply to my death for forgiveness of sin if sin never bothered them. Their enemies compel them to cry for forgiveness, and forgiveness is like a honeycomb to them, renewing love, kindling zeal, and nurturing watchfulness.[15]

If envy was, in the words of John Bunyan, 'so dangerous an enemy', let the Welsh Methodists take heart and reflect on recent events and future prospects. 'There has been lately a great revival throughout the land of Immanuel ... Prophets went out from Mount Zion, propagating the word of the kingdom, so that the sound went to the furthest corners of the earth, and every tribe, tongue, and people gathered together on Mount Zion, to see the living water issuing from under the throne, until Jerusalem overflowed with people, just as the waters of the sea ... so that never since one stone was laid upon another did Jerusalem witness such success.' Their future safety was guaranteed, 'however fierce the hostility ranged against them' in the form of a crocodile. The Prince himself gave his sure promise about the threat it posed, that 'no hair of their head would fall ... I will be a friend to them, and it shall flee from them here and there as long as their days on earth shall last.'[16] For Williams, as for any Methodist, that promise was guarantee enough.

24.

'Paths of grace and righteousness'

Establishing a biblical mindset was a matter of urgency for the Welsh Methodists following the surge of conversions during the 1762 revival. In his *Crocodil* of 1767 Williams had fortified his readers against envy as an evil, hidden tendency. In the following year it was to equip Methodists to face the pressures of materialism and the limitations of mortality that he directed his literary talent. Characteristically, his treatment of the subject is again biblical and practical, but practical in a Methodist kind of way. Knowledge of right doctrine in the head is not enough, striving for right behaviour is impossible, apart from personal faith in Christ. Whether in hymn or prose, for Williams a real relationship with Christ is the source of a godly life and a peaceful death. That complete, all-round perspective on the meaning of human destiny was very much to the fore in what Williams wrote next.

It is difficult to assess Williams's financial situation. The two farms, Cefn-coed and Pantycelyn, were held freehold by the family. In addition, Mary had brought to the marriage some lands and property. He would hardly have been an assistant to Rowland without some financial acknowledgment of his labours. He sold his books while on his travels, carrying them in saddle-bags on horseback, and these may have brought some remuneration. He was fond of tea, fond enough, it seems, to have bought and sold the commodity in large quantities. This would have supplemented his income and may have provided the communities he visited on his travels with a reasonably priced source. In an old account book William has entered this record: 'Of the two dozen and a half [pounds of tea] I took with me to Llangeitho, [I gave] seven to Mary of Llanbadarnfach, four to William Harry, six to man of Velindre, a dozen left at Cwmcynon.'[1] A lengthy footnote to the section on China in Pantheologia traces the rise in popularity, and price, of tea. In 1755 he notes that tax was raised on 4,000,000 pounds of legally imported tea, apart from vast quantities smuggled in from France. Since the East India Company had a monopoly on its supply, tea was hugely expensive. For a few years in mid-century the tax was relaxed, with the result that tea imports and consumption doubled. With the Tea Act of 1773, the tax was raised again, and it was not until a decade later that the Commutation Act reduced it from 119% to 12.5% and made up the deficit in revenue by imposing an additional duty on windows.[2] Williams's will shows that he was a man of some means, with land in Llanllawddog and Llanddeusant, as well as the two farms. Prudence and thrift, together with unremitting toil in the work of the Gospel as well as on the farm, convey a commitment to the Protestant work ethic. He had preached first to himself the message he preached in his next book in 1768.

It appeared with the title *HANES Bywyd a Marwolaeth Tri Wyr o Sodom a'r Aipht, y fan hefyd y croeshoeliwyd ein Harglwydd ni, sef, AFARITIUS, yr Awyddus; PRODIGALUS, yr Afradlon; a FFIDELIUS, y Cristion. Mewn dull o ymddiddan rhwng CANTATOR, y BARDD, a PHERCANTATOR, yr HOLIEDYDD; at ba un y chwanegwyd, MARWNAD i bob un o'r tri* ...('AN ACCOUNT of the life and death of Three Men from Sodom and Egypt, where our Lord was also crucified, namely, AVARITIUS, the covetous man; PRODIGALUS, the prodigal; and FIDELIUS, the Christian. By way of a conversation between CANTATOR, the POET, and PERCONTATOR, the ENQUIRER, to which is added an ELEGY to each one ...'). For all their quaint titles and conversational style, Williams's prose books had a serious purpose. Where previously the conversation was carried on between 'Peregrinus' and 'Percontator', here, in 'Three Men' it is between 'Cantator' and 'Percantator', but the first of these characters in each case represents someone who has travelled widely to gain insight into human behaviour. The preface begins with an affirmation that the two works are linked by a common purpose:

> Following our last meeting, I often remember the words you said about the need for the man of God to be perfect in every good work. I, too, now see more clearly that not many who profess religion are conformed to the mould of the New Testament, to have received the spirit as well as the light of the Word; simplicity as well as gifts, a heart experience of the things of God as well as their outward appearance. Oh! how few have been emptied of pride, self-conceit, false motives, burning lusts, evil desires, and all the other tendencies of the old nature. It is necessary to have grace that will shine in every part, so that the believer in every calling and circumstance will be as the salt of the earth.[3]

From such statements it is clear that Williams's aim is to encourage the pursuit of true holiness in his readers. In a world of material realities and corrupt practices the Methodist ideal was heavenly-mindedness. Next, Williams introduces the characters he is to portray in the work.

> I felt a desire to set out a saint in those gifts, graces and behaviour which Peter, James, Jude and John set him out; a saint drawn through all Paul's letters, unscathed by any of them … to set out God's soldier in all his armour under the name Fidelius, since every believer's aim is to be faithful to the one that called him. And again, seeing how men are commonly drawn to the things of this world, the unbroken desire to amass riches in both rich and poor, parents as well as children, together with the lies, deceit, perjury, treachery, oppression and greed that is applied in this pursuit, constrained me to describe the life and death of Avaritius; lest by unbroken silence the family of faith should take delight in the false way, and the inhabitants of Zion should forsake their own city to live in Sodom, and desire for themselves and their children something other than true riches. Also seeing the wastefulness that there is today in Wales as compared to the Indian States, motivated me to paint the picture of Prodigalus, who, through every excess, brought upon himself, as well as guilt and terrors of conscience when dying, many ailments that hastened his death. Whether the lives of these last two, or the example of Fidelius, will be a warning, God alone knows; but I desire a blessing upon one as much as the other. And if someone asks why I did not bring Avaritius and Prodigalus to a death-bed repentance, tell them, 'because the purpose of the book was to demonstrate how terrible it will be for those who live and die in their sin without knowing God in Christ. But for those who receive repentance to life there are a different light, spirit and effects on their last days from those of Avaritius and Prodigalus.'[4]

The setting of the three characters is the land of Egypt, the time, 'the last days of the world', and the life and death of each is summarized in an appropriate elegy. Each is different, but Avaritius and Prodigalus share the same 'spirit, aim, motivation and destiny', but the other differed in all these respects as well as in his principles. Avaritius was noted for this covetousness, Prodigalus for his riotous living and gluttony, while Fidelius was a Christian.

As always, Williams appealed to Scripture for suitable examples from which to trace the ancestry of his characters: Avaritius is a descendent of Nabal, the 'miserly and evil' husband of Abigail, 'a woman of good understanding, and of a beautiful countenance', whose encounter with David is recorded in 1 Samuel 25. Not only was Nabal covetous and hard-hearted, his deadened conscience allowed no recovery. An example of this was his cruel dealing with 'Honestus', whom he cheated by bringing against him a false accusation and hounding him to death with bribery and corruption. Robbery was to him as his daily bread, and with great subtlety he enticed many into his net. He thrived on the poverty of others, and the means he used to obtain his wicked ends were invariably unjust, wicked and cunning. Throughout his life he never gave death a passing thought, and when that 'king of terrors' came he stubbornly denied the danger to his soul. The pangs of conscience now became insistent and severe, as many of those whom he had cheated and oppressed cried 'revenge, revenge, revenge'. 'Your knees would knock together to see a man without ability, without grace or love, and with nothing but the fear of death in seeking to climb to God, which was now as impossible for him as if he attempted to get to the moon; to see a man without eyes trying to perceive; without a hand trying to hold, and without a tongue trying to shout to heaven.' Williams was not content merely to relate this particular case, because Avaritius is not alone; there are multitudes throughout the world who have been afflicted with the same poison. It is only God's grace that bestows on such a new heart that there will be deliverance, as happened in the case of Zacchaeus, whose generosity afterwards matched his covetousness previously (Luke 19: 1-10). The account of Avaritius closes with a poetic elegy, exposing his total desolation in death and his hopelessness in eternity. 'May God bless that elegy to show someone the misery of loving the world more than heaven.'

Similar treatment is given to the case of Prodigalus. Again there is biblical portrayal of bad ancestry, in his case through the Amorites to Cain. His impure heart was the den of all the wild beasts of the bottomless pit. There were hideous consequences to his drunkenness, profanity and immorality: 'they sowed multiple serious diseases, which gradually brought him to his grave: his idleness brought gout, his drunkenness and revelling affected his heart, liver, spleen and nerves; his womanising drained his energy, and wasted his spirits, so that ere he took his leave of this world he was more like a skeleton than someone having flesh and bones.' Conscience once again asserted itself as death approached, so that 'there was not one of his sins, which were many, that now did not come to remembrance', bringing deep remorse. 'Woe is me! Where was I when others were on their knees? others under the Word, and I was at the bar; other praising God in psalms, hymns and spiritual songs, while I was drunk on my bed; some were reading and meditating on the Word of Life while I was carousing among my drunken, blaspheming friends ... I am a man ... that must

227

within a few days come to judgment; the door [of mercy] is closed, with the furnace of fire and brimstone ready to receive the transgressor.' In the elegy to Prodigalus Williams dwells on the transitory nature of earth's pleasures in comparison with the excellence of those pleasures found in God's presence.

About half the work is taken up with these two characters, and the remainder extols the excellencies of Fidelius. Like the others, he comes from pagan ancestry; his mother was a Hittite, his father an Amorite. Like them he initially lived as a prodigal, 'until the time of his espousal and free grace was fulfilled, when in God's purpose his birth came about in a time of mercy; then Heaven pursued him with its call and he was compelled to listen, like Saul [of Tarsus]; he obeyed the Word of Life, and returned home to live under the wing of the Gospel of grace.' Such was Fidelius's life that it presented the most apt picture of a New Testament Christian: his graces were transparent, his spirit warm, and his life shone with an appealing beauty. He was the same man outwardly as inwardly, with a constancy and balance that was remarkable.

As Williams proceeded with his description of Fidelius's character it is hard to escape the impression that the book is written in order to portray Methodist living in a society driven by materialistic values. Separated from the spirit of the world, shunning its gossip, slander and malice, he was a peacemaker, a man of simplicity and compassion. In his home there was family worship morning and evening, with the Bible as its centrepiece, making his children as familiar with Scripture as they were at school with their Grammar, and providing the others with sound theology. The Bible was Fidelius's body of divinity, so that when he came to die, its promises were his sharpest swords against that last enemy. His generosity extended not only to God's work but also to the poor, the sick and the disadvantaged. His chief aim was to do good to God's Church, and he looked on ministers of the Gospel as sent down from heaven to feed God's flock. He excelled in spiritual discernment and counsel, and applied an appropriate remedy for spiritual ailments always with charity. In many respects he was like the Joseph who suffered much in Egypt in spite of his integrity, and bore much loss and malice with a forgiving spirit for the sake of Gospel liberty. 'I believe', Williams makes the questioner conclude, 'that Fidelius was a good and godly man.' There, in outline, were the features of a Methodist that each society member should aim at.

There are some other aspects of that godliness, however, that Williams considered it necessary to explore. He wanted his readers to be aware on the one hand of the pitfalls which lay in their path, and on the other the divine resources available to the weakest believer on the way to glory. One area where clear teaching was needed was that of the relationship between the works of the law and the life of faith.

> You might have thought, from his abhorrence of self-righteousness, that he was Antinomian, and from his commitment to obligations and his diligence in the use of the means of grace that he was an Arminian; and from the steadfastness of his life and his outward morality, that he was one of the philosophers raised from the dead. It would be hard to find anyone throughout that locality who exalted Christ more than he did; his boast was that Christ was his righteousness, sanctification, wisdom and redemption [1 Corinthians 1: 30]. And he was so clear on this matter, that the substance of his counsels, the liveliness of his doctrines, together with the entire burden of his prayers, all followed the paths of free grace and a crucified righteousness. This was the chief subject of his pleasure, this was the chord, the note which his bow especially aimed to strike; and it was chiefly on account of this basic point that he praised the old Reformers, Luther, Calvin, Hus, and Melanchthon. This doctrine, he used to say, was the greatest beauty of the old Puritans. I often heard him argue convincingly that it is because of a lack of appreciation of the exactness of God's Law, which penetrates to a man's innermost being, and judges the secret intentions of the heart, that Christians commend their own works rather than the righteousness of the cross; and also because they have not had a sight of the holiness of the Almighty.

Methodists were not to rely on their works to achieve a righteousness that would commend them to God; rather they were to trust Christ's righteousness, with which God was pleased. In this way they sought to live a righteous life before men as a matter of gratitude to God.

Another issue that caused havoc among the religious professors of the day was that of a party spirit. Williams knew well the damage done to God's flock at Cefnarthen by such prejudices, and Fidelius reflects similar grief in his blunt comment on a sectarian attitude: 'I see ministers who have been raised but a little from the dung heap in their gifts, and have won but a few people, blaze away for their sect rather than for the Gospel of God, and who desire to inflate the numbers of their congregation rather than turn souls from the error of their ways.' Williams continues: 'This ... constrained Fidelius to shun one label

229

more than another; and he would not altogether align himself with any one divine in the matter of doctrine; nor bind himself with any single article of religion composed by Arminius, Baxter, Piscator, Calvin, Luther, or any other divine more or less orthodox than these, since they all have followed too much their own understanding, and have excessively turned the Scriptures to their own emphasis.' On another issue, Fidelius partook of the Sacrament of the Lord's Supper wherever there was a gathering of believers, 'believing that the ordinance's blessing rested not so much in the worthiness of fellow-communicants as on the peace and presence of God in the soul.'[5] So much for the practice of religion.

Williams then proceeded to the life of religion in Fidelius's soul: 'his innermost experiences, the comforts and exercises of the spirit of grace, the powers of heaven, victory over the legions of hell ranged against the soul; triumph over the fear of death and the grave; the inexpressible and glorious joys, the heritage of the saint.' The narrative has close affinity with the various handbooks published to suggest questions suitable to ask society members. These spoke of the Spirit's witness to adoption into God's family, and hope of glory, but they also made it clear that the Christian faces spiritual enemies, trials, and afflictions. With regard to his troubles, Fidelius traces three sources: Satanic opposition; the world's toys with their assault upon the senses, particularly the eyes and ears; and those which stemmed from the passions and lusts inherent in the human heart.[6] His trials were many, much like those suffered by Job, but he prevailed with God for strength to overcome, and came forth as gold tried by fire.

Following this, there is a section in the work that deals with the 'inner experiences' which sustained Fidelius on his earthly pilgrimage. First among these was a constant measure of peace of conscience, 'his best treasure'; the second was 'the sweet influences of the heavenly Spirit' in his soul; the third, 'occasionally, a wonderful light to know his own heart better, but also on the Scriptures, and to discern the intentions of others'; the fourth, 'confirmation of the truth of the whole of Scripture.' Finally, however, one thing stood out in Fidelius above all else, namely,

> the delight he had in exalting the Prince of Peace ... and he found no profit in any preaching, hymns, or theological treatise, in which the Lord Jesus was not exalted in the highest way in them; he did not write a letter to friend or relative that did not savour of the salvation in the

blood of the Lamb. This was the chief subject of his meditation, the death of the cross. O! with what sweetness he spoke of man's redemption, of the infinite love of God in Christ towards miserable sinners ... This, then, is the life of one who was closest to heaven that I saw in all my pilgrimage ... as he drew closer to the grave, he drew closer to heaven ... And in short, his last hours were hours of preaching as well as hours of prayer.

The elegy to Fidelius records his eternal bliss in heaven after facing various conflicts and storms, and holds him before the reader as an example of faith, fortitude and perseverance.

Fidelius's life is lived in the rough and tumble of worldly values and satanic opposition. Herein lay the value of the work, which some commentators have recognized as among Williams's best literary productions.[7] The fellowship and discipline of the experience society is held out as indispensable for the Methodist convert, much as it was for Fidelius. It was in its atmosphere that Fidelius's godliness and piety thrived, here he matured his faith and developed his usefulness. 'Three men from Sodom and Egypt' is not a long work, and Williams might have intended it to be a tract with a double aim: to demonstrate sin's folly in the light of death's inevitability, and the infallible power of Christ to bring a sinner from the danger of an earthly 'Egypt' to the glory of a heavenly 'Canaan'.

25.

'Fly abroad, eternal Gospel'

At the end of *Gloria in Excelsis* (1771) there is the promise of another work to appear, called *Liber Miscellaneorum* because 'it would contain many unfamiliar and strange subjects which have not been written about before ... together with letters on various occasions; such as with regard to the *Aurora Borealis*, the northern lights, a sign of the success of the Gospel in the latter days.'[1] When it was published it claimed in addition that its contents were 'necessary to be made available to the Church today, which (even though the dark, cold winter is past and the sun has come to stay this side of the equator, bringing all the plants to life and filling the world with flowers) yet multitudes of weeds grow and make the careful labourer to despair of seeing a full harvest, but on lifting his head to see the Aurora Borealis, the sign of the thousand years approaching, he rejoices in a full storehouse.'[2] The two titles appeared separately, *Liber* in 1773 and *Aurora* in 1774, both in Welsh, the former incomplete, the latter a separate work in its own right, although apparently originally intended to be issued as one work. Liber is introduced with these words: 'When Theophilus the poet was ill, far away from home in the year 1769, in a lonely room on his own, he whiled away his illness in writing his last will or testament, which he signs, seals, and delivers to the world, in the year 1773.'[3]

The full title of the second work is: *Aurora Borealis: NEU, Y GOLEUNI yn y Gogledd, fel arwydd o Lwyddiant yr EFENGYL yn y Dyddiau Diweddaf, (Neu, Shekinah'r Mil Blynyddoedd:) Mewn dull o Lythyr oddi wrth ERMENEUS y Lladmerydd, at AGRUPNUS y Gwyliedydd, ('Aurora Borealis:* or the LIGHT in the North, as a sign of the Success of the GOSPEL in the Last Days, (or, The Shekinah of the Thousand Years:) in the form of a Letter from ERMENEUS the Interpreter, to AGRUPNUS the Watchman'). Two texts appear on the title page, Matthew 24:30, 'then shall appear the sign of the Son of Man in heaven'; Luke 21: 11, 'and great signs shall there be from heaven'. Williams writes with no little sense of excitement at the prospect that recent events, in Llangeitho particularly, but further afield, too, in the rest of Britain and in America, are the herald of a golden age of triumph

232

for Christ's kingdom. Interestingly, a posthumous work by Jonathan Edwards which touched on the same themes appeared in the same year, published at Edinburgh. Its title was *A History of the Work of Redemption*, and its closing sections speak of 'wonderful *revival and propagation* of religion' and *'mighty opposition'* to precede a 'national conversion of the Jews' and a *'prosperous state* of the church'.[4]

Four verses of an opening poem to *Aurora* summarize traditional views of the last days, namely, that natural phenomena would signal either the approach of a final conflagration of the world, or unparalleled success for the Gospel. Williams concludes that Scripture forbids him to believe that the world would 'melt with fervent heat' [2 Peter 3:12] before 'the Turks, Jews, and Gentiles' come to faith in Christ in multitudes [Romans 11: 25-26]. It is with the conviction that the northern lights signal the approach of a period of Gospel triumph, before the Second Advent, therefore, that Williams had written. Williams followed the position of one of his favourite Puritan authors, Thomas Goodwin, who in 1641 had drawn a distinction between the two events: 'Now the reigning with Christ a thousand years is not meant reigning with him in Heaven, for after these thousand years, there shall be many enemies raised against the Church, Gog and Magog shall gather themselves together; if it were meant of heaven, that could not be, and therefore it must be meant of Jesus Christ coming and reigning here gloriously for a Thousand years ... If there be many prophecies and promises in Scripture that are not yet fulfilled, and the fulfilling whereof will bring the Church into a more glorious condition than ever it was yet in the world: then there is a glorious time coming. Now there are such Scriptures.'[5] In the Westminster Assembly's Larger Catechism the explanation of the petition, 'Thy kingdom come' in the Lord's prayer includes 'acknowledging ourselves and all mankind to be by nature under the dominion of sin and Satan, we pray, that the kingdom of sin and Satan may be destroyed, the Gospel propagated throughout the world, the Jews called, the fullness of the Gentiles brought in ... that Christ would rule in our hearts here, and hasten the time of his second coming, and our reigning with him for ever.' For the Puritans, faced with persecution and opposition, the hope of better days was in the distant future, but for Welsh Methodists after 1762, with Williams as their spokesman, part of that hope was already being realized.[6]

Puritan and Methodist emphases inevitably built on Reformed, Calvinist convictions on God's providential ordering of the last days.

233

The issue hinged particularly on two biblical passages, Romans 11 and Revelation 20, the former relating to the position of the Jews in the purposes of God, and the latter raising the issue of a literal or figurative one thousand years of Gospel progress. On the classical text, Romans 11:15 'For if the casting away of them be the reconciling of the world, what shall the receiving of them be, but life from the dead?' Calvin comments, 'Since the rejection of the Jews has availed so much as to occasion the reconciling of the Gentiles, how much more effectual will be their resumption? Will it not be to raise them even from the dead? … Since then God has wonderfully drawn forth life from death and light from darkness, how much more ought we to hope, he reasons, that the resurrection of a people, as it were, wholly dead, will bring life to the Gentiles.' On Romans 11:12, 'Wherefore if the fall of them be the riches of the world, and the diminishing of them the riches of the Gentiles, how much more shall their abundance be?' the Geneva Bible makes this marginal comment: 'By riches he meaneth the knowledge of the Gospel to everlasting life, and by the world, all nations dispersed throughout the whole world.' Proceeding to verse 15, the comment is: 'it shall come to pass that when the Jews come to the Gospel the world shall as it were quicken again, and rise from death to life.' Until that final drama, Calvin insists that the only identifiable period of time, however spoken of in Scripture, is the broad day of grace that precedes the final day of judgment: 'the number "one thousand" does not apply to the eternal blessedness of the church but only to the various disturbances that awaited the church, while still toiling on earth.'[7]

With closer biblical investigation, Puritan convictions had inevitably moved on from those of the Genevan Reformer. Puritan responses to a time of ecclesiastical opposition, Gospel advance and sectarian excesses also had a part in forging their conclusion. Embracing both Puritan and Methodist periods, Iain H. Murray justifiably speaks of a development and eclipse of the Puritan hope of Gospel advance. [8] With the emergence of the Great Awakening in Britain and America, fresh perspectives on Gospel prospects were emerging. Thus Isaac Watts and John Guyse could claim in their commendation to Jonathan Edwards's *Faithful Narrative of the Surprising Work of God* in October 1737: 'We are taught also by this happy event, how easy it will be for our blessed Lord to make a full accomplishment of all his predictions concerning his kingdom, and to spread his dominion from sea to sea, through all the nations of the earth … Salvation shall spread through all the tribes and ranks of mankind, as the lightning from heaven in a few moment would communicate a living flame through ten thousand lamps or torches ... we entreat our readers ... to join with us in our hearty addresses to the throne of grace, that this wonderful discovery of the hand of God in saving sinners, may encourage our faith and hope of the accomplishment of all his words of grace, which are written in the Old Testament and in the New, concerning the large extent of this salvation in the latter days of the world.' [9] And Griffith Jones shortly after in Wales could write: ''Tis hoped, that more glorious times than the present are not very far off; though, perhaps a cloudy, if not a very strong day may first intervene.' By 1740 his prayers for the success of God's work were founded on passages from Isaiah 49:6, 52:10 and Romans 11: 7, 26-27 that speak of the extension of Christ's kingdom to the ends of the earth.[10] Having witnessed great things in the company of Whitefield, William Seward wrote in his *Journal:* 'I believe the Lord is working a great work upon the earth, and who knows but we are come to the dawning of the glory of the Latter Day?'[11]

Among Williams's contemporaries, Jonathan Edwards in New England believed that his generation was poised to witness unparalleled Gospel progress. The title of one section in *Some Thoughts Concerning the present Revival in New-England, and the Way in which it ought to be acknowledged and promoted*, makes the claim that *The latter-day glory, is probably to begin in America.* Its opening sentence confidently expects an expansion of its blessings: 'Tis not unlikely that this work of God's Spirit, that is so extraordinary and wonderful, is the dawning, or at least a prelude, of that glorious work of God, so often foretold in Scripture, which in the progress and issue of it, shall renew the world of mankind.'[12] Here Edwards outlined his belief that America would be in the vanguard of the work, but later, in his 1747 *Humble Attempt*, he widens its scope: 'The late remarkable religious awakenings, that have been in many parts of the Christian world, are another thing that may justly encourage us in prayer for the promised glorious and universal outpouring of the Spirit of God.' He mentioned revivals in Salzburg, Massachusetts Bay, Connecticut, 'England, Wales, and Scotland, and almost all the British provinces in North America', and concludes:

> the Spirit of God has been of late so wonderfully awakening and striving with such multitudes, in so many different parts of the world, and even to this day, in one place or other, continues to awaken men, is

what I should take encouragement from, that God was about to do something more glorious, and would, before he finishes, bring things to a greater ripeness, and not finally suffer this work of his to be frustrated and rendered abortive by Satan's crafty management; and that these unusual commotions are the forerunners of something exceeding glorious approaching; as the wind, earthquake, and fire, at Mount Sinai, were forerunners of that voice, wherein God was, in a more eminent manner ... (1 Kgs. 19: 11-12.[13]

Writing to William M'Culloch at Cambuslang, Glasgow, in May 1743, Edwards had taken up the same theme: 'We live in a day wherein God is doing marvellous things ... I cannot think otherwise, than that what has now been doing, is the forerunner of something vastly greater, more pure, and more extensive ... I believe God will revive his work again before long, and that it will not wholly cease till it has subdued the whole earth.' Some years later, at a time when the revival in New England seemed to be in decline, Joseph Bellamy encouraged his congregation with the promise that: 'Satan being conquered, and all the powers of darkness driven out of the field, and confined to the bottomless pit, ye shall reign with Christ a thousand years.'[14]

Even if it was not the source of Williams's ideas, he may have found confirmation for them in Edwards's work. The Welsh Methodists were reading *Some Thoughts* and as early as the end of 1745 Williams wrote to Harris with excitement, as if he was conveying fresh discovery and deep conviction:

The Church of God will be more glorious in the time to come. Glorious promises are not fulfilled. Is the Gospel preached through the whole world as promised in the Gospel by our Saviour Himself? No, no! All America as yet never heard such thing. Has the great Babylon fallen? No, no! Its time I hope is at hand. Has the poor, ignorant, sinful and reproachful Jew been called, Rom. 11? No! But 'tis certain to come. Has the devil been bound for 1,000 years, Rev. 19? I suppose not. Has the fullness of the Gentiles come in? Have the glorious promises of Isaiah, Ezekiel, Revelation been fulfilled? No, no! Dear brother, pray for them. We have great reason to expect these things in short. Dark cloud in the morning is no proof the day is far; hard travailing pain is no sign the delivery is far; wars, famine, pestilence; kings raging against one another is no sign the glorious Day of the Gospel is far off. Who knows but Christ's kingdom of peace may come [as a result] of the shaking [of] Empires, kingdoms, states etc. Many prayers are gone up now of late and formerly that the idolatrous Church of Rome should be pulled down, Jews converted, and Islam rooted up. May these come to pass, Amen, Amen, Amen.[15]

When the northern lights appeared in the sky over Pantycelyn with dramatic rainbow colours, rhythmic movement, and great intensity in 1774, Williams had an impressive lead-in for publishing his convictions.

Natural phenomena were often the inspiration for sermons, in the belief that God's providential control was not arbitrary but purposeful. Writing of such manifestations in this period, Alexandra Walsham concludes that an 'intrusion of the supernatural in the secular sphere', was one aspect of Protestant thinking. She quotes one Puritan writer who referred to thunder and lightning as 'visible sermons', a graphic description of popular thinking about such occurrences. [16] Under the date 16 May 1746 Harris wrote in his diary, 'At midnight when I would see lightning in the sky or the Northern Lights, my soul would be ready to burst my body with joy being in hopes Christ was coming to judgment.' Two years later, 14 July 1748, he heard Whitefield preach in London 'on the GREAT ECLIPSE'.[17] In 1750 London felt the tremors of an earthquake, and he 'ventured out at midnight to Hyde Park, where he proclaimed to the affrighted and astonished multitudes ... that there is a Saviour, Christ the Lord ... he took occasion ... to call the attention of the surrounding thousands to that most important event, in which every soul will be essentially and particularly concerned – namely, the grand, final consummation of all things, the universal wreck of nature, the dissolution of the lower world, and the confirming and fixing the eternal and unalterable state of every son and daughter of Adam.'[18] Charles Wesley's 'hymns were frequently occasioned by national events ... thus the earthquake of 1750 becomes, naturally enough, a reminder of the frailty of humanity, a call to repentance, and a plea for salvation through Jesus Christ. His *Hymns Occasioned by the Earthquake, March 8, 1750* appeared in 1750, and was reissued, presumably as a consequence of the [1755] Lisbon earthquake, in 1756.'[19] He preached at least on four occasions on the fearful events, and one of his sermons, 'The Cause and Cure of Earthquakes', was later published. He also wrote nineteen hymns related to the subject."[20]

The Lisbon earthquake resulted in the almost total destruction of the city, and the suddenness and solemnity of the occasion presented many preachers with an opportunity not to be missed. William Romaine took as his text Amos 4:12, 'Prepare to meet thy God', and fervently applied its message to issue a call to repentance in the light of God's sure judgments.[21] John Wesley's, *Serious thoughts occasioned by the earthquake in Lisbon*, appeared in the same year, and 'within a month, passed through two editions. Perhaps none of Wesley's publications contain so much fiery eloquence as this.'[22] In it he speaks of earthquakes, lightnings, winds, and comets as the work of God, and calls his readers to make their peace with God while there is still opportunity.

In Williams's *Caniadau Duwiol* ('Godly Songs'), issued with his 'Sea of Glass' of 1762, the second song, 'About the Earthquake that happened in many great lands in 1755 and 1756', mentions Persia, Portugal, Morocco, Spain, and other lands. The same countries are mentioned in *Aurora*, and all these events signalled 'the dawn of the resurrection day.' The last verse of Song 2 was often sung by the Methodists well into the next century, with great feeling and effect:

> Before the world ends by your will,
> O God, first your true Word fulfil;
> Call from all lands your chosen, 'til
> Their number is complete;
> Through all the world your Gospel send.
> And in your blood their vileness mend,
> Their ills and sicknesses all tend,
> Then take your royal seat! [23]

This was not the impersonal God of the Deists, uncaring, detached, and distant. On the contrary, His providential ordering of men's affairs was the handmaiden of His purpose of salvation in Christ.

In an elegy to Rev. Lewis Lewis in 1764, Williams answers the questions, 'What is meant by the thousand years? Will Satan be bound in heavy chains? When will he be bound and released?' with a call to possess the soul with patience, to trust in Bible promises, and to be ready for the end of the world.[24] Likewise, in his *Pantheologia* Williams sets out the biblical evidence on some of the detail:

> Eusebius.- ... do you think that the Gospel in all its purity must reach every part of that huge country [America] before the Son of Man comes in His glory? Apodemus.- There will be no corner of it, though it were three times its size, where the light of the Word will not shine in unspeakable and glorious brilliance ... who knows but that the Sun of righteousness shall run its course over the earth until it shines again on

238

the lands of the east, and old Jerusalem? And in this way the fullness of the Gentiles shall come in, and then, after the word of the kingdom has appeared for the second time in their land, all Israel shall be saved ... and the Jews, presently scattered throughout the world ... will be ripe to receive this teaching, that the Messiah has come; and then the scriptures will be fulfilled that are found in Isa. 11: 11-13; Ezek. 37: 21-3; Hosea 3: 4-5; and in Zech. 10: 6-8. Eusebius.- What you have just said is better than all else ... for it is certain that our Lord will not come until this Gospel is preached throughout the world, and it does not much matter which kingdom conquers first or last. It is pleasing to think that days of greater success shall attend the word of the kingdom, when the fullness of the Gentiles is come in, and all Israel shall be saved.[25]

With such pronouncements, one thing remained: how imminent were such days of triumph? Williams provided the Methodists with a basis to believe that the event was near.

As in America, so also in Scotland, the Great Awakening was thought to be about to usher in the millennium. A tract written by John Erskine appeared at Edinburgh in 1742 with the title, *The Signs of the Times considered: or, The high Probability, that the present APPEARANCES in New-England, and the West of Scotland, are a PRELUDE of the Glorious Things promised to the CHURCH in the latter Ages. Mat. 16: 3; Luk 21: 31; Jn 1:46.* In its Preface, Erskine wrote: 'It is not the principal design of the following sheets to vindicate the work now carrying on at Cambuslang and other places... What I chiefly aim at is, to point out the proper use which Christians ought to make of this so extraordinary a dispensation, by laying before them the high probability that the things we have seen and heard, are a prelude of greater things yet to come.' For Williams the Northern Lights were 'one of the last wonders of the world', and

one of greatest wonders ever seen in God's skies, and a particular sign of some great things that are about to happen ... a special sign of the extension of the bounds of Christ's Gospel, and of the success of the Word in the last days, the fall of Antichrist, the call of the Jews, the total destruction of paganism and Islam, and the setting up of the kingdom of Christ over the face of the whole earth, when 'the knowledge of the Lord will cover the face of the earth as the waters cover the sea.' The Lord has frequently given great wonders in the heavens and on earth of things to come; sometimes as signs of God's judgment on unrepentant sinners, but more often as a sign of the deliverance and salvation of his saints.[26]

Such considerations, then, set the scene for bringing the issue before a people whose experiences of God's dealings in revival were real and fresh. There were solid grounds for believing that God had more blessings in store.

First, however, the matter had to be set in context. From the beginning of time to its end, human events and eternal destinies, for Williams could only be understood theologically, by relating everything to God. Hence, God's eternal counsel of salvation, man's fall into sin in Adam, God's providential ordering in all of creation, redemption by Christ, the invincibility of the Church, and the ultimate, eternal reign of Christ, all held together as a unity. 'All nature was thrown into upheaval when man fell; we cannot think that prior to that there was any thunder, lightning, storms, fierce winds and earthquakes … Man's fall resulted in chaos in all of creation; and since that time God has allowed creation to be sometimes a judgment upon a stubborn and hardhearted people, and on the other hand to be a blessing, and a sign of blessing, to his elect. The same water that drowns the ungodly, now floats righteous Noah's boat; the same fiery furnace that keeps Shadrach, Meshach and Abednego alive, consumes those who cast them into it.'[27]

Next for Williams comes an explanation of the Northern Lights:

> I cannot but believe that the northern lights are a sign of the closing days of the Gospel … The fall of Babylon the great, all the erring churches in the world, in Revelation 18, together with our Lord's reign for a thousand years, chapter 20, are among the most amazing things in the Old and New Testaments … All this signifies that the Gospel of salvation, the Word of life, is to run and be glorified at the command and authority of King Jesus, to enlighten and reprove all those lands where darkness reigned, and all those churches that prostituted the faith in life, spirit, or doctrine. This is the morning of the Thousand Years, when a multitude of ministers of the Gospel will appear, all following where their glorious Teacher trod; dressed in white, pure in life, spirit and principles; prospering in Gospel triumph. Meanwhile, 'Satan will be bound for a thousand years' Revelation 20, and 'the holy city, new Jerusalem, will come down from God out of heaven, adorned with every precious jewel, prepared as a bride adorned for her husband' (Revelation 21: 2) … Is it not very likely that the northern lights … have been given by the Mediator of the New Testament as a sign to the world of his coming to set up his kingdom on the earth in greater glory than ever before?[28]

It is important, however to distinguish things that differ, and Williams says of the Northern Lights, that 'it cannot be a sign of the end of the world, since the 'fullness of the Gentiles has not come to pass, nor have the Jews been turned to the faith, nor has Satan been bound for a thousand years'; and all these must come to pass before the end of the world.' While this is for Williams a matter of conviction, it belongs to the secondary issues of the Faith, not to the essentials: 'Even though I do not believe this as a doctrine necessary to salvation, or as one of the fundamental doctrines of the Faith, nor do I impose it in this way on others, except that it seems quite reasonable to be such.'[29] Crawford Gribben concludes that within Puritanism there was a 'caution which guarded against the inclusion of such hopes within the movement's confessional documents.'[30]

Williams drew his work to a conclusion with an acknowledgment that it was the revival's ever more powerful manifestations that gave him the greatest confirmation of what God was about to do: 'The final reason why I am persuaded in these matters is the revival which came about in the churches shortly after the appearance of this light. Whoever has observed carefully the work of the Lord during the last forty years, will know that the word of the kingdom has been sown in the field; and at the beginning of that time it took root, sprang up, and grew until it became a tree, so that "the birds of the air come and lodge in its branches" … and when this light appeared in the darkness it surprised and amazed everyone, just as the Northern Lights.' God is sovereign over all things: and it is this belief that gives true meaning and real hope in a world that is to be renewed, much as summer comes after the bleakest winter: 'As the Northern Lights spread across the sky, so also the Gospel in time will cover the earth as well … All the earthquakes that happened in 1755 and 1756 … all the wars in Asia, Europe and America are merely a fulfilment of the Lord's Word … and when I see these and similar things I am ready to believe that summer is at hand. And that the sun will hasten to shine upon us is the earnest desire of your brother.'[31]

With the passing of time, Williams did not change his mind about the hope of Gospel success, as this letter of 1787 shows:

> … the harvest is great and the Lord of the harvest will have labourers for his harvest, for the fullness of the Gentiles shall come in, viz. the Gentiles round the globe, black, white, yellow, orange, tawny shall hear of a crucified Saviour; and shall believe in Him, and then all Israel, the

scattered tribes that inhabit the farthest and remotest part of the world, shall be gathered as sheep unto the sheepfold of the Gospel, as may be seen [from] Isa. 11:9-12; and as the fall of the Jews became the riches of the Gentile world, how much more riches will the Gentiles world gain by their fullness, Rom. 11:13, for if the casting away of the Jewish world became a reconciling of the Gentile world, what shall the reviving of the Jewish world be, but life from the dead – that is in plain English. Thus all the Gentile world shall receive the Gospel and believe. Then drowsiness shall fall on them in the time of their drowsiness, decay and backsliding, the Jews shall awake round the globe and believe and the sleeping Gentile Church shall be roused up by the zeal, love and faith, and catch the fire, so the whole world will be on blaze.[32]

The manner in which Williams reached his conclusions, and the emphases on Jewish and Gentile success, may vary, but there can be no doubt as to the permanence and vigour of his conviction that the Gospel would prevail. It is for this reason that his hymn, which begins with 'O'er the gloomy hills of darkness', also has a verse that begins with 'Fly abroad, eternal Gospel, Win and conquer, never cease'. [33]

26.

'Let the Lord go before you'

Not the least of the responsibilities that came with Methodist membership were those relating to marriage. All the Welsh Methodist leaders were married, and had accepted the tensions imposed on them by domestic and public constraints. They rejected a mandatory celibacy, and would have agreed with convictions expressed by Harris. 'I was enabled to excite them to industry', he says on one occasion, 'and to show them how to behave in families. I spoke for a long time to a brother regarding his marriage, and his prospects in life, showing how a minister should not be hindered by the things of the world but as little as possible.' In this respect Williams, Rowland and Howel Davies maintained an exemplary standard, while Harris came short at one period of his life. The English Methodist leaders, too, were married. Whitefield managed a modest measure of contentment in his, Charles Wesley rather more, but it was widely known that John Wesley's marriage was strained.

An area of particular difficulty was the itinerancy and absence from home to which the preachers were exposed. Gareth Lloyd even goes as far as to say that the 'marriage of Charles Wesley in April 1749 represented a watershed in his ministry ... After his marriage, domestic responsibilities started to encroach on Charles' itinerant preaching and he abandoned the travelling work entirely at the end of 1756 ... John declared just weeks after his own wedding that he could not understand a preacher travelling less as a married man than he did as a bachelor; not surprisingly, the result was a relationship with his wife that was the very opposite of his brother's.'[1] What the Wesley brothers failed to achieve, Williams managed, and the balance between ministerial labours and domestic life yielded both usefulness abroad and harmony at home.

Marriage among the Welsh Methodists was a strictly regulated affair, even though the element of romantic love was allowed. It was certainly a matter for prayer: the man and woman concerned should seek God's purpose for their lives with patience and diligence. Marriage, in Harris's words, 'the greatest act next salvation we can do',

243

should only be considered in the light of Scripture precept and example.[2] Another Methodist constraint in the matter was the involvement of parents and society leaders, a far cry from the individualism and independence of later Christian generations. But the intention was support rather than interference, to offer wise counsel rather than to pry and meddle.

In one report that Williams sent to the Association about the societies under his care, there are two instances of the sanctions imposed on the members regarding marriage. 'Two of the members are considering marriage, and have broached the subject to the society, but there is one that loves a carnal woman, so that he must either part with her or leave the society .... There is an old woman ... who has married an old man like herself; she left the society to get a husband – O! pitiful state.'[3] On occasions the Association would decide that a certain member should postpone marriage 'as not clear it is of God.'[4] This would be in line with the Association's rule, 'that none under our care are to marry without consulting the superintendent; and if he has clear light from the Lord and His providence etc., to see 'tis a temptation, he has power to forbid it, or they be turned out after bringing the matter to be laid if they desire it before the next Association.'[5]

It is not surprising, therefore, that the more timid would hesitate to make their courtship known. Take the example of Evan John, converted under Harris's ministry and enjoying Gospel privileges in 1742 under Thomas Jones, the evangelical minister of Cwm-iou, near Abergavenny. He writes to Harris: 'This is the matter I wish to set before you, since I know you are the instrument through whom God first penetrated my soul with His free grace ... For some time I believe God is calling me to the married state. As far as I can discern with the light I have so far this is in accordance with God's will, but I am fearful to put the matter to you, in case you reprove me ... I have mentioned it to Mr. Jones and some other faithful friends ... I desire to have your mind on it.'[6] Belonging to the society involved self-denial, as much as being a Christian, and this was an impression that the Methodists seemed to have deliberately encouraged. There is seemingly no record of Williams making such a request to the Association, presumably because Rowland particularly would have been party to his intentions.

For Williams, the right attitude was summarized in the closing remarks of his *Cyfarwyddwr Priodas* ('Guide to Marriage'): 'be content, fully satisfied in your state; and if heaven wills to bring about a change in your life, let the Lord go before you.' This Welsh work appeared in 1777 with 76 pages, and the translated title conveys some idea of its message, '*Ductor Nuptiarum:* or, A Guide to Marriage, in the form of a conversation between Martha Pseudogam, and Mary Eugamus, Both at first professing godliness, but the first having backslidden, marrying after the flesh; and the other holding on to the power of godliness, marrying in the fear of the Lord'. This is a Methodist document, dealing with young Methodist converts struggling to resist the social pressures and loose morals of those around them. The Scriptural injunction to believers, that they should not be 'unequally yoked together with unbelievers' (2 Cor. 6:14) comes late in the work, so that Williams builds up his case for Christian marriage in a wider framework. The document's unreserved appeal to biblical standards, however, demonstrates that for Williams their authority and relevance were unquestionable.[7]

This was not his first treatment of what he considered a serious issue, requiring urgent attention. Bound with his hymn collection, *Môr o Wydr* ('Sea of Glass') of 1762 was *Cerdd Newydd am Briodas* ('A New Poem about Marriage'). Five male fictional characters debate the issue. Its divine institution at creation is noted as a union between a man and a woman to enjoy and serve God, and to help each other in this sacred task wherein their blessedness lies. Then, after man's fall into sin, the classical Protestant ethic of the three-fold end of marriage is stated: to avoid fornication and adultery, nurture children in godliness, and to provide mutual help in the vicissitudes of life in this world.[8] There is sound advice: love to God, love for each other, earnest prayer, and trust in God's providential control of human affairs. Within marriage there will be difficulties, but God's grace will restore harmony and enable sustained discipleship.

With the great influx of young converts after a revival season in 1762, some were getting married to unbelievers; others now found themselves living with unbelieving spouses. A more practical treatment is found in William's next foray into marriage counselling, his *Theomemphus* of 1764. Here Williams works his way through a believer's typical experiences, from his unconverted days to his last in the face of death, and the subject of marriage is given appropriate attention. Within the context of the society and Christian fellowship, the Christian is to recognize the pitfalls of carnal love, of temptation to abandon God's Law and will under the pressure of lust, and to maintain love for God both as his motivation and his priority. In a lengthy footnote, Williams sets out the potential dangers: 'so many of the saints in every generation have erred in the matter of the passions of natural love. Hardly anything has enticed the godly away from the path of life more than this … May the deceit which Theomemphus found in his affections be a warning to all not to give too much credence to the fickle fire of the wayward passions of human nature.' Furthermore, even within marriage there is no perfect bliss, so that the believer must always be watchful, but also confident. With God's grace the believer will reflect God's character as a covenant-keeping God by the way in which marriage vows are honoured.

Williams's Preface to his 'Guide to Marriage' deserves to be quoted in full.

> The occasion that stimulated me to write this *Dialogue* was the spectacle of the defilement of the present age in the matter of the courtship and marriage of professing believers. Every discerning person is aware that the convictions which were held by many in recent years have been but superficial and fickle. Several came to love godliness merely on account of the little pleasure they received in hearing, singing, praying and having fellowship with people of a fervent spirit; young men of pleasant disposition who attracted their friends to the Faith. These in turn were wrought upon by the same spirit, and for a time they pursued godliness with the same fervour. They took great delight in the word when it was mixed with such excitement, which worked powerfully on their natural affections. Alas, some preachers filled their sermons with the comfort and precious promises of the scriptures to this end. They were more eager to produce such feelings in their hearers, either out of sheer ignorance, or, possibly to gain praise and multiply the size of their congregations, than to disseminate faithfully the Word of Life by 'instruction, reproof, correction, exhortation and teaching, that the man of God may be perfect, thoroughly equipped to every good work.' [2 Tim. 3:16-17.] But when, in time, the affections of these young adherents cooled, the desire for attending the means of grace, which they had hitherto displayed, declined. Then, like the seed that fell on rocky places, when the sun arose and the heat intensified, new trials appeared, and the devil, full of rage and subtlety, tempted these youngsters to various empty pleasures; among other things to wantonness and the flesh, which are attended with regrettable and shameful consequences. Eventually, religious young women, who had departed from God, now under the power of natural desire, turned their affections to unbelieving and ungodly young men. These they married, without asking the permission of their parents or the church of God. This presently became

bitter to them, having to spend the rest of their lives, possibly, in regret, guilt and unhappiness. Such considerations prompted me to write this book as a warning to all who might read its counsel, to beware of losing that spirit which they received at first, lest they should be unequally yoked with unbelievers. Also, to encourage those who are already so joined to use every means in love and tenderness to bring their marriage partner to the Faith. By prudent behaviour they may at least gain sufferance for themselves to follow the ways of godliness.[9]

There are, then, dangers to be avoided in the matter of marriage: from without, 'the defilement of the present age', and a superficial response to the Gospel; and from within, excitable 'affections', hasty decisions without consulting one's natural and spiritual families, and imprudent behaviour that might alienate an unbelieving spouse even further.

The work is in the form of four dialogues, involving fictional characters. This device was commonly used in those days for dramatic effect. The intention was that readers were to identify with whichever character came closest to portraying their own person and circumstances. An obvious example of the effectiveness of this form of literature is John Bunyan's *Pilgrim's Progress,* and Williams was fond enough of that author to have considered this way of commending truth appropriate. The first three dialogues are between the happily married Christian, Mary, and a professing believer, Martha, whose carnal love for an unbeliever has ended in a disastrous marriage. The last dialogue uses different characters to explain the biblical principle that a believer should not be 'unequally yoked' with an unbeliever. The case for Christian marriage is built on a solid Scripture foundation, using classical texts like Gen 2: 18, 21-23; Ex. 34: 11-16; Judges 3: 5-7; Proverbs 31; Mat. 19: 10-12; 1 Cor. 7; 2 Cor 6: 14-18; and 1 Pet. 3: 1-2. Reference is made to a work on marriage by Desiderius Erasmus. He is perhaps more widely known for his pioneering work on the Greek New Testament that was of such significance to the Protestant Reformers. His treatise on marriage is found in *The Colloquies, or Familiar Discourses of Desiderius Erasmus of Roterdam*, an English edition of which was published in London in 1671, and a copy of this in the 1725 edition was in Williams's library.[10] But it is scriptural exposition and application which dominates the treatment of his subject, while at the same time making a profoundly practical statement of a Christian ideal that has personal relevance in this most intimate and important area of human relationships.

In the first dialogue it emerges that Martha has married someone to whom she was physically attracted. In spite of the early warnings of conscience which she suppressed, and that of parents, 'we … decided to get married in spite of all opposition.' He turns out to be a veritable scoundrel, who outwardly 'has the form of a man rather than an animal – he has two feet and not four – but in all the moods and passions and actions of his life he is worse than an animal.' Martha accepts some responsibility for her actions: 'When I first lost the breezes of heaven, I became as wanton and carnal as before. Any man with eyes to see would know from my carnal appearance, my flirtatious eyes, my frivolous conversation, and my haughty attitude, that the love of young men rather than the love of God was in my heart.' To Mary's enquiry, 'With such wantonness did you avoid scandal?', she replies, 'More or less, in the eyes of the world, which only thinks of sin in terms of the deed; but in God's sight we were no better than those who were guilty in the fullest sense. We burned with such lust that I know not to this day how the fruit of our intentions was not exposed to the world.' But she also blames the institution of marriage: 'Oh! wretched marriage that has deprived me of all the pleasures of my youth! … Marriage makes people more worldly, more self-conscious, more dissatisfied, and often less useful in the church, and possibly as useless as I am.' For such statements she is reproved by Mary: 'do not blame the ordinance; blame yourself for the carnal manner of your own base use of it, for which you will pay dearly. For the rest of your life it will be as a rod upon your back, unless grace intervenes.'

Williams uses the second dialogue to elaborate on an ideal Methodist courtship in the case of Mary and Philo Alethius:

> These were the chief considerations that made me attractive to him: first, the integrity of the work of grace in my life, of which for many years he had been fully persuaded; secondly, the constancy of my disposition, so that he believed that I would not yield to storms of discontent and whinging, but would be kept by grace in a gentle, humble and loving frame of mind towards all, especially to good people. Thirdly, the inward warmth of affection he had towards me more than any other in the world, which came to him after prayer for a long time to the Lord for a wife of God's choice, and pleasing to himself; an affection that he was convinced would enable him to pardon my failings, sympathise and be faithful to me forever. Lastly, the liberty and light of the most solemn and substantial members of the church of God, and the counsel they had received through prayer, in

this matter ... We were not long in this state of courtship, but put our case immediately to the church and to our respective parents. With the consent of these, the door was opened, and everyone seemed in a hurry to get us before the priest.[11]

This was not pious humbug on their part; it was the mindset by which the Welsh Methodists lived, with a sense of accountability to God and His Church, and the ever-present reality of spiritual values. A book that argued for equality in the face of cultural prejudice against women, *The Woman as Good as the Man; or The Equality of Both Sexes* was in Williams's library, and may not be without significance.[12] Williams's position was neither chauvinist nor feminist; it merely set out the role of each gender in the manner God intended for mankind. This is plainly and concisely stated in a verse from Williams's 'View of Christ's Kingdom', where God the Creator sets out for Adam and Eve their mutual relationships:

> In gentleness excelling, in feature and in face,
> In reasoning and in knowledge thou hast the foremost place;
> Her beauty is external, within it holds less sway,
> Thy province is to love her, and hers is to obey. [13]

Individuals, male and female, attain their fullest dignity and fulfilment when they follow God's blueprint for life in a fallen world. Both Martin Luther and John Calvin recognized this; the former set the ideal in the context of 'vocation', a person's calling in life, while the latter places it in 'the need for order and control in society against what he believes to be the inevitable moral chaos if societal structure is removed.'[14]

Nor does it exclude romantic love: this passage comes after Mary's account of the occasion when Philo made known his love for her:

> One afternoon, which I will remember as long as I live, after hearing the word of the kingdom from a fiery evangelist on the text, 'These are they which follow the Lamb whithersoever he goeth' [Revelation 14:4], I was returning home the same way as Philo. When we arrived at the place where my way parted from his, he escorted me, and talked about the great salvation in Christ, man's misery by nature, and the bliss of the saints in the world to come. He politely asked me to turn aside a little from that way, where many were walking, as he wanted to talk to me personally. This was the first time ever that he talked privately with me. I praise God to this day for what I heard at that time, as his discourse set my heart ablaze by giving an echo of the evangelist's message with

heavenly sweetness and incomparable pleasure. As I walked along with him, before he could express his mind, I had a strong premonition as to his purpose. We sat on a grassy verge under a poplar tree, its branches spreading above us like a green canopy, the leaves rustling in the evening breeze making sweet melody in our ears. It was in the month of May, the earth's fragrance like frankincense, myrrh and cassia, shoots sprouting up, devouring the dew as drunkards swallow wine; herbs, emerging from the soil in all colours and sizes, seemed to laugh at us, blessing our friendship, as though they wished to please our every faculty. The birds, too, were singing and twittering, as if they wished to entertain us all the time. More than all these, the breeze of heaven had risen upon us, as if to bear witness to me that we were pleasing our Lord. He held my hand with the tenderness, respect and affection that some courtiers kiss the hand of the kings of the earth. He stared me in the face with such delight, that I blushed, although I knew not why, and as I said, I knew intuitively his entire purpose.

Now, in the married state, Mary is able to say, 'Our love is the same today as it was then ... it is a steady love, deep as the sea, that bears each others' heaviest burdens.'[15]

The Third Dialogue is summarized in its title: 'Containing Mary's counsel to Martha to please her husband, and in that was to make her marriage happier and more harmonious, and possibly, to win him to the faith.' Here Mary begins with a relentless catalogue of possible failure on Martha's part: neglect of duty, careless praise of others at her husband's expense, blaming him for their poverty, and such like. She adds, 'Remember that he is your husband, and that a sure covenant exists between him and you as long as you live ... your place is to entice him to love you.' At this point Martha explodes with rebellion: 'In this way you make wives to be housemaids, yes, rather, slaves ... to suffer all manner of derision, neglect and misery by their husbands ... If so, it is better to be single than to be married.' Mary's riposte is the biblical position, that wives 'should obey their husbands in everything comely and good.' She is also made to exclaim that 'she was not taken from his head, so that she should be his equal; and not from his foot, so that the husband would make the wife too much of a slave, and belittle her; but from a rib under his breast, to show that a man is to love his wife, and to take her as the most precious part of himself.'[16] It is at this point that Williams introduces his most revolutionary argument: the power that women have over men: 'But even with this measure of submission that attended womanhood, apart from several other

250

privileges, one special privilege was given to them along with this submission, namely that they possessed more influence and authority on men than men had on each other.' Female characters from the Bible are quoted to buttress the statement: the influence for good of Esther (1: 10-12, 19) and Abigail (1 Sam 25: 23-31); for evil as in the case of the Moabite women (Num. 23-24), Delilah (Judges 16:4,ff.), and Jezebel (1 Kings 18: 4).

Williams does not hesitate to spell this out in the boldest terms:

> Our sex has power, Martha, especially when we have beauty and purity, and no little subtlety, to tempt the wisest, the most discerning, the strongest of men, so that it is hard to escape our nets, unless heaven's grace prevails. Our hearts are nets all the time; and we use all the ability and means at our disposal to make our bodies the same as well. We beautify them with clothes in the most attractive manner possible; we paint and colour them, and apply cosmetics to make our skin soft, smooth and pretty; and all this to tempt men. We use every conceivable device that enables the members of our body to tempt. Sometimes our eyes are like irresistible nets, when we make them dance and flutter with unparalleled flirtation. Our feet, our hands, our cheeks, and every other part of our bodies, by vigorous application, are made into deadly traps and nets to entice all men except eunuchs. But our hands and arms are a mighty double-chain, because passion resides there, so that none will escape them except those in whom God delights. What heart, what spirit will not utterly melt like wax before the fire when we embrace the neck or waist of the object of our love? And this is what we do, if it answers our purpose, when the sun sets in the west. With this chain we can snuff out wrath and spark off love; we turn bears into babes, and wolves into lambs.

For good measure, he adds a quotation from John Milton's *Paradise Lost:*

> O Martha, if only we kept our place, and behaved worthy of Christ's Gospel, under God we would almost be able to rule the world. Listen to how Milton, in Adam's person, sets out the various faculties in Eve which overcame his wisdom, knowledge and authority, and how her beauty, comeliness and gentleness showed that all his gifts were impotent to resist her in anything:
>
> > ...when I approach
> > Her loveliness, so absolute she seems,
> > And in herself complete, so well to know
> > Her own, that what she wills to do or say,
> > Seems wisest, virtuousest, discreetest, best:

251

All higher knowledge in her presence falls
Degraded; wisdom in discourse with her
Loses, discountenanced, and like folly shows;
Authority and reason on her wait,
As one intended first, not after made
Occasionally ... [17]

Williams was not addressing a hypothetical difficulty in dealing at such length with Martha's predicament. A poignant plea in one of the society reports sent to the Association confirms the reality of its pain and at the same time shows how the Methodists faced it with deep concern: 'one Sister, a precious Christian ... is under great trials by reason of an unquiet and profligate husband, and has the greatest hindrance of the kind as ever I saw; and also she is forced to care for all things within and without. She is in great straits, but God strengthens her through and in all, and will strengthen her – I hope I can speak more at large in time – I would desire every one to sympathize with her and pray for her.'[18]

By means of this honest and thoroughly practical *Guide*, Williams met a real need with biblical counsel and personal sympathy. One of the strengths of the work lay in its honesty, dealing with sensitive issues in a candid and realistic manner. Williams's readers faced tough choices, with hormonal surges within and intimidating practices without as ever-present pressures militating against the absolute standards of God's Word written. What was the antidote to that decay in spiritual desire which opened the floodgates to a worldly attitude in life? The answer is hammered out in biblical mould on the anvil of everyday realities in eighteenth-century Wales, with no concession to prudery on the one hand or salaciousness on the other. It is this fearless exploration of feminine power as well as responsibility which drew sanctions on the book's publication in Victorian times. Above all, the work conveys a profound understanding of human nature and is written with compassion and concern. There is warning and reproof, but also encouragement and hope. It was a timely manual for young Christians in Williams's Methodist world.

The Rev: Thomas Charles.
(From The Gospel Magazine, 1797)

18. Thomas Charles of Bala.

19. David Jones of Llan-gan.

IMMANUEL:

NEU

DDIRGELWCH DYFODIAD MAB
DUW YN Y CNAWD,

WEDI EI AGOR.

AN Y GWIR BARCHEDIG DAD YN NUW
MES USHER, GYNT ARCH-ESGOB ARMAGH
YN YR JWERDDON.

A gymreigiwyd gan y diweddar Barchedig
WILLIAM WILLIAMS.

——o——

1 Tim. III. 16.

*n ddi-ddadl, mawr yw Dirgelwch Duwiol-
deb; Duw a ymddangosodd yn y Cnawd.*

——o——

DOLGELLEU:

rgraphwyd gan T. Williams, dros E. James.
[*Gwerth Pedair Ceiniog a Dimmeu.*]

1803.

20. Title page of Williams's translation of James Ussher's 'Immanuel'.

ii

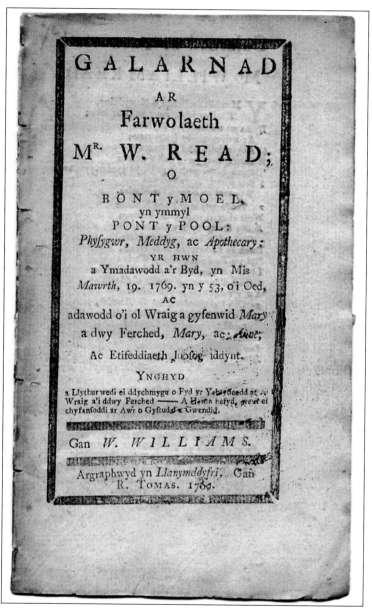

21. Williams's elegy to the physician William Read.

MARWNAD

ER

COFFADWRIAETH

Am y Parchedig

Mr. WILLIAM WILLIAMS,

Gynt o BANT-Y-CELYN.

SALM CXIV. 15.

'Gwyn ei fyd y bobl y mae'r Arglwydd yn Dduw iddynt.

CAERFYRDDIN,

ARGRAPHWYD GAN IOAN DANIEL.

M DCC XCI.

22. Title page of an elegy to Williams by David Saunders.

23. *Plaque on Col, Myddfai, the birthplace of John Thomas.*

24. *Plaque at the birthplace of Morgan Rhys, hymnwriter from Cil-y-cwm.*

25. Monument to Williams in Llanfair-ar-y-bryn churchyard.

26. Marble statue to Williams by L.S.Merrifield, Cardiff City Hall.

28. Top: Windows at Pentre tŷ gwyn Chapel.

29. Right: Window at
Crwys Chapel, Richmond Road, Cardiff.

27.

'A candle of heavenly brightness'

Williams's work 'The Door of the Experience Society' appeared in the same year as his 'Guide to Marriage'. He was sixty years of age, had been a Christian for nearly forty years, and after leaving his curacies had travelled extensively, perhaps as many as 2,000 miles a year on horseback, to preach and lead society meetings. The considered opinion of Thomas Charles is worth recording in this context: 'His imagination was lively; his insight was characterized by discernment and penetration. Many heavenly influences were brought to bear on his spirit in public ministry, and as he conversed with people about their souls in the private societies.'[1] As well as his hymn-writing, his counselling skills were recognized as exceptional and unequalled.

Published at Brecon in 1777, it had a long title: Templum Experientiae apertum; *neu, Ddrws y Society Profiad wedi ei agor o led y pen, fel y gallo y sawl a chwennycho edrych i mewn: Mewn saith Dialog. Ar Ddull o Ymddiddan rhwng Theophilus ac Eusebius, y naill fel y dychymmygir yn byw ar Dir Immanuel, a'r llall yng Ngwlad Cwsg. Yn cynnwys, (Ar ôl hanes ddychymmygol o Grefydd Gwlad Cwsg) Sylfeini, Siamplau a Gorchymmynion ysgrythurol am Society Profiad, fel y Moddion gorau i gadw Credinwyr rhag oeri; y Dysgyblaethau, yr Holiadau, a'r Trefniadau sydd i fod ynddi; y Buddioldeb a'r Adeiladaeth dduwiol sydd o'i chadw hi yng ngoleuni ac ofn yr Arglwydd, ond y canlyniadau gresynus sydd o'i chadw hi yn annoeth ac yn anystyriol ('Templum Experientiae apertum*; or, The Door of the Experience Society fully opened, so that whoever wills may enter: in seven Dialogues, by way of a conversation between *Theophilus and Eusebius*, the one in imagination living in *Immanuel's* land, and the other in the Land of Sleep. Containing, [after an imaginary account of the religion of the Land of Sleep] the foundation, examples and Scriptural rules of an Experience Society, as the best means to keep believers from growing cold; the disciplines, questions, and arrangements that are to be kept by it; the usefulness and godly edification that accompanies its exercise in the light and fear of the Lord, and the alarming consequences of conducting it flippantly and unwisely'). An English translation by Bethan Lloyd-Jones, with the title *The Experience Meeting*, was first published in 1973.

Two characters are involved in the dialogue, Theophilus and Eusebius, and both are representative of the Welsh Methodists at the time. Theophilus lives his life on 'Immanuel's Land', the spiritual Canaan promised to God's people as the inheritance of true believers. Eusebius, on the other hand, has dwelt in 'the Land of Sleep', engulfed in a spiritual slumber until recently, when God sent revival and transformed the community. R. Geraint Gruffydd considers that the work 'at least approaches that of a minor classic of our recent prose tradition … It is important because it reveals to us, possibly better than any other book, the heart of Welsh Calvinistic Methodism at its inception and in its purity. And that heart was: experience, or if you wish, feeling … The Methodists … looked, not only for a cerebral response, the concurrence of the mind with the truth of the doctrine. Rather, they looked for a response of the whole man, a response of the heart, a response that combined the will and the affections in a commitment of trust in Christ as the Saviour of sinners.'[2] It commends itself as a work of spiritual maturity, shrewd judgment and wise practical advice that dealt with matters central to the Methodist's distinctive life and witness. For that reason it deserves, first, a survey of its contents, and secondly, in another chapter, some consideration of its leading issues.

In the first dialogue, Eusebius elaborates on the consequences of the revival: 'there are obvious signs that these people are going on from grace to grace, for it can be seen that their hearts are wounded and bruised, their consciences alive and tender, their wills broken to the will of God… Godly fear grows in them, and they are careful in all their duties to God, to themselves and to their neighbours…' Their new life in Christ is characterised by two areas of growth: 'First, their view of themselves, that their hearts are deceitful above all things … This view makes them loathe themselves, and to believe always that they are the chief of sinners … believing themselves to be more unworthy than anyone. In the second place … This poor view of themselves … has made Christ, and all that pertain to Him, very precious – His righteousness, His sufferings, His power and His wisdom … the sufferings of Christ on Calvary's hill is what they sing about. This is the subject of their talk and of their study …. They were made … dead to their own gifts, graces, virtues and the opinions of other people. Today, nothing counts but Christ, and He is all in all.' The picture of their condition, however, is not yet complete, 'because their temptations are innumerable ... some within, some without ... But you will understand some of them when you consider their ages and circumstances – companies, of merry, manly youths, crowds of girls in the full strength of their feminine attractiveness and vivacity, men who for the most part are an easy prey for Satan to work upon their fleshly lusts, and to entice them to the pleasures of flesh and blood.' At this point Theophilus offers advice: 'Of all the means of grace, I know of no more profitable than the special fellowship meetings, called private societies, to correct, to direct, to edify and to encourage weak members who are ever ready to stray aside – either to lusts, pleasures or the love of vanities on the one hand, or to pride, arrogance, conceit and envy on the other ...' The stage is now set as Williams makes Eusebius give the reason for the work: 'to receive some guidance from you ... about these private societies.' He outlines objections to them: 'that there is no basis for them in Holy Scripture'; that they were not a custom 'with the Protestant Reformers, but that it is some new order introduced by the Methodists.' Furthermore, 'some say that it is not a good thing to reveal the secrets of the heart', with obvious dangers in so doing and disastrous consequences likely to follow. Confirmation of a Scriptural foundation for them, and specific directions for their conduct are therefore solicited.[3]

In the second dialogue, before Theophilus outlines biblical precedents, with obvious text like Malachi 3:16, 'they that feared the Lord spake often one to another', and Hebrews 10:25 'not forsaking the assembling of ourselves together", he gives reasons why they are profitable.

> First of all ... because they are means of keeping up this same warmth and liveliness that was ours at the beginning ... Fellowship is very effective in stimulating us to good or evil ...In the second place ... to unravel the various nets and hidden snares woven by Satan to catch the simple believer on his own ground ... Many young saints are like lambs, that run after the dogs instead of after their mothers; imagining that some sins are no sins, but grace; that the breezes of nature are the breath of heaven; that the spirit of melancholy is a truly broken heart; and pride, envy, and prejudice are a sign of zeal for God ... Thirdly, these ... meetings are good at forestalling contentions, suspicions, prejudices, discords, jealousies and all uncharitableness ... The gardener has only to neglect to visit his garden, and to refrain from weeding it, and it will be overrun with weeds in a few weeks ... fourth

... in order that we may look after and watch over each other's lives, lest any should fall into loose living and turn the grace of God into lasciviousness. The saints of the Most High God often happen to have their abodes in stony places ... where they must talk to, mix with, and work with unbelievers, and where they are in great danger of having their garments stained by their proximity to them ... fifth ... these ... meetings give us the opportunity of bearing one another's burdens ... sixth ... because it gives us the opportunity to declare the work of God on our souls, and to praise His name for it ... lastly ... for strengthening ourselves against all our spiritual enemies, and for praying together as one man against them all.

As the second dialogue draws to a close, Eusebius recites some of the pitfalls in sharing experiences, and Theophilus emphasises the need for wisdom, together with appropriate rules and 'waiting on the Lord to trouble the water.'[4]

The third dialogue is given to a consideration of the stewards or leaders and their qualifications, and includes an important section on preaching. It begins by setting out an ideal: 'It is essential that there should be stewards in every fellowship.' However, this was not always achieved. In June 1745 some north Cardiganshire societies lacked 'private exhorters to supervise them on a weekly basis; the ones they desire cannot come, and those who can they will not accept, but I hope the issue will be resolved.'[5] As a general rule, it was said, the stewards 'need to have a clear-eyed ability to recognize the temperament, emotions, troubles, and inclinations of all the different ages and ranks of the members.' In particular, 'they must have a bold spirit' to deal with one without fear or favour, and they 'must feel a sincere love to the whole fellowship.' In addition, no leader can raise the fellowship above the measure of his own spirituality: 'it is a good thing, if possible, that such ... should be lively in their faith, warm in their spirit, promoting God's work with zeal and heavenly enthusiasm – the kind that will keep the meeting alive from beginning to end.' Their responsibilities are addressed as well: 'keep the names of all the members in a register ... collect for the needs of the church ... the fellowship is to care for those who are widows indeed ... and if they are sick ... to pay for a doctor to visit them', and to ensure 'that there are teachers to minister the Word' each Lord's Day, providing them with money and hospitality as appropriate. A long discussion follows regarding the qualifications of preachers, since 'today, preachers of all denominations are more numerous than were Bibles in the dark days of our grandfathers.' On the one hand, Williams is scathing about those who leave off their secular craft with a zeal that does not correspond to or flow from knowledge. 'Many set out to preach, who are much more concerned about honours, personal gain and creature comforts ... than for the glory of God and the good of immortal souls.' On the other hand, there were some from such backgrounds who had no great learning but who 'have the substance in them – that is, the Spirit of the Lord', and these were to be charitably discerned and highly esteemed. Two other issues are dealt with: if for some reason 'the wives of any teachers have to accompany them, it is fitting that they too should be self-effacing and meek.' They should not be 'too eager for gossip over tea or coffee, after the manner of the ungodly women of the world ... slanderous; going from house to house and from one district to another with tittle-tattle, like a Gazette for Satan.' Finally, stewards should be 'suitably gifted ...to perform all the tasks that appertain to the ministry of grace in a society of separated Christians.'[6]

An echo of Williams's concern about preachers' motives and abilities is found in a letter to Thomas Charles, written in 1790:

> I rejoice to see such an attraction to Gwynedd in some preachers. Ten or twelve of them in our part have this desire, and yet there is here no deficiency, as some new ones arise daily. Some of them have received liveliness and light; let the Lord multiply their number! But others are so keen to go that all of Gwynedd would be too small for them, even though there is no good word for them at home ... I fear that some come to Gwynedd before they are mature. Many come to you without seeking the Association's sanction. It would be advisable for them to have the Association's commendation, before they adventure to stand before such mixed congregations as you have, that they possess the intelligence, enlightenment, and attitude that will enable them to fulfil such responsible work without bringing shame on it. Our Association has become quite negligent in this matter, every man is allowed to do as he wishes without any commission, and never was there greater need of reformation. I fear that some, instead of seeking and praying to God for assistance to set out that great salvation and the depths of free grace in the salvation of miserable sinners, venture forth to gain fame, a better standard of living, and to benefit their own households, to give themselves less laborious callings, and to live in greater luxury; and you encourage them, so that they return home showing the world that they have prospered greatly. But I forbear in this, hoping that you have discernment and recognize it all.[7]

The Methodists were nothing if not conscientious and careful in seeking to maintain the highest standards among themselves and in the sight of the world.

In the fourth dialogue, as well as giving advice on what form the experience meeting should take, Williams describes 'the gifted catechizer'. Part of his skill is to probe the individual's true spiritual condition, much as a good clinician takes into account a patient's case history, and considers underlying causes as well as symptoms, before making a diagnosis and prescribing a remedy. 'And so', Williams concludes, 'through the experiences of the man being questioned, the catechizer lights a candle of heavenly brightness for the entire fellowship, and provides for them a dish of sweetmeats, possibly even from a poor and muddled experience.' The ideal catechizer, then, is one who 'perceives what particular sin it is that keeps the man away from God; he can seek out those dark dens, where lurk sin and Satan, fleshly lusts and the lust of the world and its idols. In the same way as a fisherman knows where the fish are, and the mole-catcher the runs of the moles, and the fowler where to find the partridge, so does the expert catechizer recognize the cause of every fall, so does he recognize the secret ways of the temptations of the world and of the flesh, and ... all the twists and turns of human nature, between true repentance and fits of melancholy, or the state of unhappiness that overtakes us at times in this world.' He must beware of sparing his friends, of showing partiality 'to those in high positions in the world', and indulging those who generously reward God's servants. In an elegy to Christopher Bassett, Williams portrays him as one 'who questions pilgrims with solemnity how they have journeyed over steep, rocky places, and when they fell were their bruises fully healed, and their wounds washed clean with water from the fountain of Bethlehem?' Again, he would ask women young in the faith 'whether Christ had freed the root of their hearts from carnal love? ... the robust young men, full of heavenly fire, whether Christ excelled every other object in their affections?' As for more mature Christians, 'had they fully triumphed over the debilitating love of the world, and had the one talent they had received now grown to ten talents?' Such were the perception and gifts required of the religious society's catechizer.[8]

Williams now moves to the nature of the questions that are to be put to those who were to be received as members of the society. Here he was able to develop the directions and questions found in the Welsh Methodists' earlier manual, *Sail, Dibenion a Rheolau'r Societies* ('The

Basis, Purposes and Rules of the Societies') of 1742. As an important principle, 'we should not be putting the same questions to everyone – not the same question, for instance, to a beginner in Christ as to an older Christian.' He proceeds to suggest fourteen questions that would be appropriate for those seeking membership, in whom 'the light of faith and assurance' is not of the same clarity or strength as those 'who have long enjoyed the visitations of the Lord.' Their emphasis falls on matters that accompany personal repentance, faith in Christ, a faith 'which is the work of the Holy Spirit', counting the cost of discipleship, right motives in seeking membership, and submission to the society's constraints and privileges. Above all, seeking membership should stem from a deeper longing in the soul: 'though you have not received the witness of the Spirit, yet are you seeking God with all your heart, and that as a constant disposition of the soul (not in fits or waves of conviction), longing to lay hold on God, wanting nothing else but Him alone, and counting all things loss that you may gain Him, not resting till you possess Him.' The outcome of such questioning would be either acceptance or probation, but it should always be determined with charity: 'no one in the person of a seeker, and with a true desire for eternal life, should be shut out, however faint may be the revelations and visitations of God to him.' [9]

Dealing with more mature members of the society receives attention in the fifth dialogue. Among other matters, issues of assurance, love, conscience, fresh lessons learned, motives for conforming to God's Word in behaviour, and the use of God-given talents, are examined. Progress in their spiritual lives is to be measured in terms of 'new lessons ... the Lord taught them of late', and an awareness of being 'nearer heaven than they were at the beginning' of their walk with God. The pursuit of godliness is urged with vigour, always with the endeavour on the part of the leader 'to keep a spirit of light and heavenly feeling in them.' To achieve this, it is also recognized that occasions may demand 'special exhortations', or preaching, aimed at addressing specific needs and conditions that prevail in the society at the time. [10]

The thorny question of discipline receives attention in the sixth dialogue. Harsh treatment of those who fall into sin is to be avoided in the spirit of Galatians 6:1, 'If a man be overtaken in a fault, ye which are spiritual, restore such an one in the spirit of meekness; considering thyself, lest thou also be tempted.' The society should proceed with compassion and mercy, and aim at restoration. At the same time, other

259

Scriptures, such as Ephesians 5:11, 'have no fellowship with the unfruitful works of darkness, but rather reprove them', are also to be observed. It is the stubbornly unrepentant or hypocritical that is to be shunned and excommunicated:

> If he who professes religion has fallen to the same fault again and again, and that with very little provocation, and with every sign that he has never hated his fault, but loves it and fondles it in secret, so that he does not sorrow for it, but rather shows nothing but an empty, hypocritical pretence, springing more from the shame that the disgrace has caused him, than from pain for having sinned against a merciful and gracious God – it is necessary to discipline someone like this before all, as a warning, an alarm and a cause of fear to others; and if the sin is against the law of the land, and is known to the world outside, it is profitable to lay upon the guilty some public or open punishment or rebuke, so that the world may come to recognize the fact that the church of God does not suffer any to live in any sin. [11]

For the genuine backslider, no effort should be spared to plead 'with them with all tenderness, gentleness and love that they would cleave anew to the Lord.'

Practical matters, some of them delicate and calling for sensitivity, wisdom, and careful management, are the subjects of the final dialogue. Williams is concerned to set clear boundaries within which the societies should conduct their meetings, and reminds them that, 'the emphasis of the work should be on the state of the soul ... The things meant for discussion in these fellowships are the things to awaken consciences, to arouse convictions, to generate zeal, to create a godly fear, to promote love towards God and His Church, to reveal sin, and to display the length and breadth, the depth and height of the love of Christ which is beyond all knowledge.' Matters not to be related in the meeting include: 'blasphemous thoughts that Satan insinuates into our spirits ...stray, wandering thoughts ... every wild temptation that comes to arouse our passions ... our old erroneous ways before we came to know the Lord ... our every lapse ... our weaknesses ... evil consequences might follow the relating of lapses that God has hidden ... to complain much about others...' A good steward sets 'good examples' before the fellowship, does not divulge society affairs, and warns against over-eating and drinking and idleness.

Finally, the high aim for which the societies existed, says Williams, will only be achieved by prayer: 'O pray very much to the Father of spirits to lead you in every aspect of this great work, with which there is nothing under the sun to compare for its substance and its glory.'[12] This expression of dependence on God for guidance is also a confident assertion of the value of the societies. Williams believed that what God had initiated in the Great Awakening by way of lively preaching He would sustain by way of pastoral oversight. For this reason his work was intended not only to provide urgent and necessary counsel for the present, but also lasting guidelines for the future.

28.

'This inward Spring of Activity'

Society meetings were clearly concerned with the experience and fellowship of those who made a Christian profession, and whose expression of faith, love and godliness was in conformity with Methodist convictions. Williams's *Experience Meeting* dealt not only with the sifting process to establish fitness for membership, it also elaborated on the societies' leading characteristic: a sharing of experiences by 'searching the heart'. This went further than giving an account of recent encounters with God, of trials and triumphs, of Scriptures read or prayers answered. It involved a penetrating probing of the hidden life of the soul, its motives, attitudes, failures, desires, and much else beside, in the light of God's standard of purity and practice. This is why it was referred to as 'the private society'. Such 'searching' made heavy demands on both leaders and members. In the former it required wise and skilful handling; in the latter, restraint, selectivity and honesty, even though the context was that of a private rather than a public meeting. For this reason, Williams's work was a pioneering venture, breaking new ground, and designed to set out safeguards as well as justification for the practice. In his 'Introduction' to the English translation of *The Experience Meeting*, D. Martyn Lloyd-Jones speaks highly of Williams's achievement: 'The task of conducting these "experience meetings" obviously called for great wisdom, spiritual insight, tact, and discretion. They could easily degenerate into exhibitionism on the part of extroverts, and lead to scandal, as very private matters were related involving others. It was in order to obviate such troubles and disasters, and to instruct the leaders in this most important work, that the Rev. William Williams wrote this little book.' Concerning the book's author, he says that 'his genius, his spiritual understanding, and what would now be described as psychological insight stand out everywhere and are truly astonishing.'[1]

There was another reason for the book's appearance. Hitherto in Protestant churches, discipline had been exercised by means of regular pulpit ministry and by congregational scrutiny entrusted to the church's officers. Puritans, Dissenters and New England pastors operated within clearly-defined ecclesiastical structures, established or separating, whereas the Methodist societies were entering new territory. Allegiance to an Episcopal Church was fiercely defended during the lifetime of the leading Methodist clergymen, and yet their distinctive soul culture was developing outside it. This created fresh challenges and opportunities. How was their identity defined and preserved? How did they develop and protect their autonomy? Dissatisfied with the spirituality, or rather the lack of it, within the parish churches, what were the essentials of the alternative which they offered? Faced with charges of fanaticism, irregularity, emotional excess and heresy, what would be their response? Williams and the Welsh Methodists were profoundly concerned to monitor and nurture genuine Christian experience in the context of a self-regulating community. It was in this context that Williams forged for the Methodists this manual. It sought to establish the societies on a sound foundation, and was formulated so as to supply a worthy and mature alternative to what was lacking in the formal religious establishments of the day. New wine can only be safely stored in new bottles.[2]

Williams never tired of insisting that faith was an indwelling principle, planted in the soul at regeneration, rather than an isolated, once-for-all act of believing. It was by faith that Christ, freely offered in the Gospel invitation, was personally appropriated. The mind, conscience, emotions, and the will were involved in that personal commitment. Salvation by God's free grace and mercy, while repugnant to the popular religion of the day, was a foundational pillar of Methodist convictions. It was an irrevocable transaction, guaranteed by the character and promise of God. This was the beginning of a life of faith, whereby that inward principle determined priorities, standards, attitudes and everyday behaviour. One response to God's free gift of salvation was gratitude, so that faith was an active principle of love, love for God and love for others, especially the household of faith.

> There is hardly an opportunity when society members meet together in public or private, that they do not feel the power of God and His divine presence. This makes them shout for joy, and they often cry out for assistance to praise God and glorify the Lamb for their daily experience of His distinguishing love in their souls. They spend whole nights together rejoicing in God and praising His sacred name; and there are but few among them that are not in this liberty, but even those

> who have not, perceive the happiness of those that have attained liberty; and so continually groan under their bondage, longing much for liberty.[3]

As Williams claimed in *The Experience Meeting*, the societies were profitable, 'first of all ... because they are means of keeping up this same warmth and liveliness that was ours at the beginning; as iron sharpeneth iron, so a man sharpeneth the countenance of his friend.' This was often the case, and some accounts speak of the blessings received by meeting together in superlative terms: 'The Societies are in a flame in some places, and others growing gradually in the Lord. Some that have been sluggish begin to recover their strength; some are now walking in thick darkness, but groaning for the Sun of Righteousness to arise after a tedious night of desertion. Some few there are endeavouring to reconcile Christ and self, Christ and the world, and not knowing which to choose, but I hope they will choose the better part, and leave all and follow Him fully; and indeed there are many can experimentally rejoice in God their Saviour, and have no confidence in the flesh, daily thirsting after the full enjoyment of God.'[4]

A desire for close fellowship to nurture spiritual health and vigour had been recognized by Martin Bucer among the Reformers, and by Puritan pastors later. Thus Bucer at Strasbourg, and the Pietists on the Continent gathered believers together for spiritual exercises and counsel.[5] Thomas Goodwin in England favoured the sharing of Christian experiences as well as an account of conversion on admission to church membership: 'This duty of communion of saints doth not consist in giving an account of their graces in that set way, as they gave an account of their conversion, when they were first admitted into the church. But it is a communication of their experiences, as to the growth of their graces, and as to the exercise of them. The graces of a believer ... may rather appear thus, by way of a conference, than in a set narration.'[6] The Welsh Puritan, Vavasor Powell, argued strongly for gatherings of this kind: 'Experience is a copy written by the Spirit of God upon the hearts of believers. It is one of faith's handmaids, and attendants, and hope's usher, (Romans 5:3). And when Christ is withdrawn within the vail, and the wings of faith clipped, and the clouds of temptation overflow, and overwhelm the poor, distressed, doubting, despairing, and drowning soul; this barque keeps, and hold up the soul's head above water, till the Ark return. That Christian believes strongest that hath experience to back his faith, and that Saint speaks sweetest and homest, that speaks experimentally; for that which cometh from one spiritual heart, reacheth another spiritual heart. Experience is like steel to an edged tool, or like salt to fresh meat, it seasons brain-knowledge, and settles a shaking, unsettled soul.' Powell published the book from a conviction that 'herein you may see not only your own hearts, but many hearts, and heart-knowledge is both necessary and precious to sincere souls.'[7]

The Dissenting ministers, Isaac Watts and Philip Doddridge, at a date nearer the Great Awakening also recognized the importance of 'heart-religion'. Watts's *Discourses of the Love of God and the Use and Abuse of the Passions in Religion* which appeared in 1729 echoed Powell's convictions:

> Even where Reason is bright, and the Judgment clear, yet it will be ineffectual for any valuable Purpose, if Religion reach no further than the Head, and proceed not to the Heart: It will have but little Influence, if there are none of the Affections engaged ... 'Tis a sort of Life and Fire within the Hearts of Men, which God the Creator hath ordained to be ever ready there, to give Force and Spirit for present Action. He knew our Nature wanted this Spur, this inward Spring of Activity.

Having said this, Watts goes on to outline some of the dangers for Christians of 'an irregular conduct, with regard to their affections':

> *when they live entirely by their devout Passions, and make these the only Rules of Self-Inquiry concerning their Temper, their habitual State of Soul, and their present Frame of Spirit, and concerning every Thing that belongs to their Christianity* ... Let us watch against this Danger, and remember that though the Passions are of excellent Use in religion, yet they were never designed to stand in the place of Reasons and Judgment, or to supply the Room of an enlightened Understanding, a sanctified Will, and a Conversation attended with all the Fruits of Holiness. [8]

Doddridge, in the third of ten sermons on 'regeneration', identifies the power of the affections in the regenerate, to attract and repel, motivate, alarm, or rejoice: 'I readily acknowledge, that the Degree, in which the *Affections* operate, may, and will be *different*, in different Persons, according to their Natural Constitution: But as in some Degree or another, they make an essential Part of our Frame, it is impossible but they must be impressed with a Matter of such Importance, as *Religion* will appear.'[9] In this respect, Williams was following a sound tradition, but his treatment takes the nurture of 'heart-religion' to a deeper level of personal perception.

A fuller appreciation of 'heart-religion' also appeared in the early years of the Great Awakening in the work of Jonathan Edwards. Originally preached in 1742 and 1743, the substance of his *Treatise Concerning the Religious Affections* was revised for publication in 1746. One of his biographers, Iain H. Murray, says that the 'basic and recurring theme' of *The Religious Affections* is that 'the love and the pursuit of holiness is the enduring mark of the true Christian.' He adds that it is 'unquestionably one of the most important books possessed by the Christian church on the nature of true religion.'[10] Early in the book Edwards makes his position clear: 'The Holy Scriptures everywhere place religion very much in the affections; such as fear, hope, love, hatred, desire, joy, sorrow, gratitude, compassion, and zeal.' He is careful to define its character: 'in those gracious exercises and affections which are wrought in the minds of the saints, through the saving influences of the Spirit of God, there is a new inward perception or sensation of their minds, entirely different in its nature and kind, from anything that ever their minds were the subjects of before they were sanctified ... This new spiritual sense, and the new dispositions that attend it, are no new faculties, but new principles of nature ... There is ... a divine taste, given and maintained by the Spirit of God, in the hearts of the saints, whereby they are in like manner led and guided in discerning and distinguishing the true spiritual and holy beauty of actions.' The title of the work's final section summarises this point: 'Gracious and holy affections have their exercise and fruit in Christian practice.'[11] With an insistence on matters of the heart in religion, Williams was in this tradition, and his book developed the theme with thoroughness and conviction.

In writing *The Experience Meeting*, Williams had in mind the mainly young Methodist converts who found the local churches to which they belonged, if indeed they belonged to any, lacking in sympathy, and often critical of their new experience. All too often those churches lacked biblical preaching and teaching, their spirituality was formal rather than personal, and their devotion to Christ was detached rather than fervent. For the present it was enough that the Methodist society's identity was seen as having a loose affiliation, through its leaders particularly, with the Established Church, while developing its own character, priorities, and culture. For this reason, it was necessary to define and protect membership by careful scrutiny of those who sought to join, and mutual discipline among those who belonged to, the society.

Knowledge and experience featured prominently in the questions asked of those seeking membership: 'Have you had a view of your pitiful state … and that you deserve damnation? … Do you regard yourself as a greater sinner than anyone else? …and that you cannot know yourself … without the supernatural work of the Holy Spirit enlightening the eyes of your mind? … Have you seen your need of faith more than of any other grace?' There were questions, too, as to personal commitment and experience: 'Have you … counted the cost…? Are you seeking God with all your heart, and that as a constant disposition of the soul (not in fits or waves of conviction)…? Are you willing to take rebukes and chastening and instruction from us …?' For 'members of longer standing' there was a question related to assurance: 'Does the Holy Spirit bear witness with their spirit that they are the children of God? Has this witness been doubled [that is, repeated]?' This question was based on Romans 8:16, 'The Spirit itself beareth witness with our spirit, that we are the children of God', but it also implied a repeat of such episodes or seasons. At such times of intimate communion with God the awareness of belonging to Christ, of the intensity of His constant, undeserved love, and of the soul's complete security in Him, could be overwhelming. It was a ministry of the Spirit objectively spoken of as 'sealing with the Spirit' of Ephesians 1:13, and subjectively apprehended during seasons of special visitation by God. Nevertheless, as seen from society reports and questions, it conveyed a nearness to God that was to be sought and desired. Harris's early experience in the Llangasty church tower, and in 1746 'in a private society to two in the morning like a drunken man. Could say nothing but Glory! Glory! for a long time', were examples of this. Williams's hymn that begins with, 'O! llefara, addfwyn Iesu' ('Speak, I pray Thee, gentle Jesus') has a verse that begins with the line, 'Dwed dy fod yn eiddo imi' ('Tell me Thou art mine, O Saviour'). The whole is an expression of intense longing for the same intimacy. John Thomas, Tre-main, had similar experiences in various society meetings when 'it had become heaven on earth' to him, and he had felt a beam of 'sunshine' flooding his soul. [12]

In the matter of assurance, Williams followed closely one of his favourite Puritan authors, Thomas Goodwin. In his work *Of the Object and Acts of Justifying Faith* (1697), Goodwin acknowledges, 'that that act of faith which justifies a sinner, is distinct from *knowing* he hath eternal life, and may therefore be without it, because it doth not necessarily contain prevailing assurance in it. By prevailing assurance, I mean such an assurance as overpowereth doubts and sense to the contrary, so as, in the believer's knowledge, he is able to say, Christ is mine, and my sins are forgiven' [italics mine]. Goodwin then proceeds to speak of three kinds of assurance, spoken of in 1 John 5: 7-8 as 'three that bear witness in earth, the Spirit, and the water, and the blood'. 'By blood' is to be understood 'the work of justification on a poor sinner'; by water, 'sanctification, both in the habits and fruit of it; for whom Christ's blood justifies, it doth also cleanse and sanctify, and washeth away the filth of sin'; and 'the third witness is that of the Spirit, whereby is meant an immediate testimony of the Holy Ghost, superadded to all these.' In this third sense, Goodwin speaks of it as 'the special work of the Holy Ghost to comfort and assure the hearts of believers of their salvation.' He urges believers to 'sue this promise out, wait for it, rest not in believing only, rest not in assurance by graces only; there is a further assurance to be had.'[13] It was in this sense that society members were to seek more intimacy with God.

Other questions were intended to drive home the expectation of spiritual progress: 'Are they conscious of more spiritual light within ... Is their love increasing toward the church ... Is their conscience more tender ... What new lessons has the Lord taught them of late? ... Do they find that they are ... nearer heaven than they were at the beginning? ... Do they examine their motives ... whether it is for the glory of God ... or some ... satisfaction for themselves? By whose will do they walk ... Is it by the will of God?' Such questions evidently assumed that people were able to articulate their response, and that the questioner was competent to discern its credibility and also able to take the matter further for the good of the society as a whole. Society reports demonstrate that these ideals were not always achieved or achievable, as this example shows: 'These two bands can't give a very full and plain account of their conversation – first, how they were convinced of their lost and damned state by nature in the first Adam, and also how they were justified by grace in the Second; and how all their happiness lies entirely in Him; they find much sweetness in conversing with Jesus in His ordinances; some of them walk in sweet liberty, and are filled with much holy fear; but here are some much questioned by the brethren; two of them say they believe, but can give no account of how or which way they came to believe, or what effect their faith works upon their souls, or what fruit it brings forth.'[14]

Nevertheless, it is also clear that a substantial measure of success was maintained by sustained oversight of the society leaders.

Williams had spoken of the reinstatement of the soul's faculties in regeneration, so that all parts of human personality are now able to function in a God-centred way: the mind, the emotions, the conscience, memory, imagination, and importantly, the will. Williams readily granted that the feelings or 'frames' could dominate at a time of heightened spiritual activity, when powerful preaching and ervent song would be in evidence. But he maintained that emotion had its place, because human beings feel as well as think and act. The answer therefore was to evaluate emotional manifestations, and acknowledge the validity of those emotions sanctified by the Holy Spirit.

> Those who are members continue to go on pretty well; and considering the miserable and ignorant condition of men by nature, it is precious to see how much signs of grace and sanctification that is in many. But looking on the other hand on the excellency of the Christian religion and wonderful love of God in Christ, and the preciousness of those things contained in the new covenant, and God's promises and the gifts of redemption etc., it is sore to see so little knowledge, that is, spiritual and experimental; and so little of the holy, heavenly life which is answerable, and appropriate for saints, especially those that are members of the societies with us. They are but young in grace, and so had rather have a little feelings and fine frames most commonly than feed by faith on the great things of God (which we expect a full enjoyment of soon), because their faith is weak and they lose, in part, the exercise of it etc. when they lose their feelings and frames, by reason that they are but babes and have need of milk and not strong meat.[15]

An astute examiner would recognize well-founded manifestations of emotion, and in any case the aim of the experience meeting was not to exclude it, but to encourage a maturity which would secure for emotion its rightful place.

Another response was a sustained appetite for God, to know Him better, in closer acquaintance, and for godliness with the aid of divine grace: 'longing for more enjoyment of God ... longs to be more holy ... longs for a clearer sight ... walks much with God and longs to walk with Him continually ... longing for Christ.'[16] Williams was eager to encourage the exercise of spiritual senses, especially sight and sound, and he indulged his gifts to this purpose often in both Welsh and English, as the following examples show:

269

> I gaze beyond the distant hills,
> Each hour for Thee I pine;
> Come, O Beloved, the day's far spent
> My sun is in decline.
>
> The Saviour's beauty most to see
> I covet here below;
> Not even heaven's legions fair
> Can such a sight bestow.
>
> O! let me see those beams of light,
> Feel that celestial spark
> That veils the beauties of the world
> In an eternal dark.
>
> O speak the word, and all is done,
> My sins shall flee away,
> Just like the curtain of the night
> Before the rising day.

As the body's eye delights in sights of natural beauty, so the eye of the soul is ravished by the beauty of Christ. Even as words of personal recognition and worth to the natural ear create a sense of self-esteem, so to the spiritual ear, Christ's voice brings peace and reassurance.[17]

'Simplicity' was also a favourite word for Williams. It conveyed a fusion of the attributes of sincerity and humility in the soul, which manifested itself in openness to God and to His people, together with integrity and honesty in dealing with others. This was true of several society members, in the same report he can say, 'one of the warmest, simplest and most zealous and fruitful societies under my care; they truly fight against the world, the flesh and the devil'; and of another, 'the few that are here have strengthened themselves in the Lord, and grow in several graces, especially in simplicity, humility, and a longing for the Lord.'[18] The impression conveyed by these reports is that of serious dealings with God in the context of love and mutual encouragement. Society members faced trials and afflictions in their lives with the support of others in their meeting, as well as by practising close fellowship with God.

As well as listing matters not to be mentioned in the course of 'heart-searching' by the society leader, the seventh dialogue also makes a positive statement. It speaks of matters 'most suitable to be related':

270

1. Things to awaken conscience, to arouse convictions, to generate zeal, to create a godly fear, to promote love towards God and His Church, to reveal sin, and to display the length and the breadth, the depth and height of the love of Christ ... 2. it is necessary to have a clear and open view of people's condition, in order to deal impartially with their immortal souls. 3. ... things that will be helpful ... to release our spirits from bondage, guilt and the fear of death, and to bring us to the true liberty of the children of God ... 4. ... convictions and inwards suffering for sin which the Holy Spirit works in us when we sin ... 5, ... the graces, the heavenly feelings and the sweet delight that the Spirit of life produces in you from time to time ... 6. ... the shortcomings and disappointments that you find in yourselves... [19]

The whole section conveys the impression of an intense spirituality, to be shared with honesty in the context of mutual support. It assumed a measure of ability to articulate on the part of the members, and great skill on the part of their leader to turn the conversation to benefit the entire society. It was Methodism that introduced such close spiritual examination, and Williams in this work who set out its meaning in most comprehensive detail. Jonathan Edwards advanced the understanding of Christian experience in a philosophical way, while Williams practised as a physician of souls in a fallen world. Edwards spoke and wrote for settled congregations, Williams ministered to gatherings of people whose denominational affiliation was ambivalent. These differences serve to explain the originality and practicality of Williams's *Experience Meeting* when compared with Edwards's writings on revival.

At one point Williams speaks of the stewards as exercising 'the ministry of grace in a society of separated Christians.'[20] With this last phrase Williams gives the impression that as far as the Methodist were concerned the societies had an identity all of their own. The members were Christians by virtue of God's work in their lives: they believed God's Word to be true, they were justified by faith in Christ, regenerated by the power of the Holy Spirit, submitted to God's will, dependent on God's grace, and seeking God's glory. They were separated Christians because they held in common a personal experience of these things, demonstrated in a lively way that they found nowhere else. It would be another forty years before these 'separated Christians' became a distinct, separate Church. For the present it was enough for Williams to close his *Experience Meeting* with an earnest conviction and prayer, that God 'has never failed to hear His people's

271

cry when they seek Him with all their heart. Farewell, and may the God of peace bless you and prosper you and strengthen you to promote His glory.'

29.

'Preserve the gold'

This chapter's title is taken from the 'Conclusion' of the first part of John Bunyan's *Pilgrim's Progress*. It invites the reader to 'throw away' any 'dross' found in the work, 'but yet preserve the gold'. In a similar way, Williams in his elegies invites his readers to recognize the value and usefulness of the testimony of Methodist pilgrims who have passed through death into glory. These poetic compositions are meant to depict the life-changing power of Christ's salvation, the golden trophy of holiness in the flawed, weak, failing believer in this world and its unalloyed purity in the next. To preserve that gold was to provide eloquent commentary on the dealings of God's providence with God's people. However short they have fallen of that ideal of Christ-likeness which they pursued during their Christian pilgrimage, they are still God's people, the objects of His undying love and kept by His power for an eternal inheritance. Their testimonies provide a spur to godliness of life, and they are useful as cumulative evidence that believers are not abandoned by their Saviour at death. Elegies are useful because the experiences they relate are not the product of a relative subjectivism or an arbitrary mysticism, but of sound biblical truth. The people of whom Williams writes were, after all, if not actual society members, those who had the closest affiliation with Calvinistic Methodism. One writer has described them as 'mini spiritual biographies, the vitae of the saints, major and minor of the Methodist Revival.'[1]

A rehearsal of Christian experience and the achievements of grace was familiar enough territory during a person's life in the context of a Methodist society's close dealings with its members. The elegies, however, also made a clear statement that an afflicted, fearful, apprehensive believer, under the weight of mortality and facing an eternal destiny, could have a real hope that would sustain them in their conflict with the last enemy, death. Countless examples were available of triumphant grace in death as well as enabling grace in life. Providences and promises pointed to God as the guarantor of the believer's safety and glory. Faith and hope surmounted the perplexities of strange events and indefinable uncertainties. Even so, Williams still

273

asks questions: why are the young struck down, the godly taken, while others, older or less noted for these qualities are spared? How does a believer face the future encounter with death, that dreadful, invincible enemy? What is heaven like? Next to a sinner's conversion, his death as a saint deserved the most solemn consideration. Familiar Puritan practice advocated that their congregations should 'live in a constant readiness and expectation of death'. The most effective advocate among them of such a discipline was Richard Baxter. Seriously ill in 1647 and 'having no acquaintance about me, nor any book but my Bible, and living in continual expectation of death', he began to meditate on Hebrews 4:9, 'there remaineth therefore a rest for the people of God'. The result was his monumental work, *The Saints' Everlasting Rest* which first appeared in 1650 and reached a thirteenth edition by 1688. In its 'Dedication' he stated that preaching 'is but the least part of a minister's work', and that pastoral visitation 'to ... examine ... your preparations for death', among other things, 'is the great work.' [2]

The questions became more urgent by the 1760s and in the years that followed for a simple reason. Death was leaving gaps in the Methodist ranks, without respect of persons, age or gifts. By 1787 Williams reported to Thomas Charles that 'about 37 Methodist preachers are dead since Mr. H. Davies, Mr. Harris & Mr. Whitefield left us & now Mr. Davies of Neath is gone to the realms of bliss.'[3] Even before that date Williams had included three hymns 'in memory of the death of several godly persons in the Llansawel area' in the second printing of his 1749 *Aleluja*. Another elegy appeared in 1757 to persons whom he does not name, except that they were 'godly people who died in Cardiganshire, close to Llangeitho'. His first fully-fledged elegy appeared in 1761, to Griffith Jones, whose death was a great personal loss as well as a serious blow to Christian witness in Wales.

The identities of those for whom Williams wrote his elegies were as various as the causes of their death. These included clergymen, laymen, preachers, housewives, young and old; death by drowning; the death in 1781 in a flash flood of four people while at a prayer meeting; a child who died from smallpox and 'who had, from every evidence, true grace'. Two family members are among those remembered, his daughter Mary Sophia, who died a fortnight old, and Ann Price, his niece, who died of smallpox in her twenty-third year. There are in total some thirty-five elegies, and all are in Welsh, although Howel Davies, George Whitefield, and Miss Eliza Price have elegies in Welsh and English.

Besides these, there are elegies for the fictitious characters Avaritius, Prodigalus and Fidelius found in 'Three men from Sodom and Egypt'. In his *Theomemphus*, Williams has a 'farewell song' to Philomela, on whom he had set carnal love. In a sense this was an elegy, because it, too, spoke of death. Here, too, there was a past that was ended, but it spoke of a different kind of final parting. It prompted the prospect of a different kind of future, a future apart for the two 'lovers', setting them free to pursue God's will rather than their own in the present, and to survey a future in glory without the relationship of marriage. [4] For his readers, Williams says that 'the elegies of those who have crossed to the heavenly realm are an incentive to spend time in pure, quiet contemplation.'[5] As for the deceased Eliza Price, she has this message 'from the world of bliss immortal' for her parents:

> Here I live, triumphant, happy,
> Freed from misery and woe,
> Quite released from thousand follies
> That delude the world below;
> Fled from shows, and dreams, and shadows
> To realities above,
> Now I drink from holy fountains
> Draughts of everlasting love. [6]

If in his hymns Williams encouraged the pouring out of the heart in praise and prayer, through his elegies he nurtured anticipation and hope.

Symbolism abounds in the elegies: of death as a summons from God, as a marriage with attendant feasts, as a release from bondage. A 'summons' conveys the idea of a higher authority that makes an inescapable demand. Hence, for Whitefield the summons was served by angels who found him at Newburyport, Massachusetts; the summons came to Llewellyn Dafydd 'to leave his earthly labours' while he attended an Association at Builth, and died two days later. One of Williams's favourite authors, John Bunyan, had used the same symbolism in the second part of Bunyan's *Pilgrims Progress:* 'there was a Post come from the Celestial City, with matters of great importance' to Christiana, and he came again, 'and his business was with Mr. Ready-to-halt'; for Mr Stand-fast the summons was delivered by the Post 'with open hands … that he must prepare for a change of life, for his Master was not willing that he should be so far from him any longer.' If, for Williams, the imagery was familiar, for his readers it

275

was an appropriate and comforting description of the death that
awaited believers.

Of John Parry it is said, not only that he was summoned to 'return to
dust', but also that 'he was seen in heaven … without any pain or
sickness', where 'he feasts for endless ages where there is no time,
drinking deeply of pure love endless peace without constraint.' By way
of contrast, the elegies for Avaritius and Prodigalus spell out the
dreadful guilt and eternal wrath which constitutes the 'feast' that awaits
the unrepentant sinner.[7] Williams is concerned, then, not only with the
manner of death, but also with its sequel for the believer. Full
enjoyment of God embraces songs, perfect knowledge and complete
acceptance. Death ushers John Dafydd into a wedding feast; the
twenty-three-year old Ann Price's funeral was also a wedding, with the
godly crowd that attended it praising, weeping, singing, dancing, while
the preacher could hardly continue, being overcome with rapture and
love. Nor was the burial of Grace Price of Watford a funeral; it, too, was
a wedding, with angels in attendance. If Susanna Prichard, after six
weeks of suffering, died with no material wedding ring on her finger,
she was that day given an everlasting crown, and the truths of salvation,
sweet melodies of a gracious covenant, as a bridal dress for her ascent
to heaven. Williams says of Mari Jones that 'death burst asunder the
shackles, and set free your feet.' The bliss which attends John Evans in
glory is also meant to take away the fears of the believers who read
his elegy:

> Every blemish now forgotten,
> And the robe that now he wears,
> From the top to very bottom
> Has no stain, or seam, or tears;
> Woven by the King of Heaven,
> Once on Calvary with pain,
> Dwell not on his faults and failures,
> See this garment of his reign. [8]

All in all, the elegies were crafted by Williams in such a way, that the
Welsh Methodists could easily identify their destiny in Christ, and even
on earth enjoy a foretaste of that blessed prospect.

Earthly events and their attendant experiences are woven by God's
providential over-ruling into a pattern that is pleasing to God and
advantageous to the believer. Theophilus Jones speaks from the
perspective of the other side of the grave when he is made to say:

> Providence we view from glory,
> Rules creation through and through;
> Works for good in cruel happenings,
> Never fails, is always true.

'The spirit of faith' comforts Margaret Lloyd, bereaved of her ten-year-old son with smallpox, by assuring her 'that death was an angel, sent to bring her son home, and that he had an unshakeable stake in heaven':

> Gentle lady! weep no longer
> Though today there's bitterness
> With the vinegar and wormwood -
> Your Redeemer faced no less;
> All that meets you works this purpose,
> Doubles privilege in love,
> And prepares you in some measure
> For pure bliss with saints above.

Such assurances do not minimize the mystery of providence, they stem from faith not sight, but it is a faith that is founded on the Word of the God who cannot lie. [9] If in the second part of *Pilgrim's Progress*, a messenger from the Celestial City seeks out the pilgrims, in the first part it is their pilgrimage that brings them there. But there is no contradiction here: the times of God's people are in God's hand (Psalm 31: 15), purposed by free grace and realized by wise providence.

It is not without reason that Williams addressed the perplexing questions which arise when facing death. In an age when medicine was far from being an exact science able to offer prospects of success, believers and unbelievers alike had to face an uncertain outcome to illness. Here is part of the elegy to Howel Davies:

> Where love and peace in silent rivers flow,
> Where bliss abounds, where guilt and sin ne'er go.
>
> My muse, forbear, and be thou willing still
> Thy race to run, thy allotted place to fill;
> To fight thy battles, and to expect thy crown;
> To quench each flame, and quash each passion down.
> Thou shalt arrive soon on that happy shore,
> Where fears and death shall trouble thee no more;
> And meet ten thousands with their golden lyres
> To sing of Him whom all thy soul admires.[10]

So much for death; what awaits the believer on the other side of the grave? In an extraordinary piece of literature, an imaginary 'letter' from William Read in heaven to his family on earth, some of these questions are answered.

> Beloved, I left you rather suddenly; I never thought death was as near
> ... until the hours of heaven were numbered, and a summons was sent
> for me to appear in the King's Court. At that moment my beloved angel
> took my hand, and in a moment I was in the great world which has no
> end; my soul he embraced joyfully in his arms, and that worthless body,
> that mortal carcase was left with you to be placed in the earth ... And
> he bore me past a hundred thousand stars .... Until eventually we left
> behind all sight of creation ... until we came within sight of heaven's
> glory, the light of which produced within me such a blaze of pure,
> divine love that I had never felt on earth, and we then entered ... not
> even the wise congregation of cherubim and seraphim can convey to
> humanity a thousandth part of the festivity and glory in that city ...
> There is here no conflict between nature and grace. What we choose,
> we wonder at, what we wonder at, we possess ... the substance of love
> resides here ... there is no more hunger or thirst, for our life is to gaze
> on the face of our Redeemer; our sustenance is not bread, and the
> earth's wine is not our drink; but to look on Him who bought us with
> His own precious blood; we drink eternal joy as running water, and
> feast on love as an endless feast. [11]

No conflict between nature and grace? No, because the soul at death is made perfect in holiness, 'the substance of love resides', and there is complete harmony between God's nature of purity and love and 'the spirits of just men made perfect' (Hebrews 12:23). If the highest Methodist aspiration while on earth was a deeper acquaintance with the Saviour, often expressed even though feebly attained, in heaven even those who had died in infancy would 'know' instinctively and profoundly. This is how Williams comforts himself after the death of his daughter, Mary Sophia, a mere two weeks after her birth. He takes trouble first to set out the cause of human misery. Human nature is as corrupt seed even in the womb, guilty and polluted in Adam and under condemnation, so that the deepest hell lies within man's bosom, with the result that man is born to endless woe and sighs attend everything under the sun. Only then does he proceed to apply balm to the wound inflicted on her parents. First, he asks, 'what is death for those beloved of the Gentle Lamb?' Death is but a change of place; to be out of the body is to be at home; to be in the grave is to be in heaven. Then comes the confident assertion that in heaven believers 'know even as they are known' (1 Corinthians 13: 12). Mary is one of a myriad infants now in heaven who, though without education, language, achievements, or merits, sound out the pure songs of glory, and 'know' salvation's plan more comprehensively than the most gifted and mature Christians in all of Great Britain.[12] It is, however, another kind of 'knowing': intuitive, abiding and penetrating, in the manner of belonging, on the basis of personal relationship rather than by way of accumulated information. This is what constitutes the true and eternal bliss which is in prospect for God's children.

Clearly, Williams is at pains to keep before his readers the Christian hope, based on Christ's bodily resurrection and return to glory. Above all, heaven is characterized by the beauty of holiness, and this consists of the presence of Christ and the absence of sin. Heaven is a place of final triumph, unalloyed joy and uninterrupted adoration, a release 'from the world of woe to the realm of life', where God's people enjoy everlasting bliss. [13] However great earthly blessings may be, they bear no comparison with the heavenly inheritance. William Jones is reminded of this on the death of his wife, Catherine, who for godliness 'would bear comparison with the most outstanding in Wales.'

> O sweet union, strong and loving,
> Kate and William then were one,
> By a bond forged far in heaven
> Long before the world was done!
> Never was there gentler bridegroom,
> Never bride so bright and fair,
> So the yoke of holy marriage
> Always was a joy to bear.
>
> William Jones, now sad and grieving:
> There no more to share your life,
> Cruel death, that last great en'my,
> Has removed your precious wife.
> Katy, now released from suffering,
> Has attained the distant shore,
> There a glorious land once purchased
> By Christ's blood for evermore. [14]

However pleasant life on earth, heaven is to be preferred: the best is yet to be.

Another feature of the elegies is their portrayal of New Testament

279

Christianity, for which purpose Williams uses each subject as an example. There is variety in their gifts and experiences, some are public figures, others within a more confined sphere, but all show evidence of God's grace. It would be a simple matter to distil from the elegies a statement of Williams's firmly-held, biblically-sourced beliefs. They would range from the unity of the Godhead in a Trinity of Persons, providence, revelation, redemption, through to resurrection, the means of grace and eternal destinies. Such teaching is scattered throughout the compositions, in an explicit but not a systematic way, implying that they are presupposed, and provide a unifying body of conviction that undergirds Christian hope as well as Christian experience. The distinctively Christian character of each one is determined on the basis of the transformation that grace has achieved in their lives, rather than on what natural lineage had bestowed. The elegy was an eulogy only in the sense that it demonstrated the power of Christ's salvation: sainthood was the result of divine mercy rather than human merit.

It is also useful to remember that Williams wrote about his own people, the Welsh Calvinistic Methodists, with their distinctive priorities, activities and experiences. 'One of the most useful men among the people called Methodists' from Breconshire, Llewellyn Dafydd, often travelled to Llangeitho through floods and over mountains to secure preachers for his local society. He spent his money, his time, lost his health and reputation, gave his life, gifts and means, in the pursuit of one goal, all in order to exalt Christ's name and spread abroad his Gospel. It was true for Mary Morice, the wife of a preacher, that 'at the commencement of her affliction, a dark cloud came between her and the rays of heavenly light which she had enjoyed many times previously. Now this cloud plunged her into dread and hid from her the graces of heaven, and also of all the multitude of promises given in the covenant of grace, not one pierced through the darkness. The sweet is never so sweet as when it is preceded by bitterness, and she was not kept long in prison but the fetters of brass were broken. With the sun blazing afresh on her soul, she sang and praised the Saviour for her deliverance, and now the fear of death had passed.' The elegy on the death of a minister, Lewis Lewis, uses the form of a meditative 'question' and 'answer' to deal with the issue of revival manifestations:

> Question: Tell me now, if you are able,
> Since at times you witnessed here,

Singing, shouts of jubilation,
Laughter, clapping with no fear;
Does it please the King of Glory,
Jumping, dancing, without shame,
If these issue from affection
For the mighty Saviour's Name?

Answer: Only search the Holy Scripture,
You will find the answer plain;
All its words and spirit render
Life and fire of this strain;
'T would be hard to be too eager
If you follow in its light,
When your fire in love is grounded,
And your motive's pure and right. [15]

A passion for preaching, assurance, life and fire; all these were Methodist distinctives in Williams's day, and by including such elements in his elegies he was suggesting that they were not features of a passing fashion, but an enduring evidence of valid Christian witness.

Inevitably, preachers receive particular attention in the elegies, and biographical details emerge concerning them, even of Williams himself. He speaks of 'Merioneth, where the mountains compete with the clouds' by way of a descriptive travelogue. A reference to his ministry at Llansawel, birthplace of his wife, is more poignant: 'when I preach Parry is no longer on my right hand side, praising while I am preaching.' Griffith Jones's achievements get special mention since his preaching filled the parish churches to overflowing. He secured two printings of the Bible for sale at reasonable cost, and arranged for schools to teach some 120,000 scholars. No marble plaque is needed to commemorate him, his writings in print and on the souls of many, proclaim his worth. In the death of Howel Davies, 'that fixed refulgent star ... Poor Wales hath lost a bright, laborious man!' He was one who 'opposed countless heresies, and spoke words of thunder and lightning against the enemies of God's Gospel. He was sound in his principles, simple and honest in his faith, philanthropic in his life, and widely useful in his day.' Whitefield was 'the man whom heaven did adorn with glorious gifts', and,

He loudly published Gospel peace and grace,
Procured in full unto the chosen race ...
His body rests, his spirit wears the crown;

281

No more shall he resound the Gospel cries,
With hand outstretched to the lofty skies;
No more persuade the sinner to restrain
From impious deeds, and happiness obtain;
Or yet invite the intemperate to enjoy
The Gospel feast of inward peace and joy. [16]

The death in 1784 of Christopher Bassett, at the age of thirty-one, was keenly felt by Williams. He is described as 'a godly, learned and worthy man, a solemn preacher, fervent and authoritative in all the doctrines of Holy Scripture, and an enlightened leader to pilgrims in all the ways of Christ's redemption ... deeply mourned throughout south and north Wales.' It was not only his youth that moved Williams to write his elegy. Both its length and its fluency bear witness to genuine gratitude for the ministry of this man of God:

Teaching of a costly offering,
God's rich purpose he did trace;
Cream and substance from the Bible
Now by him distilled with grace;
With experience duly seasoned
Preached his sermon to the throng,
Nourished thus the sad and hungry,
Fed the weak and fed the strong.

Come and listen to him preaching,
And behold life's water clear,
Words that pour from him in plenty
Stream like light to far and near;
Gates of promises are opened,
Treasures here to give delight,
Calling sinners from their anguish
To partake both day and night.[17]

The elegies were written by Williams from a real sense of loss, but they were also written with the serious purpose of identifying Methodist priorities. Preachers were sent with an urgent message from the King of kings to all and sundry in His dominion. Even in grief and bereavement at the personal loss of such men, their public ministry as Christ's ambassadors was of eternal consequence to their congregations.

This was another reason for Williams to write elegies. He wanted to assure the Methodist constituency that others would be raised to preach that precious Gospel. In his Welsh-language elegy to Whitefield, this theme serves to fuel a concluding prayer: 'the meek Davies first departed, then [Thomas] Adams followed, now the root, Whitefield has been smitten; the wolves are celebrating that the shepherds are departing; come, gentle Jesus to your lambs, come soon, raise up gifted, worthy teachers to shepherd your dear flock.' [18] Here Williams echoes a sermon by David Edwards on Whitefield's death:

> Several ministers have been removed by death this year; some of them laboured long amongst you, and were not ashamed of the despised Methodists; faithful Mr. Howell Davies, Mr. Adams, and now Mr. Whitefield, who begun, continued, and closed their ministry, as beholding him that is invisible. Blessed triumvirate! now beyond the reach of every sorrow. When faithful labourers are called home, 'tis a sign that there is a storm coming; that judgements are drawing nigh the land ... I cannot but look upon the death of faithful ministers and godly people, as separating the Israelites from the tents of Corah; like Noah entering the ark, or Lot's going out of Sodom; and you know what followed. O let the thoughts of these things cause us to provide an ark, and get a safe refuge! Let the godly of all denominations of Christians, cry mightily to the Lord, that he would raise up young ... Timothies in the room of aged Pauls; that there may be a succession of able faithful ministers to hold forth the word of eternal life to the people ... Ministers of the greatest grace and gifts are like candles, that are soon extinguished by death, but the Sun of Righteousness shines perpetually." [19]

In the elegy to Rowland, Williams's last, he proclaims that even when that great preacher's body has returned to dust in the cemetery at Llangeitho, Gospel days would continue. An Elisha will wear Elijah's mantle until Gospel light has shone wherever the sun takes its rays. In conclusion, Williams charged the second generation of Methodists to stand in the breach for the cause of truth, now that such valiant holders of orthodoxy were passing away. They are to perpetuate the heritage of martyrs like John Hus, Thomas Cranmer and Nicholas Ridley, to defend Calvinist principles, just as Rowland did during his lifetime.[20] Like Fidelius, that ideal Methodist in 'Three Men from Sodom and Egypt', he is to receive 'a crown of glory, as everlasting as God Himself', and with his voice 'sound forth throughout eternal ages God's glorious praise.' [21]

30.

'The crystal fountain opened'

Consideration of Williams's elegies has already introduced some leading aspects of his theology. It was, after all, the heart-convictions of those people to whom he paid tribute that determined their behaviour in life and confidence in death. The second and third verses of the hymn by which he is most universally known, 'Guide me, O Thou great Jehovah', read thus:

> Open now the crystal fountain
> Whence the healing streams do flow;
> Let the fiery cloudy pillar
> Lead me all my journey through;
> Strong Deliverer,
> Be Thou still my strength and shield.
>
> When I tread the verge of Jordan,
> Bid my anxious fears subside;
> Death of death, and hell's destruction,
> Land me safe on Canaan's side;
> Songs of praises
> I will ever give to Thee.[1]

The Scriptural allusions here are clear, while Williams's favourite metaphor of 'pilgrimage' dominates. Locating the Israelite journey through the desert to the Promised Land provides instruction: the cloudy pillar, the verge of Jordan, Canaan's side, guidance, healing, deliverance, safety, triumph and praise. In small compass Williams uses these biblical figures to underpin the believer's convictions and experiences. Theology and biography for the Methodists were inseparable, as they are for every Christian. In order to understand the contemporary significance and abiding value of Williams's contribution, therefore, it will be advantageous to explore his teaching in some detail.[2] In this chapter its basic foundations are examined.

First and foremost, then, Williams's theology was biblical. It bears repeating to say that for him the Bible was true, reliable, perspicuous and authoritative. Its source was God, and its message had been revealed by the Holy Spirit through prophets and apostles. The same Holy Spirit bore witness to its integrity, enlightened the mind to understand it, applied it to the conscience, evoked a response to its message in the affections and the will, and instructed believers in God's purpose for their lives. This was neither more nor less than what Griffith Jones maintained: ''Tis the Word of Truth, contained in the sacred volume, that is the great and appointed instrument to raise the dead in sin into a life of righteousness, and whereby we come to be born of God, and begot or born again into a lively hope, and to an inheritance that fadeth not away.'[3] Passages of Scripture are diffused throughout Williams's hymns, expounded in his sermons, appealed to in his defence of the Revival, and form the basis of his teaching, whether oral or verbal. Williams rejected the Apocrypha as being a Jewish and Roman Catholic addition, rather than the true Word of God.[4] Concluding his section on 'The Holy Scriptures', Stephen J. Turner says that Williams's 'trust in the Scriptures' integrity was as much the source of his assurance and joy as his trust in the person of the Lord Jesus revealed in the Word.'[5]

At the end of his 1779 translation, *Berr Hanes James Albert* ('A Narrative ... of the life of James Albert'), Williams included a short piece, *Gloria Scripturarum, neu Ogoniant yr Ysgrythur lân* ('Glory of the Holy Scriptures'). Williams introduces the Welsh verses that follow with his conviction, that the Bible is 'an infallible standard, apart from Council or Canon, of all the doctrines of divine grace, and the certain rule of godly living; and that it is through the ministry of the Spirit, by Whom also it was given at first, effective to call, convict, reprove, comfort, and guide those elected to life from the wilderness of this world to the kingdom of heaven.'[6] He concludes his introduction with these words: 'The author's purpose is to get people to read more, meditate more, and to examine themselves more, by the Holy Scripture, lest they think that diligent attendance to hearing alone, apart from a radical change within, is enough to claim a right to eternal life.'

On another matter, Williams admits that there are some parts of Scripture less clear than others, and he offers this advice: 'When the Scriptures seem to contradict each other, understand that it is due to the darkness in our understanding, and that in reality there is no inconsistency in Holy Scripture; and that the only way for us (when something appears unclear) is to seek the Lord for heavenly illumination, since the same Spirit who wrote the Word is the only One who can unravel the Word that He gave to His Church as a pillar of fire

285

and cloud to lead us to life.'[7] Old Testament types and shadows that pre-figured Christ feature in Williams's compositions. They were viewed by him as useful because they were part of the literary armour of divine revelation. As R. M. Jones points out, for Williams 'the journey of Israel was a shadow of the journey of today's Christian from justification to glorification.'[8] Hence, in the Welsh *Aleluja*, 'Hymn XCIX' unashamedly identifies Christ with the brazen serpent of Numbers 21:9 and the gentle Manna of Numbers 11:9. A fuller exposition of these appears in 'Hymn CCLI' with the title, 'Christ's correspondence with the shadows. Noah's ark, Isaac, Jacob, Jacob's Ladder, Job, Joseph … Melchizedec, Gideon, Samson, Elijah …. David, Solomon, etc.'[9] Both Testaments are necessary to make a complete Bible, and necessary, too, for a 'complete' Christian. Christ is the theme of both, and what is foretold of Him in the Old is fulfilled in the New:

> Whate'er had been predicted since first the world began,
> Has been fulfilled, or will be, in Christ the Son of man;
> His Person and His merits, the cross with all its pain,
> Found in the first Testament, are in the New again.
>
> The graces of His person, His glory, and His fame,
> His miracles and also His death tell whence He came;
> His offices, His rising, the natures which He wore,
> Agree with that predicted of Him in days of yore. [10]

The correlation between the Testaments confirm the Bible's integrity, while the theme of Christ's Person and work confirm the Bible's unity. Together they gave Williams's theology a foundation and structure. God's truth is centred on God's Son, and there is no dichotomy between the Word incarnate and God's Word written. All Scripture points to Christ, and Christ's own view and use of Scripture establishes its authenticity and finality.

On account of his genius in dealing with Christian experience, both on a personal basis in the societies, and especially in his published works, some have wrongly concluded that his theology was subjectively derived from such exercises.[11] Nothing could be further from the truth. Williams's theology was unequivocally sourced in Scripture, but always coupled with an insistence on the power of God's Spirit to make it relevant, and on the miracle of God's grace to make it personal. D. Gwenallt Jones understood this perfectly when he concluded that for Williams,

> the Gospel was not merely a set of doctrines; it was also an experience. To think that the Methodists placed all their emphasis on experience is a mistake. They believed that one should have a subjective experience of an objective Gospel: and the objective Gospel was the most important. The relationship between them was like the relationship between cause and effect. It was in the Bible that Pantycelyn had a framework for his experience ... Having seen his sin, the sinner realizes that there is no deliverance except by faith in the Lord Jesus Christ ... and the grace of God motivates his will, enlightens his understanding, guides his conscience, and turns his affections towards God. Grace saved the whole man. [12]

Methodists avoided both theoretical intellectualism and subjective emotionalism. They *did* engage the mind, in their preaching, teaching, writing and counselling; but held with equal vigour that to stop with the intellect was to deny Scripture and abdicate ministerial responsibility. The Gospel is not only God's truth for life, it is also God's power for salvation. On the other hand, they were equally adamant that to make their appeal only to the emotions was misleading at the time and disastrous for the future. In this respect they were merely following familiar Puritan practice, the works of John Bunyan providing a notable example. John R. Knott, Jnr. writes: 'The preface of *Grace Abounding* displays an imaginative grasp of the reality of the Word and a capacity to read his own experience in its terms which Bunyan shows himself struggling in the narrative itself ... Bunyan shows an extraordinary ability to appropriate biblical language and events, especially from the Old Testament and convert them to his uses. To view his own experience from this perspective was to understand it and claim for it a kind of validity that could only be established for Bunyan by the Word.'[13] Similarly, it was because Methodist theology was objectively biblical that its practical expression could be subjectively individualistic. If the experiences of which Williams wrote in his works, and monitored in the societies, were 'earthed' in the lives of real people, he insisted that they be soundly sourced in the 'lightning' of divine revelation.

It would not be until 1823 that the Welsh Calvinistic Methodists produced their own Confession of Faith. Until that time the Thirty-nine Articles of the Established Church served the purpose of defining their doctrinal position as orthodox, Protestant, and as they insisted,

Calvinist. A letter written late in Williams's life to Thomas Charles gives advice for the next generation of Methodists: 'Exhort the young preachers to study, next to the Scriptures, the doctrines of our old celebrated Reformers, as set forth in the Articles of the Church of England, and the three Creeds, namely, the Apostles' Creed, the Nicene, and the Athanasian. They will see there the great truths of the Gospel, and the deep things of God, set forth in the most excellent and suitable manner. They are a most sound form of words on the high and spiritual things of God. The larger and lesser Catechisms of the Assembly of Divines, with the Confession of Faith, are deserving of the greatest respect and acceptance.'[14] R. Tudur Jones makes it clear that Williams's position was firmly located in this tradition: 'Williams Pantycelyn had a passionate concern for theological orthodoxy. He insisted that the Welsh Methodists stood squarely in the tradition of the early ecumenical creeds, the Protestant Reformers and Puritan Calvinism.'[15]

That theology has a systematic as well as a biblical aspect means that in the face of passing, changeable theological fashions, there is always a standard of truth by which all theological expression can be tested and, if necessary, corrected. Methodism faced theological challenges as well as varying emphases. Within Methodism there were Calvinists and Arminians, differing in their understanding of grace; and there were Moravians whose theology of the cross took Christ's humanity to the boundaries of acceptability. More serious and unacceptable to the Welsh Calvinistic Methodists there were deviations on the doctrine of the Trinity, and of faith, which required rebuttal and correction. Williams opposed Antinomianism by maintaining that the witness of the Spirit must be accompanied by the marks of grace, and that faith works by love for God and for His Law. He resisted Baxter's 'scheme' of a change in the Law of God that made faith a matter of obedience, by insisting that Christ's death was full satisfaction of its demands, and that faith is God's gift to unite the sinner to Christ. From the early 1760s, John Popkin, an exhorter, became a thorn in Williams's side, and between 1764 and 1781 Popkin's translation into Welsh of a number of titles by John Glas and Robert Sandeman created acute difficulties. Their limiting faith to a bare mental assent of Gospel truth was, for Williams, not only serious error but positively harmful. It opened the door to self-deceit and pride, and deprived the soul of real joy and comfort. In his writings, Williams repeatedly warned against its dangers: in 'The Value of the Bible' that appeared with 'The Answer of

Philo Evangelius'(1763); in 'An Account of the Late Success of the Gospel' and also in his elegy to Anne Price (both 1766); in 'The Crocodile of Egypt's River' (1767); and in the elegy to Daniel Rowland in 1790. Williams was not alone in his opposition; Rowland and Harris also took issue with the heresy. In February 1768 Harris heard Rowland preach on Psalm 51:7, 'Purge me with hyssop, and I shall be clean; wash me, and I shall be whiter than snow', and recorded in his journal:

> On hearing him preach so effectively on the blood of Christ and the necessity for it to be poured out upon the conscience, and his opposition to the views of Sandeman, earnestly inviting everyone to come to Christ, and in such a way that I never heard from him before, I felt great love for him and for the people. Having been asked, I myself spoke on looking to our Saviour and his sufferings. As Rowland had expounded upon the blood of Christ, that it sanctifies and glorifies, so I confirmed his words. I was given remarkable freedom to preach Christ.[16]

On one occasion Williams challenged Popkin to debate the issue at an Association meeting, exposing the erroneous nature of his beliefs and securing the orthodoxy of the exhorters present. Both Popkin and David Jones, Rowland's nephew, were excommunicated by the Welsh Methodists for holding Sandemanian views. [17]

Given Williams's proverbial orthodoxy, his firm belief in a Trinitarian Godhead is to be expected. Here are some verses from a hymn bearing the title 'Trinity'. As with all of Williams's works, however sublime the teaching, there is always personal application:

> Thou'rt One, my God, and yet in three,
> A myst'ry deep, too great for me;
> Co-equal with eternity
> Thy Word reveals with dignity.
>
> Since by Thy Word this truth is taught,
> My reason with its limits fraught,
> Must bow its weakness to confess,
> Thine essence own as thus, no less.
>
> Its depths I try to fathom now,
> But fail each time, and hence I bow;
> This heavenly truth beyond me lies,
> Where reason fails, there faith reclines.

Father in Son, Son in Him too,
The Spirit has this essence through;
Where One resides, others attend,
Bless'd Three in One without an end!

And this, the Trinity divine
Alone can heal this soul of mine;
Three offices in God are sought,
Ere to God's heaven I can be brought.

Election by the Father's will,
The death of Jesus on the hill;
The Spirit's effort this to seal
God's great salvation, me to heal.

Another verse is in the form of a doxology:

To the Father be all glory,
Since He gave a gift so free,
Praise eternal be to Jesus,
Coming to the world for me;
Honour to the Spirit ever,
For revealing God's sure plan;
Praise for sealing, and for pointing
To the Advocate of man. [18]

In the matter of divine revelation, where reason fails, the Christian confidently affirms that the alternative is not irrationality but mystery. The essence of faith is to submit in humility, and acknowledge that created beings can never attain perfect knowledge. The Gospel has unlocked much that was dark, and the way of salvation is clear, but the believer waits with patience for a full disclosure of God's being and ways in glory. 'Now we see through a glass darkly, but then face to face' (1 Corinthians 13: 12).

The Welsh Methodists had already faced one crisis on the issue of the Trinity, with the Patripassianism of Howel Harris. Their response had been to issue the short pamphlet, 'Conversation between an Orthodox and a Mistaken Methodist', dissociating them from that heresy. In his Preface to the first printing of 'A View of Christ's Kingdom' in 1756, Williams refers with sadness to 'those who deny our blessed Lord's deity, the merit of His blood and the worth of His death.' He added, 'thoughts of that kind about Christ fall short of those in the Holy

Scriptures ... and all the old orthodox divines in any age ... Such doctrinal departure is also at variance with the Church of England's Articles ... the Assembly's Catechism, and Puritan writings in the last one hundred and forty years.'[19]

In 1770 Peter Williams brought out an annotated Bible printed at Carmarthen, the first to be printed in Wales. In a biographical sketch after his death, Thomas Charles spoke highly of him: 'He laboured diligently and faithfully in the vineyard of the Lord. He travelled in all weathers, and suffered much for the Gospel's sake; he was the means of conferring great blessings on many souls in the dark days in which he lived. He had been given a strong physique, and a mind unflinching; he could work hard, travel long distances, and put up with indifferent lodgings and poor food. His gifts were most suitable to the dark understandings of the common people.' The Bible's comments on John 1: 1, 'In the beginning was the Word, and the Word was with God, and the Word was God', were deemed to fall short of acknowledging the deity of Christ. The heresy with which Peter Williams was charged was not new, having its roots in the Early Church, and was called Sabellianism after its originator at the end of the Second century. In it, the names 'Father', 'Son' and 'Holy Spirit' apply to the one God, but have significance only as an unfolding, successive revelation. This devalues the concept of three distinct Persons in the Trinity. Harris was still alive, reviving memories of past doctrinal deviation in the matter of Trinitarian belief, and this may have contributed to the outcome. Eventually, in 1791, after the death of Daniel Rowland, Peter Williams was excluded from the Methodist fraternity. Two years later he wrote to the Association expressing his belief in the eternal generation of the Son, and 'that the man Christ Jesus is the only begotten Son of God.' It is a poignant letter, and ends with an acknowledgment that could have been written by any of the Welsh Methodists: 'Although knowledge of God is desirable, I do not presume to be wise enough to comprehend the blessed Trinity; nor will I ever believe that my God will shut his door against me, because I cannot comprehend the incomprehensible.' The whole sad episode demonstrates the difficulty of maintaining the delicate balance between public standards of truth and personal expressions of devotion. [20]

Towards the end of Williams's life anti-Trinitarian views were widespread. A deeply-concerned Williams wrote to Thomas Charles in 1790:

I wish you all success in your Association. I can assure you that my spirit is with you; and I doubt not but that the Spirit of the Lord will, likewise, abide in and with you, to lead and direct you to all truth, love and harmony, peace and concord; and also gloriously deliver you from all envyings and strife; and at the same time enable you to keep a watchful and jealous eye over each other's life and doctrine, and behaviour, in pure love and charity. I hope the Holy Spirit will make you strong against innumerable assaults of the grand enemy, who continually tempts to some false and erroneous step in our most holy religion; sometimes to lukewarmness, indifference, and indolence on the one hand, as well as bigotry, enthusiasm, party zeal on the other. And at another time he tempts to a loose, irregular, careless life, as well as to pride, self-conceit, or false opinions, and even heresy. Know, my dear brother, that now, as well as in the Apostles' time, errors are conceived and brought forth amongst many sects and denominations of people, and boldly preached without shame or fear. But as Methodism has hitherto been kept clear from pernicious and destructive tares, I hope the Lord will preserve us to the end. And as we have continued now nearly sixty years orthodox in the faith, notwithstanding dreadful attacks from without and within, I doubt not but that we shall spend a century without erring in life or doctrine; yea I believe that God will take care of us as a body for ages and generations to come, and make us a blessing in the land as we have hitherto been to thousands of our fellow creatures. Exhort each other to search the Scriptures diligently, that you may be strong in the Word of God. Indeed, there are palpable and dreadful errors in the country, and new and destructive heresies brought to light, which for a long time have been dead and buried, such as denying the doctrine of the Trinity, which is the foundation of Christianity, and also the divinity and sonship of Christ. They say that some of the Baptists deny the divinity of our Saviour. They cannot bear the word *divine* blood. They preach that his *blood*, by which we understand His sufferings and death as a satisfaction for sin, is no better than the blood of a common man; which is horrible to think of. It is asserted also, that they do not baptize in the name of the Father, Son and Holy Ghost, but dipping the person in water, they repeat that verse in Galatians 6:14, 'God forbid that I should glory save in the cross of our Lord Jesus Christ, by whom the world is crucified unto me, and I unto the world.' Believe me, dear Charles, the antitrinitarian, the Socinian, and Arian doctrines gain ground daily. Our unwary new-born Methodist preachers know nothing of these things; therefore pray much that no drop of the pernicious liquor may be mingled with, or be privately thrown into, the good, delicious, and living water from the divine fountain, of which the honest Methodist drinks.[21]

292

This was written only a short time after he had translated into Welsh James Ussher's *Immanuel, or the Mystery of the Incarnation of the Son of God*. Ussher (1581-1656) was Archbishop of Armagh and Primate of all Ireland, Calvinist cleric, scholar noted for his biblical chronology, and a fervent apologist in the Protestant cause. He was also the leading theologian behind the influential Irish Articles of 1615, more Calvinist and ecclesiastically flexible than the Thirty-nine Articles. When Williams sent three dozen copies of the book to Thomas Charles he spoke of it as 'the best pamphlet I have ever read', and adds, 'Christ is the whole of it and we Methodists nowadays ought to study more, read more, and preach more of that divine doctrine of the Person of the Messiah God-man, the depths and the heights of the eternal covenant between God and His Son.' [22] Ussher's work was originally published at Dublin in 1638, and its first part deals with the Person and natures of Christ; the second deals with His work and offices.

> Now there dwelleth in Him not only the fullness of the Godhead, but the fullness of the Manhood also, for we believe Him to be both perfect God, begotten of the substance of His Father before all worlds, and perfect Man, made of the substance of His mother in the fullness of time. And therefore we must hold that there are two distinct natures in Him, and two so distinct that they do not make one compounded nature, but still remain uncompounded and unconfounded together. But He in whom the fullness of the manhood dwelleth is not one, and he in whom the fullness of the Godhead, another; but He in whom the fullness of both these natures dwelleth, is one and the same Immanuel, and consequently it must be believed as firmly, that he is but one Person ... the Son of God and the son of the blessed Virgin, being but one Person, is consequently but one Son; and so no alteration at all made in the relations of the Persons of the Trinity. [23]

So much for the first part of the book; in the second the relevance of this mystery for the preacher's task and the sinner's comfort is explained:

> Such was God's love to justice, and hatred to sin, that he would not have his justice swallowed up with mercy, nor sin pardoned without the making of fit reparation. And therefore our Mediator must not look to procure for us a simple pardon without more ado, but must be a propitiation for our sins, and redeem us by fine and ransom ... His surety therefore being to satisfy in his stead, none will be found fit to undertake such a payment, but He who is both God and man ... And

now we are come to that part of Christ's mediation, which concerneth the conveyance of the redemption of this purchased possession unto the sons of men. A dear [that is, costly] purchase indeed, which was to be redeemed with no less price than the blood of the Son of God ... The same God that giveth grace, is He also that giveth glory: yet so, that the streams of both of them must run to us through the golden pipe of our Saviour's humanity. [24]

By bringing the book to the notice of a predominantly Welsh-speaking Methodist constituency in 1786, Williams was not only neutralizing a potential threat to foundational theology, he was also providing a warm-hearted manual to aid their devotion to Christ.

At much the same time, Williams's son, John, was also translating into Welsh another work defending the doctrine of the Trinity. Published at Trefeca in 1794 'with the agreement of the Association' it was an abridgement of the sixth edition of a book by the high Churchman William Jones, *The Catholic Doctrine of a Trinity proved by over an hundred short and clear arguments, expressed in the terms of the Holy Scripture*. In the 'Translator's Preface' John Williams declares his intention 'to neutralize the deadly plague' which has affected several parts of England 'and that Welsh people, who have long been favoured with sound Gospel principles, are in danger of being overwhelmed, or at least injured by these dangerous heresies (if some have not already been corrupted by them)'. In the same year, Joshua Thomas the Welsh Baptist minister and historian translated *The Doctrine of the Trinity stated: in a Circular Letter of the Baptist Ministers and Messengers assembled at Olney, Bucks, May 28, 29, 1776* from its second edition.[25] In defence of orthodoxy, Calvinistic Methodists and Particular Baptists were both vigilant and of one mind.

294

31.

'The food of the children of God'

In his 1786 letter to Thomas Charles, Williams had spoken of 'the depths and the heights of the eternal covenant between God and His Son.' A similar phrase is used in his elegy to William John:

> That bless'd cov'nant entered into
> 'Twixt the Father and the Son,
> Jesus taking human nature,
> Suff'ring death for those undone;
> And as prize the Father giving
> To Him radiant Bride and pure,
> Brilliant white as any sunshine,
> That will evermore endure. [1]

It was a theme that Williams referred to again a short time before his death in 1791 as the first part of true religion: 'true light respecting the plan of salvation; God's eternal covenant with His Son to pay the debt of believing sinners, all the truths of the New Covenant by which He becomes all in all in creation, in all-embracing providence, and in redemption. With regard to this light, I had been making considerable progress in it for many years, so that I used to delight in every book, sermon, and preacher, striving to set forth the glory of Christ's Person, and the great privileges of salvation which came through Him. The books of Dr [Thomas] Goodwin, Dr [John] Owen, Dr [John] Gill, [Walter] Marshall, [James] Harvey, [James] Ussher, and others, have helped to enliven my understanding of these great truths.'[2] This was a reference to the manner in which Methodist theology was organized, and it drew heavily upon a Reformed, Puritan ancestry.

From the time of Calvin, Protestant theologians had sought to organize their doctrinal views of God's dealings with man around the framework of a Covenant, or contract, and this was known as 'Federal theology'. It allowed to the people of God, who were its object, the vital elements of cohesion and continuity throughout history. Calvin argued for this in his *Institutes*; it was developed more fully by the Continental theologians Zacharias Ursinus, Johannes Cocceius and

Herman Witsius; and its influence upon the Confession of Faith of the Westminster Assembly divines is marked. The latter's seventh chapter, with the title 'Of God's Covenant with Man', begins in this way: 'The distance between God and the creature is so great, that although reasonable creatures do owe obedience to Him as their Creator, yet they could never have any fruition of Him as their blessedness and reward, but by some voluntary condescension on God's part, which He hath been pleased to express by way of covenant.' J. I. Packer takes this further by saying, among other things, that this is a means 'of discerning that in our salvation by grace, God stands revealed as Father, Son and Holy Spirit, executing in tripersonal unity a single cooperative enterprise of raising sinners from the gutter of spiritual destitution to share God's glory for ever.' [3]

Evidence for the prominence and influence of this theology among the leaders of the Revival in Wales, is found in a variety of writers, from Griffith Jones to ordinary society members. Of Jones in 1740 it was said that, 'he has preached now about eight or ten sermons on 2 Samuel 23:5, ['he hath made with me an everlasting covenant, ordered in all things and sure: for this is all my salvation, and all my desire'] ... he showed the riches of this covenant, that all that belong to our salvation are in Christ – grace, increase of grace, faith, love, repentance, pardon, assurance ...'[4] This bedrock text for covenantal teaching was a favourite of the exhorter, Morgan John Lewis, a popular preacher who was later ordained minister of an Independent church at New Inn, Monmouthshire. He records how 'God blessed those words to me ... more than any verse that ever came to me for ought I know, and to the edification of many of the brethren; I believe the Lord called me to preach upon it about seventeen times.' Another favourite Bible passage is referred to by the exhorter William John. In a letter to Howel Harris in September 1743 after listening to Howel Davies preaching on Jeremiah 31: 2, 'The people which were left of the sword found grace in the wilderness', he says, 'I never heard the covenant of grace so clearly preached and with so much power; the Communion was there, and our dear Immanuel was there in truth.'[5] There are references to society members being 'enlightened' in the covenant of grace, to growing 'more acquainted' with it, and of one who had died 'steadfast in faith, and clear in his justification and God's unchangeableness in His everlasting covenant.'[6].

A book often mentioned by Harris was John Cotton's *A Treatise of the Covenant of Grace, As it is dispensed to the Elect Seed, effectually unto Salvation. Being the substance of divers Sermons preached upon Acts 7:8.* As early as May 1739 Harris copied extracts from its third edition of 1671 in his diary, and in the years that followed he refers to its significance and helpfulness.[7] A copy of the same edition was in Williams's library. The second chapter in Book II of Cotton's work begins with a statement 'Of the Compact between God the Father and the Son':

> That the nature of *the covenant of grace* may be the more thoroughly understood, two things are above all to be distinctly considered. 1. The Compact which intervenes between God the Father, and Christ the Mediator. 2. That testamentary disposition, by which God bestows, by an immutable covenant, eternal salvation, and every thing relative thereto, upon the Elect. The former agreement is between God and the Mediator; the latter between God and the Elect. This last presupposes the first, and is founded upon it. When I speak of the compact between the Father and the Son, I thereby understand the will of the Father, giving the Son, to be the Head and Redeemer of the Elect; and the will of the Son presenting Himself as a Sponsor or Surety for them; in all which the nature of a compact and agreement consists. The Scripture represents the Father, in the economy of our salvation, as demanding the obedience of the Son even unto death, and for it promising Him that name, which is above every name, even that He should be the Head of the Elect in glory; but the Son, as presenting Himself to do the will of the Father, acquiescing in that promise, and in fine, requiring the kingdom and glory promised to Him ... The effect of Christ's satisfaction is twofold: the first regards Christ Himself; the other, the elect. Christ, by His satisfaction, obtained for Himself, as Mediator, a right to all the elect: which the Father willingly and deservedly bestows upon Him ... The Lord Jesus obtained for the elect, by His satisfaction, an immunity from all misery, and a right to eternal life, to be applied unto them in effectual calling, regeneration, sanctification, conservation, and glorification. [8]

Joel R. Beeke says that 'for Witsius, the doctrine of the covenants is the best way of reading Scripture', and for Williams and the Welsh Methodists it became the most reliable way to navigate through their experiences.[9] Its significance has been summarised by R. Tudur Jones in this way: 'Ever since its celebration by William Williams, Pantycelyn, in the most majestic of his poems ['A View of Christ's Kingdom'], this theology has been popular amongst Calvinistic

Methodists and through the 1823 *Confession of Faith* it became the official theology of the Connexion.'[10]

It was by virtue of union with Christ, the second Adam, the head of a new humanity, with whom God had entered into a gracious covenant, that the elect, descended from the first Adam by natural descent, were given the new status of God's people. Those previously subject to the covenant of works, were brought to a relationship of grace on the basis of the covenant of redemption, the guarantor and surety of which was Christ. It was this framework that enabled Williams and others to identify the spiritual state of society members, whether 'under the law' and bondage, or 'under grace' and brought into Gospel 'liberty'. It also explains the frequent occurrence of the phrase 'free grace' in their writings, with Harris as early as 1739 saying, 'I see that the doctrine of grace is the food of the children of God.'[11] Williams speaks highly of the Westminster Assembly's doctrinal standards, and the Larger Catechism's Answer 31 states that, 'The covenant of grace was made with Christ as the second Adam, and in Him with all the elect as His seed.' John Cotton elaborates on the manner in which union with Christ is realized in the sinner's experience:

> Our faith closeth with Christ upon a promise of free grace, otherwise (as Calvin, *Institutes* III. ii. 29) my faith would always be trembling and wavering as my works be. Upon a promise of free grace, therefore, my faith is built, as upon the promise of God in Christ, reconciling the world unto Himself, 2 Cor. 5: 18-19. The word is (it may be) spoken outwardly unto all Christians: but if God do set it home particularly unto any soul, that man receiveth this gift of God, and it is made his own. First, he believeth the promise of free grace, and then afterward come other promises, that do bear witness unto the right application of that promise unto the soul; but I am first built upon a promise of free grace, or else there is no true closing with Jesus Christ. Well then, being thus united unto Christ, from this union with Christ do flow all other blessings and benefits of the Covenant of Grace; for hence springeth communion with Christ in all *spiritual blessings*, that the Lord hath wrought for us in Him; and they are two of them, *Relative blessings* (as they are called by Divines); and two of them positive blessings. The two former are laid up in God's own hand, and are not created in us; the other two positive blessings are created in us. For the uncreated blessings, they are 1. Adoption; 2. Justification... for the *Positive blessings* that are wrought in us, they are 1. Sanctification; 2. Glorification.[12]

The passage gives some indication as to why Williams and the Welsh Methodists evaluated spiritual experience in the light of God's free grace. For them it was the source of true faith and invariably issued in persevering godliness. The lasting importance of covenant theology for the Calvinistic Methodists is evident from the fact that Thomas Charles's *Hyfforddwr*, a popular and enduring catechism, devotes two early chapters to the doctrine. An extensive entry on 'covenant' also appears in his *Geiriadur Ysgrythyrol* ('Scripture Dictionary'), which began to appear in 1801.[13]

Within this covenantal framework a whole body of theology hangs together as inter-related, from the sinner's election to the sinner's glorification. 'Admittedly', says Donald Macleod, 'all attempts to impose an artificial unity on Scripture should be treated with caution. But there is no doubt that large masses of biblical truth can be organized under the covenantal principle; and that adherence to a covenant framework ensures close attention to the progressive, historical character of revelation.'[14] Another advantage lies in its consistency since it traces all salvation's benefits to the blessed Trinity. A cluster of important initiatives on the part of God describe the covenant's unfolding: purpose, election, revelation, incarnation, regeneration, redemption, and resurrection. Furthermore, it provides the believer with an understanding of the relationship between the several elements of salvation: grace, faith, repentance, justification, sanctification, and glorification.[15] A Williams hymn of the 1780s serves to outline the identity of the parties involved in the covenant, together with its terms and benefits:

> Before time a covenant done
> For my ransom;
> 'Twixt the Father and the Son
> Of His bosom,
> On conditions safe and dear;
> Not hell's fury
> Nor the world, nor Satan's ire
> Could it bury.
>
> God's delight e'er worlds were born
> Was with sinners;
> And with love undying sworn,
> To opposers;
> Full atonement by Christ given

For transgression;
Who through hatred aye are driven
To destruction.

Far before the age of man
Was created,
This divine redemption plan
Was once settled;
Jesus undertook to spill
His blood freely,
In accordance with God's will
For th'unruly.

Praise and worship now is made
For His passion;
Recompence in full was paid
For rebellion;
Now His loving Father owns
All His promise,
And His Son's blood-shedding crowns
With our release.

The Trinitarian initiative in eternity drawing up the plan of salvation in love and grace receives considerable attention in Williams's writings. This example is from a Welsh hymn with the title 'election':

My Saviour has loved me
For ages untold,
And truly has known me
As life did unfold;
He purposed quite early
To save me for sure,
When sealing His cov'nant
With blood that was pure.

With love everlasting
To me He did bind,
All praise throughout heav'n
He kept me in mind;
My name He inscribèd
In ages long past
Amongst those elected
'Ere this world was cast.

He makes it clear that covenant blessings originate in eternity and last to eternity:

> The blessings of the cov'nant,
> A covenant costly, new,
> Outlast creation's ages,
> When their course is through;
> Then only will appear
> Heav'n's goodness and its store,
> When sun, moon, and the planets
> Their brilliance shine no more.[16]

In a world of time and space, creation serves the purpose of providence, nature serves grace, but 'when their course is through', providence will have brought God's purpose to fruition and will give way to the harmonious reign of the King of kings. Williams examined his theme in depth in his 'View of Christ's Kingdom' and demonstrated the centrality of Christ in God's eternal purpose. It is likely that Williams's convictions concerning election and the sovereignty of God's grace were forged on the anvil of controversy at Cefnarthen. Biblical passages bearing on the matter would have been the subject of lively debate, and with Williams himself preparing for ordination, his conclusions would have had immense personal significance. For this reason, the Calvinist thread in his preaching and writing was firmly sourced in the Bible. Familiarity with Puritan authors would have confirmed and developed those convictions. Griffith Jones, Daniel Rowland and Howel Davies held the same truths with equal confidence and vigour. They were held, not with divisive intent, or party spirit, but with grateful hearts and missionary zeal.

Federal theology begins man's story in time with the first Adam. The first individual, created in the image of God, he possessed original uprightness, integrity and the promise of life contingent on his obedience to God's revealed will. His fall into sin was a real event with catastrophic implications for mankind, since the first Adam was a representative head of humanity. His actions are reckoned to have been on behalf of his descendants; much as when a parent acts on behalf of a child during its minority. Furthermore, what happened to him affected his descendents; the marks of his fallen nature are perpetuated and duplicated in his progeny. When Williams describes the havoc wrought by envy in the Garden of Eden, he elaborates on the blessings lost in this way:

It drags with it a multitude of companions … expelling the original
residents such as love, patience, faith, simplicity, and made expansive
room for a multitude of fiends to settle in the memory, the
understanding, the will, the conscience, and the affections, and in the
end turning God's temple into a cave of thieves … The most usual of
his companions are self-confidence, selfish ambition, self-love, wrath,
malice, suspicion, falsehood, deceit, craftiness, treachery, tyranny,
perjury, slander, contention, heresies, apart from others like hellish
jealousy, defamation, false witness, frivolous talk, vile insinuation, evil
surmising, and crowds of others too numerous to name except that they
are of the same nature and effect as envy itself.

The result on Eve, and by extension, on Adam, was devastating and
widespread:

Her understanding was darkened, her memory was deadened, her
conscience slumbered, all her affections changed their place; new
objects filled her thoughts, and all the faculties of her soul became al
together unruly, so that not one kept its proper place; the last became
first, and the first became last; the weakest, gentlest endowments took
control, as if the briar became king of all the trees of the forest, and the
understanding, the reason, and the conscience were enslaved in a dark
pit deprived of the light of day. Fears now replaced confidence, flesh
took over from spirit, love for the creature instead of love for the
Creator, and the chief structure under the heavens was demolished; it
was as if a royal palace had been reduced to a heap of earth and stone,
without beauty or glory.[17]

The ramifications of man's fall into sin are comprehensive:

The crooked, straight appears, the truth he cannot see;
He loves what's vile and tainted, and hates all purity;
Indulges every pleasure, embraces every lust,
Delights in total darkness, reject the light he must.

So that man's highest reason, and this he boasts with might,
Now sends him even further from heaven's pure shining light;
While proud, high-minded int'llect compels with one accord,
All arguments together to serve itself as lord.

Nor can the light of nature, nor eye, nor hand supply
Safe guide to heaven's glory, on them none can rely;
Desire with all its branches, the instinct that's so strong,
Drags reason's mightiest power relentlessly along.[18]

Such deep-seated problems will not be solved by human agency, hence the need for regeneration, a sovereign, irresistible and irreversible act on the part of the Holy Spirit.

It is in regeneration that the effects of the fall are reversed, and bring about man's restoration to a pristine state, with this difference, that he is no longer on probation. In Christ, the second Adam, the sinner has gained more than he lost in the first Adam:

> And if it be urged further, that God's image now is lost,
> Jesus, of Him the image, outshines the heavenly host;
> His image, too, restoring to those He calls His own,
> Beyond of old what Adam had of God's image known.
>
> And bring us into favour an infinite degree
> More than we lost in Adam from the forbidden tree;
> And on more sure foundation, as compact more of grace
> Its comfort and duration and glory beyond trace.
>
> A new law instituting the passions to control,
> Which on the heart was written, and previous to man's fall;
> The dragon's law to shatter without the least reserve,
> That once did wholly govern this heart which did it serve.
>
> This is the gracious precept whose verdict doth bestow
> Relief from sin and sorrow, grim death and endless woe;
> And now the Spirit's life-law, a sweet and heavenly voice
> Is heard arranging, ruling, becomes the creature's choice.[19]

Regeneration issues in conversion, and Williams's skill in understanding, evaluating and nurturing this in professing believers has already been noted. It is important to draw the distinction, as he did, between God's initiative in regeneration and man's response in conversion. Numerous Puritan works had set out the nature of conversion, including the popular works *An Alarm to the Unconverted* by Joseph Alleine, and *A Call to the Unconverted* by Richard Baxter. Other leading works of the period include Stephen Charnock, *Discourse on Regeneration* (1683); Thomas Cole, *Repentance, Faith and Regeneration* (1689); George Swinnock, *The Door of Salvation Opened by the Key of Regeneration* (1659); Ralph Venning, *Alarm to Unconverted Sinners* (1675); and William Whately, *The New Birth* (1618). The importance of the doctrine is stated by both Edward Reynolds and Richard Baxter in their commendations to Swinnock's work; by the former it is held to be 'of most absolute necessity to the being of a Christian'; by the latter it is framed in personal application: 'Till thou art regenerate, and hast a new heart and spirit, thou wilt disrelish those saving truths that call thee higher, and put thee upon self-denial and a holy life.'[20] The popular work by Lewis Bayly, *The Practice of Piety,* was addressed to 'the natural man whose corrupted nature has been renewed by grace in Christ, and has been made a new creature.'[21] 'Book II' of Thomas Goodwin's *The Work of the Holy Ghost in our Salvation* is introduced in this way: *'That there are two states or conditions through which God carries the elect: the state of nature, and the state of grace. – That the new birth is the passage between them, which evidenceth the necessity of the new birth, or regeneration.'*[22] Charnock helpfully explains its meaning:

> Regeneration is a spiritual change, conversion is a spiritual motion. In regeneration there is a power conferred; conversion is the exercise of that power. In regeneration there is given a principle to turn; conversion is our actual turning; that is the principle whereby we are brought out of a state of nature into a state of grace ... Conversion is related to regeneration, as the effect to the cause. Life precedes motion, and is the cause of motion ... In regeneration, man is wholly passive; in conversion, he is active ...from this principle all the acts of believing, repenting, mortifying, quickening, do spring. In all these a man is active; in the other merely passive ... understanding, will, conscience, affections: all were corrupted by sin, all are renewed by grace. Grace sets up its ensigns in all parts of the soul, surveys every corner, and triumphs over every lurking enemy; it is as large in renewing as sin was in defacing. [23]

Williams's theology of regeneration and conversion must be understood in this biblical sense, to which these Puritan works bear lucid and uniform witness. It is implied rather than explained in his writings, but his extensive theology of Christian experience cannot be understood apart from it. His exposition of salvation, accomplished by Christ on the sinner's behalf, and applied by the Holy Spirit in the sinner's life, is placed seamlessly alongside God's sovereign initiative in regeneration.

Williams published three accounts of individual conversion, drawing attention to various aspects of this work of God's grace. The first of these to appear was a reissue by Williams of a Welsh translation of the autobiography of Joseph Hart, a contemporary hymn-writer, in order to provide a corrective to two commonly-held false positions. One was the belief that Christ's atonement saves apart from the work of the Holy Spirit to illumine, comfort, lead and effectively apply Christ's redemption to the souls of the faithful. The other position maintained as sufficient for salvation a mental assent to all the Christian doctrines, without an inward, renewing work of Christ's Spirit, leaving the sinner's worldly behaviour untouched.[24] The other publications appeared five years later, in 1779. Thomas Goodwin's 'Memoir' was translated 'to show to all the churches how far men may go in some measure of elevated affections, fiery zeal, the joy and pleasure of religious duties, yet without any knowledge of God, nor genuine change, but all springing from natural instincts, and the general activity of the Spirit.'[25] The third work recounts how James Albert, an African tribal chief, was sold as a slave to a New England minister. Here he came under conviction of sin, was given John Bunyan's *Holy War* and Richard Baxter's *Call to the Unconverted* to read. The latter especially left a strong impression, and after coming to England, eventually he settled in Kidderminster, partly on account of its association with Baxter. By making it available in Welsh, Williams intended to convey the power and sovereignty of God's grace, which brings sinners from darkness to light, and from death to life by the secret workings of providence and apart from any human merit or resources.[26]

Redemption, accomplished by Christ on the cross, and applied by the Holy Spirit to the believing sinner, form another cluster of doctrines frequently present in the works of Williams. He was not only a theologian of Christian experience, but also a preacher of Christ and Him crucified. This he did not only in his sermons, but also in his writings. Consider this hymn:

> The enormous load of human guilt
> Was on my Saviour laid;
> With woes, as with a garment He
> For sinners was array'd
>
> And in the horrid pangs of death
> He wept, He pray'd for me;
> Lov'd and embrac'd my guilty soul
> When nailèd to the tree.

305

O love amazing! Love beyond
The reach of human tongue;
Love which shall be the subject of
An everlasting song.

Eternity, though infinite,
Is short enough to trace
The virtues of His healing wounds,
The wonders of His grace.

Ye men, rejoice in Jesu's blood,
Ye angels, join your lays;
In one harmonious endless choir
Sing His eternal praise.[27]

If that draws attention to the sufferings, the next example highlights the
benefits, of the cross:

Thy love is eternal,
Thy grace is all free,
My glorious salvation
Springs wholly from Thee;
All works, all endowments,
All merits are dross,
They vanish as vapours
In sight of Thy cross.

The fountain was opened
For filth and for sin,
Such as are polluted
Without and within;
Ye wretched, come hither
And wash yourselves white,
So that you'll appear
All glorious and bright.[28]

Redemption has a judicial and a practical aspect, and Williams does not
neglect these. In justification the sinner's forensic state is declared; in
sanctification the sinner's condition in terms of righteousness is worked
out. The first of these is the subject of these lines from *Theomemphus*:

I now delight in thinking that God, who is so just,
So undefiled his looking, from sin's view turn he must;
That God who is so faithful, himself he can't deny,
Can justify the ungodly, yet not be soiled thereby.

> And that same God is righteous, that man to justify
> Who puts his trust in Jesus, though fit and doomed to die;
> And such was Theomemphus, to hell-fire ripe was he,
> Ungodly and unrighteous, devoid of piety. [29]

It also has a place in Williams's preaching: 'Christ, the eternal Son of God, in the fullness of time, was born of a woman, born under the Law, as a Surety in our place, fulfilled all the conditions of the covenant, and, in a word, obeyed all the commandments of the Law; suffered its curse; and so brought in righteousness by which the guilty sinner is justified before God.'[30] So much for a statement of this great truth; here is a Welsh hymn by Williams expressing it in verse:

> Pure righteousness eternal,
> Great and endless and divine;
> This my naked, fainting spirit,
> Must possess and make it mine.
> May this robe, both bright and glorious,
> O'er my naked soul be thrown –
> Then will I no longer tremble
> To appear before Thy throne.[31]

Christ's righteousness is imputed to the sinner in justification, and is figuratively spoken of as a covering garment, hiding from God's view every natural blemish and stain. Williams states in a verse referring to the wedding garment of Matthew 22:11, that nothing less than 'the pure righteousness of God' will suffice. His sermon on the Prodigal Son of Luke 15 in 'The Crocodile of Egypt's River', speaks of 'the best robe' with which the returning prodigal was draped, as 'divine righteousness, the garment of righteousness, salvation's dress'.[32]

The practical aspect of redemption, sanctification, is inseparable although distinguishable. Williams's elegies provide ample evidence of this, showing that Methodist convictions produce a Methodist character and life-style. Theomemphus's struggles with the subtle deceit of his own heart in the way of presumption, pride, with anger in the face of opposition, with the enticements of Jezebel to licentiousness, all these demonstrate Williams's concern for his people's progress in personal holiness. One of Williams's finest hymns is in the form of an earnest prayer for divine assistance to pursue this goal:

Lord, O sanctify my spirit
In each passion and each gift;
May the sovereign will of heaven
My weak soul with strength uplift;
From vain wanderings
Save me always everywhere.

Thou alone canst keep my spirit
From the pitfalls on the right,
On the left, when in great danger,
Thou alone wilt hold with might:
O have mercy
In a desert land I live.

Plant those holy ruling forces
In this helpless soul of mine,
That are like a pleasant fragrance
In Thy nature true, divine;
Flowers of beauty,
May they fill both heaven and earth.

So that sin with all its vileness,
Flames and fumes from depths below,
Ne'er succeed to cloud my vision,
Nor to cause my overthrow;
Help me follow
A straight path by light of day. [33]

This was a thoroughly Reformed emphasis, as Mark A. Garcia concludes in his study of John Calvin: 'The Christ with whom believers are united through faith is none other than the Spirit-anointed Mediator. By virtue of the economic or functional identity of Christ and the Spirit in terms of the application of redemption, one cannot receive Christ for forgiveness without receiving the Spirit of holiness.'[34] In the matter of sanctification the guiding principles affected every area of behaviour, so that, for example, Williams denounced the slave trade in his *Pantheologia*, and advocated mission.[35] His teaching on assurance and revival have already been discussed. All in all, as Williams makes clear in the concluding remarks to *The Experience Meeting,* 'believers should ... become the salt of the earth; a sweet savour in the world in every respect of behaviour, and like lighted candles to the districts in which they live.'[36]

To mention Williams's elegies is enough proof of the adequacy of his theology on the resurrection and the redemption of the body. Hymns on 'the day of judgment', 'eternity' and 'the happiness of heaven' add to the impression that for Williams the element of hope in the Christian salvation is invigorating and important. His *Myfyrdodau ar Angeu* ('Meditations on Death') of 1785 closes with an affirmation of the resurrection of the body in a spiritual state like Christ's resurrected body, 'to spend eternity in the presence of Jesus our God.'[37] Williams's *Aurora Borealis* shows the Christian's sense of anticipation of a better future. William Read's letter 'from the eastern streets of the Holy City' confirms the blessedness of the Christian's future state. And Theomemphus's epitaph at the end of that work dispels doubts and fears even for the most timid of all believers. With this survey it is clear that Williams has a full-orbed theology in line with the whole counsel of God. It is expressed with biblical integrity, Protestant emphasis and Puritan insight. The Welsh Methodists were following in an illustrious tradition.

32.

'Glad consolation, complete bliss'

The title of this chapter is the first line of a verse in one of Williams's early Welsh hymns. The hymn has as its theme the believer's confidence in Christ, and that verse in translation reads thus:

> Glad consolation, complete bliss
> Is theirs who trust Christ's love;
> 'Tis greater than an angel's tongue
> Can sound in heaven above.

The hymn's title, 'The Christian's freedom', suggests that the Christian life is lived in an 'Egyptian night', a world that is hostile to God and godliness, but one that is about to come to an end. 'Egypt' represents the tyranny, misery and danger of sin. Its darkness conveys not only estrangement from God, but also the dread sentence of death that hangs over the sinner duly executed by 'the angel of death' on the Egyptians prior to the departure of Israel from its unremitting bondage. In an English hymn the sinner is said to be 'bound in chains of horrid darkness, Gloomy, thick, Egyptian night', and the theme of a Welsh hymn speaks of salvation as 'the journey from Egypt to Canaan'. Ahead lies 'the promised land', heaven, but meanwhile the soul is at full stretch for more of God.[1] Not only were these words an affirmation of a young convert's perception of his Saviour's future faithfulness, they also distil the impression conveyed during the closing years of William's earthly pilgrimage. Family matters, preaching and travelling, the distribution of his books, Association affairs, and leaving a clear testimony of his convictions are among his activities. These are pursued in the strength of the 'glad consolation, complete bliss' which come from Christ.

 Williams's two sons received some education at Ystrad Meurig in Cardiganshire, an endowed grammar school known for its classical scholarship and allegiance to the Established Church.[2] Of the two, William, referred to as 'Billy' by his father, was more reserved, and he is encouraged to boldness in preaching by the example of his brother John, called 'Jacky': 'Be brave, Billy; a preacher without boldness is like a steel saw without teeth, like a knife without sharpness, or a soldier without heart. Your brother Jacky went on his own to speak to the bishop on the road in Carmarthen, and was rewarded for his courage.'[3] Neither son married. The marriage of Anne, his second daughter took place in February 1784, within a week of the death and burial of his mother, Dorothy. Another daughter, Amelia Maria married the following year, and two more daughters married in later years. In 1770 Williams had bought Llwynybrain farm in Llanddeusant, the location of one of the earliest Associations, and after their marriage Anne and her husband, Philip Thomas, went there to live.[4]

In the last year of his life, Williams wrote an apologetic letter to Billy, giving an outline of his frenzied schedule:

> you must know that I have but very little time to spare to write to any; for I am most part of my time [away] from home ... I travelled through the six counties of south Wales, and some few of them very often since Michaelmas last [29 September]; and now I am just come from a long journey through Carmarthenshire, Glamorganshire, Monmouthshire, and Breconshire, being about 250 miles; and the little time I am at home is spent entirely in composing new manuscripts, and revising those already written ... I have now reprinted 2,000 shilling Hymn Books; therefore, considering all, you will forgive my apparent negligence ... and I hope you will accept of my love and best respects, and forget my neglect in not writing to you sooner; and I can do now no better service than pray for your temporal and eternal welfare, which ever shall be the real and honest principle of your loving father. [5]

Another 1790 letter speaks of the difficulties he faced while on a journey to Pembrokeshire: 'My round has been very near three weeks, and though I have been very ill of the gravel [clusters of crystals in the urinary tract] all the way, yet, notwithstanding my pain and want of sleep, I was enabled to preach constantly twice a day. I was obliged to rise 18 or 20 times out of bed each night, and often more, so that I could rest at most but half an hour! I preached in some of the churches, such as Nevern, Newport; each sermon was nearly an hour long.'[6] Visits to Llangeitho were, as always, frequent. By this time an Association was held there annually in August. On Sunday 22 December 1782, Rowland was indisposed, and Williams preached instead of him, to be joined later by Rowland who later administered communion to a large congregation.[7]

In addition to these visits to the west of Wales, Williams frequently preached at the Trefeca College Anniversary in August. Association meetings were also regularly attended by Williams. One such is mentioned by David Jones, Llan-gan, in May 1773, when he reported the event to the Countess of Huntingdon, who was at Trefeca at the time: 'We should have been truly glad to have seen you at our Association. It was a very solemn day indeed … Great power from on high attended the Word preached. Many went home rejoicing; and who would not rejoice when the Captain of our salvation Himself appeared in the field of battle, assuring the hearts of His poor people that He would conquer in and for them? I trust there were some also of the careless sort cut to the heart.' Jones mentions that Williams preached as well as others, Rowland among them, and of the latter he adds, 'surely he is the greatest preacher in Europe.' At the end of the letter Jones wrote the verse of a Welsh hymn by Williams, with a challenge to the Trefeca students to translate it for her. This was done by the wife of one of them in this way:

> Alas! how vain is mortal man,
> How fickle he appears!
> How fast he hastens to the tomb,
> Which terminates his years!
>
> So said my soul, when great distress
> Like waves burst o'er my head;
> But God for ever is the same –
> Who shall my footsteps lead.
>
> He my unchanging refuge is,
> Nor will my prayer despise;
> I know he'll save – I'll trust His grace
> To raise me to the skies. [8]

Written originally when Williams was approaching his fiftieth birthday, the hymn speaks of God's faithfulness and the believer's confidence of victory over trials and death.

Journeys further afield, to north Wales, were regularly undertaken as well. Together with Rowland and others, he preached at Associations in Pwllheli in 1777 and in Bala in 1780 he preached on 'the Green; there was a pulpit erected for that purpose.'[9] From the time of Thomas Charles becoming a member of the Methodist society in Bala in 1784 that town's significance in the Methodist movement rapidly became prominent. In effect it replaced Trefeca as the twin centre with

Llangeitho, and with Charles's gifted and expanding influence, greatly accelerated Methodist influence in the north. The previous summer Charles had married Sally Jones, daughter of the owner of a thriving business in the town. Thirty years of age at the time, she was a woman of exceptional qualities, shrewd in financial affairs and mature in spiritual matters, attractive and intelligent. The correspondence that passed between them during their courtship is remarkable for the affectionate expressions in those of Charles, ('My dear dearest heart .... My sweet Dearest Love, most affectionately your's') and the detached formality of her responses ('Dear Sir ... Your friend'). For her mother, Jane, Williams included in his elegy to William Davies, the preacher from Neath, a fitting tribute to her hospitality and generosity towards Association members.[10] Williams frequently corresponded with Sally as well, and to a 1776 letter he added some verses of admiration. 'At last I composed you these lines and I'll assure you they are out of real respect to you ... I beg you would keep these verses, perhaps you will read them when I am in the grave. I have been about 2 or 3 hours composing of them; they flowed naturally from my heart, so that my task was very easy ... I intend to come to the north to the Association and perhaps I will send a wallet of books to you before that, which I desire you to keep safe for me. You need not open the bundles for the books will be the same as those which I had last year, viz. *Môr o Wydr* and the *Haleluia*.' A representative verse reads like this:

> Blessèd is the man you'll marry, for his portion he'll have more
> Than the treasures vast, luxurious, in Japan and Borneo's store;
> His, a virgin pure and gracious, constant, loving, fair and bright,
> Of a steady disposition, and most precious in God's sight.

More verses followed in 1781, rich in spiritual counsel, advocating patience in the face of adversity. They convey a deep appreciation of the work of grace in one who was not above administering words of reproof to her hymn-writer correspondent. Williams writes to Charles in 1787: 'give my respect to your dear wife who I love in all sincerity and return her thanks for her last letter – but I imagine by a check she gave me of my putting my hand to the plough and drawing back that she thinks I sit down in my easy chair and never go out to preach. Let her ladyship know that I am as diligent now in preaching as ever, and more.'[11] Sally's encouragements continued as long as health permitted, a worthy helpmeet to a second-generation Methodist.

Among the ministers present at the Association, Thomas Charles's name appears for the first time in the minutes for that held at Llangeitho on 10 August 1778. For the next ten years the matters dealt with included collecting money for chapel building, evaluating the fitness of members to preach, defining the geographical limits of their labours, and appointing preachers to visit north Wales and London. Money was collected on a weekly basis from society members for building more permanent meeting-places. After the death of her brother, John, in 1828, Williams's daughter Elizabetha Margaretta gave sums of £10 and £20 to pay debts incurred by chapel building.[12] Williams was also involved as a trustee for some of the new chapel buildings, those at Amlwch, Anglesey, in 1777 and at Capel-y-Cwm, Llansamlet, in Glamorgan in 1782, being examples.

If organization and discipline were prominent in the Association's business, compassion was not lacking. Thus, financial help was solicited by the Association for a society member who had provided security for a 'bridge upon Cothy' which had unexpectedly collapsed. Furthermore, Associations were preaching occasions as well as business meetings, with several sermons being delivered by those appointed to do so. As a result, numbers attending had grown, and Williams comments on the generosity of one particular family in providing hospitality for the Nevern Association in Pembrokeshire in October 1786: 'Mr. Bowen of Llwyn-gwair has treated the whole Association. Hundreds of people, godly and ungodly, dined and were entertained. Sixty beds were occupied by strangers at Llwyn-gwair alone, and about six score sat down to meals there.' To avoid giving the impression of ecclesiastical separation, direction was given that no preaching occasion should be held at the same time as parish church services.[13]

By September 1787 it was obvious that travelling in the cause of the Gospel was becoming difficult for Williams. His spirit was eager enough, but his physical frame was registering increasingly its inadequacy for the task, however near to his heart. This appears in a letter to Thomas Charles at that time:

> I really intended to visit you this summer and I came some part of the way to Bala, to be at your Association there and then; but somehow or other faintheartedness prevailed, and after I travelled 20 miles, I

returned back again. I promised again anew at Llangeitho Association to come to Bala this instant, and from you to Pwllheli provided Jack Edw[ards], the man your people agreed with to come along with me would come; and now I received a letter from him that he can't come because of the harvest, and it would be impossible for me to make such a round as to encompass the counties of the north alone, especially this time of the year, when the days are shortened and the weather colder and colder every day; and it is truth to a demonstration whenever I put a foot on the northern ground that [I] must go through the whole and preach twice and often thrice a day as some of our southern preachers do, though I am now 70 years old, but I hope the Lord will enable me if I will be alive and in health next summer not only [to] promise but actually come to you, let your burdens be as heavy as they will. I long to see you all and love more those that press me to work the more. If time would allow I would be glad to stay a few days at Bala, though some time past when I was there, I was put out of breath by preaching twice, administering the sacrament once, and keeping a long private society for two hours on one Sabbath day. I was then but 67 years old … There was so much cry at Llangeitho Association for the penny hymns that I have printed 1000 of them since, and sent you a bundle of 50 by Mr John Price. Either sell them at Bala, or give them [to] William Evans etc. being worth only 4 pence.[14]

The loss of Rowland in 1790 affected Williams deeply, but the immense bond that had existed between them was motivation enough to write one of his most informative and enduring elegies. In a letter written to Charles a few days before his own death he refers to it in this way:

With much effort, I have composed an elegy on Mr. Rowland, consisting of about 44 verses; if I knew that the people of north Wales would dispose of 2 or 300 of them, I would send them to Aberystwyth; the price is one penny. I know that Shani, if possible, will sell two hundred of them in the great Association at Bala. I have here, at home, 200 of the shilling hymn-books; if they were at Bala during the great Association, I know most of them would be sold. But I know that I cannot come there, if alive; but if anyone came from Bala to fetch them, I would adequately reward him.[15]

He was owed money for his books by some of the distributors, and in the same letter he appeals to Thomas Charles to remind his debtors of their obligations: 'some in north Wales – good men, I hope – are rather careless in paying what they owe, as if they had a right to the possessions of other men, as though they were their own. Edward Pierce of Dyffryn Clwyd owes me 14s. for the last two years – Betty Mark 10s., Cornelius of Anglesey 8s. for elegies, and if you will so good as to mention the matter to them, please do so.'[16]

A reference in the same letter speaks of Williams's final effort in prose.

> Welsh schools are much needed in order to teach the Word of God. I have written and printed an address to the wealthy folk to induce them to contribute a little of their possessions for that object; and you will do well if you will devote some of the money you have for building meeting-houses to help the poor to become able to read the Word of God. I should very much like you to see those papers. But the exhorters who come to visit us from your country are unwilling to carry books from here to you, so loath are they to do one a kindness. Each one cares for his own rather than for the things of the Lord. [17]

Its lengthy title explains its purpose: *A Serious Address presented to the consideration of all charitable and well-disposed Christians, for contributing some part of their monied properties, to raise a small fund, to carry on Welsh Charity Schools, upon a plan similar with that established by the late Rev. Mr. Griffith Jones, and continued by Mrs. Bevan* (1790). Mrs Bevan's endowment of £10,000 for Welsh schools was contested after her death in 1779, and the matter was not resolved for thirty years. Williams's fervent plea for financial support was grounded on considerations of illiteracy and poverty:

> Notwithstanding we are at present more abundantly favoured with preaching and expounding of the Scriptures, and likewise have more attendants among us than in the days of our forefathers, yet an opportunity of hearing is obtained but too infrequently, and sermons cannot be supplied at all times. Again, in case preaching were to be procured at will, all could not attend it, especially at all seasons, and in every circumstance; some are so much confined by ungodly heads of families that they cannot attend one sermon in a fortnight; some are afflicted with sickness, some are debilitated by old age; some by reason of various infirmities rendered unable to walk any considerable way. This considered, how absolutely necessary it is then for such to be capable of reading the Word of God, so as to draw out their comfort, consolation, and light, personally from thence when they are left destitute of all other means? [18]

In his will, Williams left a sum of money for Nathaniel Rowland, David Jones, George Bowen of Llwyngwair, and Thomas Bowen, Gweinifor,

316

to pay any schoolmasters that were employed in the proposed charity schools.[19] Even though the project floundered, the aim reflects Williams' love of God's Word and concern for his countrymen.

Despite the fact that Williams's body was getting weaker, his passion for the salvation of souls was unimpaired. However frequent and grave the discouragement at the end of his life, the knowledge that the Gospel was still bearing fruit was cause for triumphant reporting: 'A great revival has taken place in many parts of our country – from 5 to 600, to my knowledge, have been added to the number of those who profess religion, during the last two years.'[20] He may have been referring to a powerful revival at Twr-gwyn in Cardiganshire which began in 1784 and lasted for a considerable time, or to a revival at Trecastell, between Llandovery and Brecon, which began in 1786. Two revival seasons at Llangeitho may have been in his mind; 'the great revival' of 1781, after Rowland had preached on the same text for a whole year; or one in 1790 which began with family worship in the homes of believers, but then spread throughout the community.[21] The fluency with which his mind flows from considerations of physical suffering to those of spiritual delight is astonishing. As always, so now, for Williams, news of such seasons of refreshing was a spiritual tonic that more than compensated for ill-health. Their power and frequency at that time would have enabled his spirits to soar into heaven in praise, even though his body was an earthen vessel in decline.

33.

'No more this side of eternity'

For the last five or more years of his life Williams's health was causing concern. In 1786 he wrote to Thomas Charles: 'I am very ill and by all probability I shall see you no more this side of eternity. May the Lord be with you; you will follow me very soon. Make all possible speed to carry on the great work you were called unto. I hear that the Lord blesses you more and more, and may you be an instrument to call thousands to the faith of our dear Immanuel. I beg and humbly beg you to pray publicly this day for me and I doubt not but at the hour of prayer I shall find some easing of this violent pain in my bladder. I have tried the hot water, but nothing doeth for me. Oh may the will of the Lord be done in life or death.'[1] Near the end of the year, the crisis had passed and he wrote to his son William:

> Received both your letters, and after reading them over again and again I sent them [to] Jacky [the other son, John], on condition of returning them me immediately, which he did … your mother, brother and self [are] now exceeding joyful that providence has been very favourable to you considering how black and melancholy it appeared at first. You ought to thank the Almighty, and never forget His tender mercy for your safe arrival at your long-wished home; in whose hands are all the contingencies of our life. With thanks to God and pleasure I tell you that I am indifferently recovered from my late illness; and the reason of my not writing to you sooner was that I have been three rounds from home since you left us; and was middling well in each of them; and now I am home, but intended to go, to Llangeitho next Sunday, but the weather is so cold, the wind so high and the frost so severe that I found I can't go. Your brother is at college [teaching at Trefeca] indifferently well, but we have not seen him since you left us. I return you very many thanks for the abstract from [William] Buchan [*Domestic Medicine; or the Family Physician*]; it gave me more light … to the cause and nature of my distemper than I had anywhere else, though I ran over many books on the subject. I find that the cause of suppression of urine in me is a spasm or stricture of the nerve fibres and membranes about the neck of the bladder … so that the passage of the urine in the neck of the bladder is becoming too narrow to convey it out but by drops and I find

there is no stone nor much gravel in my bladder, for the case is as above. I have desired Mr. Ross [a Carmarthen printer] to buy me Buchan which will cost 7 shillings and six pence. I shall endeavour to use every means he prescribes. And return you many thanks for your care of my life and health … We are all well, thanks be to God … November 17th. The weather has altered and your mother and self intend to go to Llangeitho tomorrow being Saturday, and if I'll go I will not return for a whole week if the Lord will give me health. This very minute news was brought to us that Ishmael died this day of a fever; he continued sick but 5 or 6 days; this violent distemper rages somewhere or other these 2 or 3 years in Wales and cuts persons' lives in a very few days. There is a woman in our village very ill in this fever; what will become of her the Lord knows, but she has quite lost her senses.[2]

In spite of health hazards and weather unpredictability, a determination to fulfil his ministry characterized Williams to the end. His interest in things medical was unabated as well, his mental faculties maintaining their integrity in a sustained and lively manner. His biographer, Edward Morgan, records of Williams that he 'was guilty of the very injurious practice of sitting up late at night to study and write. It was very seldom he went to bed before two o'clock in the morning. But some apology must be made for him as a poet; for those highly devotional strains of the heavenly Dove, were conveyed into his mind generally in the night watches.' It was a practice that Thomas Charles thoroughly disapproved of in him, adding, 'two hours of sleep before midnight is better for health than four or five after midnight … It must be admitted, that in this matter the old servant of the Lord had gone astray.'[3]

Four years later, in May 1790, another letter to Charles bears witness to both tenacity in labour and deterioration in health.

No man ever had more intense longing than I did to come to Gwynedd this year. I thought I would have at least enough health from my heavenly Father to reach your part, even though I would not manage the whole; for my heart truly is with you, even though it is unlikely that I shall ever be able to come in person. However, sadly for me and to your disappointment, it is impossible for me to reach you, even though I have been advertised in five or six places from Pant-y-celyn to Bala. It does not appear to have been the Lord's will for me to come this time. My ill-health is so grave, that during the last six weeks I cannot go much further than around the house without much pain and hazarding life itself. It is the same illness that nearly took my life at the time of the Llangeitho Association three years ago. I am convinced that my days

319

are drawing to a close, and my race nearly run; I have had a long life; I am now 73 years of age and health would still be robust were it not for this affliction which my heavenly Father has put upon me. I have been preaching for 43 years, and I know that I have travelled between 40 and 50 miles every week, and since there are 52 weeks in a year, this amounts to 2,600 each year, and in 43 years that makes a total of 111,800 miles, a 4 times round the world. This spring I managed four or five substantial journeys, each one taking two weeks and amounting to 200 miles through the south Wales counties. I had thought I would not rest until I took a journey through the Gwynedd area, but these last journeys so wearied me that it is unlikely I shall ever do this, since I my health deteriorates each time. If you pray that I shall have more relief than at present, I shall do my best to come to Bala this summer before harvest-time, but it would be impossible for me to go further as I can only travel a short distance each day; also the weather would have to be kind, as a cold temperature aggravates my complaint; it is responsible for my present condition.[4]

Meanwhile at Llangeitho, Rowland, in his seventy-ninth year was telling his congregation: 'I have some presentiments that my heavenly Father will soon release me from my labours, and bring me to my everlasting rest.' He had dismissed all his labours as 'nothing' and told his family: 'I have no more to say by way of evidence of my acceptance with God, than I have always stated: I die as a poor sinner, depending fully and entirely on the merits of a crucified Saviour for my acceptance with God.' He died on Saturday, 16 October 1790, and was buried the following Wednesday. His funeral sermons were preached by David Jones, Llan-gan and John Williams, Lledrod, which suggests that William Williams was unable, for whatever reason, to minister on the death of one with whom he had laboured for so long. Williams's thoughts, however, inevitably turned to his own encounter with 'the last enemy'. In the last two verses of the elegy he wrote to Rowland, his body often racked with pain, he speaks of death as a release:

> Here on earth my life's now ending,
> God soon calls me to depart;
> Death now holds me in a prison
> I can sense it in my heart;
> There is no release from dying,
> Nowhere here or there to flee,
> But I know all bonds will shatter
> At my coming Jubilee.

Yet, in spite of all the bondage,
Which my body feels each day;
Heaven opens wide before me
Heavy chains will melt away;
And my spirit joins in prospect
With the vast and heavenly throng
Of the first-born now in heaven.
There, by grace, I, too, belong.[5]

In the various elegies he wrote Williams had been fond of giving free rein to his imagination in identifying biblical and historical believers together in the full enjoyment of their Saviour and of each other. Death for him, too, would be a 'jubilee', a setting free from the shackles of a mortal body and the confines of a material world, to spend eternity in the perfect communion of saints in glory.

With such an awareness of death's imminence Williams could contemplate his spiritual state before God, review his life's work, and distil what mattered most for a Christian on the edge of eternity. He expands on these matters in his last letter written at Pantycelyn to Thomas Charles a few days before his death:

Accept these lines from one who cannot converse with you face to face. I have been very ill, beyond all hopes of living, to my own mind, and in the opinion of others; and yet for some secret purpose of the Lord, I am alive so far. I have for ten weeks been confined to my bedroom, nor could I risk one step from out of it without being in danger of an upset. I have taken a great deal of doctors' medicines without the slightest benefit ... nor did anything serve to assuage my pain and check my sickness until the Lord himself became a doctor of medicine to me; and that came to pass in consequence of the church taking my case in hand, and calling aloud at the door of his shop, and he, according to his promise, heard it; and I have this moment faith to believe that one earnest prayer has more efficacy than all the doctors in the world. As the apostle says, 'Is any sick among you? Let him call for the elders of the church; and let them pray over him', 'and the prayer of faith shall save the sick, and the Lord shall raise him up.' And I believe that some hundreds of prayers were offered up for me in this illness. In answer to these prayers a verse came to my mind with such force that, for the moment, I believed I was going to rise; and the verse was Ps. 118: 17, 'I shall not die, but live, and declare the works of the Lord.' Now my tender and beloved Father has made me easy, though I am still unable to leave my bedroom. I want nothing from Him but He gives it me, and I have never hitherto had so much faith to pray as I have now. I know

321

that this affliction is from the Lord, and I know that whether I live or die, it will prove a blessing to me. I have acquired more knowledge of myself and of the goodness of God during these ten weeks than during the forty previous years. The Bible, which I used to read, in a great measure, for the edification of others, I now apply entirely to myself, as the only book by which I shall be tried in the great judgment; and although I have hundreds of books, not one of them suits my taste like the Bible. I have looked for its most searching passages, for those which press hardest on flesh and nature; and I have seen that grace and mercy outweigh the threatenings even in them – and that, in the end, a way of escape and deliverance lies in the reproofs and punishments of God. I have come to see that true religion consists of three parts: first, true light respecting the plan of salvation; God's eternal covenant with His Son to pay the debt of believing sinners, all the truths of the new Covenant by which He becomes all in all in creation, in all-embracing providence, and in redemption ... but now, in this affliction of mine, I have come to see that I am very defective in a subject not less magnificent than the other, that is, being in intimate fellowship with God in all our dealings with the world, and in all the exercises and ordinances of religion. We find that the saints of old had attained this under the old Covenant. Abram is said to be the friend of God, as if God and he consulted each other ... Lastly, I have come to see the third part of true religion – life and conduct, such as would reveal to the ungodly that there is a great difference between us and them ... You will understand that though I am somewhat better as regards the pain from which I have suffered, I am still but weak and feeble, and very helpless; and I have but little hope that I will ever be able to go out much, if at all, again; because I am seventy years of age. Think what a disappointment it must be to a man who has travelled nearly three thousand miles every year for over 50 years to be now without moving more than 40 feet in a day – from the fireside to bed. This is how my God wishes to deal with me, and it is well ... A visit from some of your preachers is much need in south Wales. Of the preachers owned of God, some 6 or 7 are either dead of afflicted of the Lord; and the north Wales preachers most in favour with the people have not visited us for some time. You yourself are one of them, because your services are called for from every part of south Wales, and the Lord will reward you if you come. My dear, dear brother, work while it is day; the night will overtake you, as it has overtaken me, so that you will neither be able to travel nor preach.[6]

The medical clinician as well as the biblical theologian in Williams are obvious here. The gravel is described as coriander seed, much as manna was described by the Israelites in the desert, and Christ is compared to an Apothecary who responds to the entreaty of the church on his behalf at His shop door. [7]

So much for his deteriorating health; but his biblical mind-set takes over completely in order to concentrate on the ground of comfort for his soul, and the fervent desire that God's work would continue to prosper after his decease. According to his biographer,

> His latter days were marked by great simplicity; the pleasures of imagination ceased to delight him; the variety of studies, which used to interest him, had lost their fascinations; and we find him spending his time in a recumbent posture, with his wife ... beside him, reading portions of the New Testament and of the Psalms of David alternately ... His dying advice to all who visited him, as long as he could command utterance, was 'Cleave unto the Lord, with full purpose of heart', laying the emphasis strongly on *full purpose*. Speech failed him, but a sweet serenity of countenance, and an eye fixed towards heaven, made some who were present to say, 'May I die the death of the righteous, and may my latter end be like his.' ... Dear Mr. Williams could not utter a word for many hours before his departure, though he frequently strove to do so. This arose from the interruption of the phlegm and the difficulty of breathing which it occasioned.

It is not surprising that the same biographer reports of his funeral that 'there was a very great concourse of people ... who felt their loss exceedingly. W. Lloyd, Esq., of Henllan, Caeo, Carmarthenshire, preached a most excellent sermon to the great congregation. Though a lay-preacher, very few excelled him in the sweet experimental strains in which he set forth Christ and Him crucified. After the discourse was over, the procession moved, and the people sang solemnly and triumphantly all the way to the church.'[8] David Jones of Llan-gan expressed his reflections in a letter to the Countess of Huntingdon: 'We have had a second great loss by the death of dear Mr. W. Williams. The old oxen are taken from the field and the great work not yet accomplished. We may rest assured therefore that fresh ones shall be sent in for the plough till all be ready for the harvest. Mr. Williams, just before his death, has honoured us with the sweetest elegy on the departure of dear Mr. Rowland. I wish I could give it a translation to the English language. 'Tis the best I ever saw. He had a foretaste of heaven in every part of it. He tells us in the last verses that he was then a prisoner under the fetters of death himself, but that his spirit was solacing itself among departed saints.'[9] Such remarks expressed fitting tribute to William's faith, message and ministry.

Williams's passing was noticed in the national press of the day, with this entry in the *Gentleman's Magazine* for January 1791.

> At Pantycelyn, near Llandovery in Carmarthenshire, aged 72, Rev. William Williams, a clergyman of distinguished talents and character. In early life a pious but amiable enthusiasm induced him to adopt the itinerant and apostolic modes of Methodism; and uniting a talent for poetry to an insinuating and captivating eloquence, he contributed greatly to its prevalence and support. He is probably the last lyric poet of south Wales, the language of the country gradually giving way. His Muse was wholly religious; yet many of his hymns have all the properties of the ode, true poetic fire, striking imagery, and glowing expressions. United to the plaintive music of the country, their effect on the people is astonishing, and the veneration in which they are held little short of devotion. Of this veneration the author greatly participated; and it will not be wondered at when it is known that for fifty years he has almost incessantly traversed the Principality in the ardent discharge of the duties of his ministry; that his imagination gave variety and interest to his orations; that his piety was warm, yet candid and charitable; his manners simple, yet affectionate and obliging; and his moral conduct without blemish or imputation.

While the reference to the Welsh language has proved to be erroneous, the rest of the obituary represents a widely-held assessment of Williams and his achievements.

The following tribute was paid by Edward Morgan to Williams's wife, Mary: 'She was a truly pious, sensible, and amiable person … highly beloved and respected … She departed triumphantly rejoicing in the Lord. Her last words were: 'It is come, it is come, I never thought it would arrive this way; it dawned last night! Salvation is like the ocean! On this I have been meditating all the night.' She spent much of her time, the last year of her life, in reading the Bible, and Fox's Martyrology, which was her favourite book. She was buried by the side of her husband, in the churchyard of Llanfair-ar-y-bryn.'[10] The inscription on their tombstone reads thus:

> Sacred to the Memory of the late Reverend William Williams of Pantycelyn in this Parish. Author of several works in Prose and Verse. He awaits here the coming of the Morning Star which shall usher in the Glories of the first Resurrection when at the sound of the Archangel's Trump the sleeping dust shall be reanimated and Death for ever shall be

swallowed up in Victory. He laboured in the service of the Gospel for near half a century and continued incessantly to promote it both by his Labours and Writings, and to his inexpressible Joy beheld its influence extending, and its efficacy witnessed in the conviction and conversion of many thousands. After languishing some time he finished his course and Life together January 11th. 1791 Aged 74.

> No darts, no frights, no fears, no sorrow and no pain,
> Sounding forth the glory of the Lamb that once was slain;
> One of a throng of myriads, who sing with endless praise,
> A love-song as the anthem, a song they'll ever raise.

Also the remains of Mary the pious and beloved wife of the said William Williams who departed this life 11th of June 1799 Aged 76. Her unfeigned piety, amiable conduct and unblameable deportment through life are too well known to require any further encomium.

'The Sweet Singer' of Wales, author of the hymn 'Guide me, O Thou great Jehovah', had departed for 'Canaan's side', triumphant over death and hell, to give 'songs of praises' to the One who had delivered his soul, and would raise his mortal body to immortality.

325

34.

'The wine of heaven'

The emblem of fire is a fitting one to describe the passion with which Williams fulfilled his ministry. It is an emblem that in many respects characterises Methodist aspirations, activities and experiences. But nowhere is its intensity more dominant and sustained than in the case of Williams himself:

> 'Tis Thou I seek, Thou canst fulfil
> My infinite desire;
> Inflame my gloomy heart anew
> With Thy celestial fire.
>
> One drop of that o'erflowing stream
> That angels taste above,
> One smile from my Redeemer's face
> Would kindle all to love. [1]

For this reason his achievements are many and significant. Burning with a desire to bring the Gospel with urgency to a needy people, it explained his fervent preaching. Concerned to maintain an intense devotion to Christ among the Methodist society members, the same devotion within his own heart issued in a profuse outpouring of vigorous, soul-searching, heart-warming hymns for congregations and individuals alike to make their own. It was also a fire that purified the gold of genuine spiritual experience in revival times from the dross of mixed motives, corrupted desires and worldly idols. It drove him to define, with clear, if at times fictional, imagery, the outlines of a Christian ideal in profession and practice. It fired zeal for orthodox teaching in the church, for a biblical mind-set in everyday life, for harmony and charity between believers.

Following Williams's withdrawal from a settled curacy in 1743, the Church of England's authority over his activities effectively came to an end. In order to work alongside Rowland in particular, he accepted the constraints of an 'incomplete ordination', so that he would only assist at the communion service. On the other hand, he was no longer confined by parish boundaries or Episcopal restraints, so that he was free to adopt an itinerant ministry of counselling and preaching. He thought highly of gifted lay preachers, among them Dafydd John of Pwll-y-march, who relied on the heavenly gales for power in his preaching, and William Lloyd, who preached at Williams's funeral. Allegiance to Anglican liturgy and spirituality continued to be the official stance of the Welsh Methodists, strongest in the case of Harris, weakest in the case of Williams.

Of greater importance to Williams was the unalloyed commitment to evangelical principles, voluntary inter-dependence, and careful discipline of the societies. It was this commitment that enabled him to steer a middle course between the hierarchical structure of episcopacy and the separatist independency of the Dissenters, among whom his family had been nurtured. The carefully monitored prominence given to laymen by the Methodists created a religious democracy that emphasised both individual responsibility and corporate concern. But it was a democracy that had checks and balances within its own structures, and objective constraints for its preservation from influences without. The persistence of a vigorous Calvinistic Methodism for over a century is ample testimony that Williams and the other leaders bequeathed this as a sound spiritual heritage to posterity.

The geographic spread as well as the powerful impact of Methodism created new tensions. With chapel buildings mushrooming across the country, the issue of identity was rapidly becoming unavoidable. Spiritual liveliness and careful oversight with a network of linked fellowships had served their purpose for many years.[2] But at the end of the century, the maturity, both in leadership and membership, as well as the success of the societies, demonstrated the need to define their character as well as their purpose. The deaths of Rowland and Williams early in the last decade of the century spared them the agonies of facing that crisis. It was left for another generation of Methodists to separate by ordaining their own ministers in 1811. Even then it was taken as a painful, if necessary, step, with some evangelical clergymen, hitherto owning allegiance to both Methodism and Anglicanism, unable to join the new denomination.[3]

In many respects the important events in Williams's life are also landmarks in Welsh religious history. His conversion and the first revival at Llangeitho coincided closely in 1738, and were an earnest of greater things to follow. His first collection of hymns, the *Aleluja*, appeared a matter of months after leaving his curacy in 1743 to assist Rowland, loosening his affiliation to the Established Church and providing a new vehicle for worship. During the testing years of the Disruption, in 1756 his 'View of Christ's Kingdom' was published, providing young Methodists with a sound theological foundation. By it he was also staking a firm claim to be following in the Protestant and Puritan tradition. It was a steadying influence in tempestuous times. Close on the heels of the 1762 revival he issued his apologetic works 'Martha Philopur's Letter' and 'The Answer of Philo Evangelius', followed in 1764 by his careful account of Christian conversion in *Theomemphus*, works that convincingly rebuffed criticisms of the revival's phenomena. Two prose works at the end of the 1760s, 'The Crocodile of Egypt's River', and 'Three Men from Sodom and Egypt', bore ample witness to Methodist awareness of the need to walk worthy of the Gospel they so fervently and widely preached. A decade later, Williams wrote two works of practical guidelines for the societies, 'A Guide to Marriage' and 'The Experience Meeting'. His memorable elegy to Rowland in 1790, followed by his own death marked a triumphant end to two of that period's most illustrious figures. Methodism's biblical message which centred on Christ's person and work, the evangelical fervour of their insistence on the new birth and on faith, and the close, if charitable, self-imposed discipline of their societies drew criticism from their contemporaries, religious and otherwise. But there is no question that the period of its ascendancy in Wales transformed the nation's culture and society. In this transformation, it is no exaggeration to say that Williams's part was pivotal. Griffith Jones's schools were pioneering and important; Harris's itinerancy and organizing ability opened up new pathways for the spread of the Gospel; Rowland's preaching was well-known for its authority and penetration; but it is Williams's memorable verbal legacy in poetry and prose that has most permanence and usefulness.

The strength of Williams's contribution to Methodism lay in his insights into the nature of Christian experience. There were several facets to this, not least his hymn-writing, but also in his defence of religious revival, its meaning and manifestations, and in his exposition of Christian assurance. He readily acknowledged his debt to Puritan authors, and to the names of those he mentioned in his 1791 letter to Thomas Charles should be added that of John Bunyan. He thought highly of Rhys Prichard, Jonathan Edwards, and the Erskine brothers. On all these he drew freely: on Prichard for an example of effective communication; on Edwards with his theology of true revival; on the Erskines for their understanding of spiritual devotion and progress. His immense debt to Edwards is freely acknowledged, but Williams never indulged in the philosophical sophistication to which Edwards was prone. There were other authors that Williams used: Isaac Watts, Charles Wesley and James Hervey for their hymns; Desiderius Erasmus and his work on marriage; Elisha Coles on divine sovereignty; William Durham for his Astro-theology; John Cotton on the Covenant; and James Ussher on the Person of Christ. But there is no question that Williams had made all knowledge derived from such sources very much his own; it is Williams the Welsh Methodist that the reader meets in his work.

The language of his Welsh hymns is that of the common people, often identifiably colloquial and idiomatic, because he wants to communicate to them what is of supreme urgency and importance. His concern is for the Welsh people; he may rebuke them for their tardiness in reading, or the parochial extent of their interests, yes, but he has their eternal welfare at heart. The entire organization of Welsh Methodism has a Welsh flavour to it; there is no pomp or ceremony, but a down-to-earth simplicity for a people who enjoy equality and freedom to be themselves without any pretence to superiority or importance. It is a Methodism that is not only Welsh in its exuberance and sensitivity, but it is also a Methodism that is Calvinist in its God-exalting insistence on the priority and triumph of grace to all conditions of men.

Williams seems to have held a fascination for biblical types, metaphors, and figures. For him they were reason enough to exercise his imagination to create the vivid imagery which peppers and enriches his hymns. It is necessary to qualify this statement somewhat, since his was no ordinary, fictional or fantastic imagination. On the contrary, it was a sanctified imagination that stirred Williams, and that imparted an elevating, memorable quality to what he wrote. In other words, it was an imagination that took Scriptural precedents and skil-fully wove them into new thought-forms and fresh connections, giving an edge to their personal relevance and practical usefulness, in medita-tion, worship and everyday behaviour. Williams was as convinced as Jonathan Edwards, that the soul's senses, in particular through the affections, were profoundly affected in any genuine work of the Holy Spirit. Williams's hymn-writing gift enabled him to present the Word of God, dressed in powerful imagery, to the mind and heart to work its powerful spiritual office. In this way, memory and conscience were stirred, the will was subdued, and saving influences followed. It is to Williams's credit that he never abused that gift. His writings rigorously and consistently observed biblical boundaries, and his aims are invariably subservient to God's purpose. Master of his poetic art, he laid his crown at the feet of the God who gave it.

In writing his hymns Williams deliberately avoided classical forms, language and regulations in the belief that spiritual usefulness had precedence over literary excellence. He aimed not to impress with the medium but to inspire with the message. 'I have written for you some hymns, composed as near as possible to the sound and language of the Scriptures, so that in song they might come more easily to mind and be more effective in working on your affections.' For this he had any number of biblical precedents: 'It was not the learning of Deborah, Barak, and Miriam that made them, nor that of David either, that made him such a notable poet in God's Book, but the spirit, zeal, and enjoyment of God and experience, together with the power of the heavenly breeze stirring within, until the fire burst forth into sweet melodies that will last forever.' Hymn-writers should study poetry, especially biblical examples, yes, but such discipline in and of itself would not achieve the desired goal of meaningful hymnology, any more than knowledge of the original languages and careful exposition of a biblical text would guarantee powerful preaching. For hymns to have the quality of spiritual compositions and to realize a truly godly purpose, they had to conform to inner constraints of the soul rather than to external conventions of poetry. For this reason the hymns 'as far as possible had been framed with the sound of CHRIST and his gracious Gospel like blood flowing through all their veins, and man, his learning and perception as nothing.' That purpose according to Williams, was quite simply, 'for the eternal good of your souls', and 'to stir up the affections with love to God.' Rhys Prichard in the previous century had written 'in the common dialect – catchy, carol-like songs, in which any and every word, however corrupt as to form and origin, was consecrated to service.'[4] Likewise, Williams wrote in the way that he did, not because he could not conform to poetic norms, but because he would not, in the conviction that to do so would have seriously compromised those aims.

The hymns written by Williams after 1762 are particularly memorable. He was at the height of his productive brilliance, with years of mature experience behind him. Derec Llwyd Morgan summarises their excellence when he says of them: 'Neither before nor since throughout our land has there been such a powerful whirlwind of creative energy. In all these collections there are magnificent, outstanding hymns.'[5] Here is Thomas Charles's appreciation of his genius:

> In his youth he was in person comely, vivacious, and of average height; in temperament he was rather heated; but usually gentle, and pleasant to everybody. Putting everything together, he was one of most gifted, respected, and useful men of his age. His gift of poetry was naturally and abundantly given him by the Lord. He would frequently mount on very strong wings, which would lift him into heights of splendour. The cross and its great sacrifice are the chief topics and substance of his writings; and while there is love in the hearts of the Welsh people for that great Sufferer, his work will be in favour among them – especially his hymns. Little did he study of Welsh metrical theories, of the purity of diction; but he would mount on the breeze of heaven, take up the words nearest to hand, and absolutely familiar to the masses, who were passionately fond of his songs. Though neglecting the purity of Welsh diction to the degree he did was not a thing to be commended in him, yet, in his homely language he is intelligible to all, and captures their minds and hearts by the force and excellence of his matter and high soarings. His hymns wrought a remarkable change in the religious aspect of Wales, and in public worship. Some verses in his hymns are like coals of fire, warming and firing every passion when sung, and impelling the people to repeat them many times, until they break forth, shouting and leaping for joy. These strong effects are definite proofs of the power of the forces which cause them. Mr Daniel Rowland's sermons, and the hymns of Mr. William Williams, made the age in which they lived more remarkable than almost any age in the history of Wales. These four things were marked in him: the strength and abundance of his natural gifts; his great diligence in the use of them, night and day; the very great extent to which he enjoyed the influence and power of the Holy Spirit in his own work; and the immense blessing which the people received through him. [6]

This assessment, by one who perhaps knew Methodist congregations better than any, and whose spiritual discernment was second to none, bears ample witness to the validity and effectiveness of Williams's priorities in composing hymns.

Like Harris, but for a more sustained period of time and in a more skilful and compassionate manner, Williams travelled indefatigably to set up new societies and encourage established ones by regular visits. He combined regular visits to the Llangeitho Sunday communion occasions with the oversight of the nearby Tregaron society on the previous Friday. In 1747 he established a new society at Soar y Mynydd in the sparsely-populated mountainous region between Ystradffin and Tregaron, his usual route to Llangeitho. From 1774 he made the journey to Aberystwyth, further north, to provide the Methodist converts with society privileges. There were always privileges; on many occasions there was also delight: 'God's people come away from such a meeting as this like drunkards from the wine-shop – contentedly happy, having drunk the wine of heaven; all comforted, guided and edified.' [7]

In his relationship with the other Welsh Methodist leaders, Williams was cordial and supportive. He was the wise intermediary that facilitated Harris's reconciliation and reinstatement to the Welsh Methodist fold. For Rowland he was a humble helper, generous with his time, unremitting in his labours. Numerous elegies testify to the ease with which he related to ordinary people, and paid tribute to their gifts and achievements. Apart from those elegies, however, original material about his dealings with other people is lacking, so that he appears somewhat detached. Short in stature, his body movements and speech rapid, and occasionally quick-tempered, he had a sense of humour but he could also descend into a measure of melancholy. He was at ease on horseback, enjoyed the countryside, and frequently drew on the seasons and the changes in nature to convey spiritual lessons. Nevertheless, from the time of his conversion it was the marvels of divine grace that became his supreme delight.

Unwavering in his commitment to Calvinist theology, his emphasis was, consequently, on the glory of God. It is not without reason that the final part of 'A View of Christ's Kingdom' has the title, 'Christ delivering the kingdom to the Father':

> Christ will yield the kingdom whole to His Father, God,
> Which He had gained through conquest, and purchased
>   with His blood;
> Each office He had taken for earth's weal to provide,
> My all-sufficient Saviour doth now lay all aside. [8]

Drawing always on the Bible, he strenuously avoided secondary issues of the Church's teaching and practice, and made Christ's Person and work the constant theme of his writings. This is evident from his advice to young preachers:

It would be desirable for young preachers to read books that have much of Christ in them; to study more of that great salvation which highly exalt the divine attributes, and give complete satisfaction to the Father for all He demands by way of propitiation and the payment of the debt owed by the chief of sinners to His righteousness; to His divine holiness and truth. Matthew 3:17, 'This is my beloved Son, in whom I am well pleased', bringing inexpressible glory to the Son, in His amazing love coming into the world, taking a human body, suffering, dying, rising again, clearing the debt, receiving remission for His people, ascending to heaven, sitting on the right hand of the Father, where He was before; and all this before we had either being or life; and now sending the Holy Spirit to enlighten, lead, and sanctify those people whom He justified when still ungodly. This glory our Lord has merited, expects the Father to give, and which the Father confirms by promises, John 13: 31-32, 'Jesus said, now is the Son of Man glorified, and God is glorified in Him. If God be glorified in Him, God shall also glorify Him in Himself, and shall straightway glorify Him.' He bestows on the believer ultimate riches, meeting his needs, however boundless, with present and eternal treasures of grace and glory that are laid up in Christ's Person, hidden in Him before we existed, 2 Timothy 1:9, 'Who hath saved us … according to His own purpose and grace, which was given us in Christ Jesus before the world began'; Ephesians 3:8, 'unto me … is this grace given, that I should preach … the unsearchable riches of Christ'. [9]

A faithful ministry of God's Word draws on God's truth, depends on God's power and exalts God's Son.

Bible words were true words because the Bible was 'the Statute Book of Christ's kingdom', having the King's authentication, inspired by the King's Executor, the Holy Spirit. The words were not only true, they were good; the Gospel is good news because it offers the King's pardon to rebels, reconciliation with God to undeserving sinners. Such redemption, wrought by Christ, was at great cost, and Williams's gifts are stretched to the full when he presents the death of Christ as newsworthy, trustworthy, and praiseworthy. For the kingdom to be realized in personal experience, God must take the initiative in regeneration, yes, but this is always accompanied by conversion: the humbling, transforming response of repentance and faith in the sinner as that wonderful release is appropriated. In this way the kingdom is set up in the heart, Christ comes to reign and to stay. And this is only the beginning for the believer. There is more, much more: more of God, more grace, more peace and joy in believing. There will be adversity, disappointment and failure, but the King rules all for the good of His people. Such trials are by way of rebuke and discipline, to hone the soul's faculties and return them to God when they go astray. Finally, for Williams, the kingdom of grace issues in the kingdom of glory. In new, immortal bodies, believers will enjoy forever the blessed Trinity, and God will be all in all.

> In the life that lasts forever,
> I shall gaze upon His face,
> Search His love, beyond all measure,
> And the branches of free grace;
> Heavenly mysteries
> Shall my soul delight for aye. [10]

Christian salvation and Christian hope are inseparable because the author of both is the King, who accomplished the first by His death, and is the earnest of the other by His resurrection. If Williams could not accept all of the Puritan Richard Baxter's theology, he was Baxterian in other respects. In both there was a passion to provide ordinary people with biblical teaching in an accessible way that had popular appeal, Baxter by his evangelistic tracts, Williams by his memorable hymns. What Baxter had done by regular catechising of his flock, Williams achieved by careful counselling in the societies. Both dwelt much on Christian hope. While Williams did not write a sustained treatise of the calibre of *The Saints Everlasting Rest*, he scattered throughout his published works pearls of rich meditation on heaven. It was meditation suffused with confidence and triumph, because the believer's hope is immovably anchored on Christ's finished work on the cross:

> See myriads sealed above
> Who feared once, as I,
> That overcame the journey's woes
> Through strength of Christ's supply;
> They now in heaven reside,
> Sing praise without alloy,
> The songs of Calv'ry's costly death,
> And hail the Lamb with joy. [11]

A true physician of souls would hardly neglect their eternal welfare.

Above all, Williams was a man of deep personal piety. His relationship with Christ was one of close, sustained devotion. His soul was frequently ravished by the ineffable beauty of Christ's Person, and filled with amazement at Christ's undying love. Fresh views of the mysteries of God's saving grace transported his soul into raptures of pleasure and praise. His most eloquent and gripping hymns convey nothing less than wonder at the communion, little short of ecstatic, that he enjoyed at such seasons. Its intimacy could only be conveyed by referring to Christ in terms used by the Song of Solomon: 'Rose of Sharon'; 'Lily of the valleys'; 'beloved', 'the chiefest among ten thousand'. His other hymns and writings may be less intimate, but they, too, give the impression that the writer is not a detached spectator of what is objectively pleasant or astonishing; on the contrary, he is a closely involved participant, willing, and engrossed, in what is inexpressibly delightful.

Theologian of Christian experience and revival, soul physician, hymn-writer, man of discernment, vision and compassion: Williams was all these to the Welsh Methodists. By his ministry of preaching and writing he gave cohesion to the Methodist movement in Wales. His orthodox theology, expressed in rhyme, became the staple of the society meetings, giving expression to their unity, and identity. His hymns were vehicles of worship and instruction. He could be relied on to provide spiritual nourishment to the soul, and wise counsel for everyday behaviour. What Jonathan Edwards was to New England, George Whitefield and the Wesley brothers to England, this, Williams was in Wales: leader of a revived Christianity.

Notes

Preface
Pages xi-xvii

1. R. M. Jones, *Highlights in Welsh Literature: Talks with a Prince*, Llandybïe, 1969, 62, 226, 68-9.
2. 'Dylanwad Williams Pantycelyn', *Taliesin*, Gwanwyn (Spring), 1991, 47.
3. Saunders Lewis, *Williams Pantycelyn*, Llundain, 1927, Pennod (Chapter) X, 'Rhamantiaeth'; R. Tudur Jones, *Saunders Lewis a Williams Pantycelyn*, Abertawe, 1987.
4. 'The Evangelical Revival in Wales: A Study in Spirituality', in James P. Mackey, *An Introduction to Celtic Christianity*, Edinburgh, 1989, 238.
5. 'Marwnadau William Williams, Pantycelyn', *Llên Cymru,* 17 (1993), 254.
6. *Williams Pantycelyn*, Caernarfon, 1983, 4, 7, 9.
7. CH. xix.12.
8. 'The Author's Preface' to *Commentary on the Book of Psalms*, Baker Book House, Grand Rapids, Michigan, 1989, Volume IV, xlix.
9. Kathryn Jenkins, 'Chums â'r Arglwydd', *Taliesin*, Gwanwyn (Spring), 1991, 58.
10. *David Martyn Lloyd-Jones: The Fight of Faith 1939-1981,* Edinburgh, 1990, 208-10.
11. *The Puritans: Their Origins and Successors*, Edinburgh, 1987, 196.

1. 'Truth in the Head'
Pages 1-8

1. *Trysorfa,* 445;
2. NLW MS 14916A, Morgan Williams, 'Llyfr Cofnodion Cefnarthen'. See also Rhys Davies, *Cefnarthen, - y comin, y capel, a'r ysgol,* [Clydach] 1983, 43-56.
3. John Ogilby, *The Traveller's Guide*, [1712?], 144.
4. See J. E. Lloyd (ed.), *A History of Carmarthenshire*, Vol. II, Cardiff, 1939, 348-55; and Anthony H. T. Lewis, 'The Early Effects of Carmarthenshire's Turnpike Trusts, 1760-1800', in *The Carmarthenshire Historian*, 1967.
5. Geraint H. Jenkins, *The Foundations of Modern Wales*, Oxford, 1993, 117.
6. Quoted in GMR1, 67, n.1, from *Transactions of the Carmarthenshire Antiquarian Society*, iv. 42. An article on the same subject by G. Milwyn

Griffiths in *The National Library of Wales Journal* in 1974 states, 'Of 156 families...'

7. GMR1, 24, 42-3; Theo, 81.

8. A tract with the title *Family Devotion* by Edmund Gibson (1669-1748) published in 1705 was widely distributed at the time and became a minor classic. Gibson became bishop first of Lincoln, and then of London. Its 8th edition appeared in 1730, with a Welsh translation of 32 pages available from 1725 bearing the title *Duwiol Swyddau Teuluaidd*. In 1707 a correspondent spoke of Gibson's 'exhortations to Family Prayer which have done so much good in Carmarthenshire.' For similar books see Mary Clement (ed.), *Correspondence and Minutes of the S.P.C.K. Relating to Wales 1699-1740*, Cardiff, 1952, s.v. 'Exhortations'.

9. For an account of translations of the Welsh Bible see Isaac Thomas in R. Geraint Guffydd (ed.), *A Guide to Welsh Literature*, c.1530-1900, Cardiff, 1997; and Eryn M. White, *The Welsh Bible*, Stroud, 2007. Lewis Lupton, *A History of the Genevan Bible: Welcome Joy*, London, The Olive Tree, 1975, 184.

10. For a survey of the religious literature available to Williams's generation, see Geraint H. Jenkins, *Literature, Religion and Society in Wales 1660-1730*, Cardiff, 1978, especially Chapters III-VI..

11. An English translation by William Evans was published at Carmarthen in 1771 with the title *The Welshman's Candle*, and again in 1815 at Merthyr Tydfil with the title *The Morning Star*. A poem, 'Thanks for our Election, and several Spiritual Gifts' appears on pages 285-7 of the 1771 translation. See also R. Brinley Jones, *A Lanterne to Their Feete*, Llanwrda, 1994, 17. For Prichard, see *ODNB* and *DWB*; Nesta Lloyd, 'Rhys Prichard, c.1579-1644/5', in *The Carmarthenshire Antiquary*, Vol. xxxiv, 1998, 25-37; and D. Gwenallt Jones, *Y Ficer Prichard* a *'Canwyll y Cymry'*, Caernarfon, d.d.

12. *Y Seren Fore neu Ganwyll y Cymry*, Trydydd Argraffiad, Wrexham, d.d., 19; 'Y prydydd pena' i gyd', Cyn1, 627; Theo, 15-16.

13. T. Rees a J. Thomas, *Hanes Eglwysi Annibynol Cymru*, Cyf. III., Liverpool, 1873, 583; GMR1, 21. In a letter to an anonymous correspondent early in March 1740, Howel Harris favoured Jones's involvement at Cefnarthen 'in the borders of Carmarthenshire Arminians to stop their proceedings.' (CH. xx, No.3. [TMS. i. 295]).

14. R. Tudur Jones, *Congregationalism in England 1662-1962*, London, 1962, 145.

15. The SPCK volume of 1700 was a translation by Charles Mutel from the French of Jean Frédéric Osterwald's *Traité des sources de la corruption qui règne aujourd'hui parmi les chrétiens*. It also appeared in Volume 6 of the Bishop of Llandaff's (Richard Watson), *Collection of Theological Tracts*.

16. For Saunders's views see the Cardiff, 1949 reprint of his work, pp. 23-4; 38, 48, 59-60. The Methodist contention that pre-revival eighteenth century Wales was in deep spiritual decline is defended in Eifion Evans,

'The Methodist Revival: tradition and revision', CH. 32 (2008), 12-18. See also David Ceri Jones, '"A Glorious Morn": Methodism and the Rise of Evangelicalism in Wales', in Mark Smith (ed.), *British Evangelical Identities Past and Present*, Milton Keynes, 2009.

17. Another fifteen editions would appear by the end of the century. For the proliferation of catechisms see Ian Green, *The Christian's ABC: Catechisms and Catechizing in England* c.1530-1740, Oxford, 1996; for Welsh Catechisms, see Geraint H. Jenkins, *Literature, Religion and Society*, 74-84.

18. D. E. Jenkins, *The Life of the Rev. Thomas Charles B.A. of Bala*, Volume 2, Denbigh, 1908, 71.

19. For Ellis Wynne (1671-1734) see *ODNB* and *DWB*.

20. Rees a Thomas, *Eglwysi Annibynol*, Cyfrol III, 588; GMR1, 40, n.74, see Morgan Williams's 'Llyfr Cofnodion Cefnarthen'.

21. David B. James, *Myddfai Its Land and Peoples*, [Aberystwyth, n.d.], p.40. For the legendary 'Physicians of Myddfai', see Morfydd E. Owen, 'The Medical Books of Medieval Wales and the Physicians of Myddfai', in *The Carmarthenshire Antiquary*, Volume XXI, 1995; and Howard E. F. Davies and Morfydd E. Owen, 'Meddygon Myddfai', in John Cule (ed.), *Wales and Medicine*, Llandysul, 1975, pp.156-67. Howel Harris records Jones's death in his diary entry for 16 December 1739: 'I hear of a Persecutor at Llandovery, John Jones the Surgeon, that died miserably, and was for having me and others to pray for him then, poor soul. The Lord might have left me to be so.' CH. xxviii. 118. By 1761 Llandovery could boast of four apothecaries and by the end of the century Brecon and Carmarthen were also amply served by the medical profession. See Geraint H. Jenkins, *Foundations*, 274.

22. *Trysorfa*, 445. For Llwyn-llwyd see Pennar Davies, 'Episodes in the History of Brecknockshire Dissent', *Brycheiniog*, III (1957), 32-8.

23. Pennar Davies, *Brycheiniog*, 36; *Scientific Progress and Religious Dissent*, Open University, Unit 8 'Nonconformity and the Growth of Technology', p.100, quoting from Irene Parker, *Dissenting Academies in England*, Cambridge, 1914, 86. In a Welsh article by Derec Llwyd Morgan on 'Pantycelyn a Gwyddoniaeth' (Pantycelyn and Science), the author sets Williams's scientific knowledge in the context of Christ's rule, particularly in Williams's work *Golwg ar Deyrnas Crist*; for Williams, God's power in nature is subservient to God's purpose in grace. The article is in J. E. Wynne Davies (gol.), *Gwanwyn Duw: Diwygwyr a Diwygiadau*, Caernarfon, 1982,164-83. For Ephraim Chambers, see *ODNB*.

24. Rees a Thomas, *Eglwysi Annibynol*, Cyfrol IV, Liverpool, 1875, 267, 269, 272; Richard Bennett, *Howell Harris and the Dawn of Revival*, Bridgend, 1987, 99.

25. *The Dissenters: from the Reformation to the French Revolution*, Oxford, 1999, 391-2.

26. Theo, 82-3.

2. 'The Language of Canaan'

Pages 9-16

1. *Trysorfa*, 445.
2. Bennett, *Dawn of Revival*, 24-7; *A Brief Account of the Life of Howell Harris, Esq.*, Trevecka, 1791, 10-24.
3. Richard Baxter, *Five Disputations of Church Government*, 1659, p.165.
4. CH. v (TMS1, 68, 69, 94-7, [Letter to Griffith Jones, dated 31 July 1736]).
5. *GWP2*, 112; *The Pilgrim's Progress*, Edinburgh, 1977, 100.
6. M. G. Jones, *The Charity School Movement: A Study of Eighteenth Century Puritanism in Action*, Cambridge, 1938, 313. See also Eryn M. White, 'Popular Schooling and the Welsh Language 1650-1800', in Geraint H. Jenkins (ed.), *The Welsh Language Before the Industrial Revolution,* Cardiff, 1997, 324-37; Glanmor Williams, *Pioneers of Welsh Education*, Swansea, 1964.
7. Cyn1, 440. The claim made for his greatness is found in Henry T. Edwards, *Wales and the Welsh Church*, London, 1889, 319, and other writers have echoed this. For Jones, see *ODNB; DWB*; Gwyn Davies, *Griffith Jones, Llanddowror: Athro Cenedl*, Bridgend, 1984; Geraint H. Jenkins, *Cadw Ty Mewn Cwmwl Tystion*, Llandysul, 1990, 153-74.
8. CH. v (TMS1, 95); *Brief Account ...Howell Harris*, 41-2; Tom Beynon, *Howell Harris's Visits to London*, Aberystwyth,1960, 187.
9. Edward Morgan, *The Life and Times of Howel Harris, Esq.*, Holywell, 1852, 293-4.
10. GWP1, 108, [*Golwg ar Deyrnas Crist*, ('A View of Christ's Kingdom')]; Cyn1, 499.
11. Theo, 17.
12. Theo, 95-6.
13. See Theo, 181.
14. GWP2, 136.
15. GWP1, 162.
16. GWP2, 2, 3.
17. Theo, 96, 97.
18. GWP2, 145-6, 148.
19. *Golwg ar Deyrnas Crist* was first published in 1756. The faithful Gospel preacher in question was David Jones, of Llan-gan and the phrase occurs in Williams's elegy to him. Williams's later aim in hymn-writing is found at the end o his *Rhai Hymnau a Chaniadau* ('Some Hymns and Songs') of 1757; see GMR2, 62-3.
20. B. B. Warfield claimed that 'from beginning to end, [John] Calvin conceived the confidence of the Christian in Scripture, wrought by the Holy Spirit, as one of the exercises of saving faith.' (*Calvin and Augustine*, Philadelphia, Pennsylvania, 1956, p.108, n.75.) Calvin's most explicit statement of this is found in his *Institutes* Book I Chapter 7 paragraphs 4 and 5: 'the Word will not find acceptance in men's hearts before it is sealed by the

inward testimony of the Spirit. The same Spirit, therefore, who has spoken through the mouths of the prophets must penetrate into our hearts to persuade us that they faithfully proclaimed what had been divinely commanded … Let this point therefore stand: that those whom the Holy Spirit has inwardly taught truly rest upon Scripture, and that Scripture indeed is self-authenticated; hence it is not right to subject it to proof and reasoning. And the certainty it deserves with us, it attains by the testimony of the Spirit.' (ed. John T. McNeill, Philadelphia, Pennsylvania, 1973, 79, 80.)

21. Eifion Evans, *Fire In the Thatch: The True Nature of Religious Revival*, Bridgend, 1996, 111. Several Puritan writers taught this. In William Perkins's *A Golden Chain, or The Description of Theology*, faith is defined as 'a miraculous and supernatural faculty of the heart, apprehending Christ Jesus being applied by the operation of the Holy Ghost and receiving him to itself.' (Ian Breward (ed.), *The Works of William Perkins*, Abingdon, 1970, p.228.) John Preston (1587-1628) speaks of justifying faith 'as a grace or habit infused into the soul by the Holy Ghost, whereby we are enabled to believe, not only that the Messiah is offered to us, but also to take and receive him as our Lord and Saviour.' (*The Breast-plate of Faith and Love*, [first published in 1630], Edinburgh, 1979, 42.) The statement of John Bunyan (1628-1688) in his *Christian Behaviour; being the Fruits of True Christianity*, (1663), is more general: 'Faith is a principle of life, by which a Christian lives, Gal.2:19-20; a principle of motion, by which it walks towards heaven in the way of holiness, Rom. 4:12; 2 Cor.5:7. It is also a principle of strength, by which the soul opposeth its lust, the devil, and this world, and overcomes them, 1 Jn. 5:4-5.' (*The Works of John Bunyan* (ed.) George Offor, Glasgow, vol.ii (1848), p. 551.) The posthumous work of Stephen Charnock (1628-1680), *Discourses on Regeneration* of 1683, though not as massive as his famous *Excellence and Attributes of God*, is still comprehensive, and in it he speaks of faith as 'the first discovery of all spiritual life within us, and therefore the immediate principle of all spiritual motion … The new creature being begotten by the seed of the word, and having thereby an evangelical frame, hath therefore that which is the prime evangelical grace, upon which all other graces grow; and consequently all the acts of the new creature spring from this principle immediately.' (*The Complete Works of Stephen Charnock*, vol. III, Edinburgh, 1865, p.98.)

3. 'Ruffi, Gymmos, and Asafetida'
Pages 17-23

1. CH. iii. 97.
2. CH. iii. 44.
3. Theo, 94.
4. Cyn1, 492.
5. Tom Beynon, *Howell Harris's Visits to Pembrokeshire*, Aberystwyth, 1966, 117.

6. *Yr Haul*, 1887, p.19 says he spent some time as an apprentice to a doctor in Hay-on-Wye. In P. J. Wallis and R. V. Wallis, *Eighteenth Century Medics: Subscriptions, Licences, Apprenticeships*, Newcastle upon Tyne, 1985, pp. 331, 619, 1187, mention is made of John Jones at Myddfai in 1721, with Richard Jenkins as apprentice, and at Hay on Wye, Edward Wellington in 1737 with Richard Baker as apprentice. Neither Williams nor William Read appear in these lists.

7. While Kilsby Jones makes the suggestion that Williams taught at Llansawel, he places the period of his doing so *after* he severed his connection with the Episcopal Church. See Kilsby, ix. Cf. NLW Ffrwdfal MS 111b, p.132, 'Rev. W. Williams, Pantycelyn kept school at Llansawel when a young man, probably about 1740 – David Jones Cwmgogerddan.' This William Williams, writing to Thomas Davies, rector of Coety in 1773, speaks as one who had been at the College in Trefeca, and had subsequently taught at Aberystwyth, Machynlleth and Aberdovey, before moving to Llansawel. The letter, written from Llansawel and dated 28 April, 1773, is at the Glamorgan Record Office County Hall, Cardiff (D/D St 16, 'Collection relating to Methodism in Glamorgan'.). In it he also says that 'there is preaching at present in every corner' of Aberystwyth, despite recent opposition to Howel Harris, and commends Thomas Boston's *Fourfold State* as 'a very experimental little piece.'

8. GMR1, 21, 23.

9. Stuart Anderson, *Making Medicines: A brief history of Pharmacy and Pharmaceuticals*, London, 2005, 64, 66.

10. J. H. Davies (ed.), *The Letters of Lewis, Richard, William and John Morris, of Anglesey (Morrisiaid Môn) 1728-1765)*, Vol. 2, Aberystwyth, 1909, 393. A 'John Pugh of Llandovery, Apothecary' is mentioned in an indenture dated 2 February 1755. See Alfred Theodore Arber-Cooke, *Pages from the History of Llandovery,* Volume One, Llandovery, 1975, 285.

11. 'A Summary of the Life and Character of the Rev. Mr. Griffith Jones', in *A Collection of Valuable Tracts*, 1780, 39.

12. Dorothy Porter and Roy Porter, *Patients' Progress: Doctors and Doctoring in Eighteenth-century England*, Oxford, 1989. The full title of Wesley's work is, *Primitive Physic; or an easy and natural Method of curing most Diseases*. According to Luke Tyerman, one of Wesley's biographers, 'the publication of this remarkable book arose out of the great success of Wesley's dispensary, opened in 1746. At the time of his death, it had reached its twenty-third edition … Wesley says, "For six and twenty years, I had made anatomy and physic the diversion of my leisure hours … I took into my assistance an apothecary, and an experienced surgeon."' *The Life and Times of the Rev. John Wesley*, Fourth Edition, Volume I, London, 1878, 563-4. See also Deborah Madden, 'Pristine Piety: primitive and practical piety in the art of John Wesley's Physick', Oxford D. Phil. Thesis, 2003; and Barbara Prosser, 'An Arrow from a Quiver; Written Instruction for a Reading People: John

Wesley's *Arminian Magazine* (January 1778-February 1791)', Manchester Ph.D. thesis, 2008, 150-165. Daniel Neal (1678-1743) was an Independent minister and author of the four-volume *History of the Puritans* that appeared 1732-38. He wrote a pamphlet in 1722 that explained the novel practice of inoculation against smallpox introduced from New England. Rowland Hill (1744-1833) was refused ordination as priest for his extra-parochial preaching, and known chiefly as a preacher at Surrey Chapel, London, from 1783. He was a strong advocate of vaccination, and published a tract on the subject in 1806. For Neal and Hill see *ODNB*.

13. *GWP*1, 107, 112.

14. *GWP*2, 82, from *Crocodil Afon yr Aifft* ('The Crocodile of Egypt's River') in which jealousy is portrayed as a crocodile.

15. *GWP*1, 244; Cyn1, 161; Cyn2, 215, 216. Cf. Philip W. Ott, 'Medicine as Metaphor: John Wesley on therapy of the soul', in *Methodist History*, 33 (1995), 175-91. See also Eifion Evans, 'Medicine for the Soul', *Foundations*, 45 (2000), 37-41.

16. Cyn1, 464, 465, 466, 472. For Read see Joan Read Moseley, 'A Pontypool Doctor of the 18th Century', *Pontypool & District Review*, No. 8 (October, 1971), 9-14. A memorial tablet to Read in Trefethin Church, near Abersychan, Monmouthshire, reads: 'Here underneath in silent slumber lies / Read the Physician, pure, meek and wise; / In faith, in patience and in hope who ran / His steady race, a friend to God and man.'

17. A listing of books from Williams's library is found in NLW Calvinistic Methodist Archive Trefeca 752. An account of the Williams library is in GMR1, 'Atodiad IV'.

18. Morgan, 66-7. William Buchan (1729-1805) was an Edinburgh doctor, and his *Domestic Medicine, or the Family Physician*, first published in 1769, quickly went through several editions and was translated into many languages, including Welsh. For Buchan, see *ODNB*.

19. *GWP*1, 390, 386-99; Theo, 176-9.

4. 'An office of vast importance'

Pages 24-34

1. Morgan, 11.

2. *GWP*2, 141.

3. *GWP*2, 12.

4. *Templum Experientiae apertum; neu Ddrws y Society Profiad*, translated by Bethan Lloyd-Jones, and issued under the title *The Experience Meeting – an Introduction to the Welsh Societies of the Evangelical Awakening*, London and Bridgend, 1973. The quotations are on page 28.

5. Theo, 67, 87, 103; cf. Williams's elegy to Daniel Rowland: 'His name was Boanerges, Son of thunder, flaming, true.' Cyn1, 582.

6. GWP2, 95. The similarities to the 'Shepherds' on the 'Delectable

Mountains' in Bunyan's famous work, both in number and character, are striking: 'The Shepherds, I say, whose names were *Knowledge, Experience, Watchful,* and *Sincere.*' (*Pilgrim's Progress*, Edinburgh, 1977, 135, 137.)

7. Cyn1, 653, 658. For Whitefield see *ODNB*. Arnold A. Dallimore's two volume biography, *George Whitefield*, (London 1970, Edinburgh 1980), is sympathetic and convincing. More recent biographies include: Harry S. Stout, *The Divine Dramatist: George Whitefield and the Rise of Modern Evangelicalism*, Grand Rapids, Michigan, 1991; and Frank Lambert, *Pedlar in Divinity: George Whitefield and the Transatlantic Revivals*, Princeton, 1994. For Whitefield's close links with Wales see David Ceri Jones, *'A Glorious Work in the World': Welsh Methodism and the International Revival, 1735-1750*, Cardiff, 2004, passim.

8. *George Whitefield's Journals*, London, 1960, 229.

9. Cyn1, 475, 477, 478. For Howel Davies (c. 1716-70), see *DWB*; John Morgan Jones and William Morgan, *The Calvinistic Methodist Fathers of Wales*, Translated by John Aaron, Volume 1, Edinburgh 2008, Chapter 6; and CH. 11 (1987), 2-14.

10. Cyn1, 527, 588. For David Jones (1736-1810), see *DWB*; Jones and Morgan, Fathers, Chapter 19; and R. Brian Higham, *The Rev. David Jones, Llan-gan, 1736-1810, and his contribution to Welsh Calvinistic Methodism*, Lewiston, Queenston, Lampeter, 2009.

11. CH. v (TMS1, 85).

12. 'Preface' to *Theomemphus*, originally published in 1764. See Theo, 58.

13. Eryn M. White, *Praidd Bach y Bugail Mawr*, Llandysul, 1995, 3; CH. xxiv.57.

14. Cyn1, 456 (Elegy on the death of Lewis Lewis, an Anglican clergyman); Edmund Jones, *A Sermon ... occasioned by the death of Mr. Evan Williams*, London, 1750, 96; CH. xx. 125. For Edmund Jones (1702-93) and Evan Williams (1719-48) see *DWB*.

15. CH. iii. 44; xxix. 101. In August 1741 Thomas became vicar of Merthyr Cynog, 'a focal point for Methodists' in that area of Breconshire. NLW Church in Wales records, SD/BR/11, 12 August 1741; Gomer Morgan Roberts (gol.), *Hanes Methodistiaeth Galfinaidd Cymru*, Cyfrol 1, Caernarfon, 1973, 106.

16. See under the respective parishes in NLW MS 1626; Beynon, *Visits to Pembrokeshire*, 235; 276-8.

17. Eifion Evans, *Daniel Rowland and the Great Evangelical Awakening in Wales*, Edinburgh, 1985, 1, 51-2.

18. For Theophilus Evans (1693-1767), see *DWB*; A. H. Williams, 'Theophilus Evans, Chaplain', *National Library of Wales Journal*, 16 (1969-70), 264-71; Bedwyr L. Jones, 'Theophilus Evans', yn Geraint Bowen (gol.), *Y Traddodiad Rhyddiaeth*, Llandysul, 1970, 265; Geraint H. Jenkins, *Theophilus Evans* (1693-1767): *y dyn, ei deulu, a'i oes*, Llandysul, 1993; GMR1, 47.

19. Eiluned Rees, *Libri Walliae A Catalogue of Welsh Books and Books Printed

in Wales 1546-1820, Aberystwyth, 1987, Items 2141 and 5181; L. Tyerman, *The Life of the Rev. George Whitefield*, Second Edition, Volume1, London, 1890, 291-3.

20. CH. xlvi (TMS2, 178-9).

21. Geraint Dyfnallt Owen, *Ysgolion a Cholegau yr Annibynwyr*, [Abertawe, 1939], 27-8;

22. GMR1, 45.

23. Morgan, 12, 45-6.

24. Quoted in Charles J. Abbey, *The English Church and its Bishops, 1700-1800*, Vol.2, London, 1887, 27; cf. Mary Clement, *Correspondence and Minutes of the S.P.C.K. relating to Wales 1699-1740*, Cardiff, 1952, 189, 190, 241, 314. For Claggett, see *ODNB*; for documents relating to Williams's ordination, see GMR1, 44-5.

25. Evans, *Rowland*, 154-60; Harris and Rowland wrote a reply to the article, but the publisher either lost or withheld it. Roberts, *Letters* (1742-1747), 2; CH. xxx.50-1; CH. xlviii (TMS2, 229-30).

26. *Trysorfa*, 447.

27. CH. iii. 44; xxix. 119-20.

28. CH. xx.126.

29. CH. xxx.50, 52, 53; CH. xlviii (TMS2, 232).

30. CH. iii. 46 [4 December 1742]; *Account of the Progress of the Gospel*, Vol. II, No.2, p.27.

31. CH. iii. 46; Beynon, *Visits to Pembrokeshire*, 94-5, 99; *The Christian History*, Volume V, No.1, 41-2; CH. xxx. 108; Beynon, *Visits to London*, 86; *Christian History*, Vol. V, No. 1, p.40.

32. Tyerman, *Whitefield*, Volume 2, 51-2.

33. CH. lv (TMS2, 298); Morris Davies, *Deuddeg Pregeth ar Bynciau Ymarferol Gan ... Daniel Rowland ... hefyd Cofiant yr Awdwr*, Dolgellau, 1876, 309; CH. 4 (1980), 26. For a discussion of the attitude of the Church of England towards Methodism in Wales, see Glanmor Williams, William Jacob, Nigel Yates, and Frances Knight, *The Welsh Church from Reformation to Disestablishment 1603-1920*, Cardiff, 2007, 165-83.

34. *Trysorfa*, 446.

35. GMR1, 58-63, 65, 66.

36. R. T. Jenkins, *Yr Apêl at Hanes ac Ysgrifau Eraill,* Wrecsam, 1930, 42; A. H. Williams, *National Library of Wales Journal,* 16 (1969-70), 268; and *idem. Bathafarn,* 24(1969), 36-7.

5. 'The despised Methodists'

Pages 35-42

1. CH. 4 (1980), 26 (Sep. 1742).

2. CH. xlviii.38. One historian has suggested that the Association's proposal in asking Williams to assist Rowland was to replace David Jenkins, curate of

Cellan, who had died in the spring of 1742. CH. i. 27; Roberts, *Letters (1742-1747)*, 14.

3. *Trysorfa*, 446-7.

4. *George Whitefield Sermons*, Volume III, Pietan Publications,. New Ipswich, New Hampshire, 1994, 235 (Sermon on Mark 10:52, 'Blind Bartimeus'); *A Select Collection of Letters of the late Reverend George*, London, 1772, Volume 2, 17; Vol. 3, 24.

5. *An Account of the Progress of the Gospel*, Vol. iv. No.1, 77.

6. NLW MS 9145F 'Returns of Rural Deans of St. David's 1717-1828', Return for 1745 under 'Llangeitho'.

7. *George Whitefield's Journals*, 48, 67, 300; see Eifion Evans, 'The Society People: Developing a Methodist Mind', CH. 29-30 (2005-06), 25-42; D. M. Lloyd-Jones, *The Puritans: Their Origins and Successors*, Edinburgh, 1987, 191-214, 'William Williams and Welsh Calvinistic Methodism'.

8. *Bathafarn* 4 (1949), 58; cf. Eryn White, *Praidd Bach*, 3.

9.   CH. li. 64-5; lii. 45; John Hughes, *Methodistiaeth Cymru*, Cyf. 2, Gwrecsam, 1854, 2, 4.

10. Harris claimed, even in 1743, that the numbers were 'above 2,000, whereof a great part are brought to glorious liberty and walk solidly in clear light in the clear enjoyment of God without moments of darkness.' Roberts, *Letters* (1742-1747), 82; Rowland's servant is said to have reckoned the numbers to have been about 1,500.   (W. G. Hughes-Edwards, 'The Development and Organisation of the Methodist Society in Wales 1735-50', M.A. Thesis, University of Wales, 1966, 59.)

11. For Lewis see Richard Bennett, *Dawn of Revival*, 130; for Jones, CH. 8 (1985), 24-30; for John Powell (1708-95), see *DWB*; for John Hodges, see *DWB* and Roberts, *Hanes Methodistiaeth*, Cyf.1, 206-07; for John Davies, see Roberts, *Hanes Methodistiaeth*, Cyf.1, 207.

12. Church in Wales SD O/2890; *A Letter to the Reverend Mr. George Whitefield, occasioned by his Remarks upon a Pamphlet Entitled The Enthusiasm of Methodists and Papists Compared*, London, 1750, p.6.

13. Curnock, *Journal*, Vol. 2, 1911, 319.

14. *GWP2*, 23.

15. Dallimore, *Whitefield*, 233; cf. Evans, *Rowland*, Chapter 8.

16. F. A. Cavenagh, *The Life and Work of Griffith Jones of Llanddowror*, Cardiff, 1930, 12; Edward Morgan, *Letters of the Rev. Griffith Jones*, London, 1832, 86-7.

17. E. Morgan, *Ministerial Records; or Brief Accounts of the Great Progress of Religion under ... the Rev. D. Rowlands, of Llangeitho...*, London, 1840, 38-9.

18. Richard Bennett, *Methodistiaeth Trefaldwyn Uchaf*, Y Bala, 1929, 14; *A Brief Account of ... Howell Harris*, 113.

19. *Account of the Progress of the Gospel*, Vol. II. No 2, 27, 28, 29.

20. Roberts, *Letters (1742-1747)*, 68, 69; GMR1, 84.

21. Theo, 58, from 'The Preface' to the work, dated 1764.

22. Tyerman, *Whitefield*, Vol. 1, 318, 319.

23. CH. lii.12, John Harris's account of the societies in Pembrokeshire, September 1743.

24. D. E. Jenkins, *Calvinistic Methodist Holy Orders*, Carnarvon, 1911, 100. For the issue of identity, see Eifion Evans, 'The Society People, Developing a Methodist Mind', CH. 29-30 (2005-06), 25-42.

25. HHD, 13-15 February, 1741; Bennett, *Trefaldwyn Uchaf*, 34-5.

26. See Evans, *Rowland*, Chapter 17; Evans, *Fire*, Chapter 7.

27. Its claim to 'classic' status is echoed by Dr D. M. Lloyd-Jones in his 'Introduction' to the work.

28. For conversion narratives see Michael J. Crawford, *Seasons of Grace: Colonial New England's Revival Tradition in Its British Context*, New York and Oxford, 1991, Chapter 9; D. Bruce Hindmarsh, *The Evangelical Conversion Narrative*, Oxford, 2005; and David Ceri Jones, 'Narratives of Conversion in English Calvinistic Methodism', in Kate Cooper and Jeremy Gregory (eds), *Revival and Resurgence in Christian History*, Studies in Church History, 44, Woodbridge, 2008, 128-41.

6. 'Association no separaton'

Pages 43-52

1. *Evangelical Magazine*, 1826, 469-70. This is also in Tyerman, *Whitefield*, Vol. 1, 541-2; and D. E. Jenkins, *Holy Orders*, 52-4.

2. Tyerman, *Whitefield*, Vol. 2, 50; Cyn1, 520-28. Black and white photographs of the original oil painting by Hugh Williams are to be found in Dallimore, *Whitefield*, Volume 2, between pages 144 and 145; and in CH. 6: 62 and 21: 28. Articles on Watford are in CH. xxviii. 22-33; 34-40; and xxxix. 55-62. The figures portrayed are, from left to right, John Cennick, Joseph Humphreys, John Powell, William Williams, George Whitefield, Daniel Rowland and Howel Harris. The last four show resemblance to known portraits. Two other clergymen were present, Howel Davies and Thomas Lewis; and nine other laymen: Thomas Adams, Herbert Jenkins, James Beaumont, Thomas James, Morgan John Lewis, John Jones, Richard Tibbott, William Richard and Thomas Lewis. Whitefield, Humphreys, Cennick and Adams represented the work in England. For an account of *Joseph Humphreys's Experience of the work of grace upon his heart*, which appeared in 1742, see D. Bruce Hindmarsh, *The Evangelical Conversion Narrative*, Oxford, 2008, 80-7.

3. See article by Gomer M. Roberts in CH. xxxviii.15-20, 'Llyfrau o Waith Awduron Methodistaidd, 1739-1753'; and his chapter, 'Llenydda a Chyhoeddi 1737-62', in *Hanes Methodistiaeth*, Cyf. 1. As early as November 1740 Harris was 'in Miles Harry's [house], consulting about printing brother [William] Seward's *Journal* in Welsh.' *Bathafarn*, 4 (1949), 55. For Harry see *DWB*; for Seward see *ODNB*. Seward's English *Journal* was published in 1740, but it

does not appear that a Welsh translation was published.

4. *HMGC*1, 407-9. For John Lewis (*fl.* 1728-55), see *DWB*. See also David Ceri Jones, 'John Lewis and the promotion of the international evangelical revival, 1735-56', in Dyfed Wyn Roberts (ed.), *Revival, Renewal and the Holy Spirit*, Milton Keynes, 2009, 13-26.

5. TL. 713, and cf. TL. 715, Harris to Richard Jenkins, 'Sent Erskine's sermons via Thomas James.' See *Cal*, 110.

6. GMR1, 82-3. The references to 'pilgrims' (a familiar image with Williams), to 'a sight of His love', and to the mortification of 'self', lend credence to Gomer Roberts's conclusion that 'without doubt' the letter is from Williams.

7. TL. 470 from *The Weekly History*, No. 46; The letter was to Elizabeth Paul, a member of the Tabernacle Society in London. See Cal. 75; Jones, *Glorious Work*, 254.

8. Roberts, *Hanes Methodistiaeth*, Cyf.1, 408-09; Jones, *Glorious Work*, 83; CH. xxxv (TMS2, 40).

9. CH. xlviii. 37; xlix. 24.

10. Kilsby, 510, *Pantheologia: sef Hanes Holl Grefyddau'r Byd...*, 'Rhagymadrodd'.

11. CH. li. 28.

12. Quoted in Richard Green, *Anti-Methodist Publications Issued During the Eighteenth Century*, London, 1902, 56, 100.

13. CH. xxxv. 54.

14. Tyerman, *Wesley*, Vol. 1, 277. G. C. B. Davies concludes on this issue between the Wesley brothers and Walker: 'The keystone of the whole matter rested on the advisability or otherwise of the appointment of lay preachers. Had these been withdrawn, small difficulty would have arisen. But to preserve such an organization within the framework of the Church of England was an impossibility.' (*The Early Cornish Evangelicals 1735-60: A Study of Walker of Truro and Others,* London, 1951, 129.)

15. Tyerman, *Wesley*, Vol. 1, 277.

16. Its full title was *The preacher sent: or, A vindication of the liberty of publick preaching, by some men not ordained. In answer to two books: 1. Jus divinum ministerii euengelici. By the Provincial Assembly of London. 2. Vindiciae ministerii euangelici. By Mr. John Collings of Norwich.   Published by Iohn Martin, minister of the Gospel at Edgfield in Norfolk. Sam. Petto, minister of the Gospel at Sand-croft in Suffolk. Frederick Woodal, minister of the Gospel at Woodbridge in Suffolk*, London, 1658. The book's Puritan authors were Samuel Petto, John Martin, and Frederick Woodall. Matthew Poole, the Puritan commentator published a response to this in the same year, *Quo warranto; or, A moderate enquiry into the vvarrantablenesse of the preaching of gifted and unordained persons ... at the desire and appointment of the Provinciall Assembly of London.* The Presbyterian Poole maintained that ordination was necessary for right discipline and order, with ordination

authorised by, and providing benefit to, multiple congregations. See CH. 23 (1999), 44, 57; GMR1, 57, 68.

17. Tyerman, *Whitefield*, Vol.1, 291-3; Evans, *Rowland*, 96-7. Albert M. Lyles reckoned that 'of 200 anti-Methodist publications ... issued during 1739 and 1740, 154 were aimed at Whitefield'; *Methodism Mocked*, London, 1960, p.127. See also Evans, *Fire*, Chapter 8.

18. John Thickens, *Howel Harris yn Llundain*, Caernarfon [1934], 268; Jones, Glorious Work, 170. See also Griffith T. Roberts, *Dadleuon Methodistiaeth Gynnar*, Abertawe, 1970, Pennod (Chapter) II, 'Moddion Gras'; the anonymous letter, TL 2790, dated July 1740 which refutes the Moravian practice of 'stillness'; W. R. Ward, *The Protestant Evangelical Awakening*, Cambridge, 1996, 57ff, for the 'Origins of Pietism'; and F. Ernest Stoeffler, *The Rise of Evangelical Pietism*, Leiden, 1971, 180-246, 'The Advent of Lutheran Pietism'; and Eifion Evans, 'Pietism and Welsh Calvinistic Methodism', CH. 25 (2001), 7-17. For Moravianism see Clifford W. Towlson, *Moravian and Methodist: Relationships and Influences in the Eighteenth Century*, London, 1957; and Colin J. Podmore, *The Moravian Church in England*, 1728-1760, Oxford, 1998.

19. *A Select Collection of Letters of the late Reverend George Whitefield*, Vol.1, London, 1772, 87, 90. See Dallimore, *Whitefield*, Vol.1, Chapter 24, 'The Doctrines of Grace'.

20. Bennett, *Dawn of Revival*, 114, 134-5; CH. lx. 12.

21. The Harris letter to Wesley is in CH. xlii. 139-47. *Bathafarn*, 6 (1951), 52, 54-7.

22. Beynon, *Visits to London*, 119; CH. vii. 33, 34. See also Frank Baker, *John Wesley and the Church of England*, London, 1970, 126-8.

23. The early hymn on 'election' is in Welsh and appears in NLW MS 18435B, the Richard Tibbott MS. For the hymn, see CH 33 (2009), 40. Williams's hymn is in a later edition of *Aleluia*, and in Cyn2, 82. See also David Ceri Jones, '"The Lord did give me a particular honour to make [me] a peacemaker": Howel Harris, John Wesley and Methodist infighting, 1739-1750', in *Bulletin of the John Rylands University Library of Manchester*, 85, Nos. 2 and 3 (Summer and Autumn, 2003), 73-98; and *idem.*, '"We are of Calvinistical principles": How Calvinist was early Calvinistic Methodism?', *The Welsh Journal of Religious History*, 4 (2009), 37-54.

24. Roberts, *Hanes Methodistiaeth*, Cyf. 1, 194-5; Lloyd, *Carmarthenshire*, Vol. II, 195-6; cf. Eifion Evans, 'Daniel Rowland a Methodistiaeth Gynnar Sir Gaerfyrddin', CH. xlviii. 57-65; xlix. 2-9.

25. *Trysorfa*, 446.

26. CH. iii. 67; GMR1, 86. For Harris, Gambold and Sparks see Roberts, *Hanes Methodistiaeth*, Cyf. 1, 265-9.

27. CH. xxvii. 1, 5, 6; cf. *ib*. 105.

7. 'Preaching, persecution and prayer'
Pages 53-62

1. CH. xxv. 13, 99; Roberts, *Hanes Methodistiaeth*, Cyf. 2, 479; CH. xlviii. 74; 1. 45, 49. The most famous and enduring catechism produced by a Welsh Calvinistic Methodist, Thomas Charles, was *Hyfforddwr, yn Egwyddorion y Grefydd Gristionogol*, which first appeared in 1807. Its English translation, *The Christian Instructor; or Catechism on the Principles of the Christian Religion* was published in 1867.

2. Paul S. Seaver, *The Puritan Lectureships: The Politics of Religious Dissent, 1560-1662*, Stanford, California, 1970, 171, 100-1.

3. Gomer Morgan Roberts, *Bywyd a Gwaith Peter Williams*, Caerdydd, 1943, 26; Roberts, *Hanes Methodistiaeth*, Cyf. 1, 440, 441; Thomas Richards, *A History of the Puritan Movement in Wales*, London, 1920, 151-8; Geoffrey F. Nuttall, *The Welsh Saints 1640-1660*, Cardiff, 1957, 36; Goronwy Wyn Owen, *Cewri'r Cyfamod: Y Piwritaniaid Cymreig 1630-1660*, Caernarfon, 2008, 59-61.

4. CH. xix.105-06.

5. GMR1, 54, 71.

6. Cyn1, 649-50.

7. Tyerman, *Whitefield*, Vol. 2, 51-2; Others, too were persecuted about this time, and the Methodists seriously considered seeking legal protection, see Roberts, Letters (1742-1747), 84. See also John Walsh, 'Methodism and the Mob in the eighteenth century', in G. D. Cuming and D. Baker (eds), *Popular Belief and Practice*, Studies in Church History, 8, Cambridge, 1972, 215-27.

8 CH. xxvii. 108-09; TL. 1001 and TL.1003 (both dated 8 October); Cal.157, 158; *Y Lladmerydd*, 1889, 113-14; CH. i. 23.

9. *Gwaith Robert Jones, Rhos Lan*, Gwrecsam, 1898, 57.

10. Charles Wesley had a similar experience at Devizes, commenting in the face of imminent danger, 'If ever we felt faith, it was now.' See Gary Best, *Charles Wesley: A Biography*, Peterborough, 2006, 192.

11. Morgan, 21-2; Hughes, *Methodistiaeth Cymru*, Cyf. 2, 446-7.

12. Roberts, *Letters* (1742-1747), 124-5; Dallimore, *Whitefield*, Vol. 2, 165, 170-2.

13. Best, *Charles Wesley*, 180; Curnock, *Journal*, Vol. 2, 123.

14. [A. C. H. Seymour], *The Life and Times of Selina Countess of Huntingdon*, Volume 1, London, 1844, 67-8. Boyd Stanley Schlenther's opposite view is unconvincing (*Queen of the Methodists: The Countess of Huntingdon and the Eighteenth-Century Crisis of Faith and Society*, Durham, 1997, 27-30). Lady Huntingdon's misgivings about the King were moral, not political, and the whole thrust of Methodist conviction, to which she subscribed, was unequivocally loyalist. cf. Edwin Welch, *Spiritual Pilgrim: A Reassessment of the Life of the Countess of Huntingdon*, Cardiff, 1995, 62, 'Neither the Earl nor the Countess was ever suspected of Jacobite sentiments, but it must have been a difficult time.'

15. CH. xx. 132-3.

16. CH. l. 45.

17. John Owen, *Hanes Bywyd a Gweinidogaeth y Parchedig Daniel Rowlands*, Caerlleon, 1814, 83.

18. Gomer Morgan Roberts, Selected *Trevecka Letters (1747-1794)*, Caernarvon, 1962, 21.

19. GMR1, 163.

20. CH. xxv (TMS1, 417).

21. CH. xix (TMS1, 266).

22. CH. l. 27-8. See George M. Marsden, *Jonathan Edwards: A Life*, New Haven, 2003, 334-9.

23. Edwards, Works, Volume 5, *Apocalyptic Writings*, Stephen J. Stein (ed), 309-436. Stein notes that 'Edwards became an organizer of the movement in America', but that it was 'far from successful' (pp. 38, 48). Edwards's *Some Thoughts Concerning the Present Revival in New England*, published in 1742, is found in Edwards, Works, Volume 4, 365-430. My article, 'A Concert for Prayer: Consolidating the Great Awakening', is to appear in CH. 34 (2010).

24. It appears in Volume III of his *Works*, published at London in 1731, p. 123.

25. Edinburgh, p. 37.

26. See John Macinnes, *The Evangelical Movement in the Highlands of Scotland 1688* to 1800, Aberdeen, 1951, 157, 158, 160.

27. *Traethawd i brofi ac i gymmell ar yr holl Eglwysi y Ddyletswydd Fawr Efangylaidd o Weddïo dros Weinidogion, Ps. 122: 6,7,8,9; Esa. 62:1; Ps. 132: 15,16; 1 Thes. 5:25*, ('An essay to prove and urge on all the Churches the Great Evangelical Obligation to Pray for Ministers'), Llundain, 1733, iv.

28. Arthur Fawcett, *The Cambuslang Revival*, London, 1971, 223, 233.

29. GMR1, 200.

30. Cyn2, 213 (Hymn CCCCLII, 1 and 2).

8. 'The fragrance of the Bridegroom's robes'

Pages 63-72

1. *Trysorfa*, 447.

2. Bennett, *Trefaldwyn Uchaf*, 80; CH. xvii.97; xxxi. 21.

3. Goronwy P. Owen (gol.), *Atgofion John Evans y Bala*, Caernarfon, 1997, 106.

4. Cyn2, 655-8; for John Calvin's 'wonderful exchange', see *Institutes*, IV. xvii. 2.

5. Cyn2, 664.

6. TL 1099, Anne Williams to Harris, 1 Feb 1744; Cal,173; Bennett, *Trefaldwyn Uchaf*, 80.

7. Jones and Morgan, *Fathers*, Vol.1, 400.

8. GMR1, 73.

9. GMR1, 74; Jones and Morgan, Fathers, Vol. 1, 413-14; HHD 115b for Thursday, 3 January 1745.

10. *Christian History*, VIII (1745), No. 1, 61.

11. The first part was published by John Morgan, at Carmarthen. See GMR2, 50-6. Whitefield may have suggested Farley to Williams, since his *Nature and Necessity of Society* of 1737 was printed by Samuel and Felix Farley. Felix died in 1753 and the name of his wife, Elizabeth, appears as the printer of *Hosanna i Fab Dafydd* in 1754. The family published various newspapers and journals in the Bristol area. See *http://www.devon.gov.uk/library/locstudy/bookhist/devexf.html*

12. Thomas Jackson (ed.), *Journal of Charles Wesley*, Volume 1, London, 1849, 455; D. Young, *The Origin and History of Methodism in Wales and the Borders*, London, 1893, p.280; A. H. Williams, 'Theophilus Evans, Chaplain', in the *National Library of Wales Journal*, 16 (1969-70), 264-271; id., *Bathafarn*, xxiv, 16-37; Arnold A. Dallimore, *A Heart Set Free: the Life of Charles Wesley*, Durham, 1988, 149-159; Curnock, Journal, Vol. 3, 1912, 333-6; GMR1, 78-9; Bennett, *Trefaldwyn Uchaf*, 127, 130.

(13) *GWP2*, xxi. The passage dealing with the Prodigal Son is found on pp. 68-77.

14. Theo, Chapter 2 – 6, and pp. 74-5, 93.

15. *The Experience Meeting*, 25-29.

16. Beynon, *Visits to London*, 207; cf. Tyerman, *Whitefield*, Vol. 2, 189.

17. CH. xlviii. 34, 74.

18. *Whitefield Journals*, 220, 223, 302; *Memoirs of the late Reverend George Whitefield...* compiled by ... John Gillies ... Revised ... by John Jones, London, 1811, p. 41.

19. Beynon, *Visits to London*,102; Tom Beynon (ed.), *Howel Harris Reformer and Soldier* (1714-1773), Caernarvon, 1958, 133; Beynon, *Visits to Pembrokeshire*, 96.

20. Cyn1, 508.

21. Jones and Morgan, *Fathers,* Vol.1, 666. This is in a chapter that deals with Peter Williams.

9. 'Geneva jigs and a Welsh *Aleluja*'
Pages 73-81

1. GMR1, 19-20; 2, 41. Both books were published in London, the first, *Britain's remembrancer: containing a narration of the plague lately past; a declaration of the mischiefs present; and a prediction of iudgments to come; (if repentance prevent not.) It is dedicated (for the glory of God) to posteritie; and, to these times (if they please) in 1628; and the second, Halelviah, or, Britans [sic] second remembrancer bringing to remembrance (in praisefull and poenitentiall hymns, spirituall songs, and morall-odes) meditations, advancing the glory of God, in practise of pietie and vertue: and applyed to easie tunes to be sung in families &c*, in1641. For Wither (1588-1667) see *ODNB*.

2. Cyn1, 525.

3. *A Brief Account of the Life of Howell Harris, Esq.*, 22-4; CH. iii (TMS. i. 69-70). Parishes often made their own arrangements to teach Psalm singing. In April 1774, for example, 'the inhabitants' of Llandrillo-yn-Rhos agreed to pay John Thomas 'Seven Pounds Seven Shillings for teaching the Parishioners that has a mind to sing Psalms from this time to All Saints every Saturday Eve and Sundays'. (R. D. Griffith, *Hanes Canu Cynulleidfaol Cymru*, Caerdydd, 1948, 39.) GMR2, 11-18 gives a synopsis of psalm-singing in Wales up to 1736.

4. From the time of James I the Charter of the Parish Clerks' Company required that 'every person that is chosen Clerk of a Parish shall first give sufficient proof of his abilities to sing at least the tunes which are used in parish Churches.' (Percy A. Scholes, *The Puritans and Music in England and New England*, London, 1934, 262.) Bishop Edmund Gibson of London in 1742 in his *Directions Given to the Clergy* gave fuller directions for a 'Course of Singing Psalms' and recommended that the youth of a parish be instructed in psalmody. (Maurice Frost, Historical Companion to *Hymns Ancient and Modern*, London, 1962, 89.)

5. *Crynodeb y Salmau Canu*, 1774 (Yr Ail Argraffiad), iii-iv. This was first published in 1743. The Kyffin brothers, Morris and Edward, had blazed the trail for Prys's labours; Morris with his appeal in 1594 that Psalms for singing should be available 'in every land which had been reformed on receiving the bright light of the Gospel ... which would be for their delight and comfort', and Edward by publishing in 1603 the first 13 Psalms in metre. (*Deffyniad ffydd Eglwys Loegr ...drwy waith M. Kyffin*, 'Annerch at yr howddgar ddarlleydd Cristnogawl'; *Rhan o Psalmae Dafydd Brophwyd yw Canu ar ôl y dôn arfaredig yn Eglwys Loegr.*) For Edmund Prys (1544-1623), Morris Kyffin (c. 1555-1598), and Edward Kyffin (c. 1558-1603), see *DWB*.

6. John Calvin, Commentary on the Psalms, 'The Author's Preface' in *Calvin's Commentaries*, Volume IV, Grand Rapids, Michigan, 1989, xxxvii. The quotation is from W. Stanford Reid, 'The Battle Hymns of the Lord: Calvinist Psalmody of the Sixteenth Century', in Carl S. Meyer (ed.), *Sixteenth Century Essays and Studies*, Saint Louis, Missouri, 1971, 39. In his *Institutes*, III. xx. 32. Calvin adds, 'Yet we should be very careful that our ears be not more attentive to the melody than our minds to the spiritual meaning of the words." At Geneva in 1537 Calvin and William Farel "presented to the Council a scheme for the organization of the Church, in which he suggested the introduction of singing into divine service, with the object of infusing into it more warmth and life.'(*The Musical Times*, 1 July 1881, p.1.)

7. W. Stanford Reid, 'Battle Hymns'. 42-7.

8. G. R. Woodward, 'The Genevan Psalter of 1562; Set in Four-part Harmony by Claude Goudimel, in 1565', in *Proceedings of the Musical Association*, 44 (1918), 184; Hastings Robinson (ed.), *Zurich Letters*, Cambridge, Vol. 1 (1842), 71 (Letter of John Jewel to Peter Martyr, 5 March 1560). In his *Singing Psalmes a Gospel Ordinance* of 1647, John Cotton speaks of Roman Catholics

calling the metrical Psalms 'Geneva Gigs' (p.61).

9. See Stanley Sadie (ed.), *The New Grove Dictionary of Music and Musicians*, London, Second Edition, 2001, art. 'Anglican and Episcopalian Music'; 'Calvin, Jean'; 'Elizabeth I'; 'Protestant'; 'Psalms, metrical'; 'Reformed and Presbyterian Church Music'.

10. J. M. Lloyd-Thomas (ed.), *The Autobiography of Richard Baxter*, London, 1931, 79.

11. Michael R. Watts, *The Dissenters From the Reformation to the French Revolution*, Oxford, 1999, 312-13. For Watts's contribution to hymnody, see Louis F. Benson, *The English Hymn: Its Development and Use in Worship*, London, 1915, Chapters III and IV; Madeleine Forell Marshall and Janet Todd, *English Congregational Hymns in the Eighteenth Century*, Lexington, Kentucky, 1982, Chapter II; J. R. Watson, *The English Hymn: A Critical and Historical Study*, Oxford, 1999, Chapter 7.

12. R. Tudur Jones, *Congregationalism in England 1662-1962*, 224.

13. GMR. ii. 27. For Owen and Baddy, see *DWB*.

14. 'Emynau'r Piwritaniaid', *Bwletin Cymdeithas Emynau Cymru 3* (1999), 236.

15. CH. xiv. 7 – 8. A hymn written by Dorothy Jones appears in one of the exhorter, Richard Tibbott's manuscripts, see GMR2, 34, and CH. 33 (2009), 26-7.

16. Benson, *The English Hymn*, 235, 236.

17. *The Weekly History*, No. 9, p.4.

18. *Account of the Progress of the Gospel*, No.III, Vol.II: 61-74.

19. CH. iii. 44.

20. GMR2, 32-40; Goronwy Prys Owen, 'Canu'r Seiadau Cynnar', CH. 33 (2009), 21-5; CH. xxviii. 122.

21. See GMR2, 38-40. This document is NLW MS 78A. On the inside front cover, 'William Williams's Book' is inscribed in Pantycelyn's handwriting after two inscriptions by Rowland; on the inside back cover in Pantycelyn's writing, there appears the date 'March: 25: 1745', and underneath it the name 'Llanwrtyd', with a few financial accounts.

22. E. Wyn James, 'Salmau, a hymnau, ac odlau ysbrydol: brasolwg ar y cefndir emynyddol i waith Williams Pantycelyn', *Llên* Cymru, 17 (1993), 217, quoting Griffith, *Canu Cynulleidfaol*. A survey of early Nonconformist hymnology is given by Garfield H. Hughes, 'Emynyddiaeth Gynnar yr Ymneilltuwyr', in *Llên Cymru*, 2 (1953), 135-46.

23. *GWP2*, 16.

24. *Trysorfa*, 454.

10. 'Nine hymns for a penny'
Pages 82-91

1. The book was a translation by Morgan of *John Bunyan's Last Sermon*.

Originally published in 1689, the text was John 1:13, and in it Bunyan sets out the consequences of the new birth, and urges self-examination. It is found in Offor, *John Bunyan*, Volume Second, 755-8. For John Morgan, see GMR2, 50-4.

2. GMR2, 256; TC1, 146.

3. GMR2, 247-64 lists Williams's printed works in chronological order. See also J. H. Davies, *Rhestr o Lyfrau gan y Parch. William Williams Pantycelyn a Argraffwyd rhwng 1744 a 1800*, Caerfyrddin, 1918. Morris Davies wrote a series of article on Williams's hymnology in the *Traethodydd*, 1870, 63-73, 208-21; 389-417; and a 'diplomatic printing' of all six parts of Aleluja with introductory notes by Llewelyn Jones appeared in 1926, published at Liverpool. The literature on Williams's hymns is extensive, and reference will be made to some of these at the appropriate place.

4. R. Brinley Jones, Songs of Praises: *English Hymns and Elegies of William Williams Pantycelyn* 171-1791, was published at Felinfach in 1991. Translations of 76 of the Welsh hymns were issued by R. R. Williams under the title *Popular Hymns of Pantycelyn*, Liverpool, Brython Press, n.d.

5. Daniel Sedgwick (ed.), *Hosannah to the Son of David ... & Gloria in Excelsis ...With an Introductory Sketch by E. Morgan*, London, 1859, x; D. E. Jenkins, *The Life of the Rev. Thomas Charles*, Vol. II, 1908, 186.

6. Preface to *Aleluia*, Yr Ail Ran, 1745.

7. Cyn2, 424; 427,431: *Gloria in Excelsis*, LXXVI (2); LXXXVI (3); XCVII (2).

8. Jenkins, *Thomas Charles*, II, 52.

9. Cyn2, 231; 397; 399; 412: *Ffarwel Weledig* CCCCXCIX, (tr. by Bobi Jones); *Hosannah* IX (1); *Hosannah* XVI (1); Hosanna XLIX (5).

10. Evans, *Daniel Rowland*, 299-300.

11. Evans, *Daniel Rowland*, 300.

12. Theo, 33, from Cyn2, 128-9; see GMR2, 67.

13. Cyn2, 128; GMR2, 72.

14. The first part of *Ffarwel Weledig* appeared in 1763, a second in 1766, and a third part in 1769.

15. 'Williams Pantycelyn: Y Grafel a'r Gwaed', CH. 14-15 (1990/91), 57, 60.

16. '"Salmau, a Hymnau, ac Odlau Ysbrydol": Brasolwg ar y Cefndir Emynyddol i Waith Williams Pantycelyn', *Llên Cymru*, Cyf. 17, Rhifyn 3 a 4 (Ion-Gorff, 1993), 225.

17. Cf. Henry D. Rack, *Reasonable Enthusiast: John Wesley and the Rise of Methodism*, Third edition, Peterborough, 2002, 415: 'The earliest printed Methodist tune-book, the "Foundery Collection" of 1742, contained thirty-six tunes, mostly psalm settings and German chorales, with one secular piece from a Handel opera. Later collections included some contemporary hymn tunes ... There are also persistent stories that the Methodists ... were liable to adapt popular folk tunes, ballads and operatic hits, and a few appear in published collections.' See also Dallimore, Charles Wesley, 214: 'Charles and John turned

first to certain of the music used in the church for the singing of the metrical Psalms … Secondly, they turned to the works of the masters …Purcell … Haydn … Handel … third … the tunes used by the Moravians.' It is claimed that 'Handel wrote three hymn-tunes for the Methodists, of which one (*Gopsal*, to 'Rejoice, the Lord is King') is still in frequent use.' (Percy A. Scholes, *The Oxford Companion to Music*, Oxford, 1938, 451; and cf. James T. Lightwood, *The Music of the Methodist Hymn-Book*, London, 1938, 177-8.)

18. *Hanes Canu Cynulleidfaol Cymru*, Caerdydd, 1948, 30, 116. The discussion on tunes used by Williams is found on pp.27-37, and 116-29. Glyn Tegai Hughes reckons that Williams 'introduced some twenty six or twenty seven new measures into Welsh.' (*Williams Pantycelyn*, Cardiff, 1983, 79-80.)

19. Gomer M. Roberts, 'Dylanwad Rhai o Fethodistiaid Lloegr ar Emynau a Mesurau Pantcelyn (sic)', *Bathafarn*, 2 (1947), 56-62; GMR2, 102, where Roberts goes on to deal with Williams's metres and tunes, pp. 103-24; Alan Luff, *Welsh Hymns and Their Tunes*, London, 1990, 136-40.

20. John Williams acknowledged his indebtedness to the tune names listed in John Rippon's *A selection of hymns from the best authors, including a great number of originals: intended to be an appendix to Dr. Watts's Psalms and hymns*, the first edition of which appeared in London in 1787, with a tenth edition in 1800.

11. 'The eyes of speech'
Pages 92-103

1. The quotation is from one of five articles, 'Dylanwad y Beibl ar Emynau Pantycelyn', in *Yr Eurgrawn*, 146 (1954), 14-18; 35-42; 59-62; 88-92;121-3, and is found on p. 41.

2. Evans, Fire, 155; GWP1, 121, 140; Glyn Tegai Hughes, *Williams Pantycelyn*, 86-9.

3. Beynon, *Reformer and Soldier*, 136; see Eifion Evans, 'The Evangelical Spirituality of Howel Harris', in *Foundations*, 55 (Spring 2006), 29; cf. J. R. Watson, *The English Hymn* 233-43, for the book's influence on Charles Wesley's hymns.

4. 'Pantycelyn y Diwinydd', Diwinyddiaeth, XLII (1991), 89.

5. A discussion of Williams's debt to English sources is found in Llewelyn Jones, *Aleluia gan y Parch. William Williams, Pant y celyn*, Lerpwl, 1926, xxx – xliii; Gomer M. Roberts, 'Dylanwad', *Bathafarn*, 2 (1947), 56; Glyn M. Ashton, 'Cerdd Dafod Pantycelyn', *Llên Cymru*, 7 (1962-63), 62-91; GMR2, 124-35.

6. Kathryn Jenkins, 'Motiffau Emynau Pantycelyn', yn Derec Llwyd Morgan (gol.), *Meddwl a Dychymyg Williams Pantycelyn*, Llandysul, 1991, 114.

7. Tracts… Volume Second, Edinburgh, 1849, 512, 513. Calvin himself used figurative terms, using the word 'abyss' and 'labyrinth', for example, to convey horror, anxiety and confusion. See William J. Bousma, John Calvin: *A*

Sixteenth-Century Portrait, Oxford, 1988, 45-7.

8. Henri Talon, *John Bunyan: The Man and his Works*, Cambridge, MA., 1951, 182.

9. For Williams's Library see CMA Trefeca 752. Taylor's work was reprinted at Trefeca in 1766. For these authors see *ODNB*.

10. For biblical symbolism see Leland Ryken, James C. Wilhoit, Temper Longman III (eds), Dictionary of Biblical Imagery, Leicester, 1998. Among those used by Williams, see the entries for the following: 'Army', 'Character types', 'Darkness', 'Disease and healing', 'Divine warrior', 'Egypt', 'Fire', 'Jordan river', 'Lamb', 'Lion', 'Morning', 'Pearl', 'Pharaoh', 'Pilgrim', 'Promised land', 'Rock', 'Serpent', 'Treasure', 'Wilderness', and 'Wind'.

11. See, for example, Hughes, *Williams Pantycelyn*, 86-106; id. 'Delweddau Pantycelyn', *Adroddiad Cyfarfod Caerdydd Mehefin* 11-13, 1984, *Undeb yr Annibynwyr Cymraeg*, Abertawe, 1984, 75-79; T. J. Morgan, 'Iaith ffigurol Emynau Pantycelyn', *Ysgrifau Beirniadol*, VI, Dinbych, 1971, 98-114.

12. 'Motiffau Emynau Pantycelyn', Derec Llwyd Morgan (gol.), *Meddwl a Dychymyg Williams Pantycelyn*, 115.

13. *The English Hymn*, 275.

14. Cyn2, 407; 408; 417; 431; 434. Hymns referring to Exodus 14:2 are found in Cyn2, 172 and 325.

15. 'Rhyfel a Gorfoledd yng ngwaith William Williams Pantycelyn', in J. E. Wynne Davies, *Gwanwyn Duw: Diwygwyr a Diwygiadau*, 154.

16. Cyn2, 398; 371.

17. Theo, 91.

18. 'Motiffau', 114.

19. Translated by R. R. Williams, in his collection, *Popular Hymns of Pantycelyn*, 31.

20. Cyn2, 41-2.

21. *Commentaries*, Grand Rapids, Michigan, 1989, Vol. XXII, 214.

22. R. M. Jones, *Cyfriniaeth Cymraeg*, Caerdydd, 1994, 119-20.

23. Translated by Graham Stuart Harrison.

24. *GWP*1,172, 173.

25. Cyn2, 431; 322 (translated by Richard Morris Lewis); 416; 397.

12. 'The enjoyment of God'
Pages 104-111

1. CH. xlviii. 32, 33, 34, 41.

2. GMR1, 53; CH. xlix. 22; Beynon, *Visits to Pembrokeshire*, 111-12.

3. Geraint Tudur, *Howell Harris: From Conversion to Separation 1735-1750*, Cardiff, 2000, 168, 189.

4. CH. xx. 133, 134; GMR1, 83-5.

5. GMR1, 39, n.52; CMA Trefeca 2156; Cal, p. 367. Harris's wife died in March 1770 aged 58, and was buried at Talgarth. (CH. xii, December, 1927,

'The Itinerary of Howel Harris, Trevecka for the Years 1753-1773', 43).

6. GMR1, 99.

7. *Trysorfa*, 445-6.

8. GMR1, 194.

9. Cyn1, 446, 447, 448.

10. GMR1, 99, 104.

11. GMR1, Chapter IV, gives details of the family; see also Roberts, *Hanes Methodistiaeth Galfinaidd Cymru*, Cyf. 2, Caernarfon, 1978, 156-7; Maurice Davies, *Coffadwriaeth, neu Hanes Byr o Fywyd a Marwolaeth y Parchedig John Williams, Gynt o Bant-y-celyn*, Pontypool, 1831, 17, 20, 21, 25, 27.

12. GMR1, 86, 128-9; CH. xxvi.95ff; xxxix. 22, 24, 27; xxvii. 101. For Morgan Rhys (1716-1779), see *DWB* and Gomer Morgan Roberts, *Morgan Rhys, Llanfynydd*, Caernarfon, 1951; the quotation is on pages 6-7. For the latter part of his life he lived in Llanfynydd, and is buried there; Cyn1, 550-51.

13. CH. li. 73; lii. 21, 45; liii. 21; liv. 24, 57.

13. 'The roaring wolves of night'

Pages 112-122

1. Roberts, Letters (1742-1747), 163-6.

2. GWP2, 24 (*Ateb Philo-Evangelius*); Cyn2, 424.

3. The Disruption is dealt with in Jones and Morgan, *Fathers*, Vol.1, Chapter 16; GMR1, 123-8; Alun Wyn Owen in Roberts, *Hanes Methodistiaeth*, Cyf. 1, Pennod IX; Evans, *Harris*, Chapter VI; Evans, *Rowland*, Chapter 25; Tudur, *Howell Harris*, Chapters 7 and 8; and by Graham Harrison, 'Howell Harris – Division and Restoration', in *The Voice of God*, The Westminster Conference 2002, 83-102.

4. Bennett, *Trefaldwyn Uchaf*, 86, 90.

5. Roberts, *Letters* (1742-1747), 169.

6. Beynon, *Visits to Pembrokeshire*, 111-12; 128-9; GMR1,77.

7. Jones and Morgan, *Fathers*, 508-9; Tudur, *Howell Harris,* 178.

8. Jones and Morgan, *Fathers*, Vol. 1, 552, 553, 555.

9. Beynon, *Visits to London* 251-2.

10. Cyn1, 493.

11. Tudur, *Howell Harris*, 153.

12. Beynon, *Visits to London*,181.

13. Jones and Morgan, *Fathers*, Vol.1, 506.

14. Bennett, *Trefaldwyn Uchaf*, 210-11.

15. Bennett, *Trefaldwyn Uchaf*, 142-3; Tudur, *Howell Harris*, 182-3.

16. Jones and Morgan, *Fathers*, Vol.1, 508; CH. xlviii. 76-7; TL 1836, Letter of Rice Williams dated 24 December; CH. xli. 34. Evans, *Rowland*, 275-6. See also Geraint Tudur, ' "Like a right arm and pillar": the story of James Beaumont', in Robert Pope (ed.), *Honouring the Past and Shaping the Future: Religious and Biblical Studies in Wales. Essays in Honour of Gareth Lloyd*

Jones, Leominster, 2003, 133-58.

17. A Brief Account of the Life of Howell Harris, p.59. The author was J. Taylor, 'a member of a religious society of the Established Communion', of 'Wotton-under-edge, Gloucester'. Published in 1742, its full title was *A Sling and a Stone; or, The Sword of the Lord and of Gideon, Being a Defence of the All-glorious Trinity, and the eternal Divinity of God the Son ... in answer to a daring pamphlet ... by Ed. Elwall.   The pamphlet in question was, A declaration against all the kings and temporal powers under heaven. ... Also Dagon fallen before the ark of God; Shewing that they have no authority over their subjects in spiritual things*, by the Unitarian, Edward Elwall, the fourth edition of which had appeared in 1741. Taylor refers to the Arian contention that Colossians 2:9, 'For in Him dwelleth all the fulness of the Godhead bodily', 'is to be understood, not of Christ's Person, but his doctrine.' He then asks, 'If by the Son of God, and the *him* here mentioned, is meant only Christ's doctrine, in ch. 1:13, we must read thus, he hath translated us into the kingdom of his doctrine, we have redemption and forgiveness of sins through the blood of a doctrine, v. 14 ...?' The argument required that the blood of Christ, shed on the cross, may be referred to as the blood of God, in the way in which in Acts 20: 28 speaks of 'the church of God, which he hath purchased with his own blood.' (p.89.)

18. *A View of the Kingdom of Christ*, translated by Robert Jones, London, 1878, 182, 184.

19. Beynon, Visits to London, 63-4.

20. CH. xxxvii. 22; cf. Jones and Morgan, *Fathers*, Vol.1, 417.

21. Jones and Morgan, *Fathers*, Vol.1, 422, 424.

22. Morris Davies, *Deuddeg Pregeth...gan y Parchedig Daniel Rowlands*, Dolgellau, 1876, tud. 338. For a discussion of Patripassianism see Herman Bavinck, *The Doctrine of God*, Edinburgh, 1977, pp. 285-96; and in Welsh, John Gwili Jenkins, *Hanfod Duw a Pherson Crist*, Liverpool, 1931, Pennod VI. For an English translation of the document, see Hugh J. Hughes, Life of Howell Harris, the Welsh Reformer, London, 1892, 334-8.

23. Roberts, *Portread,* Pennod IX; TL2821; Beynon, *Visits to Pembrokeshire*, 166; Beynon, *Visits to London*, 235.

24. Beynon, *Visits to London*,14, 17, 234.

25. Cyn1, 586.

26. E. Morgan, *Ministerial Records ...of ...Rowlands*, London, 1840, 46.

27. Edward Morgan, *The Life and Times of Howel Harris*, Esq., Holywell, 220-21.

28. Curnock, *Journal*, Vol. 4, 1913, 432. Details of the Trefeca Family are found in Roberts, *Hanes Methodistiaeth*, Cyf. 1, Pennod (Chapter) X; and in Roberts, *Portread*, Pennod X. Details of his military service are in Roberts, *Portread*, Pennod XI, and in M. H. Jones, 'Howell Harris, Citizen and Patriot', in *Transactions of the Honourable Society of Cymmrodorion*, 1908-09, 1-37. See also Beynon, *Reformer and Soldier*, 58-146.

29. For Peter Williams see Roberts, *Peter Williams*; Jones and Morgan, *Fathers*, Vol. 1, Chapter 18; and *DWB*.

30. Roberts, *Hanes Methodistiaeth*, Cyf. 1, 393. Some of the other verses sent by Charles Wesley are in Morgan, *Howell Harris,* 296, 297. They bear the date 3 March 1755.

31. Roberts, *Hanes Methodistiaeth*, Cyf. 1, 394.Williams's 'Preface' to this work is dated 5 June 1756.

32. Curnock, *Journal*, Vol. 3, 153; *Cal.* 366.

14. 'Faint, and yet pursuing'
Pages 123-130

1. *Select Letters*, (1747-1794), 230,247, 252, 258, 261, 262, 264, 265. For Whitefield's ministry in Wales, see Evans, *Fire*, Chapter 6.

2. *Select Letters*, (1747-1794), 373.

3. Seymour, *Life and Times*, Vol.1, 172.

4. *Select Letters*, (1747-1794), 406.

5. *Select Letters*, (1747-1794), 410.

6. *Select Letters*, (1747-1794), 437; *Select Letters,* Vol. 3, 14, 35, 178, 196, 197, 237.

7. Curnock, *Journal*, Vol. 3, 463; Curnock, *Journal*, Vol. 4, 283; J. H. Cooper (ed.), *Extracts from the Journals of John Cennick: Moravian Evangelist,* Glengormley, Co. Antrim, [1996], 58.

8. *Y Drysorfa*, 1931: 393, 394; 1932: 117; 1933: 234; CH. lvii. 16.

9. *Y Drysorfa*, 1931: 433; 1932: 389.

10. Gomer M. Roberts, *Dafydd Jones o Gaeo*, Aberystwyth, 1948, 30, 31, 38; Evan Isaac, *Prif Emynwyr Cymru*, Lerpwl, 1925, 71-91; John Thickens, *Emynau a'u Hawduriaid*, Caernarfon [1945], 33-7. The translated hymn is from Jones's *Difyrrwch i'r Pererinion o Fawl i'r Oen*, 1763.

11. Gomer M. Roberts, *Morgan Rhys, Llanfynydd*, Caernarfon, 1951, 22; Thickens, *Emynau*, 144-151. The translated hymn is from the second edition of Rhys's *Golwg o Ben Nebo*, 1764. See also Rhidian Griffiths, 'Emynau Morgan Rhys', *Bwletin Cymdeithas Emynau Cymru*, Cyf. 3 (2003), 311-17.

12. Isaac, *Prif Emynwyr*, 91-116; Thickens, *Emynau*, 144-51.

13. Isaac, Prif Emynwyr, 137-50; Thickens, Emynau, 125-7; Guto Prys ap Gwynfor, 'John Thomas, Rhaeadr Gwy', *Bwletin Cymdeithas Emynau Cymru*, Cyf. II. 4 (1981), 101-12. The translated hymn is from Thomas's *Caniadau Sion* of 1788.

14. GMR1, 133, and compare Hughes, *Howell Harris*, 359.

15. TL 2472, Cal, 410; GMR1, 134.

16. GMR1, 133, 134, 135, 136; Beynon, *Reformer and Soldier*, 157.

15. 'A View of the Kingdom'

Pages 131-138

1. London, 1595. The work is not paginated, but the quotation appears at D3.
2. *The Welsh Outlook*, 1917, 91.
3. *Trysorfa*, 447-8.
4. This is found in Vol. 1, London, (Tenth edition) 1753, 145, footnote.
5. The titles of Derham's works were: *Astro-theology: or, A Demonstration of the being and attributes of God, from a survey of the heavens; and Physico-theology: or, A Demonstration of the being and attributes of God, from his works of creation*, both of which appeared in several editions during the eighteenth century. For a discussion of similar works see William Powell Jones, *The Rhetoric of Science*, London, 1966.
6. For a discussion of the Puritan use of figurative language see Mason I. Lowance Jnr., *The Language of Canaan: metaphor and Symbol in New England from the Puritans to the Transcendentalists*, Cambridge, MA, 1980, especially Chapter 2 'The Puritan Figural Imagination', and Chapter 4, 'Samuel Mather: Figures, Types, and Allegories'. Glyn Tegai Hughes deals with the subject comprehensively in Derec Llwyd Morgan (gol.), *Meddwl a Dychymyg Williams Pantycelyn*, 'Pantycelyn a'r Piwritaniaid', 31-54.
7. 'Dylanwad *Paradise Lost* Milton ar *Golwg ar Deyrnas Crist* Pantycelyn', *Ysgrifau Beirniadol*, XI, Dinbych, 1979, 165-75.
8. This and the following extracts from the 'Preface' are found in Welsh in Cyn1, 69-73.
9. 'Pantycelyn a Gwyddoniaeth', in J. E. Wynne Davies, *Gwanwyn Duw*, 179. See also his discussion of the work in *The Great Awakening in Wales*, London, 1988, Chapter VII.
10. *The Redemption & Restoration of Man in the Thought of Richard Baxter*, Vancouver, 2003, 262, 251.
11. *GWP*1, 144; Theo, 27; *GWP*1, 147; Evans, *Daniel Rowland*, 302.

16. 'The King must reign'

Pages 139-150

1. *GWP*1, 3.
2. *GWP*1, 5.
3. Robert Jones, *A View of the Kingdom of Christ*, 3 , 7, 8 (altered). Henceforth shortened to RJ.
4. *Scottish Theology in Relation to Church History Since the Reformation*, Edinburgh, 1974, 147. For Thomas Boston (1676-1732) see Nigel M. de S. Cameron (ed.), *Dictionary of Scottish Church History and Theology*, Edinburgh, 1993; and for James Hervey (1714-1758) see *ODNB*.
5. GWP1, 14-15. These footnotes in defence of the doctrine of the Trinity appear in Jones's translation on page 231. The reference to Goodwin is found

in the James Nichol edition of his works, Vol. 4, Edinburgh, 1861, 489.

6. RJ, 15, 16, 20 (altered).

7. RJ, 24, 25, 29, 31 (altered).

8. GWP1, 29; RJ, 32.

9. RJ, 44, 49, 50, 57 (altered).

10. RJ, 94-5, 104 (altered), 108.

11. RJ, 121, 122, 126 (altered).

12. Verses 3 and 4 from the hymn that begins 'Boed fy mywyd oll yn ddiolch', translated by R. R. Williams.

13. *The Complete Works*, Vol. 1, Edinburgh, 1864, 111. Rowland uses the same analogy in his sermon on Hebrews 1: 9, *Eight Sermons upon Practical Subjects*, London, [1774], 212-13.

14. *GWP1*, 121.

15. Cyn2, 116-18; CH. xxxii. 72 and HHD, 244; Cyn1, 70; RJ, 157 (altered). See Joseph A. Galdon, *Typology and Seventeenth-Century Literature*, The Hague, 1975. Catherine Jones lived in Trefethin in Monmouthshire, the same parish as William Read the Apothecary. Converted at 18 years, she enjoyed hymns and elegies as means of grace for the next forty years, and traced the significance of Old Testament types. Above all she enjoyed those preachers who were full of heavenly fire, and her soul feasted on Jesus only and Jesus always (Cyn1, 570).

16. RJ, 163 (altered). See Kilsby, 762-3, 'Gwerthfawrogrwydd y Beibl'; Kathryn Jenkins, 'Williams Pantycelyn a'r Beibl' in *Y Traethodydd*, CXLIII (Gorff. 1988), 159-69.

17. RJ, 168, 169 (altered); Theo, 27; RJ, 182, 192 (altered).

18. GWP1, 152.

19. Evans, *Daniel Rowland*, 302; GWP1, 173.

20. RJ, 219, 188 (altered).

21. Bennett, *Trefaldwyn Uchaf*, 234.

17. 'Sound and sweet and heart-searching'
Pages 151-162

1. Cyn2, 395, 400, 403.

2. The issue dealt with here is also discussed in Evans, *Rowland*, 247-9.

3. CH. 1980, 28; For a discussion of the relationship between the Erskine brothers, Ralph and Ebenezer, and Calvinistic Methodism see Evans, *Daniel Rowland*, 247-52; Tyerman, *George Whitefield*, Vol. 1, 491-518; Dallimore, *Whitefield*, Vol. 2, 83-92. For Ralph Erskine (1685-1752) and Ebenezer Erskine (1680-1754) see *ODNB*; Cameron (ed.), *Dictionary*; and A. R. Macewen, *The Erskines*, Edinburgh, 1900.

4. GMR2, 52; Eiluned Rees, *Libri Walliae*, Item No. 1873.

5. *National Library of Wales Journal*, 1992, 303, 309; Roberts, *Letters* (1742-1747), 166; *Cal*, 133, 169; CMA Trefeca 752 (Williams's Library list.).

6. *Law-death, Gospel-life*, 1724, 10.

7. *Sermons and other Practical Works*, Glasgow, 1765, 50-1.

8. *Law-death, Gospel-life*, 31.

9. *Gospel Sonnets, or Spiritual Songs*, London, 1734, 221, 222, 224: 'the harmony between the Law and the Gospel'.

10. *Law-death, Gospel-life*, 67, 77.

11. CH. xlviii. 76-7; Roberts, *Letters* (1742-1747), 137; Beynon, *Visits to Pembrokeshire*, 102; Jones and Morgan, *Fathers*, 386. Chapter III in the Welsh MA Thesis of 1934 by R. Gele Williams discusses 'Antinomianism and the Methodist Revival, 1735-91'.

12. Beynon, *Visits to London*, 69; cf. Cal, 208, 211 (Letters 1285, 1303, and 1306.)

13. *Select Letters*, Vol. 2, 79-80, Letter to Harris dated 2 May 1745.

14. Roberts, *Letters* (1742-1747), 195; TL 1516 dated 30 August 1746.

15. Jones and Morgan, *Fathers*, Vol. 1, 504, 508; Tudur, *Howell Harris*, 178; Roberts, *Letters* (1742-1747), 160-1; Evans, *Rowland*, 275-6; *Cal*, 259 (Letter 1575); 309 (Letter 1836). For a discussion of 'The Errors of Antinomianism' in its seventeenth-century context see Packer, *Redemption and Restoration*, Chapter 14.

16. Theo, 152. This is found in an extensive footnote in the original (GWP1, 345.)

17. *Hymns, &c. composed on various subjects. With a preface, containing a brief and summary account of the author's experience, and the great things that God hath done for his soul*, London, 1759. xvi-xvii, xviii, xix.

18. Anthony Burgess, *Vindiciae legis, or, A vindication of the morall law and the covenants, from the errours of Papists, Arminians, Socinians, and more especially, Antinomians in XXX lectures*, London,1647, 201.

19. For Popkin see *DWB*; GMR1, 142,ff.; Roberts, *Hanes Methodistiaeth*, Cyf. 1, 395-402. For John Glas (1695-1773) and Robert Sandeman (1718-1771) see Cameron (ed.), *Dictionary*. For a discussion of the controversy, see John Macleod, *Scottish Theology in Relation to Church History since the Reformation*, Edinburgh, 1974, 187-8; Lloyd-Jones, *The Puritans and their Successors,*170-90; Robert Strivens, 'Sandemanianism Then and Now', *The Faith that Saves*, The Westminister Conference 2004, 47-68; and John Howard Smith, *The Perfect Rule of the Christian Religion: A History of Sandemanianism in the Eighteenth Century,* New York, 2009.

20. Cyn1, 263-4.

21. GWP2, 33-4; GMR1, 142, 145, 146; cf. E. Morgan, *Ministerial Records … of … Rowlands*, 97-8; Morgan, 20-1. In the elegy to Rowland, Williams speaks of 'proud Sandemanians, boasting of their power and great light' (Cyn1, 585).

22. Ebenezer Erskine, *The Whole Works*, Vol. I, Falkirk, 1791, 154, 160, 163-9. For a discussion of assurance in the works of the Erskines, see Joel R. Beeke, *Puritan Reformed Spirituality*, Grand Rapids, Michigan, 2004, Chapter 12, 'Ebenezer and Ralph Erskine: Preachers With a Message of Promise', especially pp. 282-4.

18. 'Rude and rustic idols'

Pages 163-171

1. For publishing details of the seven parts see GMR2, 250-1. Roberts deals with the work's contents and reception on pages 221-5. The word, *Pantheologia*, had appeared in the title of a work in 1653, *BEING OBSERVA-TIONS Upon the Fourth, Fifth, Sixth, and Seventh Chapters of St. MATTHEW*, by Thomas White (1607/08-72), q.v. A. G. Matthews, Calamy Revised, Oxford,1988, 525). But it is more likely that he modified the title of a work by Alexander Ross (1591-1654, q.v. *DNB*): OR, *A View of all Religions in the WORLD*, published in London in 1653. A 1775 re-issue of the book states on the title-page that it was 'written in the year 1640'.

2. Kilsby, 635, 765. See E. Wyn James, 'The New Birth of a People': Welsh Language and Identity and the Welsh Methodists, c. 1740-1820', in Robert Pope (ed.), *Religion and National Identity: Wales and Scotland c.1700-2000*, Cardiff, 2001. For Robert Ferrar (d. 1555) and Rawlins White (d. 1555) see *DWB*.

3. Kilsby, 512, 518. Marsden, *Jonathan Edwards*, 486. See Edwards, *Works*, Volume 23, 325-34. See Gerald R. McDermott, *Jonathan Edwards Confronts the Gods: Christian Theology, Enlightenment Religion and Non-Christian Faiths*, New York, 2000.

4. Casas was a Spanish Dominican priest, and Bishop of Chiapas, a southern Mexican State, and the book was published in London in 1583; Hariot's book appeared in 1590; Harris's two volume work, published in London in 1744-48 drew on "above six hundred of the most authentic writers"; Bosman's work was published in 1705.

5. Beynon, *Reformer and Soldier*, 143. Alwyn Prosser examines Williams's use of other sources, Paul Ricaut's *Present State of the Greek and Armenian Churches Anno Christi*, and H. Reland's *Four Treatises Concerning ... Mahometans*, in 'Diddordebau Lleyg Williams Pantycelyn' (The secular interests of Williams Pantycelyn), *Llên Cymru*, 3 (1955), 201-14; See also Cyril G. Williams, 'The Unfeigned Faith and an Eighteenth Century Pantheologia', *Numen*, 15 (1968), 212-17; Glyn Tegai Hughes, *Williams Pantycelyn*, 9-10; Derec Llwyd Morgan, *The Great Awakening in Wales,* 229-34.

6. From an advertisement to the Second Part, found at the end of the 1764 edition of *Môr o Wydr* (Sea of Glass).

7. Advertisements in the 1764 issue of *Môr o Wydr*; and in the 1769 *Ffarwel Weledig*.

8. Kilsby, 510.

9. Kilsby, 561.

10. Kilsby, 510. cf. Derec Llwyd Morgan (gol.), *Meddwl a Dychymyg Williams Pantycelyn,* Llandysul, 1991, 'Pantycelyn a'i Gynulleidfa: yr Emynydd a Mirandus', 82-101.

11. Alwyn Prosser provides evidence of this tension among the Methodists between the knowledge of nature and that of grace in his article 'The secular interests of Williams Pantycelyn', noted above. Bobi Jones, in an article on '"Byd" Pantycelyn' ('Pantycelyn's "World"'), comments that 'Williams distinguishes between the knowledge of the natural man, a science of the flesh or the wisdom of the world, and the true knowledge that comes through the enlightenment of sanctified truth.' *Ysgrifau Beirniadol*, II, Dinbych, 1966, 88.

12. Kilsby, 625; 586, fn. The case of the 'Salzburgers', as they came to be known, was a cause célèbre in religious circles in the 1730s. Over 20,000 in number, Protestant believers were driven from Salzburg by the Roman Catholic Archbishop. Most settled in Prussia, but a considerable number came to Britain, and some eventually settled near Savannah in colonial Georgia, America. Their cause was vigorously argued by the SPCK, Griffith Jones being a strong advocate in Wales. He was instrumental in collecting £120 in one year alone in Carmarthenshire and Pembrokeshire, and by 1735 a total of £33,000 had been received by the Society for their support. (Mary Clement, *Correspondence and Minutes of the S.P.C.K. Relating to Wales 1699-1740*, Cardiff, 1952, 167, n.332; *id., The S.P.C.K. and Wales 1699-1740*, London, 1954, 88-9.) W. R. Ward goes as far as to say that 'The religious shock administered by the Salzburgers' march across Europe was tremendous. The simple knowledge that they were coming inspired "moving awakenings" (*bewegliche Erweckungen*) … There is no doubt that the great Salzburger emigration contributed immensely to the promotion of religious revival.' (*The Protestant Evangelical Awakening,* Cambridge, 1996, 106.)

13. Kilsby, 597-8; See Janet Glenn Gray, The French Huguenots: *Anatomy of Courage*, Grand Rapids, Michigan, 1992, Chapter 3, 'St. Bartholomew's Day – Inquiry into a Massacre'; Menna Prestwich (ed.), *International Calvinism* 1541-1715, Oxford, 1986, 91-100.

14. Kilsby, 591; Tyerman, *George Whitefield*, Volume 2, 325-30.

15. Kilsby, 620.

16. Kilsby, 634.

17. Kilsby, 622.

18. Quoted in GMR2, 223-4.

19. Kilsby, 512.

20. Jones, *View of the Kingdom*, 199.

19. 'A deluge of grace'
Pages 172-182

1. Cyn1, 650.

2. *Ministerial Records … of … the Rev. D. Rowlands of Llangeitho*, London, 1840, 79-80. Robert Jones had made this connection between the appearance of Williams's collection of hymns and the 1762 revival in his 1820 *Drych yr Amseroedd*. Gomer M. Roberts mentions that he saw a copy of the hymn

collection at the National Library of Wales bearing a signature dated 'December the 6, 1761', even though its title page dates it 1762. GMR2, 250.

3. *Ministerial Records ... of ... Rowlands*, 79-80, 92; cf. Jones and Morgan, Fathers, Vol.1, 85, which attributes this account to Nathaniel Rowland. Llangeitho chapel, also known as Capel Gwynfil, had been built in 1760, three years before Rowland was deprived of his curacy. See also Evans, Rowland, 325; Roberts, *Hanes Methodistiaeth*, Cyf. 2, 12.

4. Beynon, *Reformer and Soldier*, 189, 209.

5. *The Experience Meeting*, 8-9; cf. Eryn M. White, '"I will once more shake the heavens": the 1762 Revival in Wales', in Kate Cooper and Jeremy Gregory, *Revival and Resurgence in Christian History*, Woodbridge, 2008, 157.

6. *The Experience Meeting*, 9, 10. For this revival see also Evans, *Rowland*, Chapter 28, '1762: "Blessed Summer's Day"'; and Gruffydd, *Revival and its Fruit*, 19-40.

7. *GWP2*, 16; 179.

8. HHD 240; in part in CH. xxxii. 34-5; Jones and Morgan, Fathers, Vol.1, 607-9. and Beynon, *Reformer and Soldier*, 156-7.

10. Beynon, *Reformer and Soldier*, 156-76.

11. HHD 262; CH. xxix.47; Jones and Morgan, *Fathers*, Vol. 1, 637; Cyn1, 494.

11. *Gwaith Robert Jones, Rhos Lan*, Gwrecsam, 1898, tud. 90; quoted in Gruffydd, *Revival*, 21-2.

12. Owen Thomas, *Cofiant y Parchedig John Jones, Talsarn*, Cyf. 2, Wrexham, (1874), 804.

13. Cyn2, 586-7; Jones and Morgan, *Fathers*, Vol.1, 85 (altered).

14. CH. 2 (1978), 37. Letter of Nathaniel Rowland to the Countess of Huntingdon, dated 25 Sep 1790: '... since I have known the Lord which is now about 28 Years ago.'

15. Jones and Morgan *Fathers*, Vol. 1, 633.

16. *Lloyd's Evening Post and British Chronicle*, 27-29 June 1763, quoted in Gruffydd, *Revival*, 23.

17. G. Eyre Evans (ed.), *Lloyd Letters* (1754-1796), 1908, 52; R. T. Jenkins, *Yng Nghysgod Trefeca*, Caernarfon, 1968, 48.

18. Curnock, *Journal*, Vol. 5, 1914, 27-8; Tyerman, *Wesley*, Vol. 1, 469.

19. Evans, *Rowland*, 318; GWP2, 28. See Peter Howell Williams, 'Jumpers – Blessed Enthusiasts or Bizarre Episodes?', CH. 29-30 (2005-06), 43-72.

20. Cyn1, 626; GMR2, 163-5; Geraint Gruffydd, *Revival*, 33 (translation by Edmund T. Owen).

21. *GWP2*, 29-30.

20. 'A kind of heavenly elysium'

Pages 183-194

1. HHD for 22, 23 February and 27 November 1738.

2. CH. xx. 134. Originally published at Boston, MA., *Some Thoughts Concerning the present Revival of Religion in New England*, has been reprinted by Yale University Press in *The Works of Jonathan Edwards*, Volume 4, 'The Great Awakening', C. G. Goen (ed), 289-530, New Haven and London 1972. According to Goen, 'Introduction', even though the title-page gives 1742 as the date of publication, it did not appear until March the following year. William M'Culloch, the minister of Cambuslang near Glasgow, told Harris in November 1743 that it contained 'many excellent things ... But ... has some things ... that would need to be taken with caution.' Harris does not seem to have read the book until May 1748. See STL1, 119-20; Beynon, *Visits to London*, 184. See also David W. Kling and Douglas Sweeney (eds), *Jonathan Edwards at Home and Abroad: Historical Memories, Cultural Movements and Global Horizons*, Columbia, SC., 2003.

3. Edwards, *Works*, Volume 4, 332.

4. Edwards, *Works*, Volume 4, 341.

5. Edwards, *Works*, Volume 4, 266-7. Williams's two pamphlets are discussed in GMR2, 217-21. See also Evans, *Rowland*, Chapter 8; Gruffydd, *Revival*, 27-31; and Glyn Tegai Hughes, *Williams Pantycelyn*, 53-7. Perceptive analyses of Edwards's teaching on Revival are found in D. M. Lloyd-Jones, *The Puritans: Their Origins and Successors*, 348-72, 'Jonathan Edwards and the Crucial Importance of Revival'; and J. I. Packer, *Among God's Giants*, Eastbourne, 1991, 408-32, 'Jonathan Edwards and Revival'. More comprehensive studies of Edwards are: Marsden, *Jonathan Edwards*, and Iain H. Murray, *Jonathan Edwards: A New Biography*, Edinburgh, 1987. A survey by D. Elwyn Edwards of Edwards's 'influence on the religious life of Wales and England' was published at Caernarfon in 1989 with the title Jonathan Edwards 1703-1758 : *yn cynnwys golwg ar ei ddylanwad ar fywyd crefyddol Cymru a Lloegr*.

6. Eryn Mant White, ' "The World, the Flesh and the Devil" and the Early Methodist Societies of South West Wales', *Transactions of the Honourable Society of Cymmrodorion*, 3 (1997), 50. See also id., '"Myrdd o Wragedd': Merched a'r Diwygiad Methodistaidd', *Llên Cymru*, 20 (1997), 62-74; id., '"Little Female Lambs": Women in the Methodist Societies of Carmarthenshire, 1737-1750', *The Carmarthenshire Antiquary*, XXVII (1991), 31-6; id. 'Women in the Early Methodist Societies in Wales', *The Journal of Welsh Religious History*, 7 (1999), 95-108; id., 'Merched, Methodistiaeth a Llythrennedd yng Nghymru'r Ddeunawfed Ganrif', CH. 33 (2009), 8-20; Kathryn Jenkins, 'Pantycelyn's Women Fact and Fiction: An Assessment, *The Journal of Welsh Religious History*, 7 (199), 77-94.

7. *Experience Meeting*, 11; GWP2, 1; Edwards, *Works*, Volume 22, 412.

8. GWP2, 43-4.

9. GWP2, 165.

10. GWP2, 3.

11. Edwards, *Works*, Volume 2, 200, 204, 205, 206.

12. The views of Perry Miller to this effect are found in his books, *Jonathan*

Notes

Edwards, New York, 1949, and *The New England Mind: The Seventeenth Century*, Cambridge, MA., 1954. These views have been challenged by Paul Helm, 'John Locke and Jonathan Edwards: A Reconsideration', *Journal of the History of Philosophy*, 7 (1969), 51-61; and by Brad Walton in his thesis, '"Formerly Approved and Applauded": The Continuity of Edwards's *Treatise Concerning Religious Affections* with Seventeenth-Century Puritan Analyses of True Piety, Spiritual Sensation and Heart Religion' (Doctor of Theology, Toronto, 1999). Walton's thesis was published by the Edwin Mellen Press, Lewiston, NY, in 2002. Two recent biographies of Edwards have also rejected Miller's conclusions. Iain Murray says that Miller's attempt 'to reconstruct the whole of Edwards' outlook in terms of Lockean philosophy has long since been abandoned as untenable'; (*Jonathan Edwards*, 64). More recently, George M. Marsden, while agreeing that for Edwards, 'Locke opened up exciting new ways of looking at things', adds, 'yet Edwards was no Lockean in any strict sense' (*Jonathan Edwards*, 63). For further discussion, see David Bebbington, *Evangelicalism in Modern Britain*, London, 1989, especially chapter 1; and Michael A. G. Haykin and Kenneth J. Stewart (eds), *The Emergence of Evangelicalism*, Nottingham, 2007.

13. For Shephard (1605-49) and Stoddard (1643-1729), see Daniel G. Reid (ed.), *Dictionary of Christianity in America*, Downers Grove, Illinois, 1990.

14. *Works*, Vol. VIII, Edinburgh, 1988, 80; Vol. VII, 395. Another Puritan, Thomas Watson, claims that 'the affections are by divines called "the feet of the soul"' (*The Lord's Prayer*, London, 1965, 139). Mark E. Dever, described the early Puritan, Richard Sibbes, as 'An Affectionate Theologian', for whom 'Love is the weight and wing of the soul, which carries it where it goes.' (*Richard Sibbes: Puritanism and Calvinism in Late Elizabethan and Early Stuart England*, Macon, GA, 2000.) The quotation is from Sibbes's sermons on the Song of Songs, 'Bowels Opened', *Works*, Vol. 2, Edinburgh, 1983, 129.

15. *Works of Thomas Goodwin*, Vol. 6, Edinburgh, 1979, 166, 231; *The Complete Works of Stephen Charnock*, Vol. III, Edinburgh, 1865, 95; *The Works of John Owen*, Vol. III, Edinburgh, 1988, 329.

16. Both works were originally published in London. The Reynolds title was reprinted in 1996 as Volume 6 of his works at Morgan, PA. Williams possessed a copy of the 1658 edition of Fenner's *Works*, and the 1640 edition of Reynolds.

17. Edwards, *Works*, Volume 2, 95.

18. Williams possessed the original London edition of 1652. The quotation is from a reissue, published with the title *Spiritual Refining: The Anatomy of True and False Conversion*, at Ames, Iowa, in 1996, p. 143.

19. John Owen, *Hanes Bywyd a Gweinidogaeth y Parchedig Daniel Rowlands*, Caerlleon, 1814, 98-100.

20. Revival, 30, from *GWP2*, 26-7.

21. *GWP2*, 24-5.

22. *One Hundred and Ninety Sermons on the Hundred and Nineteenth Psalm*, Vol II,

Edinburgh, 1990, 550.
23. *GWP2*, 24, 26-7, 29.
24. Edwards, *Works*, Volume 4, 230, 218, 249-50, 266-7; cf. *GWP2*, 28, 31-2.

21. 'Pursued by God'

Pages 195-205

1. *Institutes*, III. vi. 4.
2. Doumergue is quoted by Charles Partee in the *Scottish Journal of Theology*, 26 (1973), 173, in an article on 'Calvin and Experience'.
3. Cyn2, 426.
4. Translated by Eifion Evans, and published at Bridgend. See also Glyn Tegai Hughes, *Williams Pantycelyn*, 22-40; and Morgan, *The Great Awakening in Wales*, 149-57; and in Welsh, GMR2, 155-60; and Meredydd Evans, 'Pantycelyn a Throedigaeth', in Morgan, Meddwl a Dychymyg Williams Pantycelyn, , 55-81.
5. Geraint H. Jenkins, *Literature, Religion and Society in Wales*, 127-8, notes that the use of fictional characters was a favourite with the early Welsh Nonconformist, Stephen Hughes (1622-88) in making Welsh books available to his generation. See also Benjamin Boyce, *The Theophrastian Character in England to 1642*, Cambridge, MA.,1947; and Glyn Tegai Hughes, *Williams Pantycelyn*, 61-2.
6. For Bunyan's influence on eighteenth-century Welsh literature, see Mairwen Lewis, 'Astudiaeth gymharol o'r cyfieithiadau Cymraeg o rai o Weithiau John Bunyan, a'u lle a'u Dylanwad yn llên Cymru', MA thesis, University of Wales, 1957.
7. *The Works of George Swinnock*, Vol. I, Edinburgh, 1992, 326; Bradford is quoted in Ian Breward (ed.), *William Perkins*, Appleford, 1970, 366; Edwards, *Works*, Volume 4, 389-94; 246-48.
8. Preface 'To the Reader', *A Treatise of Conversion*, in *The Practical Works of Richard Baxter*, Vol. II, Ligonier, PA, 1990, 399.
9. See, for example, Geraint H. Jenkins, 'The New Enthusiasts', in Trevor Herbert and Gareth Elwyn Jones (eds.), *The Remaking of Wales in the Eighteenth Century*, Cardiff, 1988, 43, 50.
10. *Eight Sermons upon Practical Subjects*, London, [1774], 173, 174.
11. Theo, 86.
12. Theo, 93, 97.
13. Theo, 114, 115.
14. Theo, 122.
15. Theo, 152. Jezebel, the infamous wife of King Ahab, in Scripture stands for the epitome of evil, 2 Kings 9: 7; Revelation 2:20.
16. Theo, 156.
17. Theo, 172, 173, 175.
18. Theo, 178.

19. Theo 178-9.

20. See for example, Theo, 95 [252/1], 146 [336/5], 163 [366/7], [368/1], and John Bunyan's *Grace Abounding to the Chief of Sinners,* paragraph 204, in George Offor (ed.), *The Works of John Bunyan*, Volume First, Edinburgh, 1991, 32.

21. Theo, 117. See Evans, *Rowland*, 133-4; Rack, *Reasonable Enthusiast*, 395-401.

22. Theo, 179. The original Welsh is found in GWP2, 399, and is as follows:

> *Wel dyma'r dyn a garwyd, a gannwyd yn y gwa'd,*
> *Deng miliwn lawn o feiau faddeuwyd iddo'n rhad;*
> *Ei dynnu wnawd o'r danllwyth, ac yntau'n mynd i lawr, -*
> *Fe gadwyd hwn o uffern, mae e'n y nef yn awr.*

> *Fi ga' fy nghorff i fyny, fel fy Anwylyd cu,*
> *Heb nwydau drwg byth mwyach i'm blino fel y bu;*
> *'Does dyn ŵyr is yr wybyr ddedwydded yw fy lle,*
> *Ac nis gall dyn ddychmygu dim am bleserau'r ne'.*

> *Heb saeth, heb fraw, heb ofon, heb ofid ac heb boen*
> *Yn canu o flaen yr orsedd ogoniant pur yr Oen;*
> *Yng nghanol myrdd myrddiynau yn caru oll heb drai,*
> *Yr anthem ydyw cariad, a chariad i barhau.*

22. 'A school of the prophets'

Pages 206-215

1. CH. xxxii.73-4.

2. *Select Letters*, Vol. 3, 348.

3. Cyn1, 438, 451, 648, 652.

4. CH. xxv, 108; Jones and Morgan, *Fathers*, Vol. 1, 613.

5. Higham, *Jones Llan-gan*, Chapter 2.

6. *Marwnad*, &c, 1791; Seymour, *Life and Times*, Vol. 2, 118-19.

7. Geoffrey F. Nuttall, *The Significance of Trevecca College 1768-91*, London, 1969; id., 'The Students of Trevecca College, 1768-1791', in *The Transactions of the Honourable Society of Cymmrodorion*, 1968, 249-77.

8. Beynon, *Visits to London*, 287.

9. For William Seward see CH. xxv.67,f; xxxviii. 18; lviii.12; lx. 17-21; Curnock, *Journal,* Vol. 2, 395-6; Dallimore, *Whitefield*, Vol. 1, 251-2, 582-5.

10. Beynon, *Visits to Pembrokeshire*, 158; Beynon, *Reformer and Soldier*, 114, 197.

11. Dallimore, *Whitefield*, Vol. 2, 458.

12. Jones and Morgan, *Fathers*, Vol. 1, 621.

13. See Faith Cook, *Selina Countess of Huntingdon*, Edinburgh, 2001, 232-53;

Schlenther, *Queen of the Methodists*, 75-7; Welch, *Spiritual Pilgrim*, Chapters 7 and 11.

14. Letter of Francis Okely to Harris, 10 April,1765 in Roberts, *Letters* (1747-1794), 102.

15. *Significance of Trevecka College*, 5-6, 7, 9. Further details are given by Dr Nuttall in *The Transactions of the Honourable Society of Cymmrodorion*, Session, 1968, 249-77. This is supplemented by Gomer M. Roberts in CH. liii. 88-9.

16. Tyerman, *Whitefield*, Vol. 2, 554-5.

17. Seymour, *Life and Times*, Vol. 2, 99; Trysorfa, 448.

18. Curnock, *Journal*, Vol. 5, 334; Tyerman, *Whitefield*, Vol. 2, 570.

19. Seymour, *Life and Times*, Vol. 2, 107-8, 112-14; Beynon, *Visits to London*, 285. In 1791 the College was taken over by the Apostolic Society and moved to Cheshunt in Hertfordshire. Cheshunt College, as it was now called, moved to Cambridge in 1904. In 1967 its premises were closed and students were transferred to the seminary of The Presbyterian Church of England, Westminster College, in the town.

20. CH. liii. 56-7, 58.

21. Cyn1, 652.

22. CH. lvi. 47.

23. Edwin Welch, *Two Calvinistic Methodist Chapels 1743-1811: The London Tabernacle and Spa Fields Chapel*, London, 1975, 72-3.

23. 'So dangerous an enemy'

Pages 216-223

1. *George Whitefield's Journals*, 516-17.

2. John Gillies, *Historical Collections Relating to Remarkable Periods of the Success of the Gospel*, Kelso, 1845, 361. This was re-issued by Banner of Truth Trust, Edinburgh and Carlisle, PA,1981.

3. Buell's letter to Eleazar Wheelock, 20 April 1742, in Richard Bushman (ed.), *The Great Awakening*: *Documents on the Revival of Religion, 1740-1745*, New York, 1970, 44.

4. Marsden, *Jonathan Edwards*, 317.

5. *A Faithful Narrative of the Remarkable Revival of Religion in the Congregation at East-Hampton on Long-Island, in the Year of our Lord 1764*, published at New York.

6. Quoted in Alan Heimert, *Religion and the American Mind from the Great Awakening to the Revolution*, Cambridge, Mass., 1968, 224.

7. *A Copy of a Letter*, 1-2, 3, 4, 5.

8. The pamphlet was published by the SPCK and distributed gratuitously, with three editions called for by the following year. Tyerman, *Wesley*, Vol. 1, 475-6; Lyles, *Methodism Mocked*, 47-8, 94; Roberts, *Hanes Methodistiaeth*, Cyf. 2, 28-9.

9. *GWP2*, 78.

10. Topsell's work was published in London in 1608, and the quotation appears on p.135. The 'P. Martyr' of the quotation is Peter Martyr, the Protestant Reformer. Greenhill's work of 1649 was reissued at Edinburgh in 1994, and the comment is on Ezekiel 29: 3 at p. 629 of this edition. Glyn Tegai Hughes considers that Williams's source was Nathan Bailey's *Universal Etymological English Dictionary* of 1735, which Williams possessed, where the entry for 'envy' notes that 'an envious person was represented by the
water-serpent *Hydra*, because of its proceeding from corruption and mud.' ('Rhyddiaith Williams Pantycelyn', *Llên Cymru*, 17 (1993), 273).

11. *GWP2*, 39.

12. *GWP2*, 41, 35, 36, 98-101, 83-4, 95.

13. In *Pilgrim's Progress* the shepherds' names were 'Knowledge, Experience, Watchful, and Sincere.' Offor, *The Works of John Bunyan*, Vol. 3, 144. For the use in *Holy War* of titles similar to those in *Crocodil*, see p. 297.

14. Cyn1, 493.

15. *GWP2*, 115.

16. John Bunyan, *Pilgrim's Progress*, in Offor, *The Works of John Bunyan*, Vol. 3, 211; *GWP2*, 111, 112; 116.

24. 'Paths of grace and righteousness'
Pages 224-231

1. Kilsby, x.

2. GMR1, 112. For contemporary accounts of the story of tea, see *Advice to the Unwary*, 1780; and Richard Twining, *Observations on the Tea and Window Act and on the Tea Trade*, London, 1784.

3. *GWP2*, 117.

4. *GWP2*, 117-18.

5. *GWP2*, 145-8.

6. *GWP2*, 149-52.

7. D. Myrddin Lloyd, 'Tri Wŷr o Sodom', in *Y Llinyn Arian i Gyfarch Urdd Gobaith Cymru*, Aberystwyth, 1947, 103; Glyn Tegai Hughes, 'Rhyddiaith Williams Pantycelyn', *Llên Cymru*, 17 (1993), 277.

25. 'Fly abroad, eternal Gospel'
Pages 232-242

1. GMR2, 228.

2. Kilsby, 780.

3. Cyn1, 628. There is a strong tradition that many of Williams's papers were burnt, and it is now impossible to know whether *Liber* was ever completed.

4. See Dewi Arwel Hughes, 'William Williams Pantycelyn's Eschatology as seen especially in his *Aurora Borealis* of 1774', *The Scottish Bulletin of*

Notes

Evangelical Theology, 4 (Spring, 1986), 49-63; *id., Meddiannu Tir Immanuel: Cymru a Mudiad Cenhadol y Ddeunawfed Ganrif*, Pen-y-bont ar Ogwr, 1990. JE*Wks*1, 605, 606, 607.

5. *A Glimpse of Sions Glory*, 14, 17. See A. R. Dallison, 'The Latter-day Glory in the Thought of Thomas Goodwin', *Evangelical Quarterly* 58:1 (1986), 53-68.

6. See Crawford Gribben, *The Puritan Millennium: Literature and Theology, 1550-1682*, Milton Keynes, 2008; Peter Toon, 'Puritan Eschatology: 1600 to 1648', *The Manifold Grace of God*, Puritan and Reformed Studies Conference 1968, 49-60; Robert Godfrey, 'Millennial Views of the Seventeenth Century and beyond', *God is Faithful*, The Westminster Conference, Stoke-on-Trent, 1999, 7-26.

7. *Institutes*, III. 25. 5; cf. H. Quistorp, *Calvin's Doctrine of the Last Things*, London, 1955, 159: 'Thus Calvin is concerned about the exclusive orientation and concentration of hope on the ultimate appearance and revelation of the Lord for the general resurrection and the last judgment on all.'

8. *The Puritan Hope: A Study in Revival and the Interpretation of Prophecy*, London, 1971.

9. Edwards, *Works*, Volume 4, 132, 133, 137.

10. *Selections from the Welch Piety*, Cardiff, 1938, 23; Dewi Arwel Hughes, *Meddiannu Tir Immanuel*,11-12.

11. *Journal of a Voyage ...1740*, London, 1740, 64.

12. Published in Boston, 1742; Edwards, *Works*, Volume 4, 353. American religious writers tended to appropriate the millennium almost exclusively to their country. Mason I. Lowance claims that New England studies of the subject reflect 'the conventional Puritan conviction of national election ... Indeed, during the eighteenth century, the Great Awakening ... enlarged what had been a parochial New England idea into a national conception of America as the location of Christ's millennial fulfilment.' *The Language of Canaan: Metaphor and Symbol in New England from the Puritans to the Transcendentalists*, Cambridge, Mass., 1980,119.

13. Edwards, *Works*, Volume 5, 363f.

14. Edwards, *Works,* Volume 4, 539-40; *Sermons on Several Subjects: The Millennium*, Boston, 1758, quoted in Heimert, *Religion and the American Mind*, 346. cf. Mason I. Lowance, Jr., *The Language of Canaan*, 189 ff.

15. CH. xx. 133-4.

16. *Providence in Early Modern England*, Oxford, 1999, 3, 116. The phrase is used by a correspondent of Joseph Mede in a newsletter dated 12 Feb 1627, reporting a thunderstorm in Boston, Lincolnshire, twelve days previously. BL. Harleian MS 390, fo. 205.

17. Beynon, *Visits to London*, 96, 205.

18. Seymour, *Life and Times*, Vol. 1, 130.

19. Watson, *The English Hymn*, 228.

20. Dallimore, *A Heart Set Free*, 174. Vivid descriptions of the scenes

witnessed in London at the time were published in the London Magazine. See Tyerman, *Wesley*, Vol. 2, 71-2; Curnock, *Journal,* Vol. 3, 453, 456-7.

21. *An alarm to a careless world. A discourse occasioned by the late earthquake, preached November 30*, 1755, London, 1755.

22. Tyerman, *Wesley*, Vol. 2, 225.

23. Cyn1, 237, 238. Gomer M. Roberts mentions the singing of this verse at the time of the French invasion at Fishguard in 1797, and its catalytic effect to bring about a revival in the Bontuchel area in North Wales in 1821. See GMR2, 141.

24. Cyn1, 457.

25. Kilsby, 530-31.

26. *GWP2*, 163,164.

27. *GWP2*, 164,165.

28. *GWP2*, 172, 173.

29. *GWP2*, 174.

30. *The Puritan Millennium: Literature and Theology,* 261, and see the Appendix, 'Millennialism in the Puritan Confessions'.

31. *GWP2*, 177, 179.

32. GMR1, 162.

33. Cyn2, 428.

26. 'Let the Lord go before you'
Pages 243-252

1. Jones and Morgan, *Fathers*, 382; Gareth Lloyd, '"My Dearest Sally": The Marriage of Charles Wesley and Sally Gwynne', *Proceedings of the Wesley Historical Society*, 56 (2007), 114, 123; Dallimore, *A Heart Set Free*, Chapters 13 and 14; Rack, *Reasonable Enthusiast*, Chapter VI. For Whitefield's marriage see Dallimore, *Whitefield*, Vol. 2, Chapter 6; and Stout, *The Divine Dramatist*, Chapter 9. See also Doreen Moore, *Good Christians Good Husbands?* Fearn, Rosshire, 2004.

2. Beynon, *Reformer and Soldier*, 84.

3. GMR1, 92.

4. Jones and Morgan, *Fathers*, Vol. 1, 182.

5. CH. 1. 52-3.

6. CMA Trefeca 497; Cal, 78. For Thomas Jones, see CH. 8 (1985), 24-30.

7. *GWP2*, 303. Some of the material on this work appeared in my article, 'The "Guide to Marriage" of William Williams, Pantycelyn', in *The Welsh Journal of Religious History*, 2 (2007), 105-205, and is used here with the kind permission of the Editors.

8. For Puritan responses to 'The Three-fold Purpose of Marriage', see Robert Victor Schnucker, 'Views of Selected Puritans 1560-1630, on Marriage and Human Sexuality', Ph.D. Thesis, University of Iowa, February, 1969, 126-140; James Turner Johnson, *A Society Ordained by God: English Puritan Marriage*

Doctrine in the First Half of the Seventeenth Century, Nashville, 1970, 93-104; and Leland Ryken, *Worldly Saints: The Puritans As They Really Were*, Grand Rapids, MI, 1990, Chapter 3, 'Marriage and Sex'.

9. *GWP2*, 243-4.

10. For Erasmus (1467? – 1536), see Hans J. Hillerbrand, *The Oxford Encyclopedia of the Reformation*, Volume 2, Oxford, 1996.

11. *GWP2*, 257, 259.

12. The French original by François Poulain de la Barre (1647-1723) was translated into English and Williams's copy is dated 1677. An edited edition, with an 'Introduction' by Gerald M. Maclean appeared in 1988, published at Detroit by Wayne State University Press. For a study of de la Barre, see Siep Stuurman, *François Poulain de la Barre and the Invention of Modern Equality*, Harvard University Press, Cumberland, Rhode Island, 2004.

13. Jones, *A View of the Kingdom*, 89.

14. Michael Parsons, *Reformation Marriage: The Husband and Wife Relationship in the Theology of Luther and Calvin*, Edinburgh, 2005, 214.

15. *GWP2*, 256, 260.

16. Variations of this statement about Eve being taken from Adam's rib are found in William Perkins (Ian Breward (ed.), *The Work of William Perkins*, Appleford, 1970, 428); Robert Cleaver (*A Godly Form of Householde Government*, 1598, 201); and William Gouge (Domesticall Duties, 1622, 271). Its subsequent familiarity may have been widely propagated by its appearance in Matthew Henry's commentary on Genesis 2:22, which appeared in 1706.

17. *GWP2*, 268, 269-70. The Milton quotation is from Paradise Lost, Book VIII, lines 540-559. For Milton, see *ODNB*.

18. CH. lii. 61 (Morgan John Lewis's Report for Glamorganshire, March, 1744).

27. 'A candle of heavenly brightness'

Pages 253-261

1. *Trysorfa*, 447.

2. '"Drws y Society Profiad" Pantycelyn', *Adroddiad Cyfarfodydd Caerdydd, Undeb Annibynwyr Cymru, Mehefin 11-13, 1984*, Abertawe, 1985, 71.

3. *The Experience Meeting*, 10-11, 12.

4. *The Experience Meeting*, 13-15, 21.

5. GMR1, 89 (TL 3026).

6. *The Experience Meeting*, 22-30.

7. GMR1, 164, 165.

8. *The Experience Meeting*, 32, 33; Cyn1, 533.

9. *The Experience Meeting*, 34, 35, 37.

10. *The Experience Meeting*, 40, 41, 43.

11. *The Experience Meeting*, 48.

12. *The Experience Meeting*, 55, 51-4, 62.

28. 'This inward Spring of Activity'

Pages 262-272

1. *The Experience Meeting*, 5, 6.
2. For a discussion of this work see Derec Llwyd Morgan, 'Williams Pantycelyn: Sylwadau ar ystyr a diben ei waith', yn J. E. Caerwyn Williams (gol.), *Ysgrifau Beirniadol*, Dinbych, VIII, 1974, 130-159; Glyn Tegai Hughes, *Williams Pantycelyn*, 67-70; and Eifion Evans, 'The Nature of Christian Experience: The Great Awakening in Wales', *Reformation and Revival Journal*, Vol. 11, No. 3 (Summer 2002), 74-95.
3. CH. liv. 60.
4. *The Experience Meeting*, 13; CH. liii. 50-51.
5. See Eifion Evans, 'Pietism and Welsh Calvinistic Methodism', CH. 25 (2001), 7-17. See also Ward, *The Protestant Evangelical Awakening*, 316-24.
6. *The Works of Thomas Goodwin*, Vol. XI, Edinburgh, 1865, 358. For a discussion of 'Puritanism among the English Puritans', see F. Ernest Stoeffler, *The Rise of Evangelical Pietism*, Leiden, 1971, Chapter 2.
7. *Spirituall Experiences of Sundry Believers ... The Second Impression; enlarged with the Experiences of forty two Beleevers, wherein is wonderfully declared Gods severall workings in the various conditions of his chosen ones*, London, 1653, 'The Epistle'. Studies of Puritan works on religious experience include the following: C. F. W. B. Bullock, *Voluntary Religious Societies 1520-1799*, St Leonards on Sea, 1963; Paul Delaney, *British Autobiography in the Seventeenth Century*, London, 1969; Owen Watkins, *The Puritan Experience: Studies in Spiritual Autobiography*, New York, 1972; Patricia Caldwell, *The Puritan Conversion Narrative: The Beginnings of American Expression*, Cambridge, 1983; Charles Lloyd Cohen, *God's Caress: The Psychology of Puritan Religious Experience*, New York and Oxford, 1986; and Norman Pettit, *The Heart Prepared: Grace and Conversion in Puritan Spiritual Life*, Middletown, Connecticut, 1989.
8. Published in London; pp. 164,167; 240, 241.
9. *Practical Discourses on Regeneration, in ten sermons*, London, 1742, Sermon III, 'Of the nature of regeneration, with respect to the change it produces in men's affections, resolutions, labours, enjoyments, and hopes, 2 Cor. 5:17', 65, 76, 77, 78. Isabel Rivers raises the issue of the place of the affections in the human psyche in these two writers: 'The problem essentially is whether the affections are concerned primarily with action or with feeling. This ought not to be a problem, since the basic assumption of Watts's *Doctrine of the Passions* is that the passions are instigators of action. However, the favourite images of Watts and Doddridge suggest release, dissolution, annihilation of a sense of self, passive enjoyment of a "frame": the emphasis as a result often appears to rest on feeling rather than action.' (*Reason, Grace, and Sentiment: A Study of the Language of Religion and Ethics in England 1660-1780*, Vol. 1, 'Whichcote to Wesley', Cambridge, 1991,192.) In so far as

both writers were heirs of the Puritans, it would be reasonable to expect that for them affections were properly ruled by the mind to create a driving force in determining behaviour.

10. *Jonathan Edwards*, 259, 267.

11. Edwards, *Works*, Volume 2, 102, 205, 206, 283, 383. For a consideration of Edwards's work on 'heart-religion' see Brad Walton, "'Formerly Approved and Applauded": The Continuity of Edwards's *Treatise Concerning Religious Affections* with Seventeenth-Century Puritan Analyses of True Piety, Spiritual sensation and Heart-Religion', Doctor of Theology Thesis, Toronto School of Theology, 1999; Garry J. Williams, *Jonathan Edwards and Authentic Christian Experience*, Evangelical Library, London, Annual Lecture, 2003.

12. *The Experience Meeting*, 34ff; Bennett, *Dawn of Revival,* 26-7; Beynon, *Visits to London*, 108; *Y Drysorfa*, 1931: 433; 1932: 389.

13. *The Works of Thomas Goodwin*, Vol. 8, Edinburgh, 1985, 338, 361, 366; Vol. 1, Edinburgh, 1861, 245, 248 (exposition on Ephesians 1:13). D. M. Lloyd-Jones gives further historical examples of this teaching, from Goodwin and John Flavel, to Jonathan Edwards, George Whitefield and John Wesley, in his sermons on Ephesians 1:13 (*God's Ultimate Purpose*, Edinburgh, 1978, 274-8.)

14. CH. lii. 87.

15. CH. liii. 23. Some of the reports sent to the Association are found in Jones and Morgan, *Fathers*, Vol.1, 348-56.

16. CH. li. 82.

17. Cyn2, 334, 186, 401, 416; cf. R. M. Jones, *Cyfriniaeth Gymraeg*, Caerdydd, 1994, 109-12.

18. GMR1, 91-3 (TL 3058).

19. *The Experience Meeting*, 54-7.

20. *The Experience Meeting*, 30.

29. 'Preserve the gold'
Pages 273-283

1. R. Brinley Jones, *Songs of Praises: English Hymns and Elegies of William Williams Pantycelyn* 1717-1791, Felinfach, 1991, 41. See GMR2, Pennod V; also pp. 142-3; CH. xix. 12 ff., *id.* 'Gwerth hanesyddol rhai o farwnadau Williams Pantycelyn'; Dafydd Elis Thomas, 'Agweddau ar y Cywydd Marwnad', Ph.D. thesis, University of Wales, 1986; R. Geraint Gruffydd, 'Marwnadau William Williams, Pantycelyn', *Llên Cymru*, 17 (1993), 254-71.

2. See Gordon S. Wakefield, *Puritan Devotion: Its Place in the Development of Christian Piety*, London, 1957, Chapter 9; David E. Stannard, *The Puritan Way of Death: A Study in Religion, Culture and Social Change*, Oxford, 1977; Ralph Houlbrooke, 'The Puritan Death-bed, c. 1560-1660', in Christopher Durston and Jacqueline Eales (eds), *The Culture of English Puritanism*, 1560-1700, Basingstoke and London, 1996, Chapter 4; *The Practical Works of*

Richard Baxter, Ligonier, Pennsylvania, 1990, 3: 1, 3, 5. The Puritan funeral sermon was a means of displaying the triumph of grace in the life of the deceased, in their conversion, perseverance, godliness, and at their end, for the encouragement of the congregation; cf. T. J. Morgan, *Ysgrifau Llenyddol*, Llundain, 1951, 67, 84.

3. GMR1,161, letter of September 1787.
4. *GWP*1, 342-3.
5. Cyn1, 568.
6. Kilsby, 733.
7. GWP2, 128-30; 135-6.
8. Cyn1, 461; 482, 483; 511; 527; 537; 574, 551; *Galarnad ar Farwolaeth Mari, gwraig John Jones, o Llandilo-Fach ... a ... John Philip o Lwyngyfarthwch, yn agos i Lanelli*, Brecon, 1782, yn *Y Drysorfa*, Mawrth 1920, 81-2.
9. Cyn1, 437; 499; 546, 548.
10. Cyn1, 650-1.
11. Cyn1, 470, 471.
12. Cyn1, 445-7.
13. Cyn1, 435, 471.
14. Cyn1, 570-1, 567.
15. Cyn1, 541, 563; 456-7.
16. Cyn1, 653, 658.
17. Cyn1, 528, 530.
18. Cyn1, 490-1.
19. *A Minister dead; yet speaking. Being the substance of Two Discourses preached November 11, 1770. Occasioned by the death of the Rev. George Whitefield,* Second Edition, London (1770), 23-4. This was translated into Welsh by Peter Williams and published at Carmarthen in 1771 with the title *Gweinidog wedi marw yn llefaru eto*; cf. Catherine A. Charnell-White, 'Galaru a gwaddoli ym marwnadau Williams Pantycelyn', *Llên Cymru*, 26 (2003), 40-62.
20. Cyn1, 587, 588.
21. *GWP*2, 158.

30. 'The crystal fountain opened'

Pages 284-294

1. Cyn2, 444-5.
2. Elfed ap Nefydd Roberts speaks of Williams as a 'creative', 'spiritual' and 'practical' theologian. 'Before all else', he says, 'Pantycelyn is the poet and theologian of the spiritual life.' ('Pantycelyn y Diwinydd', *Diwinyddiaeth*, XLII (1991), 78, 83, 90.) There are a number of studies on specific aspects of Williams's theology, but the fullest is the unpublished M.Th. thesis by Stephen

J. Turner: 'Theological themes in the English Works of Williams, Pantycelyn', University of Wales, 1982.

3. W. Moses Williams (ed.), *Selection from the Welch Piety*, Cardiff, 1938, 23.

4. Kilsby, 573, fn.

5. 'Theological themes in the English Works of Williams, Pantycelyn', 69-148.

6. *Cymru*, 1891, 105. There are 31 verses in all, and they appeared at the end of another of Williams's work, *Berr Hanes ... James Albert*. See GMR2, 160-1; cf. the elegy to Ann Pugh on the loss of her son, now that she is bereft of his counsel, speaks of the Bible as her companion, 'my perfect, clear guide and leader to the promised land.' (Cyn1, 515.)

7. *GWP*2, 224-5.

8. *Cyfriniaeth Gymraeg*, 121.

9. Cyn2, 57, 116-18. cf. Glyn Tegai Hughes, 'Pantycelyn a'r Piwritaniaid', in Derec Llwyd Morgan (gol.), *Meddwl a Dychymyg Williams Pantycelyn*, 36-56.

10. GWP1, 139; Jones, *A View of the Kingdom of Christ*, 163 (first verse altered).

11. For example, Glyn Tegai Hughes, *Williams Pantycelyn*, 7: 'The theology of the revivalists was first felt and then intellectualized'; and Derec Llwyd Morgan, *The Great Awakening in Wales*, 113, where he speaks of Williams 'as spokesman of a movement whose literature, like its life, is rooted in experience.' The source of Methodist teaching was not the subjective perception of truth, however powerfully experienced, but the objective revelation of the Word of God.

12. 'William Williams, Pantycelyn – Ei Gerddi Hir', in Dyfnallt Morgan (gol.), *Gwyr Llên y Ddeunawfed Ganrif a'u Cefndir*, Llandybïe, 1966, 98.

13. Knott, *The Sword of the Spirit*, 136.

14. Jenkins, *Thomas Charles*, Vol. 2, 71.

15. 'The Evangelical Revival in Wales: A Study in Spirituality', in James P. Mackey, *An Introduction to Celtic Christianity*, Edinburgh, 1989, 242. A study in Welsh of Williams's spirituality by a Catholic author, Saunders Lewis, appeared in 1927 (*Williams Pantycelyn*, Llundain). It argued that Williams had close affinities with Bonaventura, St John of the Cross, and Saint Teresa, and that the society meetings were a substitute for the Confessional. The claims were convincingly refuted by R. Tudur Jones in his Henry Lewis Memorial Lecture delivered at Swansea University College in 1987 (*Saunders Lewis a Williams Pantycelyn*, Abertawe, 1987). Cf. Glyn Tegai Hughes, 'Pantycelyn a'r Piwritaniaid', *Meddwl a Dychymyg Williams Pantycelyn*, 31-54.

16. Jones and Morgan, *Fathers*, Vol. 1, 630; For Popkin (fl. 1759-1824) see *DWB*. Further details about Popkin are found in GMR2, 266-7.

17. GMR1, 142-8; Roberts, *Hanes Methodistiaeth*, Cyf. 2, 428-9.

18. Cyn2, 115-16; 385.

19. Cyn1, 70.

20. Jenkins, *Thomas Charles*, Vol. 2, 59-83. See Jones and Morgan, *Fathers*, Vol. 1, Chapter 18; John Gwili Jenkins, *Hanfod Duw a Pherson Crist*,

Liverpool, 1931, Pennod (Chapter) VIII; Roberts, *Peter Williams*, Pennod (Chapter) VII; R. T. Jenkins, *Yng Nghysgod Trefeca*, Caernarfon, 1968, 154 – 171; Roberts, *Hanes Methodistiaeth*, Cyf. 2, Pennod VII; Derec Llwyd Morgan, 'Helynt Peter Williams, 1791', *Y Traethodydd, Hydref*, 1972.

21. Morgan, 59-61; Jenkins, *Thomas Charles*, Vol. 2, 70-1; GMR1, 167-8.

22. Morgan, 69; GMR1, 159. Its Welsh title was *Immanuel. Neu Ddirgelwch Dyfodiad Mab Duw yn y Cnawd*, and it was published at Trefeca in 1786.

23. *Immanuel*, 7, 8. A selection from the work is found in Edward Hindson (ed.), *Introduction to Puritan Theology: A Reader*, Grand Rapids, Michigan, 1976. The quotations appear on pages 109 and 110 of this work.

24. *Immanuel*, 23, 24, 38, 67; Hindson, *Introduction*, 118, 134.

25. For Jones see *ODNB*; for Thomas see *DWB*. For a discussion in Welsh of the controversy on the doctrine of the Trinity during this period, see Jenkins, *Hanfod Duw*, 234-376.

31. 'The food of the children of God'

Pages 295-309

1. Cyn1, 552.

2. Jenkins, *Thomas Charles,* Vol. 2, 52.

3. Book II, Chapters IX – XI. See J. I. Packer, 'Introduction: on Covenant Theology', in *The Economy of the Covenants between God and Man: Comprehending a Complete Body of Divinity*, reprinted in 1990, Escondido, California. The second edition of Witsius's *The oeconomy of the covenants between God and man* in 3 volumes was in Williams's library, but this was not published until 1775. Thomas Charles refers to Witsius's work in his *Geiriadur Ysgrythyrol* on several occasions, s.v. 'adenedigaeth', 'edifeirwch', etholedigaeth', 'ffydd', 'maddeuant', 'sarph'. See also the article, 'Covenant Theology' in Nigel M. de S. Cameron (ed.), *Dictionary of Scottish Church History and Theology; John von Rohr, The Covenant of Grace in Puritan Thought,* Atlanta, Georgia, 1986*; David McKay, The Bond of Love: Covenant Theology and the Contemporary World*, Fearn, Rosshire, 2001; and in Welsh, R. Tudur Jones, 'Athrawiaeth y Cyfamodau', in D. Densil Morgan (gol.), *Grym y Gair a Fflam y Ffydd,* Bangor, 1998, Pennod 1; Goronwy Wyn Owen, *Cewri'r Cyfamod: y Piwritaniaid Cymreig* 1630-1660, Caernarfon, 2008, 92-5.

4. CH. xx (TMS. i. 300).

5. CH. liv. 24; Roberts, *Letters* (1742-1747), 102.

6. CH. liv.24; lii. 9, 85; liv. 61.

7. Thickens, *Howell Harris yn Llundain*, 121; Beynon, *Visits to Pembrokeshire*, 16, 32, 58; Roberts, *Letters* (1742-1747), 6. For Cotton see *ODNB*; the book was published in London.

8. *A Treatise of the Covenant of Grace*, 3rd edn, 1671, 222, 317, 318.

9. Joel R. Beeke, *Puritan Reformed Spirituality*, Grand Rapids, Michigan, 2004, 339, in a chapter on 'The Life and Thought of Herman Witsius'.

10. *John Elias: Prince amongst Preachers*, Bridgend, 1975, 20. See also Euros Wyn Jones, 'John Calvin (1509-1564): Agweddau ar ei Ddylanwad ar Gymru', CH. 33 (2009), 140-86; and D. Densil Morgan, 'Calvinism in Wales: c. 1590-1909', *The Welsh Journal of Religious History*, 84 (2009), 22-36.

11. Beynon, *Visits to Pembrokeshire*, 14.

12. Covenant of Grace, 20-21, 23.

13. s.v. 'cyfammod'. The *Hyfforddwr* appeared in 1807, and an English translation, *The Christian Instructor* was available from 1867. The *Geiriadur* entry quotes Bishop [William] Beveridge. A copy of T*he Works of ... William Beveridge*, Vol. 1, which appeared in London in 1729, is in Williams's library, and Sermon XXX, on 1 Timothy 2:5 under the title 'Christ the only Mediator', stresses that Christ, the second Adam, is the Mediator 'of a better covenant' than that entered into with the first Adam. One of his sermons, on 2 Corinthians 5: 17, was translated into Welsh and printed at Trefeca in 1776 with the title, *Y Creadur Newydd*. For Beveridge (1637-1708), see *ODNB*.

14. Nigel M. de S. Cameron, *Dictionary of Scottish Church History and Theology*, 218.

15. These doctrines have substantial treatment in Charles's *Geiriadur*, see for example: adenedigaeth, adgyfod, arfaeth, cyfiawnhad, dadguddiad, edifeirwch, ethol, ffydd, gras, prynedigaeth, sancteiddio.

16. Cyn2, 381; 82; 287.

17. GWP2, 41-2; 43-4.

18. Cyn1, 630, from *Reliquiae Poeticae*.

19. Jones, *A View of the Kingdom*, 175, 180, 196 (altered).

20. *The Works of George Swinnock*, Vol. 5, Edinburgh, 1992, 9, 11-12.

21. *Yr Ymarfer o Dduwioldeb*, Caerdydd, 1930, 57.

22. *Works of Thomas Goodwin*, Vol. 6, Edinburgh, 1979, 73.

23. *The Complete Works of Stephen Charnock*, Vol. 3, London, 1865, 88, 89, 95. In 1878 Lewis Edwards maintained that faith preceded regeneration in the thought of Williams (*Yr Arweinydd*, 49-53, 73-78, 97-101), as did J. Cynddylan Jones later (*Athrylith a Gras*, Caernarfon, [1975], 46-73). Once the distinction between regeneration and conversion is recognized, as Williams did, the conclusion of Edwards and Jones cannot be supported. See also Meredydd Evans, 'Pantycelyn a Thröedigaeth', Derec Llwyd Morgan (gol.), *Meddwl a Dychymyg Williams Pantycelyn*, 55-81.

24. GMR2, 241; for Joseph Hart (1712-68) see Donald M. Lewis, The Blackwell *Dictionary of Evangelical Biography 1730-1860*, Oxford, 1995; John Julian, Dictionary of Hymnology, Vol. 1, Grand Rapids, Michigan, 1985; and *ODNB*. The Welsh title of 1767 for the work, now re-worked in 1774 by Williams, was *Pererindod: sef Hanes y Parchedig Mr. J. Hart*.

25. Thomas Goodwin's 'Memoir' appears in Vol. 2 of his *Works* (1861), pp. li, ff; cf. p.lxvii where his son states that Goodwin 'left it with a design ... to give from his own experience a testimony of the difference between common grace, which by some is thought sufficient, and that special saving grace, which

indeed is alone sufficient, and always invincible and effectually prevails.' In Welsh the title of Williams's translation is *Hanes Troedigaeth Ryfedd a Hynod y Parchedig Mr. Thomas Goodwin.*

26. James Albert's account had been presented to the Countess of Huntingdon by Walter Shirley to demonstrate that none come to faith except by a knowledge of the truth, to which in the purposes of grace, God's providence is subservient. The full title of the Welsh translation was *Berr Hanes o'r Pethau mwyaf hynod ym mywyd James Albert Ukawsaw Groniosaw, Twywysog o Affrica.*

27. Cyn2, 395. Chapter 4 of Stephen Turner's thesis deals with 'The Atonement' in Williams's thought.

28. Cyn2, 434.

29. Theo, 104-5.

30. Cyn2, 655-6 (Sermon on Psalm 89:16).

31. Cyn2, 166. The verse was spoken on his death-bed by the Welsh Baptist minister, Christmas Evans (1766-1838). See Owen Jones, *Some of the Great Preachers of Wales,* London, 1886, 190.

32. GWP2, 74.

33. Cyn2, 268, translated by R. R. Williams, *Popular Hymns of Pantycelyn*, 1.

34. *Life in Christ: Union with Christ and Twofold Grace in Calvin's Theology*, Milton Keynes, 2008, 255.

35. See his *Pantheologia* in Kilsby, 517, fn; 527; and E. Wyn James, 'Welsh ballads and American Slavery', *The Welsh Journal of Religious History*, 2 (2007), 61-4. John Wesley's pamphlet, *Thoughts on Slavery* appeared in 1774. Eric Metaxas, *Amazing Grace: William Wilberforce and the Heroic Campaign to End Slavery,* San Fransisco, 2007, 96; Tyerman, *Wesley*, Vol. 3, 183; Rack, *Reasonable Enthusiast*, 362.

36. *The Experience Meeting,* 62.

37. Cyn1, 597.

32. 'Glad consolation, complete bliss'

Pages 310-317

1. Cyn2, 35, 65, 430.

2. GMR1, 100,104. For the schoolmasters at the time, Edward Richard (1714-1777), and John Williams (1745/6-1818), see *DWB*.

3. GMR1, 101. The bishop duly appointed him an assistant teacher at the Carmarthen Grammar School where he had been educated. (Maurice Davies, *Coffadwriaeth ...John Williams, gynt o Bant-y-Celyn*, Pont-y-pool, 1831, 7-8.)

4. GMR1, 23, 99, 106, 108; GMR2, 42, 265.

5. Kilsby, 768; GMR1, 163.

6. Morgan, 66.

7. CH. i. 34.

8. The verses were not translated until some time later by the wife of James

Bloomfield, a student at Cheshunt. He opened the Countess's chapel at Ashford in Kent in 1823. Seymour, *Life and Times*, Vol. 2, 119; 135. The Welsh rendering given in the Countess's biography is imperfect. The original had appeared as the third verse of a hymn published in the second part of *Ffarwel Weledig* in 1766.

9. John Jones, Cofiant ... *y Parch. Michael Roberts*, Pwllheli, 1883, 151; D. E. Jenkins, *Thomas* Charles, Vol. 1, 195.

10. GMR1, 151; Cyn1, 558; For the correspondence between Thomas Charles and Sally Jones see D. E. Jenkins, *Thomas Charles*, Vol.1, Chapters IX-XIX.

11. GMR1, 152, 153, 162.

12. GMR1, 107.

13. CH. xi. 48-61; Roberts, *Hanes Methodistiaeth*, Cyf. 2, 76,ff; Morgan, 49. See also Eryn M. White, 'The Material World, Moderation and Methodism in Eighteenth-century Wales', *Welsh History Review*, 2007.

14. GMR1, 161-2.In the event, Williams managed to visit Bala on 23 September and Pwllheli on the following Friday. The reference to hymns would have been to the collection that were printed at Trefeca in 1787 with the title, 'Some new hymns on new measures' (*Rhai Hymnau Newyddion ar Fesurau Newyddion*); GMR1, 161, 162; 180; GMR2, 168, 172, 267.

15. Jenkins, *Thomas Charles*, Vol. 2, 53-4.

16. GMR2, 168, 267; Jenkins, *Thomas Charles*, Vol. 2, 54.

17. Jenkins, *Thomas Charles*, Vol. 2, 54.

18. Kilsby, 765; GMR1, 173-4; Roberts, *Hanes Methodistiaeth*, Cyf. 2, 125-6; G. J. Thomas, 'Madam Bevan's Will: the Chancery Action', *Transactions of the Carmarthenshire Antiquarian Society*, 68 (1939), 43-52. Nothing came of the Chancery action as the charity ceased to exist. For Bridget Bevan (1698-1779), see *DWB*; cf Eryn White, 'Piety and Charity in Eighteenth-century Wales', in *The Welsh Journal of Religious History*, 2 (2007), 45-58.

19. GMR1, 222.

20. Jenkins, *Thomas Charles*, Vol. 2, 54.

21. Evans, *Rowland*, 352; Hughes, *Methodistiaeth Cymru*, Cyf. 2, 17-18, 35; Hughes, *Methodistiaeth Cymru,* Cyf. 3, 354.

33. 'No more this side of eternity'

Pages 318-325

1. GMR1, 158-9.

2. CH. iii. 73-4; GMR1, 159-60.

3. Morgan, 73; GMR1, 170-2; GMR2, 267; *Trysorfa*, 448.

4. GMR1, 164.

5. Evans, *Rowland*, 363, 364; Cyn1, 588.

6. Jenkins, *Thomas Charles,* Vol. 2, 51-5.

7. GMR1, 170; Derec Llwyd Morgan has an interesting article on this aspect of Williams's theology in CH. 14-15 (1990/91), 50-68, 'Williams Pantycelyn:

Y Grafel a'r Gwaed'.

8. Morgan, 71, 72, 73-4.
9. Higham, *David Jones*, 133.
10. GMR1, 176; Morgan, 74.

34. 'The wine of heaven'

Pages 326-336

1. Cyn2, 400, 401.
2. See Eifion Evans, 'The Society People: Developing a Methodist Mind', in CH. 29-30 (2005-06), 25 – 42.
3. See Jenkins, *Thomas Charles*, Vol. 3, 242ff; Jenkins, *Holy Orders*; John Morgan Jones, *Ordeiniad 1811 Ymysg y Methodistiaid Calfinaidd*, Caernarfon, n.d.; Gomer M. Roberts, 'Ymwahanu oddi wrth Eglwys Loegr', *Hanes Methodistiaeth*, Cyf. 2, Pennod (Chapter) VI.
4. Preface to the Second Part of *Aleluja*, 1745; to *Ffarwel Weledig*, 1766; to *Hosanna i Fab Dafydd*, 1751; Preface to the third printing of *Aleluia*, 1758; to *Ffarwel Weledig*, 1766; Gruffydd Evans, *The Story of the Ancient Churches of Llandovery*, London, [1913], 158.
5. Roberts, *Hanes Methodistiaeth*, Cyf. 2, 517.
6. Jenkins, *Thomas Charles*, Vol. 2, 56-7.
7. NLW Add. MS. 361A; John Evans, *Hanes Methodistiaeth Rhan Deheuol Sir Aberteifi*, Dolgellau, 1904, 55; Hughes, *Methodistiaeth Cymru*, Cyf. 2, 42, 61; *The Experience Meeting*, 13.
8. Jones, *A View of the Kingdom*, 226 (altered).
9. GMR1, 164-5. Letter to Thomas Charles in 1790.
10. Cyn2. 346.
11. Cyn2: 247.

Select bibliography

A full bibliography to 1991 by Huw Walters is found in Derec Llwyd Morgan, (gol. [ed.]), *Meddwl a Dychymyg Williams Pantycelyn* ('The Mind and Imagination of Williams Pantycelyn'), Llandysul, 1991.

Manuscripts at the National Library of Wales, Aberystwyth include the following:
Calvinistic Methodist Archives
The Trevecka Letters
Howel Harris's Diaries

Contemporary periodicals, edited by John Lewis:
The Christian's Amusement Containing Letters Concerning the Progress of the Gospel both at Home and Abroad, (London, 1740-1)
The Weekly History: Or an Account of the Most Remarkable Particulars Relating to the Present Progress of the Gospel, (London, 1741-2)
An Account of the Most remarkable Particulars of the Present Progress of the Gospel, (London , 1742-3)
The Christian History or General Account of the Progress of the Gospel in England, Wales, Scotland and America, (London, 1743-7)

Published Works
A Brief Account of the Life of Howell Harris, Esq., Trevecka, 1791
Richard Bennett, *Howell Harris and the Dawn of Revival*, Bridgend, 1987
Richard Bennett, *Methodistiaeth Trefaldwyn Uchaf*, Y Bala, 1929
Louis F. Benson, *The English Hymn: Its Development and Use in Worship*, London, 1915
Tom Beynon, *Howell Harris, Reformer and Soldier* (1714-1773), Caernarvon, 1958
Tom Beynon, *Howell Harris's Visits to London*, Aberystwyth, 1960
Tom Beynon, *Howell Harris's Visits to Pembrokeshire*, Aberystwyth, 1966
C. F. W. B. Bullock, *Voluntary Religious Societies 1520-1799*, St. Leonards on Sea, 1963

Patricia Caldwell, *The Puritan Conversion Narrative: The beginnings of American Expression*, Cambridge, 1983
John Calvin, *Institutes of the Christian Religion*, (ed.) John T. McNeill and Ford Lewis Battles, 2 volumes, Philadelphia, 1973
Nigel M. de S. Cameron (ed.), *Dictionary of Scottish Church History and Theology*, Edinburgh, 1993
Thomas Charles, 'Buchwedd a Marwolaeth y Parch William Williams, o Bant

y Celyn, Sir Gaerfyrddin', *Trysorfa, &c.*, Ionawr, 1813

Charles Lloyd Cohen, *God's Caress: The Psychology of Puritan Religious Experience*, New York and Oxford, 1986

Faith Cook, *Selina Countess of Huntingdon*, Edinburgh, 2001

Nehemiah Curnock (ed.), *The Journal of the Rev. John Wesley, M.A.*, 8 volumes, London, 1909-1916

Cylchgrawn Cymdeithas Hanes y Methodistiaid Calfinaidd (Caernarfon, 1916-). The Trevecka Manuscript Supplement. This appeared in two series issued at intervals as part of CH.

Arnold A. Dallimore, *A heart set free: the life of Charles Wesley*, Durham, 1988

Arnold A. Dallimore, *George Whitefield*, 2 volumes, London, 1970; Edinburgh, 1980

G. C. B. Davies, *The Early Cornish Evangelicals 1735-60 A Study of Walker of Truro and Others*, London, 1951

J. E. Wynne Davies (Gol.), *Gwanwyn Duw: Diwygwyr a Diwygiadau*, Caernarfon, 1982

J. H. Davies, *Rhestr o Lyfrau gan y Parch. William Williams Pantycelyn a Argraffwyd rhwng 1744 a 1800*, Caerfyrddin, 1918

Pennar Davies, 'Episodes in the History of Brecknockshire Dissent', *Brycheiniog*, III (1957), 32-8

Paul Delaney, *British Autobiography in the Seventeenth Century*, London, 1969

Jonathan Edwards, *The Works of,* Yale University Press, New Haven and London, Volume 1, *Freedom of the Will*, Paul Ramsey (ed.), 1957; Volume 2, *Religious Affections*, John E. Smith (ed.), 1959; Volume 3, *Original Sin*, Clyde A Holbrook (ed.), 1970; Volume 4, *The Great Awakening*, G. C. Goen (ed.), 1972; Volume 5, *Apocalyptic Writings,* Stephen J. Stein (ed.), 1977; Volume 22, *Sermons and Discourses 1739-1742*, Harry S. Stout, Nathan O. Hatch, with Kyle W. Farley (eds), 2003; and Volume 23, *The 'Miscellanies 1153-1360'*, Douglas A. Sweeney (ed.), 2004.

Eifion Evans, *Daniel Rowland and the Great Evangelical Awakening in Wales,* Edinburgh, 1985

Eifion Evans, *Fire in the Thatch: The True Nature of Religious Revival*, Bridgend, 1996

Eifion Evans, *Howel Harris, Evangelist 1714-1773*, Cardiff, 1974

Eifion Evans, *Pursued by God: A selective translation with notes of the Welsh religious classic, Theomemphus by William Williams of Pantycelyn*, Bridgend, 1996

Arthur Fawcett, *The Cambuslang Revival*, London, 1971

Lawrence Goldman, Brian Harrison, Colin Matthew (eds), *Oxford Dictionary of National Biography*, Oxford, 60 volumes, 2004.

Select bibliography

Richard Green, Anti-Methodist Publications Issued During the Eighteenth Century, London, 1902

R. D. Griffiths, *Hanes Canu Cynulleidfaol Cymru*, Caerdydd, 1948

Alan Heimert, *Religion and the American mind From the Great Awakening to the Revolution*, Cambridge, Massachsetts, 1968

D. Bruce Hindmarsh, *The Evangelical Conversion Narrative*, Oxford, 2008

R. Brian Higham, *The Rev. David Jones, Llan-gan, 1736-1810, and his contribution to Welsh Calvinistic Methodism*, Lewiston, Queenston, Lampeter, 2009

Garfield H. Hughes (gol.), *Gweithiau Williams Pantycelyn*, Caerdydd, 1967

Glyn Tegai Hughes, *Williams Pantycelyn*, University of Wales Press, 1983

Hugh J. Hughes, *Life of Howell Harris the Welsh Reformer*, Newport and London, 1892

John Hughes, *Methodistiaeth Cymru*, Gwrecsam, Cyfrol 1, 1851, Cyfrol 2, 1854, Cyfrol 3, 1856

Evan Isaac, *Prif Emynwyr Cymru*, Lerpwl, 1925

Thomas Jackson (ed.), *Journal of Charles Wesley*, Volume 1, London, 1849

D. E. Jenkins, *Calvinistic Methodist Holy Orders*, Carnarvon, 1911

D. E. Jenkins, *The Life of the Rev. Thomas Charles B.A. of Bala*, 3 volumes, Denbigh, 1908

Geraint H. Jenkins, *The Foundations of Modern Wales*, Oxford, 1993

Geraint H. Jenkins, *Literature, Religion and Society in Wales 1660-1730*, Cardiff, 1978

D. Gwenallt Jones, *Y Ficer Prichard a 'Canwyll y Cymry'*, Caernarfon, d.d.;

David Ceri Jones, *'A Glorious Work in the World' Welsh Methodism and the International Evangelical Revival, 1735-1750*, Cardiff, 2004

J. Gwilym Jones, *William Williams, Pantycelyn*, Caerdydd, 1969

J. R. Kilsby Jones, *Holl Weithiau y Diweddar Barch. William Williams, Pant-y-celyn*, Llundain, [1867]

John Morgan Jones and William Morgan, *The Calvinistic Methodist Fathers of Wales*, translated by John Aaron, 2 volumes, Edinburgh, 2008

N. Cynhafal Jones, *Gweithiau Williams Pant-y-celyn*, Treffynon, Cyfrol 1, 1887, Cyfrol 2, 1891

R. Brinley Jones, *A Lanterne to Their Feete*, Llanwrda, 1994

R. Brinley Jones, *Songs of Praises: English Hymns and Elegies of William Williams Pantycelyn 1717-1791*, Felinfach, 1991

R. Tudur Jones, *Congregationalism in England 1662-1962*, London, 1962

Robert Jones, *A View of the Kingdom of Christ, London*, 1878

Saunders Lewis, *Williams Pantycelyn*, Llundain, 1927

J. E. Lloyd (ed.), *A History of Carmarthenshire*, Vol. II, Cardiff, 1939

J. E. Lloyd and R. T. Jenkins (eds.), *The Dictionary of Welsh Biography Down to 1940*, London, 1959

Nesta Lloyd, 'Rhys Prichard, c.1579-1644/5', in *The Carmarthenshire Antiquary*, Vol. xxxiv, 1998

Bethan Lloyd-Jones, (tr.), *The Experience Meeting – an Introduction to the Welsh Societies of the Evangelical Awakening*, Bridgend and London, 1973, and Vancouver, 2003.

Mason I. Lowance, Jr., *The Language of Canaan: Metaphor and Symbol in New England from the Puritans to the Transcendentalists*, Cambridge, Massachusetts, 1980

Alan Luff, *Welsh Hymns and Their Tunes*, London, 1990

Albert M. Lyles, *Methodism Mocked: The Satiric Reaction to Methodism in the Eighteenth Century*, London, 1960

John Macinnes, *The Evangelical Movement in the Highlands of Scotland 1688 to 1800*, Aberdeen, 1951

Madeleine Forell Marshall and Janet Todd, *English Congregational Hymns in the Eighteenth Century*, Lexington, Kentucky, 1982

Derec Llwyd Morgan, *Y Diwygiad Mawr, Llandysul,* 1981, translated as *The Great Awkening in Wales*, London, 1988

Derec Llwyd Morgan (gol.), *Meddwl a Dychymyg Williams Pantycelyn*, Llandysul, 1991

Derec Llwyd Morgan, *Williams Pantycelyn*, Caernarfon, 1983

E. Morgan, *Ministerial Records ...of ... The Rev. D. Rowlands...*, London, 1840

E. Morgan, *Ministerial record: or, Brief Account of the Great Progress of Religion under the Ministry of Rev. W. Williams, of Pantycelyn, Carmarthenshire*, London, 1847

Edward Morgan, *The Life and Times of Howel Harris, Esq.*, Holywell, 1852

Geoffrey F. Nuttall, *The Welsh Saints 1640-1660*, Cardiff, 1957

Goronwy Wyn Owen, *Cewri'r Cyfamod: Y Piwritaniaid Cymreig 1630-1660*, Caernarfon, 2008

J. I. Packer, *The Redemption and Restoration of Man in the Thought of Richard Baxter*, Vancouver, 2003

Norman Pettit, *The Heart Prepared: Grace and Conversion in Puritan Spiritual Life*, Middletown, Connecticut, 1989

Henry D. Rack, *Reasonable Enthusiast: John Wesley and the Rise of Methodism*, Third edition, Peterborough, 2002

Eiluned Rees, *Libri Walliae A Catalogue of Welsh books and Books Printed in Wales 1546-1820*, Aberystwyth, 2 Volumes, 1987

T. Rees a J. Thomas, *Hanes Eglwysi Annibynol Cymru*, Cyf. III., Liverpool, 1873; Cyfrol IV, Liverpool, 1875

Select bibliography

Thomas Richards, *A History of the Puritan Movement in Wales*, London, 1920
Isabel Rivers, *Reason, Grace, and Sentiment: A Study of the Language of Religion and Ethics in England 1660-1780*, Volume 1, Whichcote to Wesley, Cambridge, 1991

Gomer Morgan Roberts, *Y Per Ganiedydd [Pantycelyn]*, Cyfrol 1, 'Trem ar ei fywyd', Aberystwyth, 1949; *Y Per Ganiedydd [Pantycelyn]*, Cyfrol 2, 'Arweiniad i'w waith', Aberystwyth, 1958.
Gomer Morgan Roberts (gol.), *Hanes Methodistiaeth Galfinaidd Cymru*, Caernarfon, Cyfrol 1, 1973, Cyfrol 2, 1978
Gomer Morgan Roberts (gol.), *Gweithiau Williams Pantycelyn*, Caerdydd, 1964
Gomer Morgan Roberts (ed.), *Selected Trevecka Letters (1742-1747)*, Caernarvon, 1956; *Selected Trevecka Letters (1747-1794)*, Caernarvon, 1962
Gomer Morgan Roberts, *Portread o Ddiwygiwr*, Caernarfon, 1969
Gomer M. Roberts, *Dafydd Jones o Gaeo*, Aberystwyth, 1948
Gomer M. Roberts, *Morgan Rhys, Llanfynydd*, Caernarfon, 1951
Gomer Morgan Roberts, *Bywyd a Gwaith Peter Williams*, Caerdydd, 1943
Griffith T. Roberts, *Dadleuon Methodistiaeth Gynnar*, Abertawe, 1970

Boyd Stanley Schlenther, *Queen of the Methodists: The Countess of Huntingdon and the Eighteenth-Century Crisis of Faith and Society*, Durham, 1997
Boyd Stanley Schlenther and Eryn Mant White, *Calendar of the Trevecka Letters*, Aberystwyth, 2003
[A. C. H. Seymour] *The Life and Times of Selina Countess of Huntingdon*, 2 volumes, London, 1844

John Thickens, *Emynau a'u Hawduriaid*, Caernarfon [1945]
John Thickens, *Howel Harris yn Llundain*, Caernarfon (1934)
Geraint Tudur, *Howell Harris From Conversion to Separation 1735-1750*, Cardiff, 2000
L. Tyerman, *The Life of the Rev. George Whitefield*, 2 volumes, Second Edition, London, 1890
L. Tyerman *The Life and Times of the Rev. John Wesley*, 3 volumes, Fourth Edition, London, 1878

W. R. Ward, *The Protestant Evangelical Awakening*, Cambridge, 1996
Owen Watkins, *The Puritan experience: Studies in Spiritual Autobiography*, New York, 1972
J. R. Watson, *The English Hymn: A Critical and Historical Study*, Oxford, 1999
Michael R. Watts, *The Dissenters From the Reformation to the French Revolution*, Oxford, 1999

Edwin Welch, *Spiritual Pilgrim: A reassessment of the life of the Countess of Huntingdon*, Cardiff, 1995

George Whitefield's Journals, London, 1960

A Select Collection of Letter of the late Reverend George Whitefield, 3 volumes, London, 1772

R. R. Williams, *Popular Hymns of Pantycelyn*, Liverpool, Brython Press, n.d.

D. Young, *The Origin and History of Methodism in Wales and the Borders*, London, 1893

Index

Lloyd, Gareth, 243
Lloyd, W. Esq., 323
Lloyd, William, 109, 327
Lloyd-Jones, Bethan, 254
Lloyd-Jones, D. Martyn, 262
Llwyd, Morgan, 54
Llwyn-gwair, 316
Llwyn-llwyd, 6
Llwynybrain farm, 311
Locke, John, 7, 8, 187, 188
London earthquake, 1750, 237
London Missionary Society, 83
Lucifer, 221
Luther, Martin, 229, 230, 249

M
Macleod, Donald, 299
Macleod, John, 141
Manton, Thomas, 191
marriage, 243–252
Marsden, George H., 165
Marshall, Walter, 189, 295
'Martha,' 247, 248, 250, 251, 252
'Martha Philopur,' 24, 88, 181, 182, 184, 185, 186, 189, 328
'Mary,' 247, 248, 249, 250, 251
Mather, Samuel, 94, 134
M'Culloch, William, 42, 236
Melanchthon, Phillipp, 229
Merioneth, 281
Methodism
aims, ideals and heaven-mindedeness, 9-10, 53, 69, 92, 95-95, 189, 152-153, 183-184, 198-199, 225-226, 228
Anglicanism and established church, 37, 41, 43, 49, 206, 263, 266, 310, 327
associations and societies, 37-51, 87, 90, 115, 184, 253-272, 327, 328
Bible, approach to, 38, 53-54, 118, 132-133, 187, 328
Confession of Faith 1823, 287, 288, 298
decline, 112-113, 131, 163
definition and theology, 38-39, 49, 53, 64, 204, 284-309
denomination and ordination, 1811, 327
'despised Methodists,' 36, 41, 92
development of, 36-42, 263, 327
differences within, 48, 112-122, 288, 327
distinct issues, 38, 43-44, 48-49, 53, 59, 61, 72, 75-76, 102, 125, 164, 171, 329, 335

403

Amlwch ●

Rhydyspardyn ●

Conw

● Bangor

● Caernarfon

Dolwyddelan ●

● Nefyn

Tudweiliog ●

● Pwllheli

Llanuwchl

● Dolge

NORTH WALES

A detailed map of the Llandovery area can be found on pages 22-23

Machynlleth ●

Aberystwyth ●